A Devil and Her Love Song

Story & Art by
Miyoshi Tomori

Volume 5

A Devil and Her Love Song

Volume 5
CONTENTS

Song 27......................5

Song 28...................33

Song 29..................59

Song 30..................85

Song 31................113

Song 32................138

Song 33................173

The devil
makes me
LOVELY!!!

STORY THUS FAR

Despite the ongoing conflict with her classmates and teacher, Maria tries to bring the class together in time to participate in the school choral competition. Meanwhile, Hana works against her, subtly manipulating her until Maria winds up even more isolated than before.

However, between Shin, Yusuke and Tomoyo's support for Maria and Ayu's heartfelt plea to the class, things begin to change by the day of the competition. Maria goes out on stage alone and begins to sing. The earnestness of her performance touches everyone who hears her, and her classmates begin to gather around her.

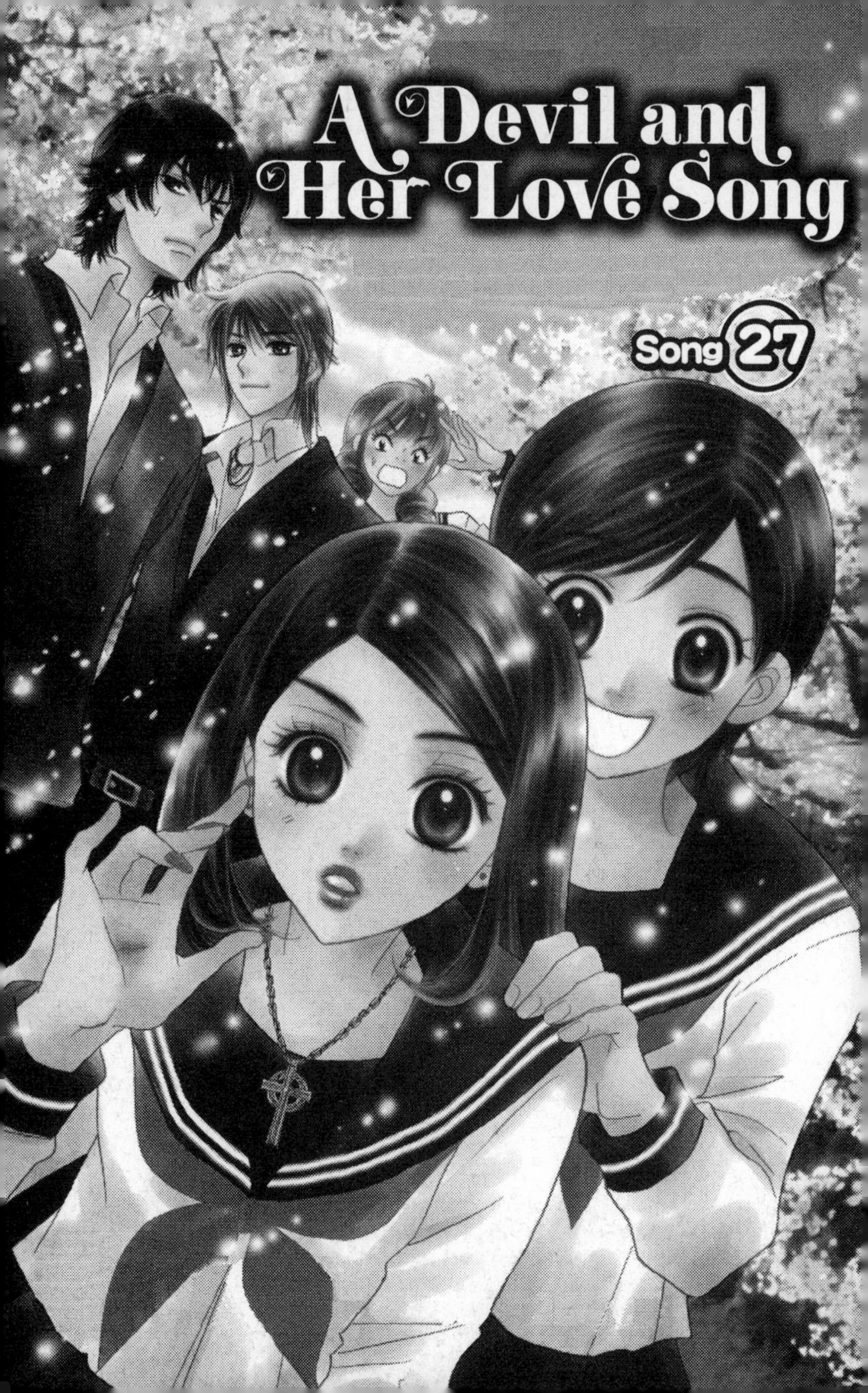
A Devil and Her Love Song
Song 27

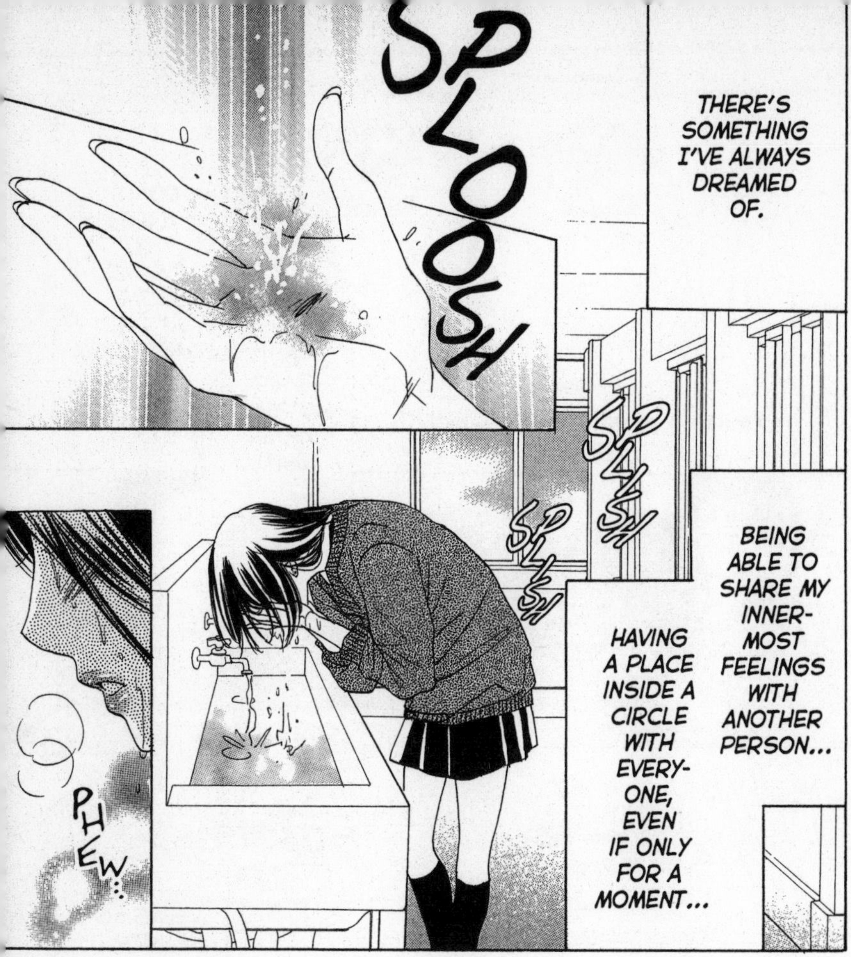
THERE'S SOMETHING I'VE ALWAYS DREAMED OF.
SPLOOSH
BEING ABLE TO SHARE MY INNER-MOST FEELINGS WITH ANOTHER PERSON...
HAVING A PLACE INSIDE A CIRCLE WITH EVERY-ONE, EVEN IF ONLY FOR A MOMENT...
SPLISH
SPLISH
PHEW...

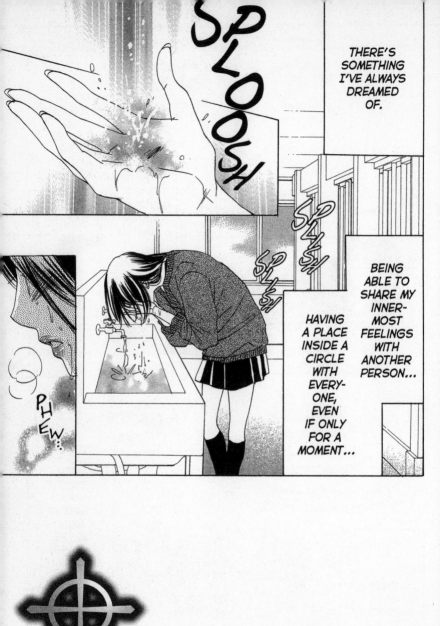

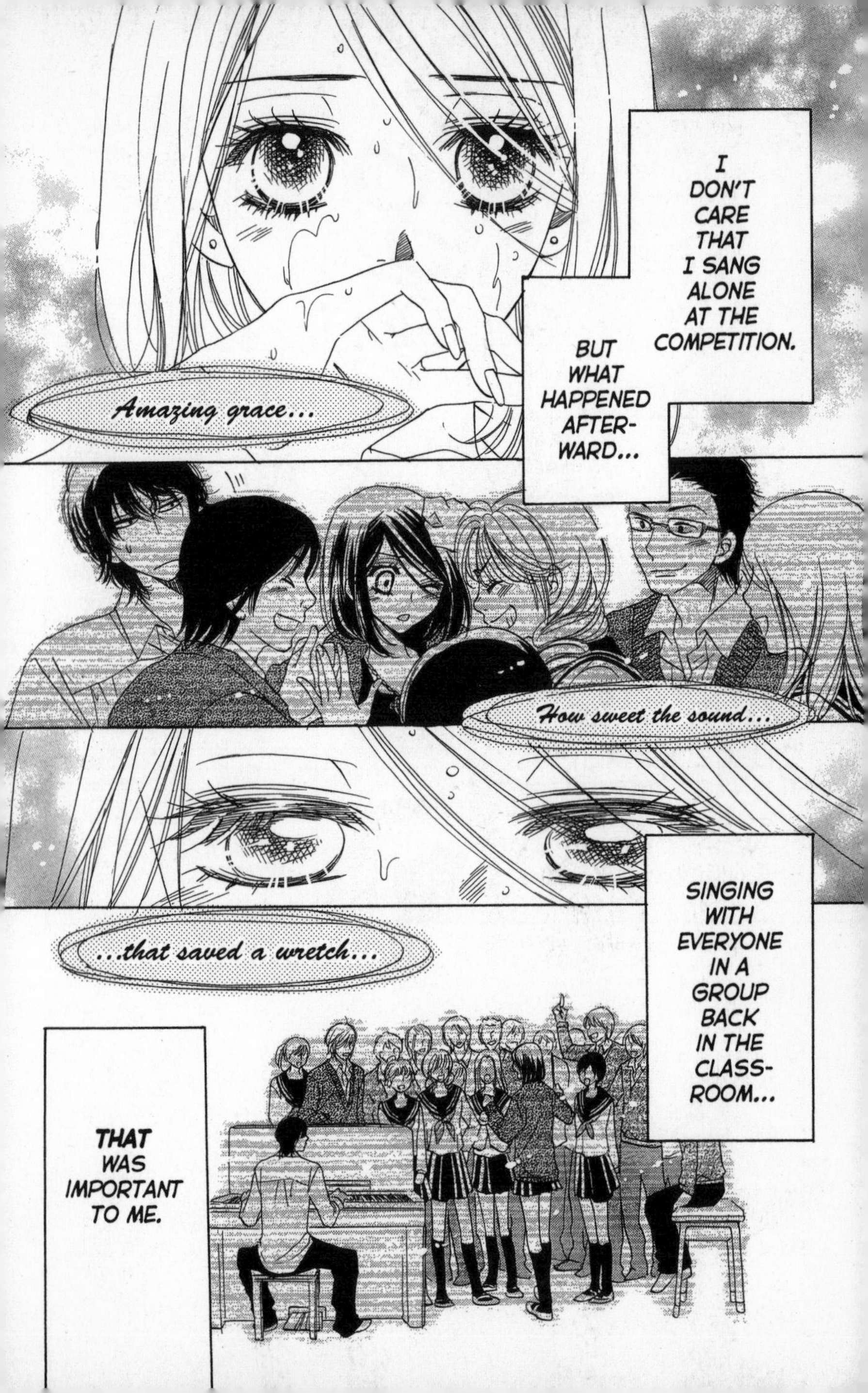
I DON'T CARE THAT I SANG ALONE AT THE COMPETITION.
BUT WHAT HAPPENED AFTER-WARD...
Amazing grace...
How sweet the sound...
SINGING WITH EVERYONE IN A GROUP BACK IN THE CLASS-ROOM...
...that saved a wretch...
THAT WAS IMPORTANT TO ME.

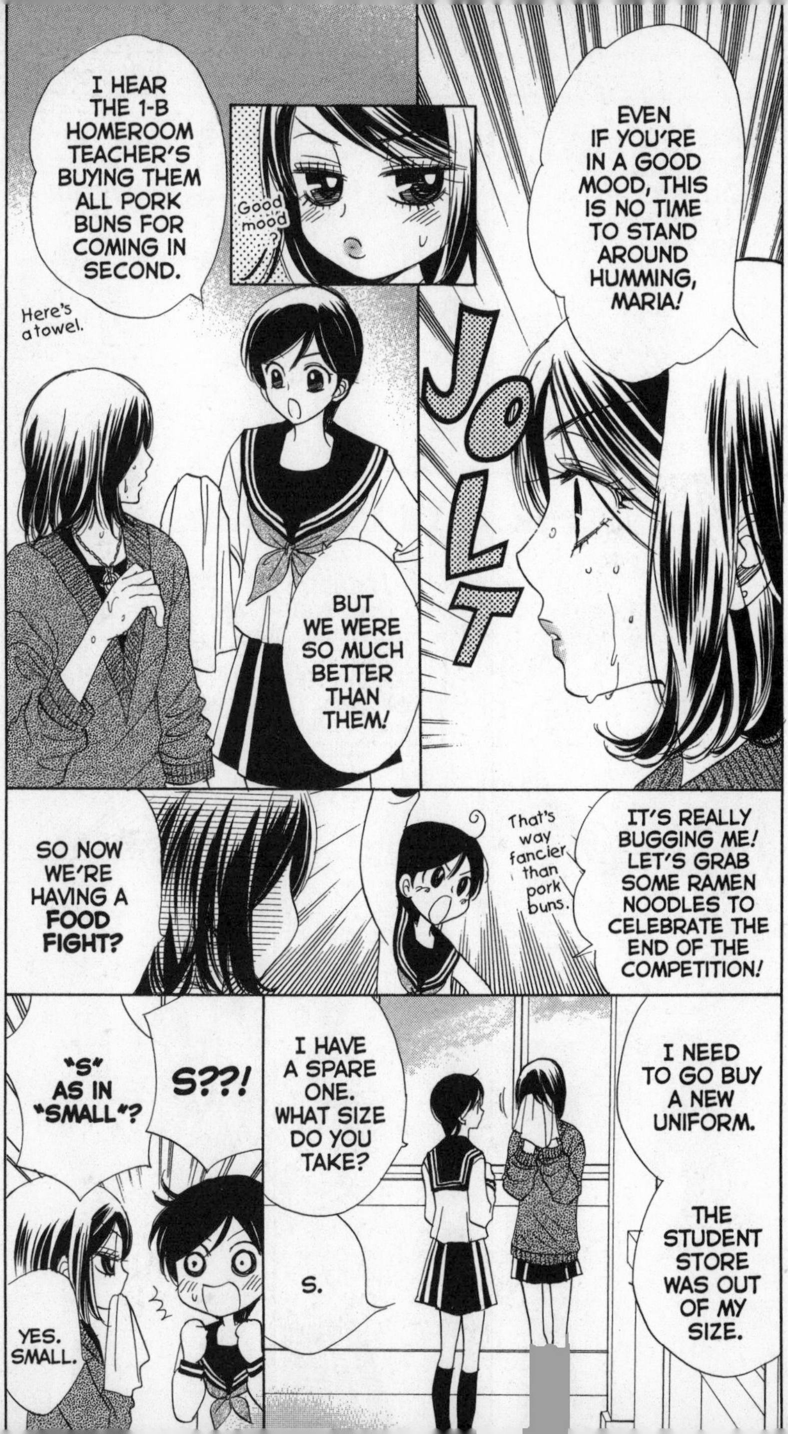
EVEN IF YOU'RE IN A GOOD MOOD, THIS IS NO TIME TO STAND AROUND HUMMING, MARIA!
JOLT
Good mood?
I HEAR THE 1-B HOMEROOM TEACHER'S BUYING THEM ALL PORK BUNS FOR COMING IN SECOND.
Here's a towel.
BUT WE WERE SO MUCH BETTER THAN THEM!
IT'S REALLY BUGGING ME! LET'S GRAB SOME RAMEN NOODLES TO CELEBRATE THE END OF THE COMPETITION!
That's way fancier than pork buns.
SO NOW WE'RE HAVING A FOOD FIGHT?
I NEED TO GO BUY A NEW UNIFORM.
THE STUDENT STORE WAS OUT OF MY SIZE.
I HAVE A SPARE ONE. WHAT SIZE DO YOU TAKE?
S.
S??!
"S" AS IN "SMALL"?
YES. SMALL.

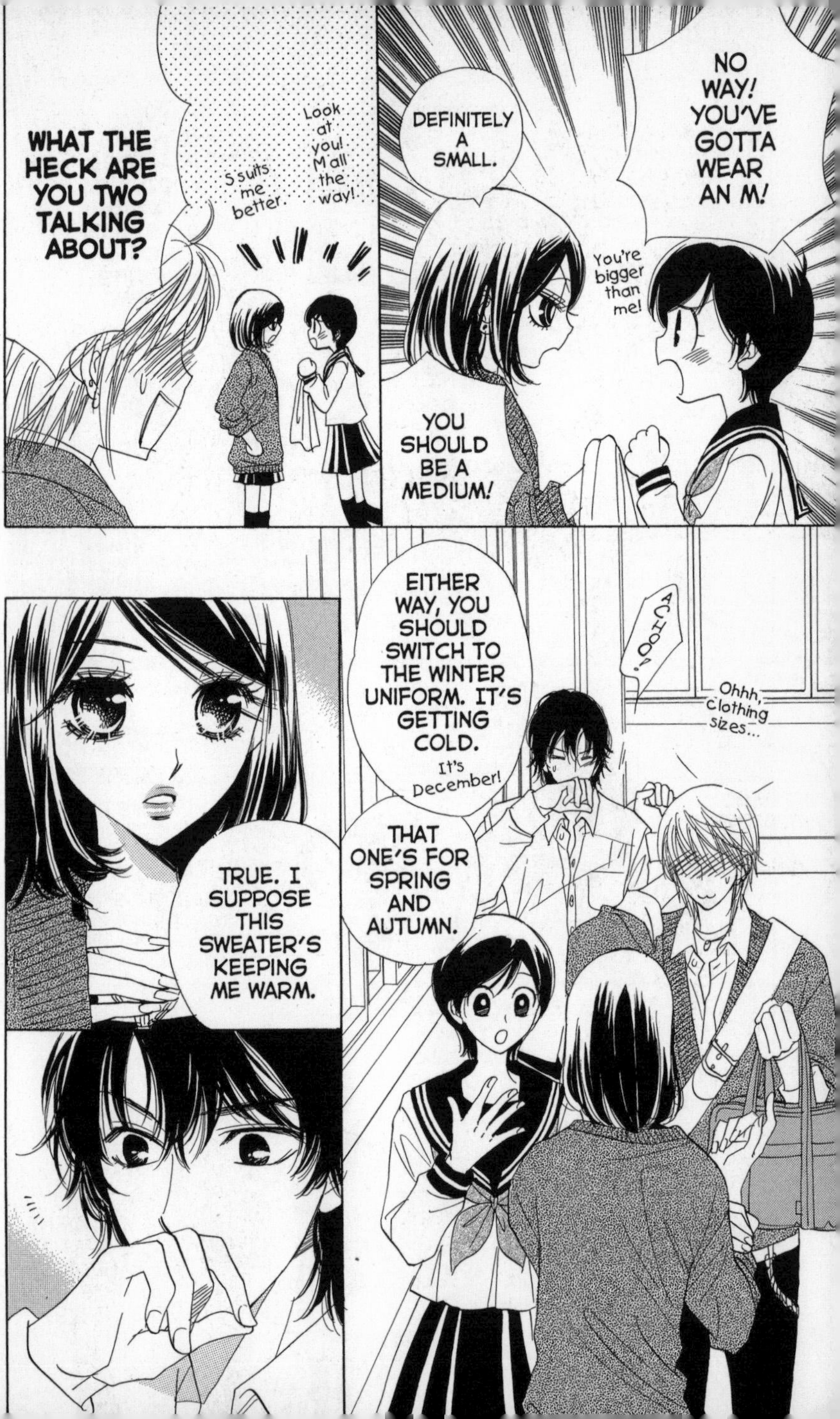
NO WAY! YOU'VE GOTTA WEAR AN M!
DEFINITELY A SMALL.
You're bigger than me!
YOU SHOULD BE A MEDIUM!
Look at you! M all the way!
S suits me better.
WHAT THE HECK ARE YOU TWO TALKING ABOUT?
ACHOO!
Ohhh, clothing sizes...
EITHER WAY, YOU SHOULD SWITCH TO THE WINTER UNIFORM. IT'S GETTING COLD.
It's December!
THAT ONE'S FOR SPRING AND AUTUMN.
TRUE. I SUPPOSE THIS SWEATER'S KEEPING ME WARM.

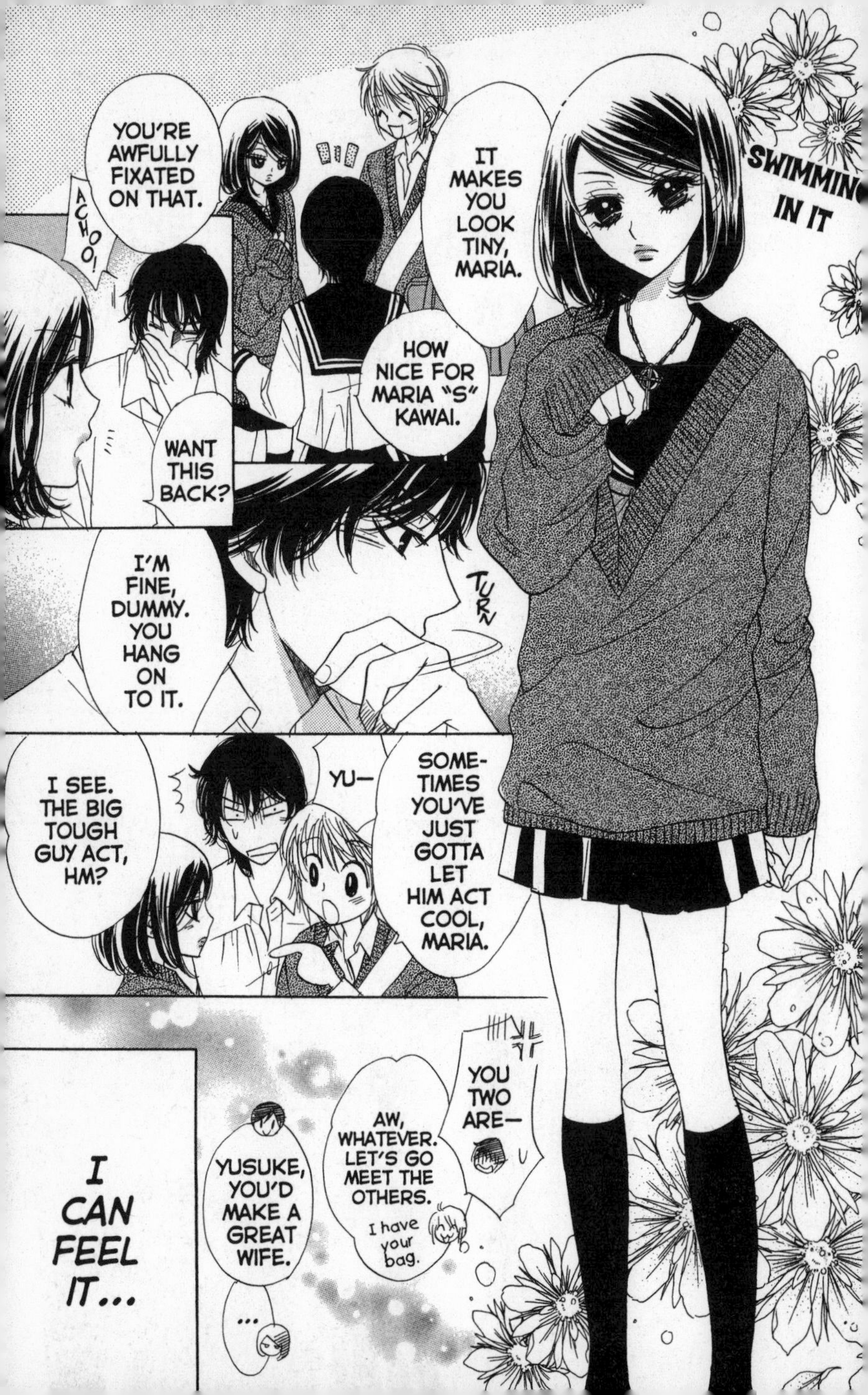
SWIMMING IN IT
IT MAKES YOU LOOK TINY, MARIA.
HOW NICE FOR MARIA "S" KAWAI.
YOU'RE AWFULLY FIXATED ON THAT.
ACHOO!
WANT THIS BACK?
TURN
I'M FINE, DUMMY. YOU HANG ON TO IT.
SOMETIMES YOU'VE JUST GOTTA LET HIM ACT COOL, MARIA.
YU—
I SEE. THE BIG TOUGH GUY ACT, HM?
YOU TWO ARE—
AW, WHATEVER. LET'S GO MEET THE OTHERS.
I have your bag.
YUSUKE, YOU'D MAKE A GREAT WIFE.
...
I CAN FEEL IT...

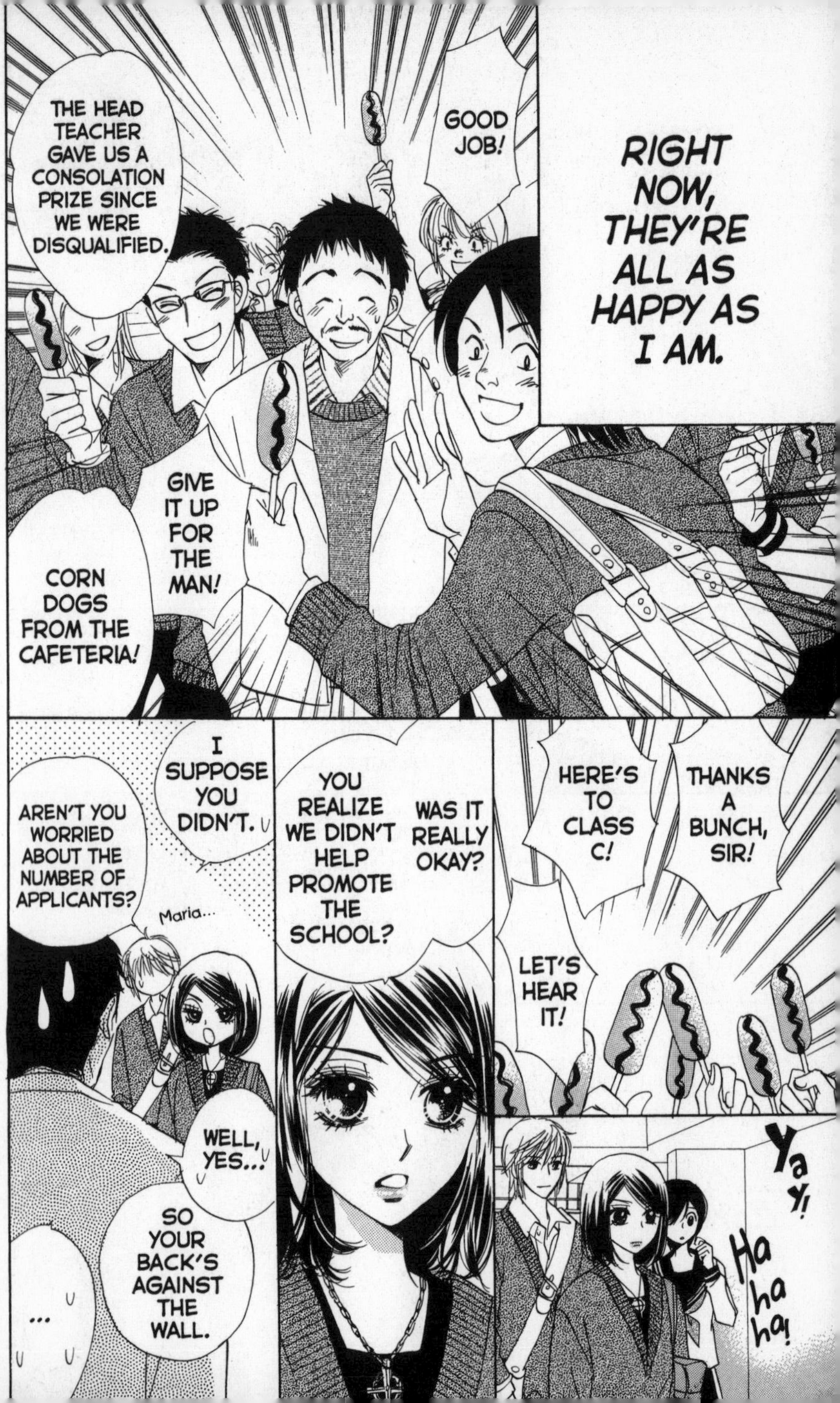
RIGHT NOW, THEY'RE ALL AS HAPPY AS I AM.
GOOD JOB!
THE HEAD TEACHER GAVE US A CONSOLATION PRIZE SINCE WE WERE DISQUALIFIED.
GIVE IT UP FOR THE MAN!
CORN DOGS FROM THE CAFETERIA!
THANKS A BUNCH, SIR!
HERE'S TO CLASS C!
LET'S HEAR IT!
Yay!
Ha ha ha!
WAS IT REALLY OKAY?
YOU REALIZE WE DIDN'T HELP PROMOTE THE SCHOOL?
I SUPPOSE YOU DIDN'T.
AREN'T YOU WORRIED ABOUT THE NUMBER OF APPLICANTS?
Maria...
WELL, YES...
SO YOUR BACK'S AGAINST THE WALL.
...

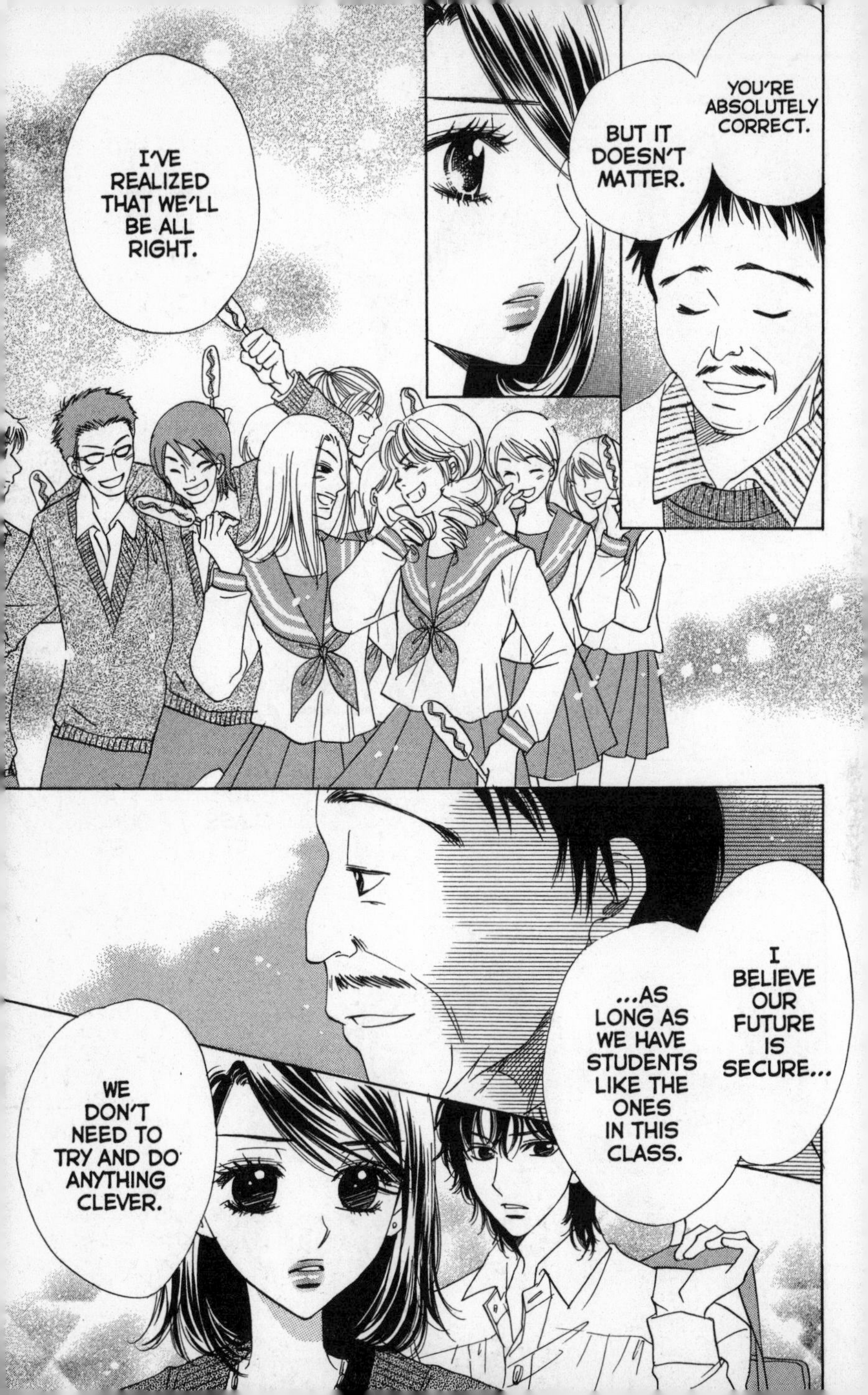
YOU'RE ABSOLUTELY CORRECT.
BUT IT DOESN'T MATTER.
I'VE REALIZED THAT WE'LL BE ALL RIGHT.
I BELIEVE OUR FUTURE IS SECURE...
...AS LONG AS WE HAVE STUDENTS LIKE THE ONES IN THIS CLASS.
WE DON'T NEED TO TRY AND DO ANYTHING CLEVER.

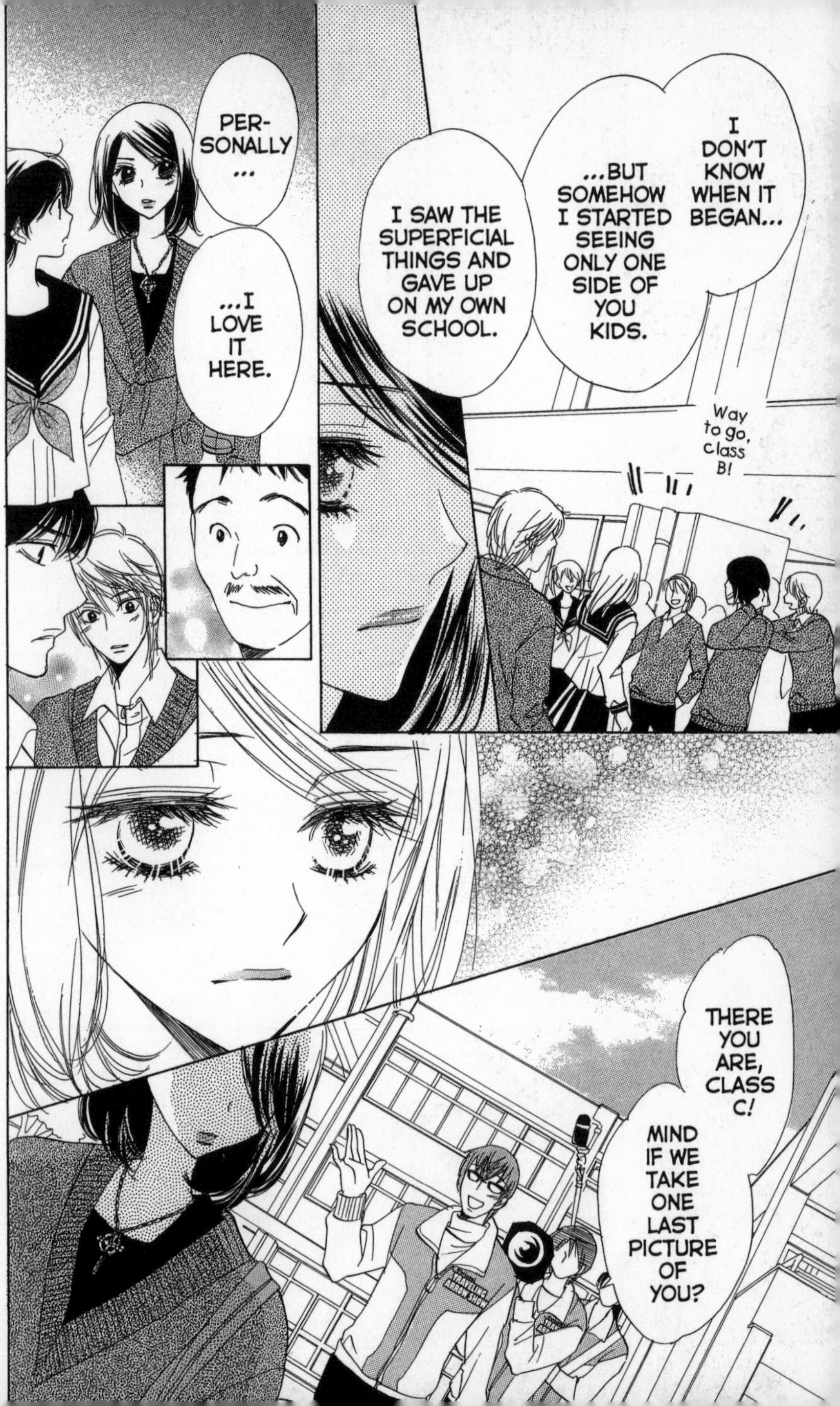
I DON'T KNOW WHEN IT BEGAN...
...BUT SOMEHOW I STARTED SEEING ONLY ONE SIDE OF YOU KIDS.
Way to go, class B!
I SAW THE SUPERFICIAL THINGS AND GAVE UP ON MY OWN SCHOOL.
PER-SONALLY...
...I LOVE IT HERE.
THERE YOU ARE, CLASS C!
MIND IF WE TAKE ONE LAST PICTURE OF YOU?

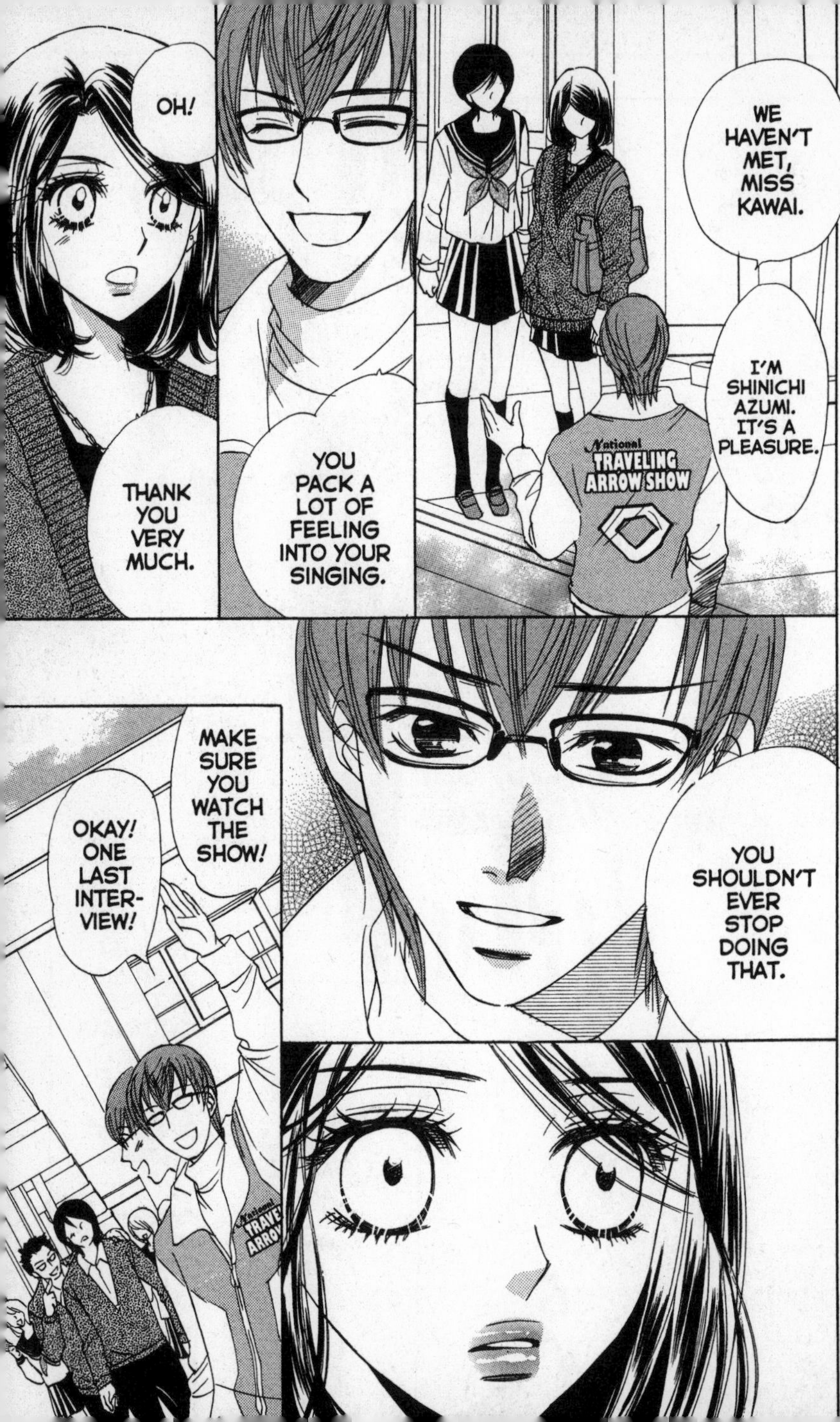
WE HAVEN'T MET, MISS KAWAI.
I'M SHINICHI AZUMI. IT'S A PLEASURE.
National TRAVELING ARROW SHOW
YOU PACK A LOT OF FEELING INTO YOUR SINGING.
OH!
THANK YOU VERY MUCH.
YOU SHOULDN'T EVER STOP DOING THAT.
MAKE SURE YOU WATCH THE SHOW!
OKAY! ONE LAST INTER-VIEW!

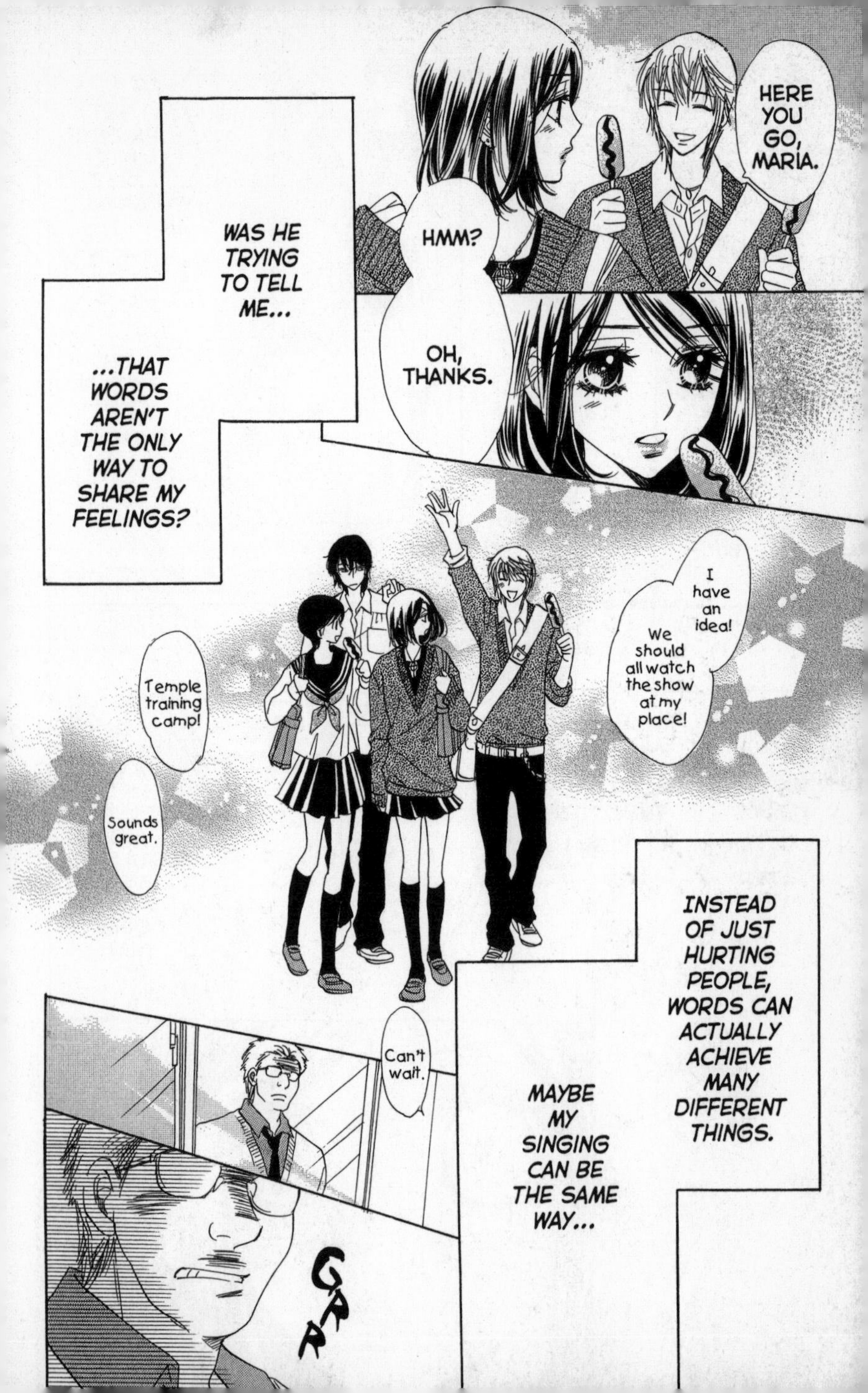
HERE YOU GO, MARIA.
HMM?
WAS HE TRYING TO TELL ME...
OH, THANKS.
...THAT WORDS AREN'T THE ONLY WAY TO SHARE MY FEELINGS?
I have an idea!
We should all watch the show at my place!
Temple training camp!
Sounds great.
Can't wait.
INSTEAD OF JUST HURTING PEOPLE, WORDS CAN ACTUALLY ACHIEVE MANY DIFFERENT THINGS.
MAYBE MY SINGING CAN BE THE SAME WAY...
GRR

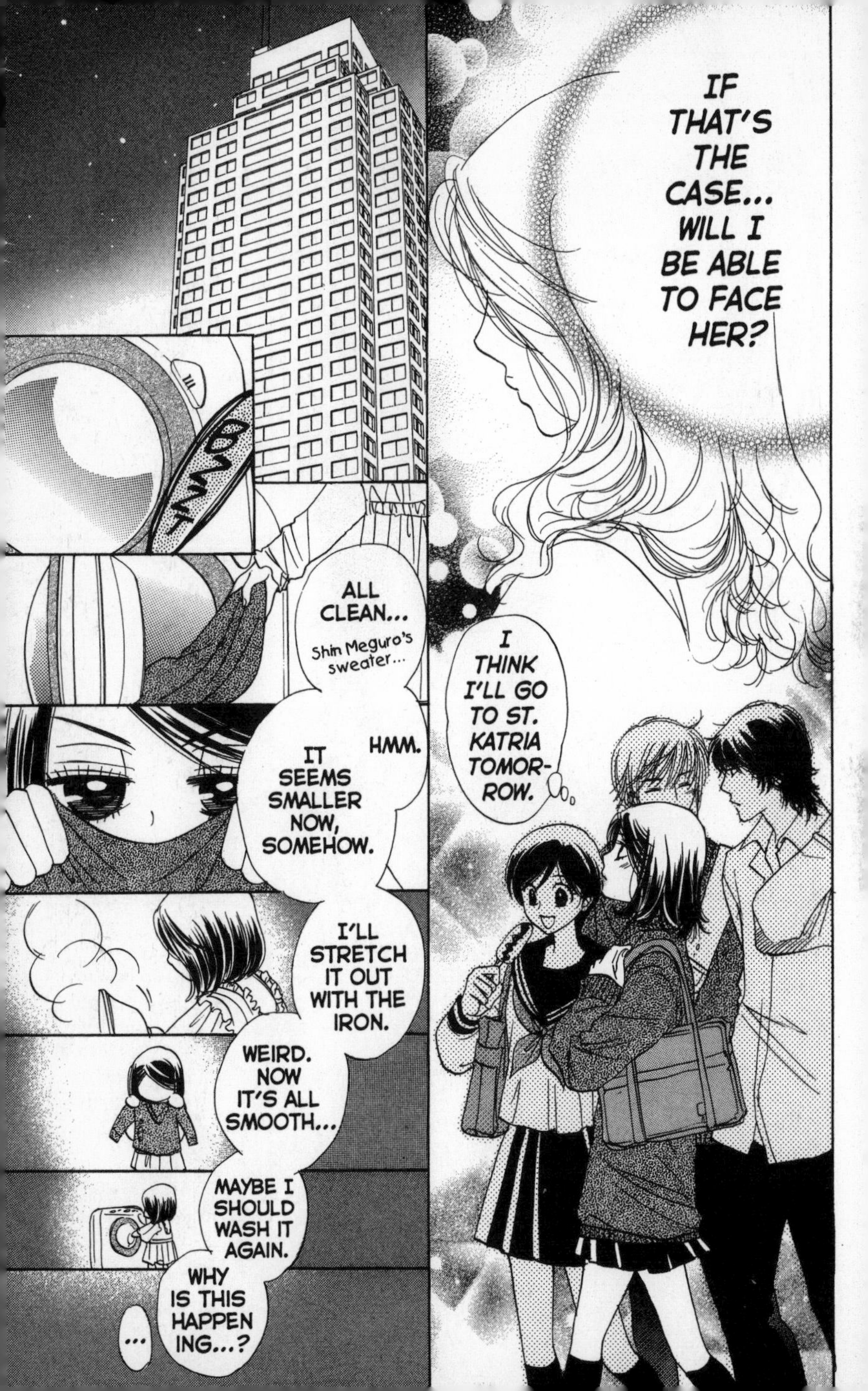
IF THAT'S THE CASE... WILL I BE ABLE TO FACE HER?
I THINK I'LL GO TO ST. KATRIA TOMORROW.
ALL CLEAN...
Shin Meguro's sweater...
HMM.
IT SEEMS SMALLER NOW, SOMEHOW.
I'LL STRETCH IT OUT WITH THE IRON.
WEIRD. NOW IT'S ALL SMOOTH...
MAYBE I SHOULD WASH IT AGAIN.
WHY IS THIS HAPPENING...?
...

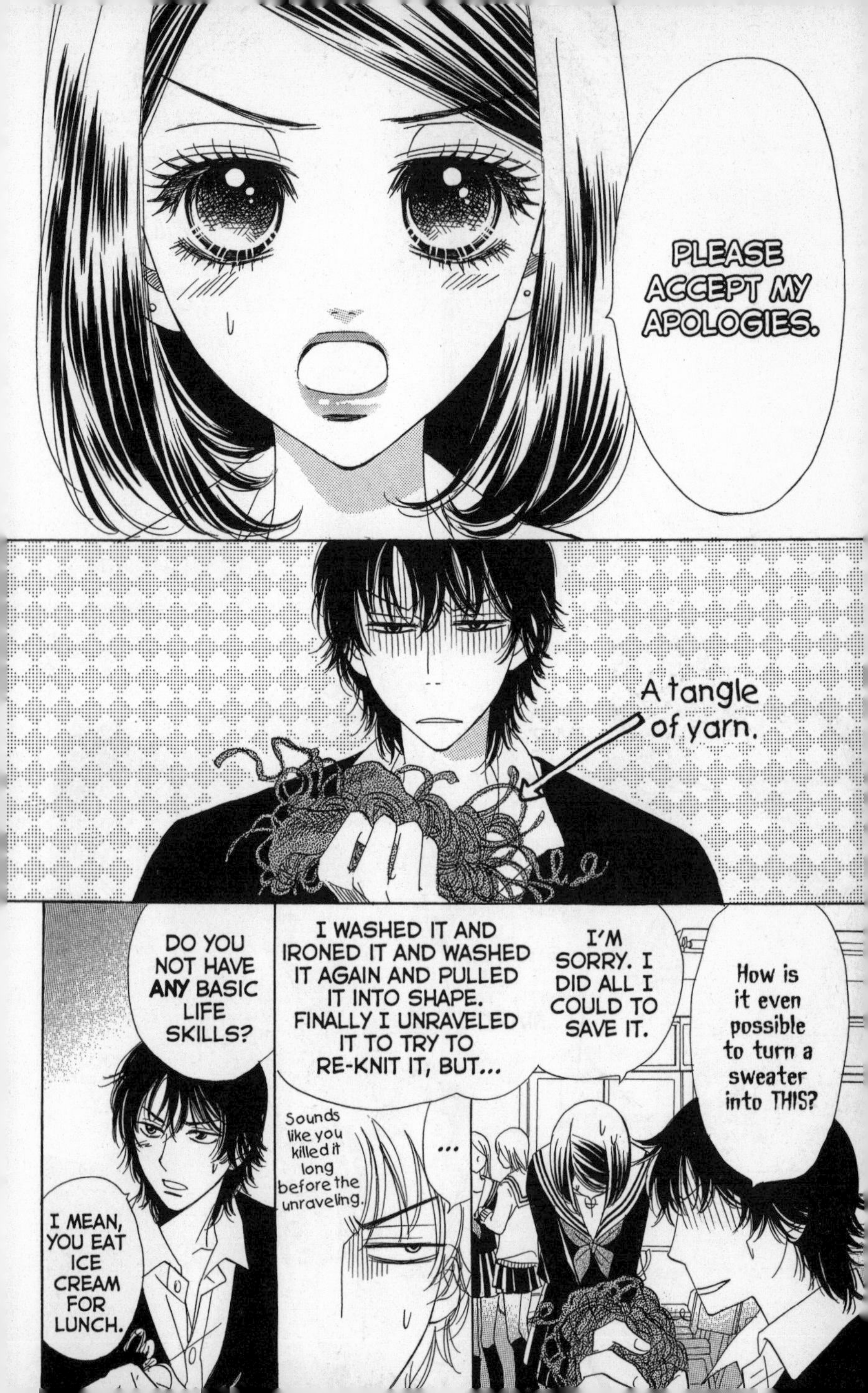
PLEASE ACCEPT MY APOLOGIES.
A tangle of yarn.
How is it even possible to turn a sweater into THIS?
I'M SORRY. I DID ALL I COULD TO SAVE IT.
I WASHED IT AND IRONED IT AND WASHED IT AGAIN AND PULLED IT INTO SHAPE. FINALLY I UNRAVELED IT TO TRY TO RE-KNIT IT, BUT...
...
Sounds like you killed it long before the unraveling.
DO YOU NOT HAVE ANY BASIC LIFE SKILLS?
I MEAN, YOU EAT ICE CREAM FOR LUNCH.

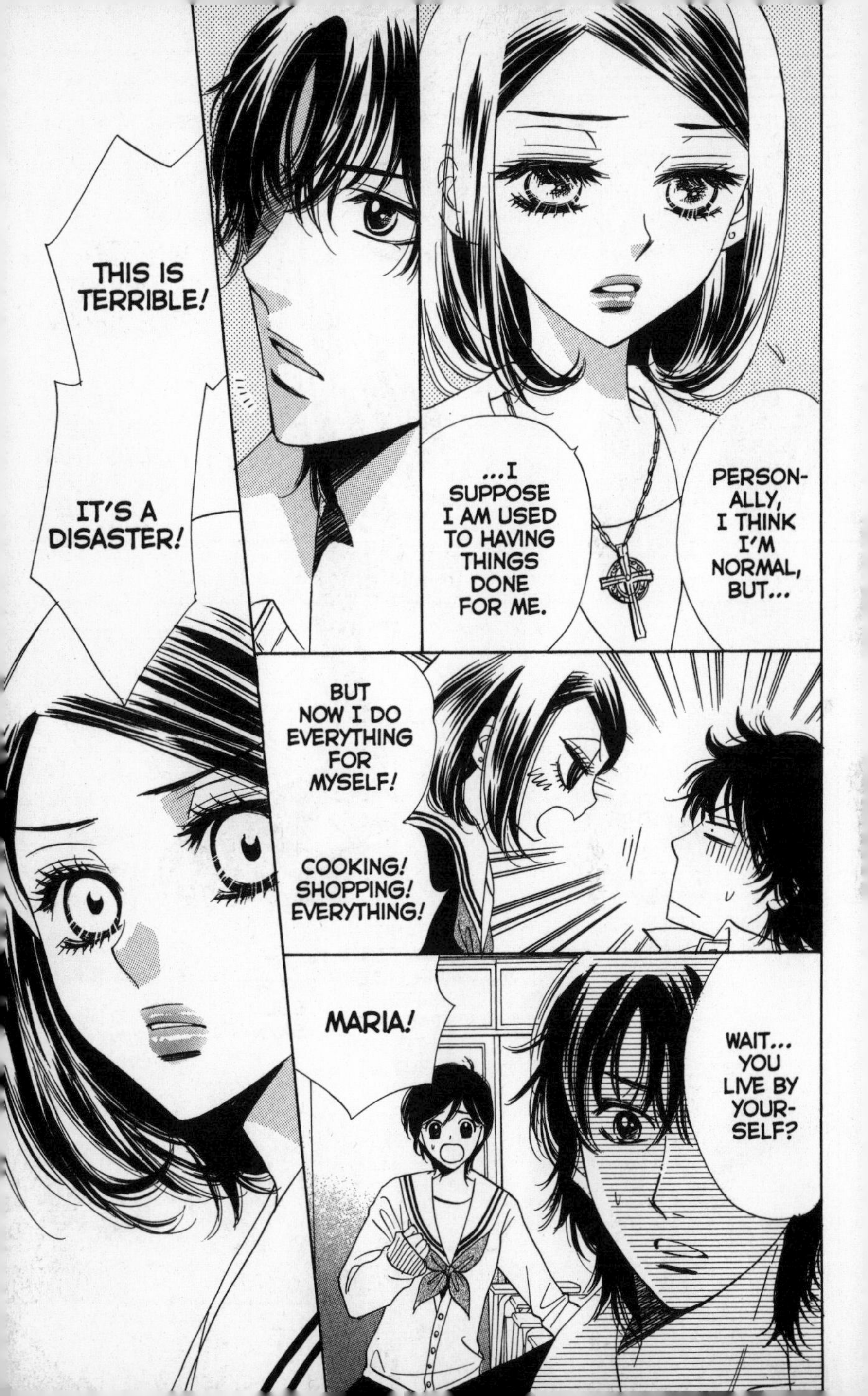
PERSONALLY, I THINK I'M NORMAL, BUT...
...I SUPPOSE I AM USED TO HAVING THINGS DONE FOR ME.
THIS IS TERRIBLE!
IT'S A DISASTER!
BUT NOW I DO EVERYTHING FOR MYSELF!
COOKING! SHOPPING! EVERYTHING!
WAIT... YOU LIVE BY YOURSELF?
MARIA!

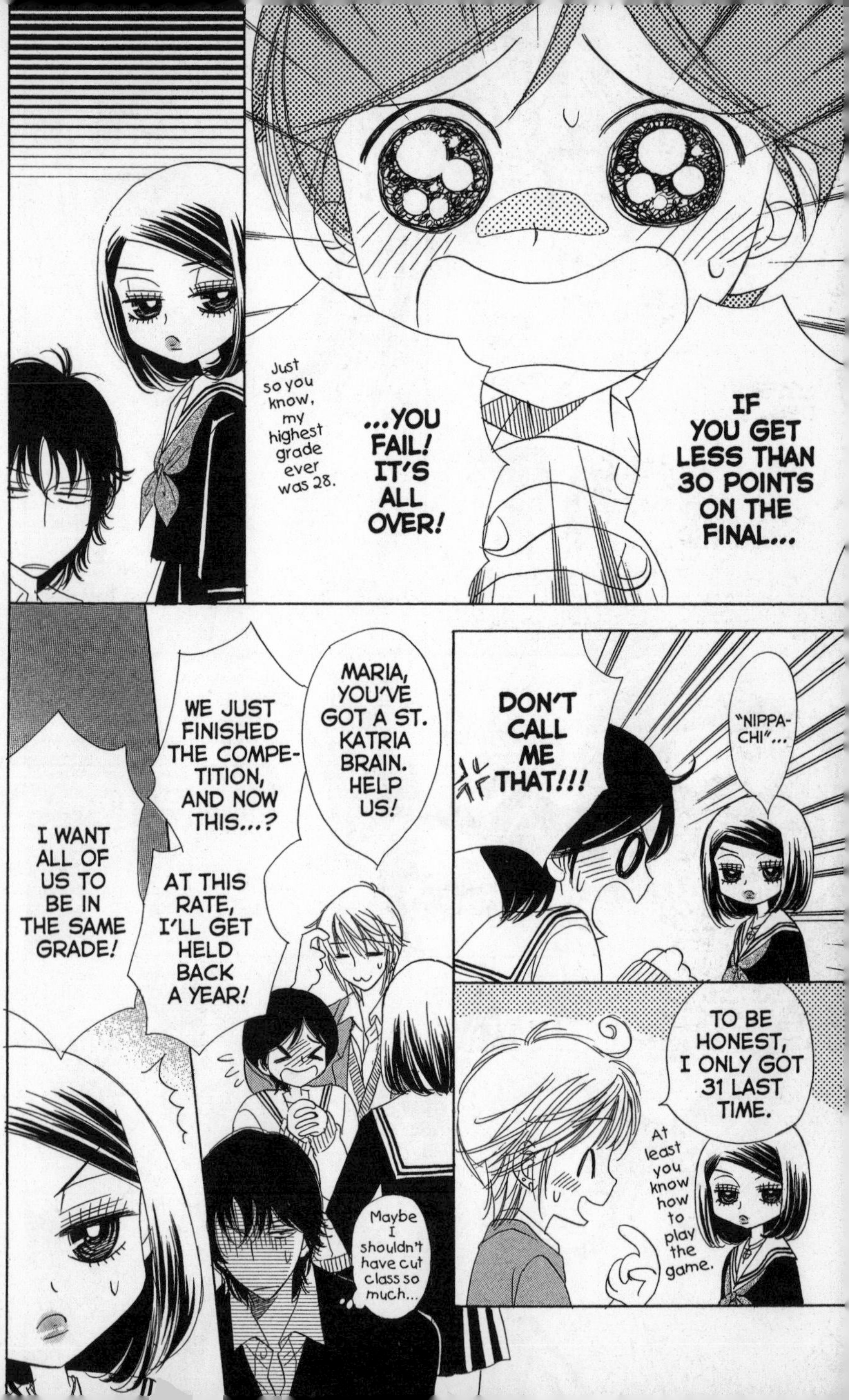
IF YOU GET LESS THAN 30 POINTS ON THE FINAL...
...YOU FAIL! IT'S ALL OVER!
Just so you know, my highest grade ever was 28.
"NIPPA-CHI"...
DON'T CALL ME THAT!!!
TO BE HONEST, I ONLY GOT 31 LAST TIME.
At least you know how to play the game.
MARIA, YOU'VE GOT A ST. KATRIA BRAIN. HELP US!
WE JUST FINISHED THE COMPETITION, AND NOW THIS...?
AT THIS RATE, I'LL GET HELD BACK A YEAR!
I WANT ALL OF US TO BE IN THE SAME GRADE!
Maybe I shouldn't have cut class so much...

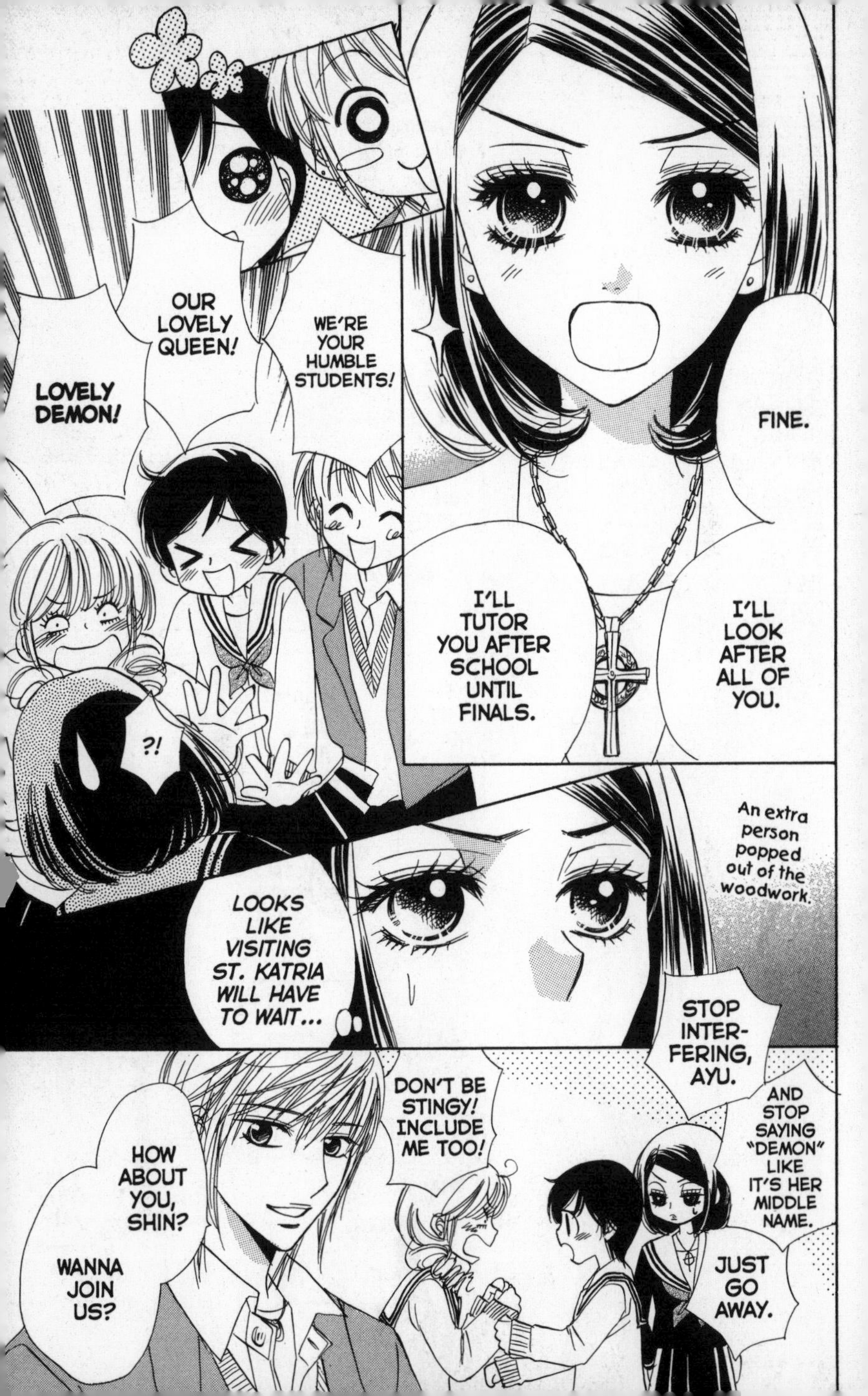
FINE.
I'LL LOOK AFTER ALL OF YOU.
I'LL TUTOR YOU AFTER SCHOOL UNTIL FINALS.
WE'RE YOUR HUMBLE STUDENTS!
OUR LOVELY QUEEN!
LOVELY DEMON!
?!
An extra person popped out of the woodwork.
LOOKS LIKE VISITING ST. KATRIA WILL HAVE TO WAIT...
STOP INTERFERING, AYU.
AND STOP SAYING "DEMON" LIKE IT'S HER MIDDLE NAME.
JUST GO AWAY.
DON'T BE STINGY! INCLUDE ME TOO!
HOW ABOUT YOU, SHIN?
WANNA JOIN US?

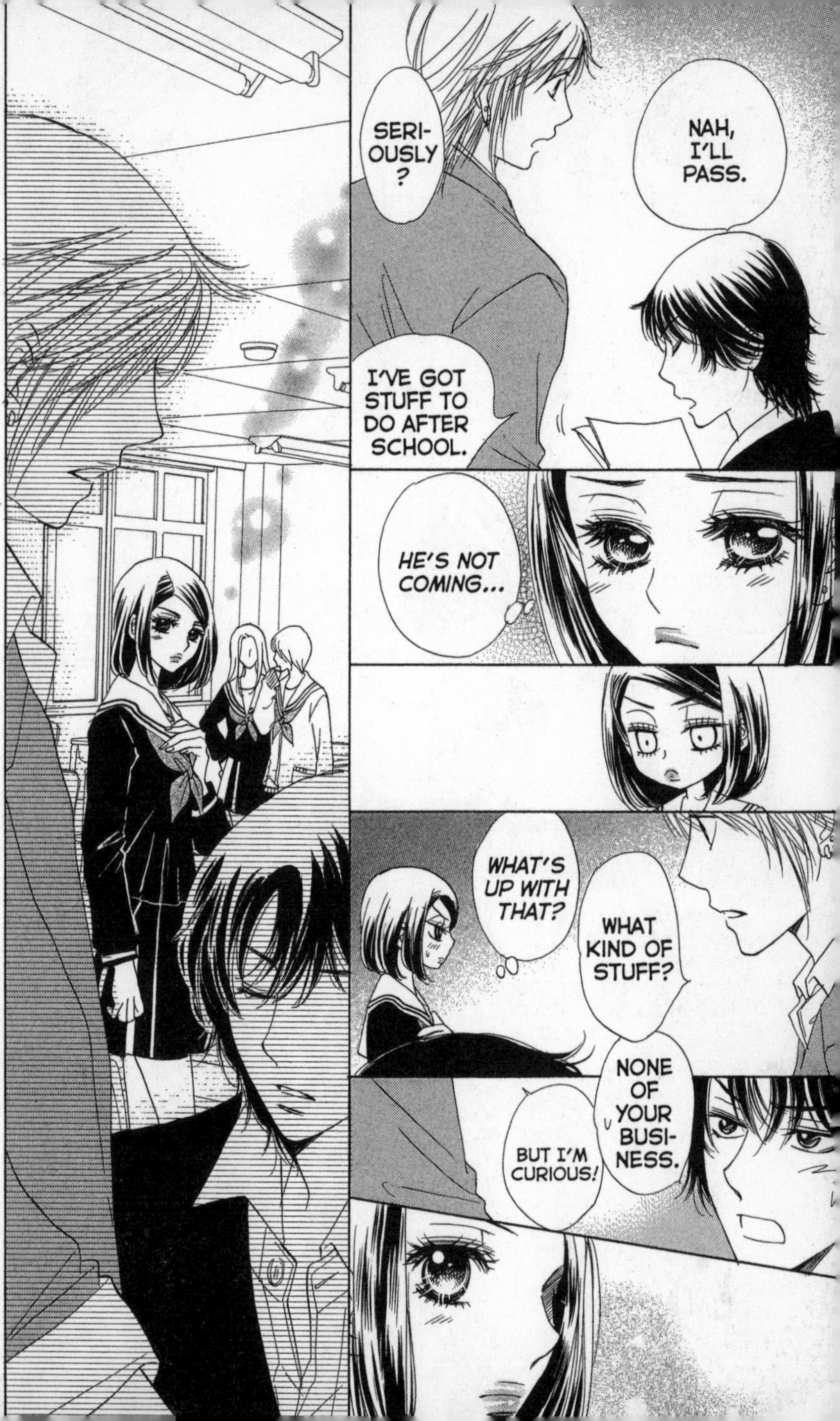
NAH, I'LL PASS.
SERI-OUSLY?
I'VE GOT STUFF TO DO AFTER SCHOOL.
HE'S NOT COMING...
WHAT KIND OF STUFF?
WHAT'S UP WITH THAT?
NONE OF YOUR BUSI-NESS.
BUT I'M CURIOUS!

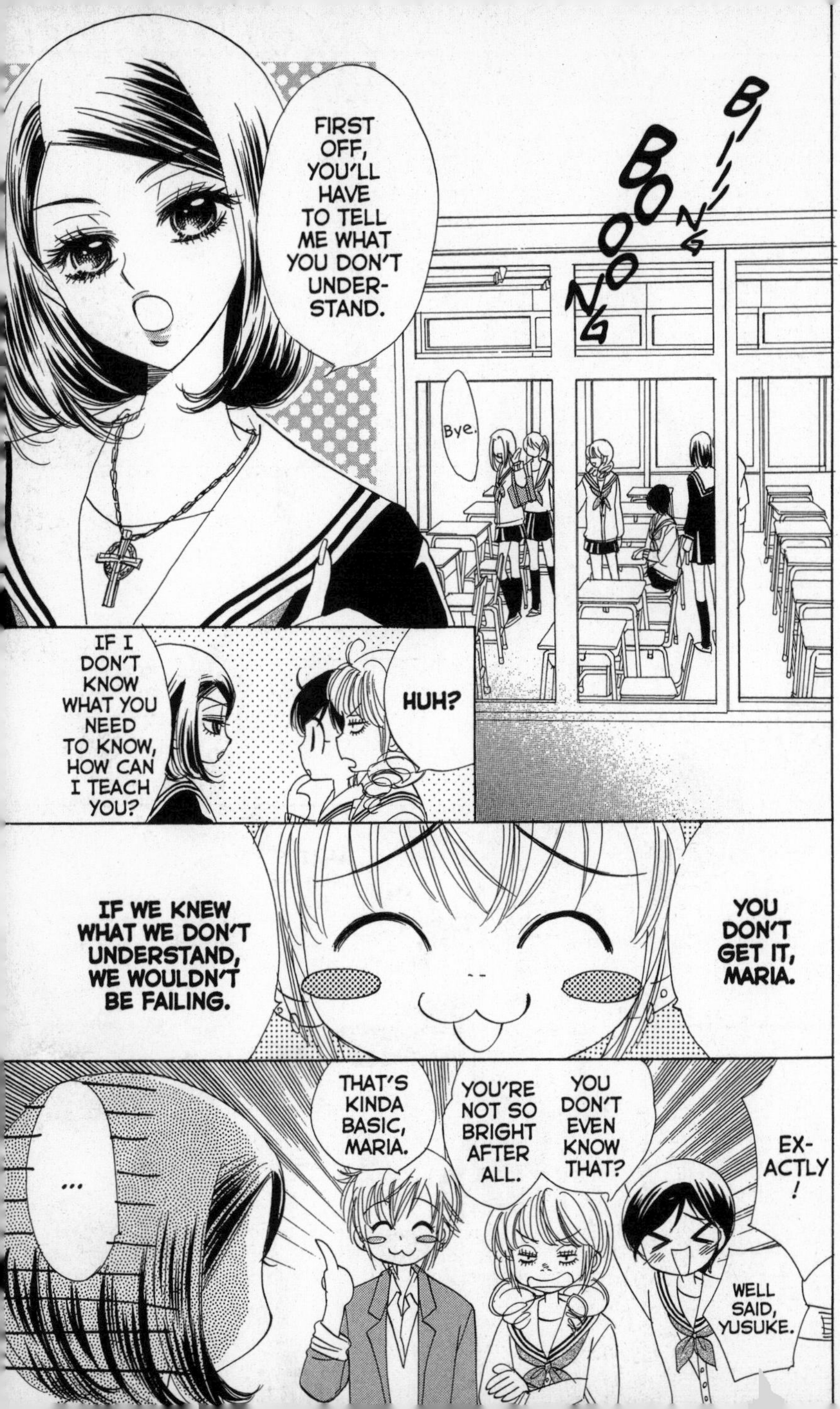
BIING
BOOOONG
Bye.
FIRST OFF, YOU'LL HAVE TO TELL ME WHAT YOU DON'T UNDER-STAND.
HUH?
IF I DON'T KNOW WHAT YOU NEED TO KNOW, HOW CAN I TEACH YOU?
YOU DON'T GET IT, MARIA.
IF WE KNEW WHAT WE DON'T UNDERSTAND, WE WOULDN'T BE FAILING.
EX-ACTLY!
WELL SAID, YUSUKE.
YOU DON'T EVEN KNOW THAT?
YOU'RE NOT SO BRIGHT AFTER ALL.
THAT'S KINDA BASIC, MARIA.
...

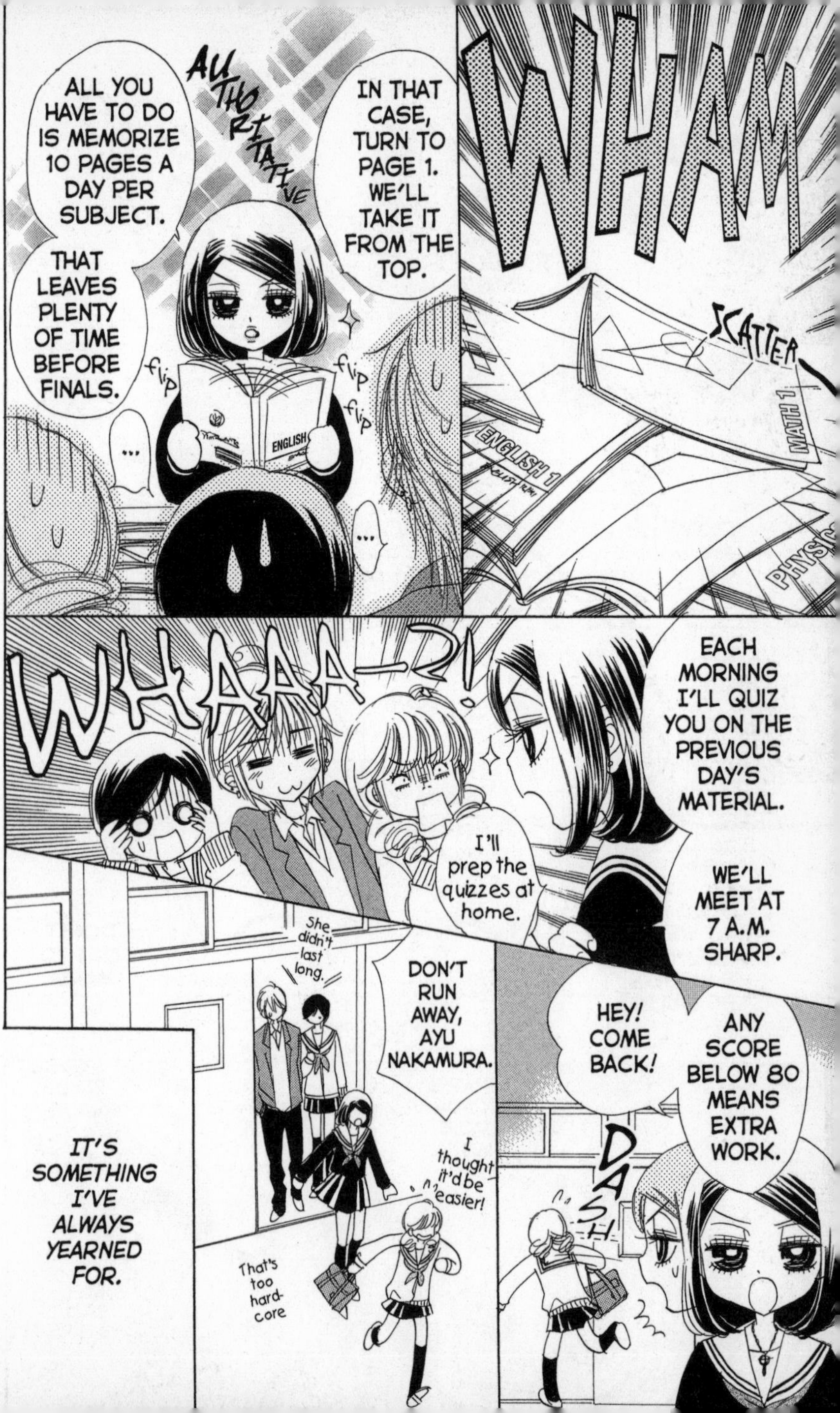
WHAM
SCATTER
MATH 1
ENGLISH 1
IN THAT CASE, TURN TO PAGE 1. WE'LL TAKE IT FROM THE TOP.
AUTHORITATIVE
ALL YOU HAVE TO DO IS MEMORIZE 10 PAGES A DAY PER SUBJECT.
THAT LEAVES PLENTY OF TIME BEFORE FINALS.
flip
flip
flip
ENGLISH
...
...
EACH MORNING I'LL QUIZ YOU ON THE PREVIOUS DAY'S MATERIAL.
WE'LL MEET AT 7 A.M. SHARP.
I'll prep the quizzes at home.
WHAAA--?!
ANY SCORE BELOW 80 MEANS EXTRA WORK.
HEY! COME BACK!
DASH
DON'T RUN AWAY, AYU NAKAMURA.
She didn't last long.
I thought it'd be easier!
That's too hard-core
IT'S SOMETHING I'VE ALWAYS YEARNED FOR.

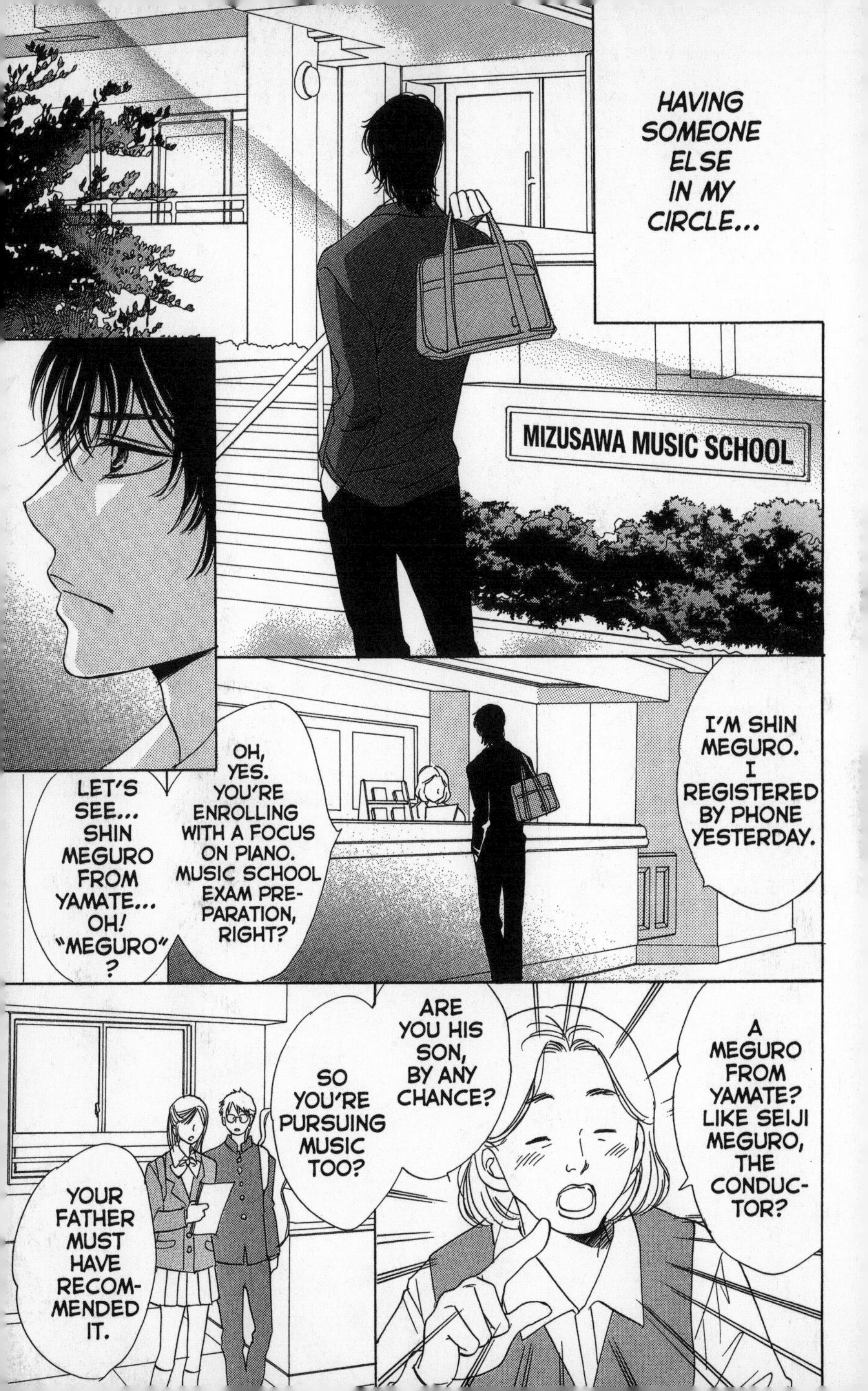
HAVING SOMEONE ELSE IN MY CIRCLE...
MIZUSAWA MUSIC SCHOOL
I'M SHIN MEGURO. I REGISTERED BY PHONE YESTERDAY.
OH, YES. YOU'RE ENROLLING WITH A FOCUS ON PIANO. MUSIC SCHOOL EXAM PRE-PARATION, RIGHT?
LET'S SEE... SHIN MEGURO FROM YAMATE... OH! "MEGURO"?
A MEGURO FROM YAMATE? LIKE SEIJI MEGURO, THE CONDUC-TOR?
ARE YOU HIS SON, BY ANY CHANCE?
SO YOU'RE PURSUING MUSIC TOO?
YOUR FATHER MUST HAVE RECOM-MENDED IT.

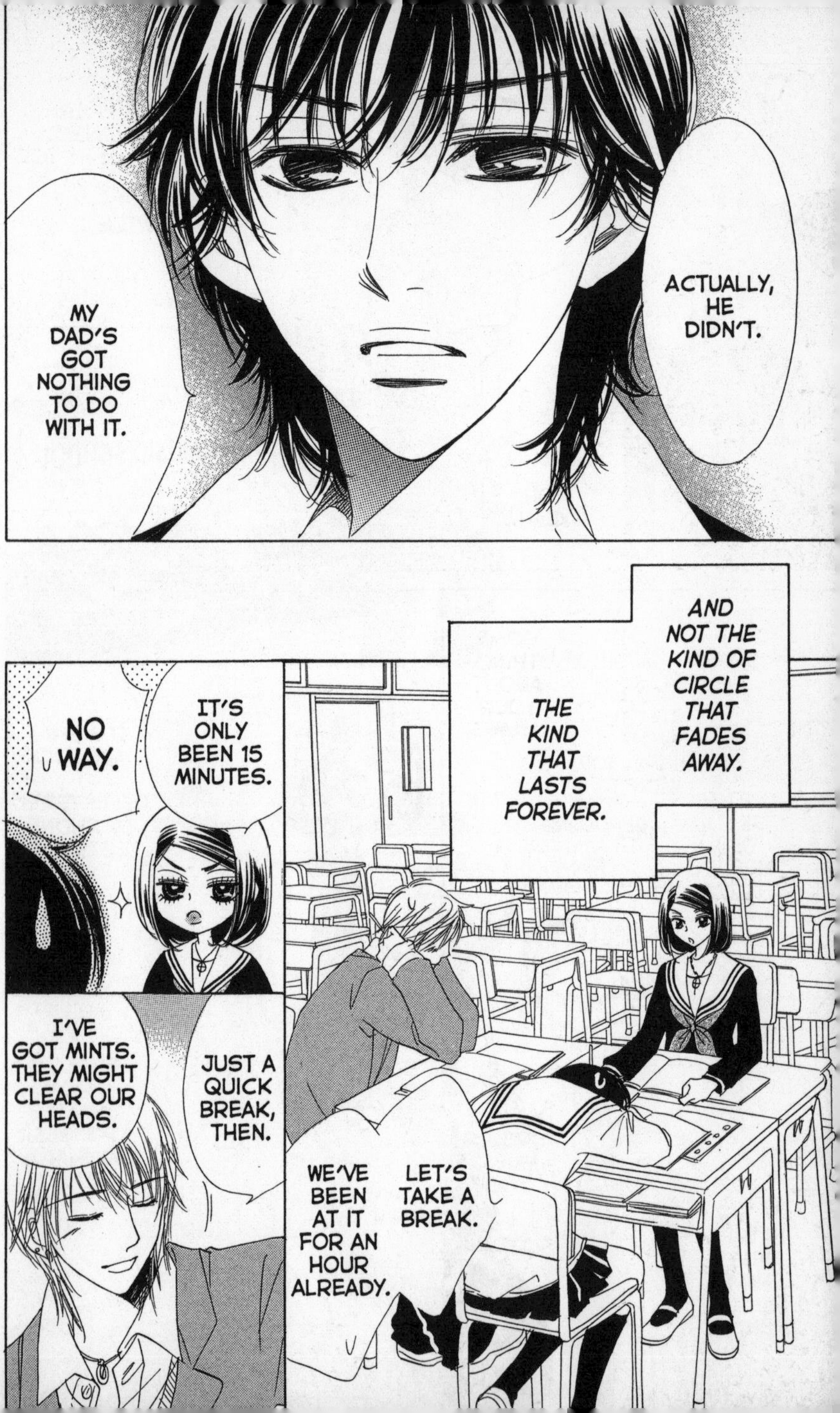
ACTUALLY, HE DIDN'T.
MY DAD'S GOT NOTHING TO DO WITH IT.
AND NOT THE KIND OF CIRCLE THAT FADES AWAY.
THE KIND THAT LASTS FOREVER.
LET'S TAKE A BREAK.
WE'VE BEEN AT IT FOR AN HOUR ALREADY.
IT'S ONLY BEEN 15 MINUTES.
NO WAY.
JUST A QUICK BREAK, THEN.
I'VE GOT MINTS. THEY MIGHT CLEAR OUR HEADS.

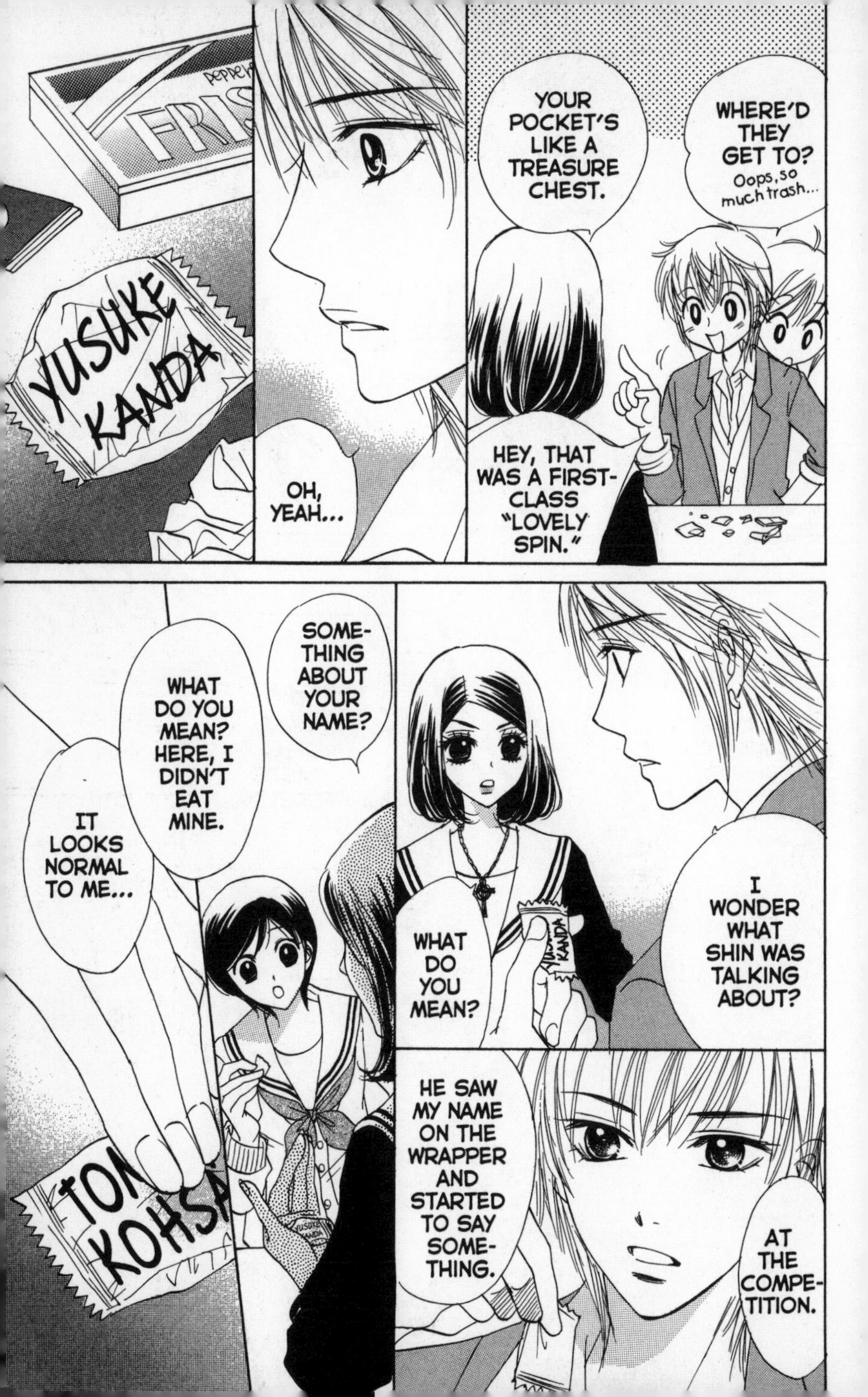
WHERE'D THEY GET TO? Oops, so much trash...
YOUR POCKET'S LIKE A TREASURE CHEST.
HEY, THAT WAS A FIRST-CLASS "LOVELY SPIN."
OH, YEAH...
YUSUKE KANDA
I WONDER WHAT SHIN WAS TALKING ABOUT?
WHAT DO YOU MEAN?
AT THE COMPETITION.
HE SAW MY NAME ON THE WRAPPER AND STARTED TO SAY SOME-THING.
SOME-THING ABOUT YOUR NAME?
WHAT DO YOU MEAN? HERE, I DIDN'T EAT MINE.
IT LOOKS NORMAL TO ME...

Note: In the Japanese edition, a part of the kanji characters for both names resemble circled crosses.

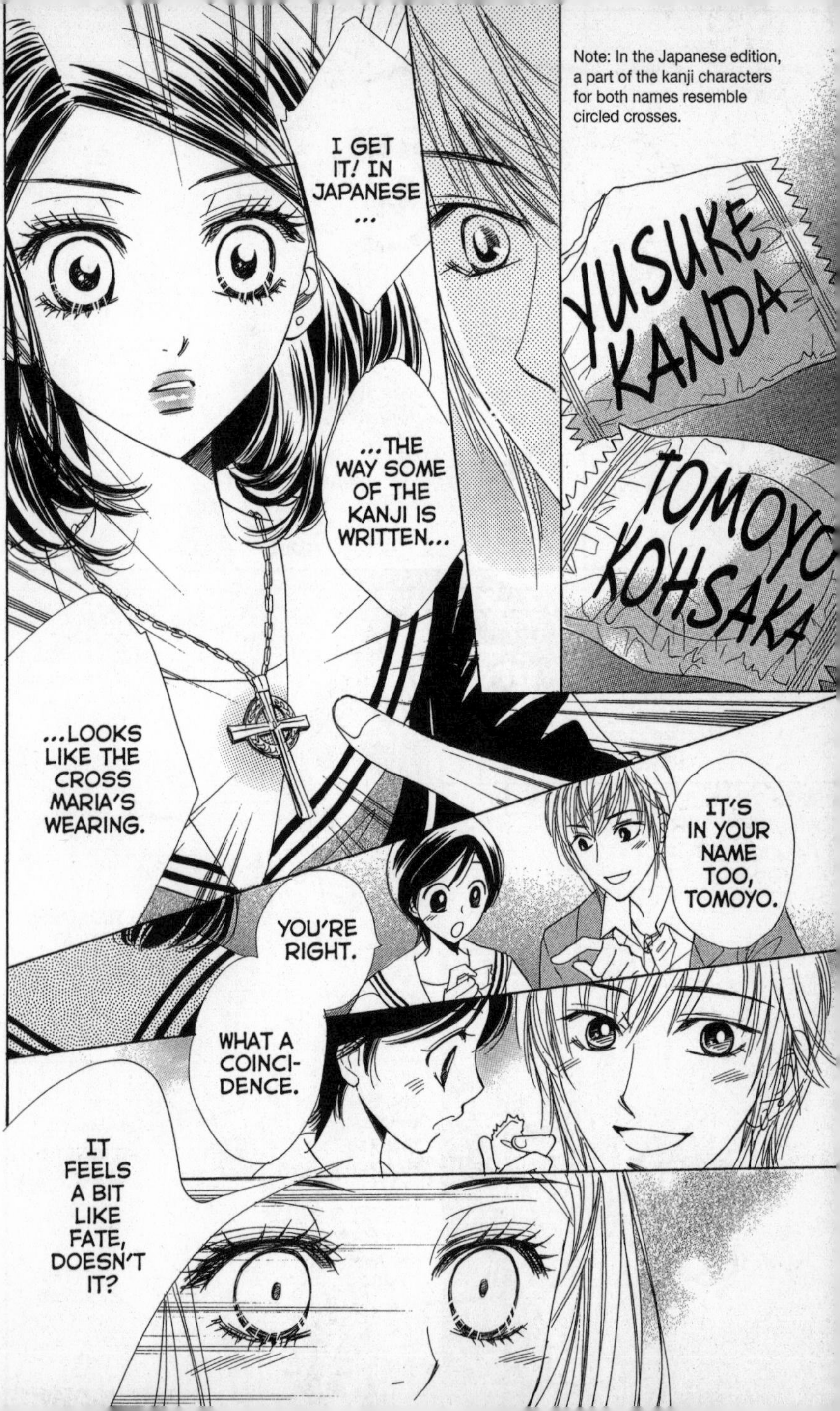
YUSUKE KANDA
TOMOYO KOHSAKA
I GET IT! IN JAPANESE...
...THE WAY SOME OF THE KANJI IS WRITTEN...
...LOOKS LIKE THE CROSS MARIA'S WEARING.
IT'S IN YOUR NAME TOO, TOMOYO.
YOU'RE RIGHT.
WHAT A COINCIDENCE.
IT FEELS A BIT LIKE FATE, DOESN'T IT?

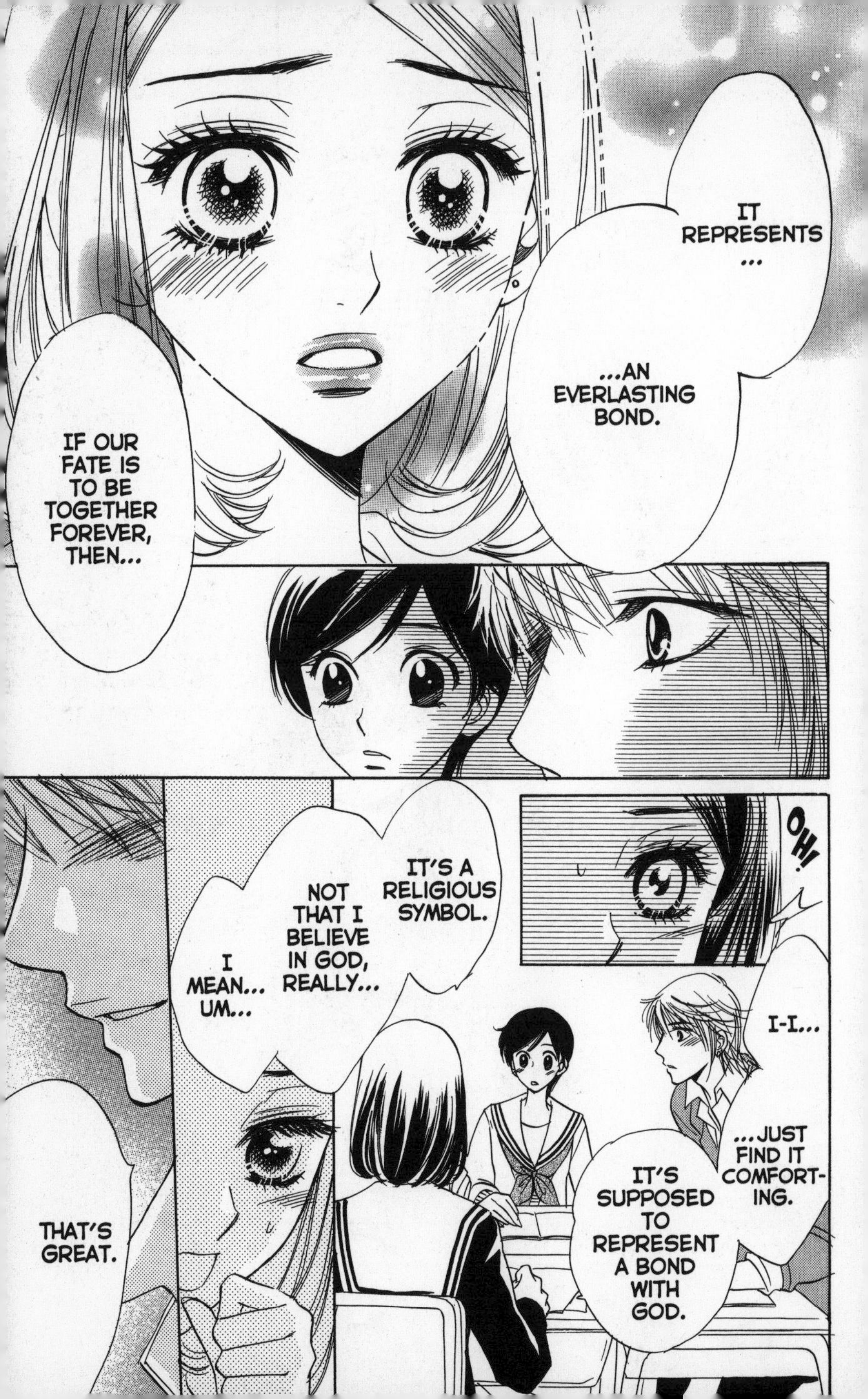
IT REPRESENTS...
...AN EVERLASTING BOND.
IF OUR FATE IS TO BE TOGETHER FOREVER, THEN...
OH!
I-I...
...JUST FIND IT COMFORT-ING.
IT'S SUPPOSED TO REPRESENT A BOND WITH GOD.
IT'S A RELIGIOUS SYMBOL.
NOT THAT I BELIEVE IN GOD, REALLY...
I MEAN... UM...
THAT'S GREAT.

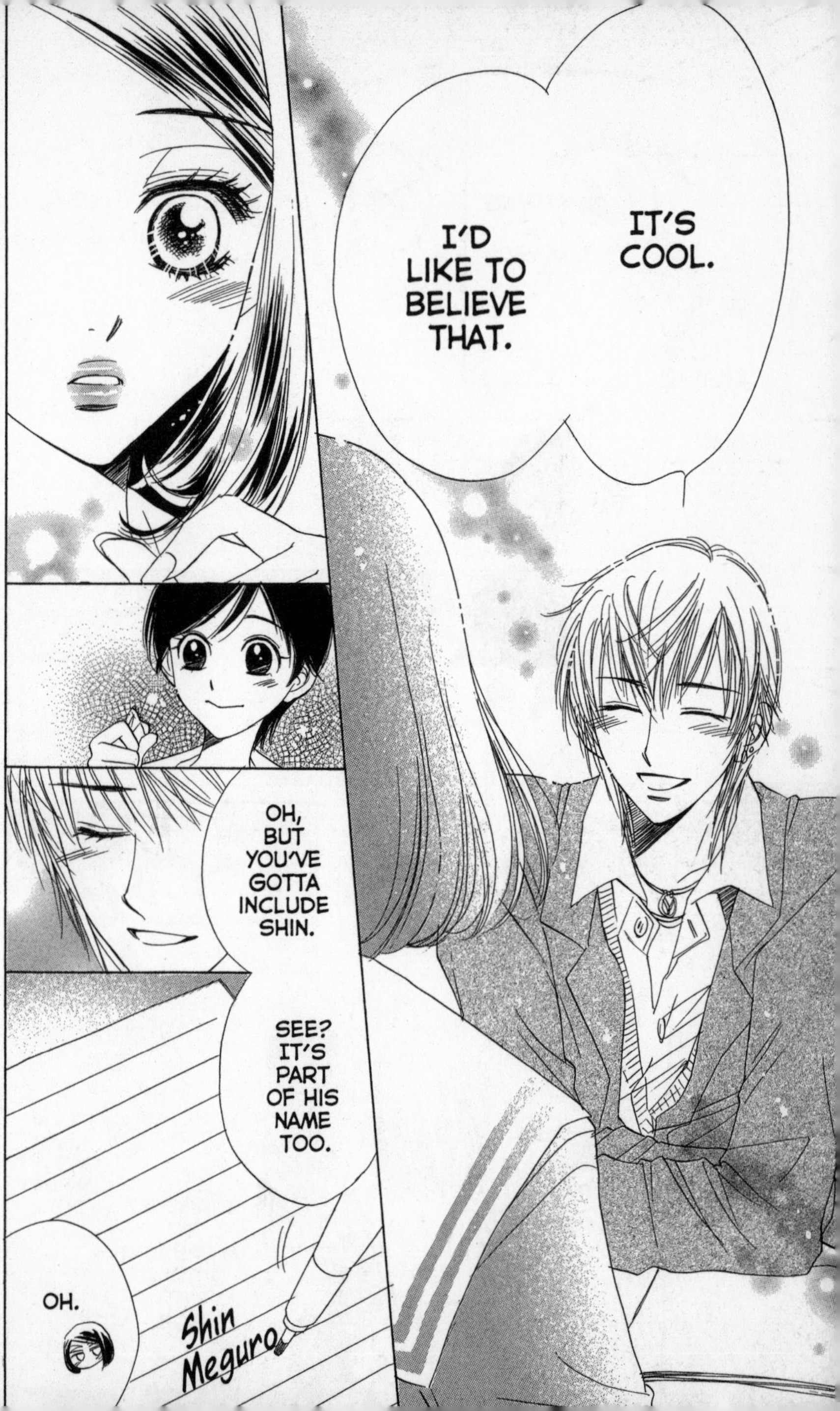
IT'S COOL.
I'D LIKE TO BELIEVE THAT.
OH, BUT YOU'VE GOTTA INCLUDE SHIN.
SEE? IT'S PART OF HIS NAME TOO.
OH.
Shin Meguro

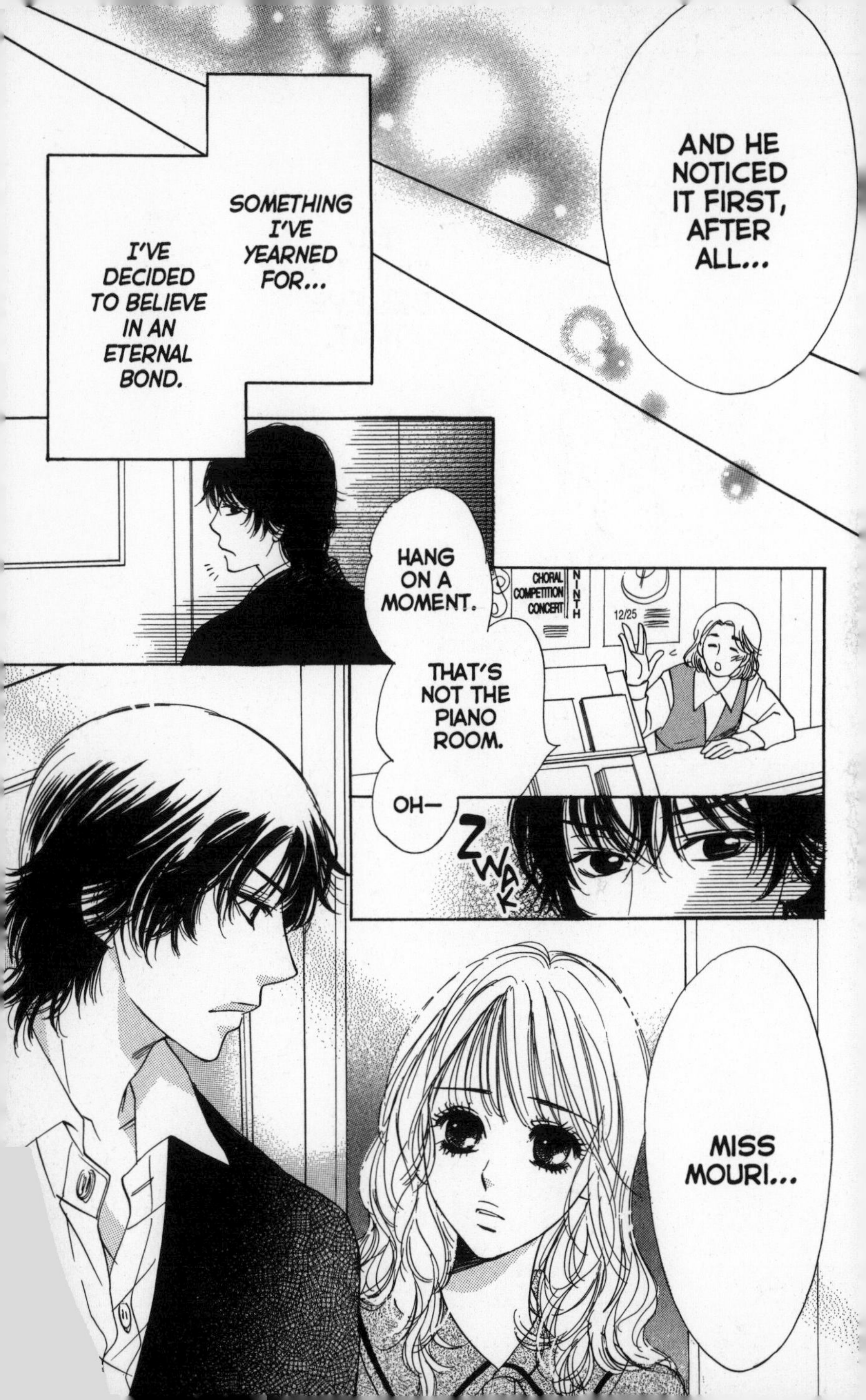
AND HE NOTICED IT FIRST, AFTER ALL...
SOMETHING I'VE YEARNED FOR...
I'VE DECIDED TO BELIEVE IN AN ETERNAL BOND.
HANG ON A MOMENT.
NINTH
CHORAL COMPETITION CONCERT
12/25
THAT'S NOT THE PIANO ROOM.
OH—
ZWAK
MISS MOURI...

A Devil and Her Love Song

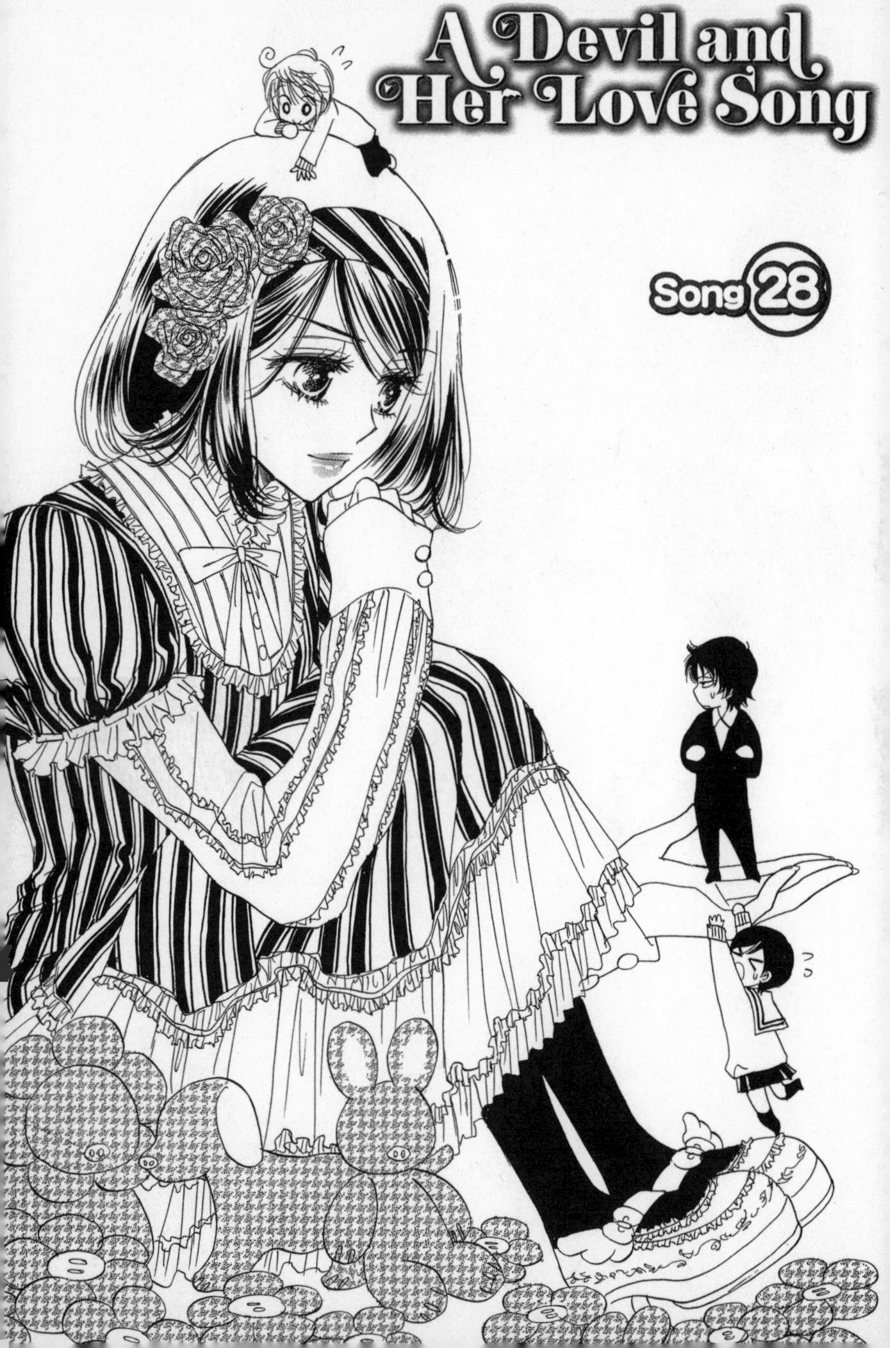
A Devil and Her Love Song
Song 28

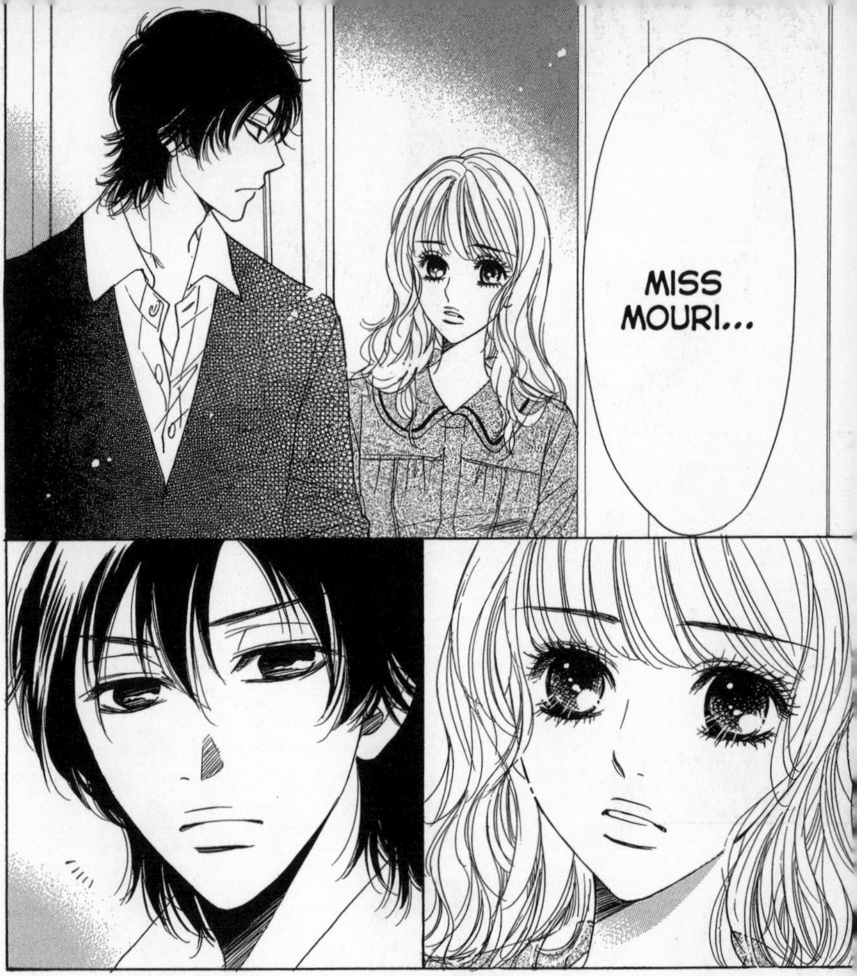
MISS MOURI...

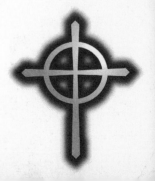

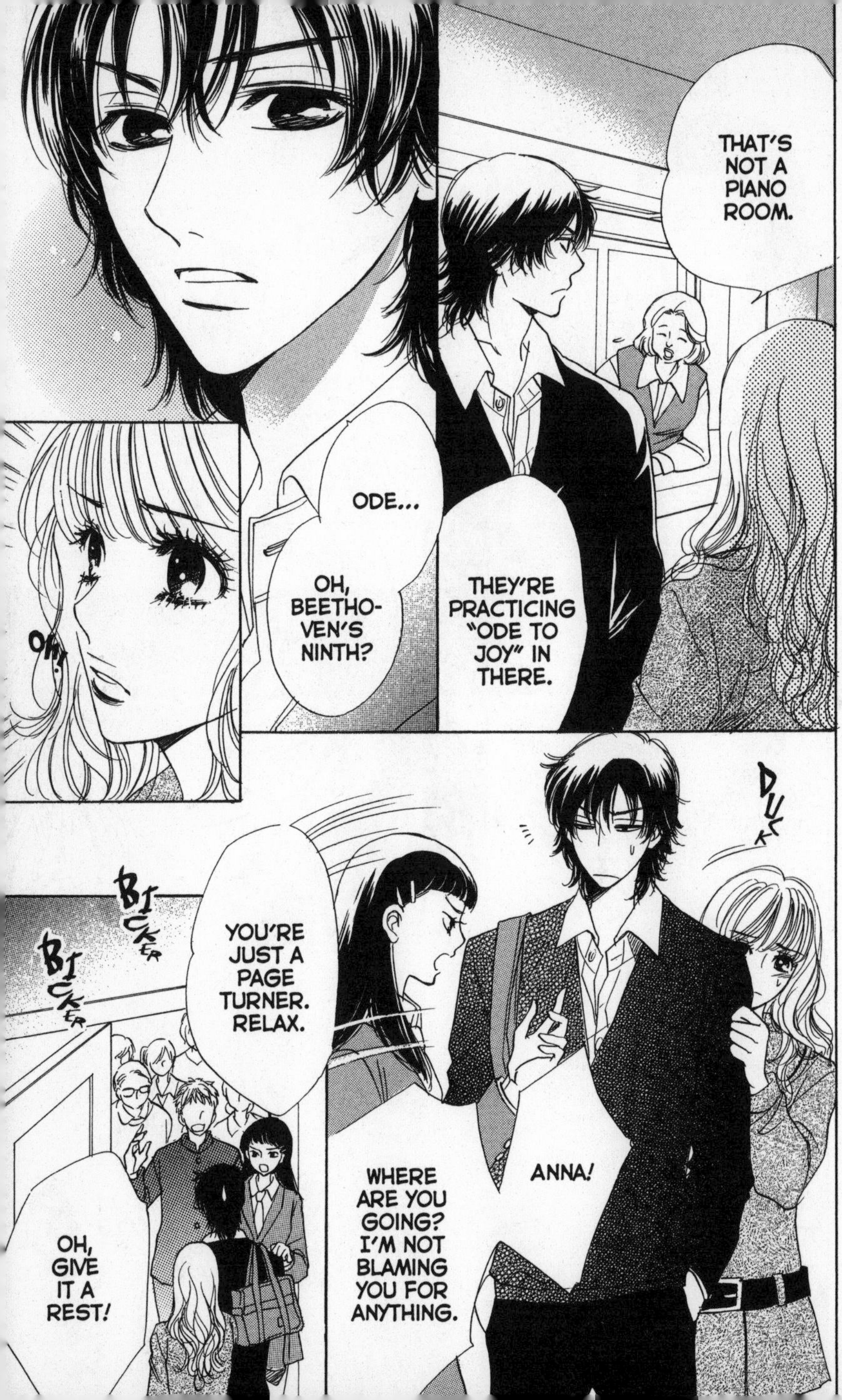
THAT'S NOT A PIANO ROOM.
THEY'RE PRACTICING "ODE TO JOY" IN THERE.
ODE...
OH, BEETHOVEN'S NINTH?
OH!
DUK
YOU'RE JUST A PAGE TURNER. RELAX.
ANNA!
WHERE ARE YOU GOING? I'M NOT BLAMING YOU FOR ANYTHING.
BICKER
BICKER
OH, GIVE IT A REST!

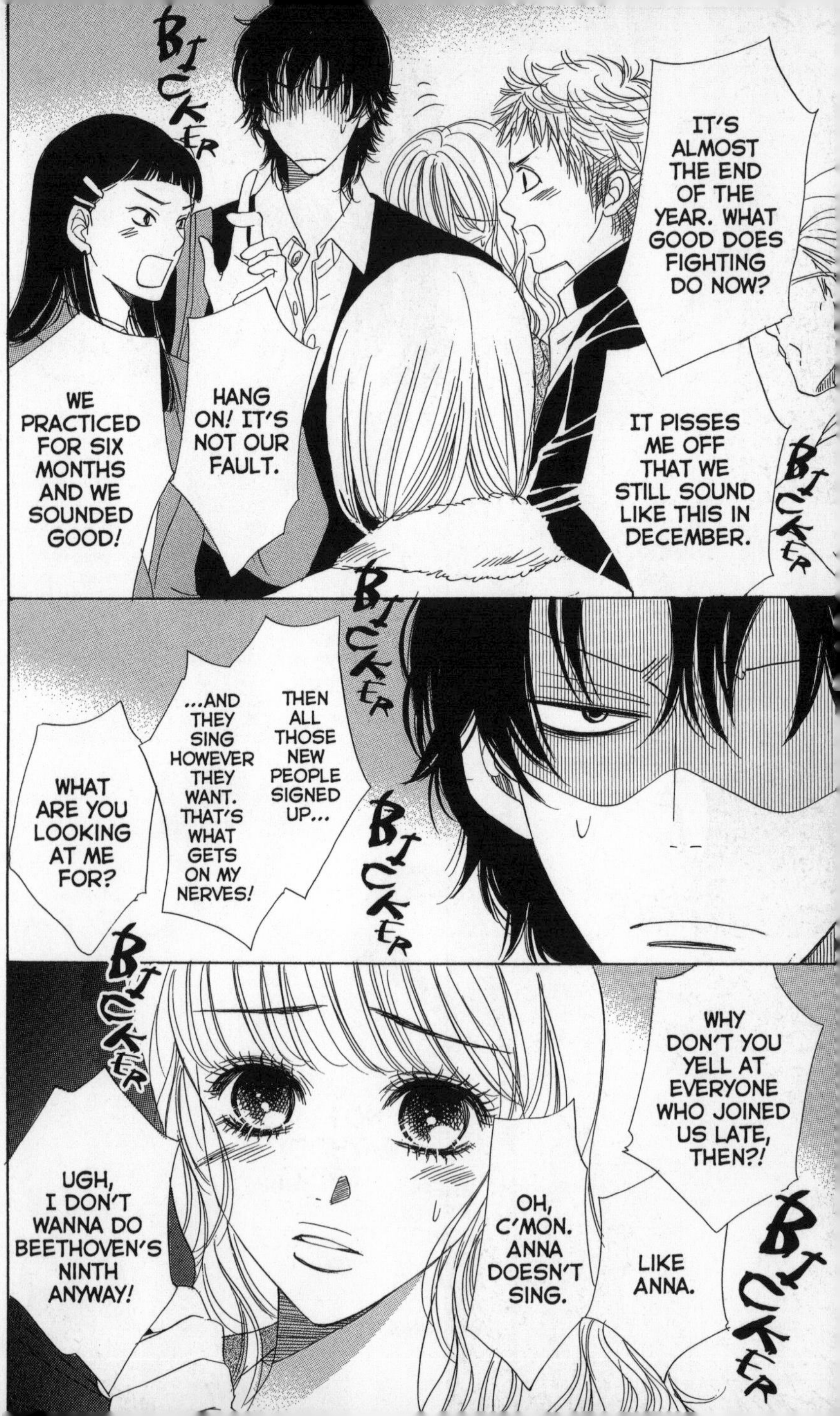
IT'S ALMOST THE END OF THE YEAR. WHAT GOOD DOES FIGHTING DO NOW?
IT PISSES ME OFF THAT WE STILL SOUND LIKE THIS IN DECEMBER.
BICKER
BICKER
HANG ON! IT'S NOT OUR FAULT.
WE PRACTICED FOR SIX MONTHS AND WE SOUNDED GOOD!
BICKER
THEN ALL THOSE NEW PEOPLE SIGNED UP...
...AND THEY SING HOWEVER THEY WANT. THAT'S WHAT GETS ON MY NERVES!
BICKER
WHAT ARE YOU LOOKING AT ME FOR?
WHY DON'T YOU YELL AT EVERYONE WHO JOINED US LATE, THEN?!
BICKER
LIKE ANNA.
OH, C'MON. ANNA DOESN'T SING.
BICKER
UGH, I DON'T WANNA DO BEETHOVEN'S NINTH ANYWAY!

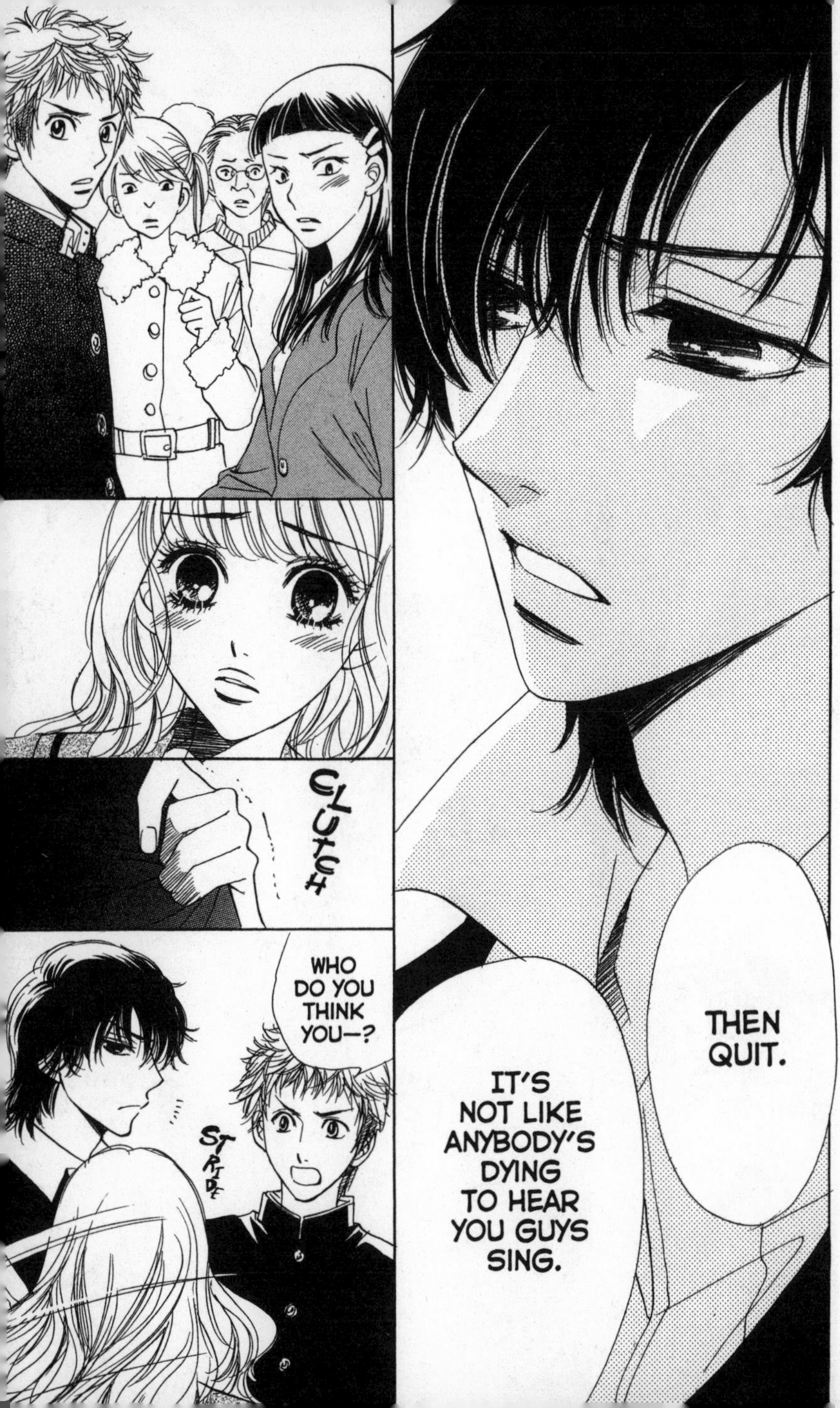
THEN QUIT.
IT'S NOT LIKE ANYBODY'S DYING TO HEAR YOU GUYS SING.
CLUTCH
WHO DO YOU THINK YOU—?
STRIDE

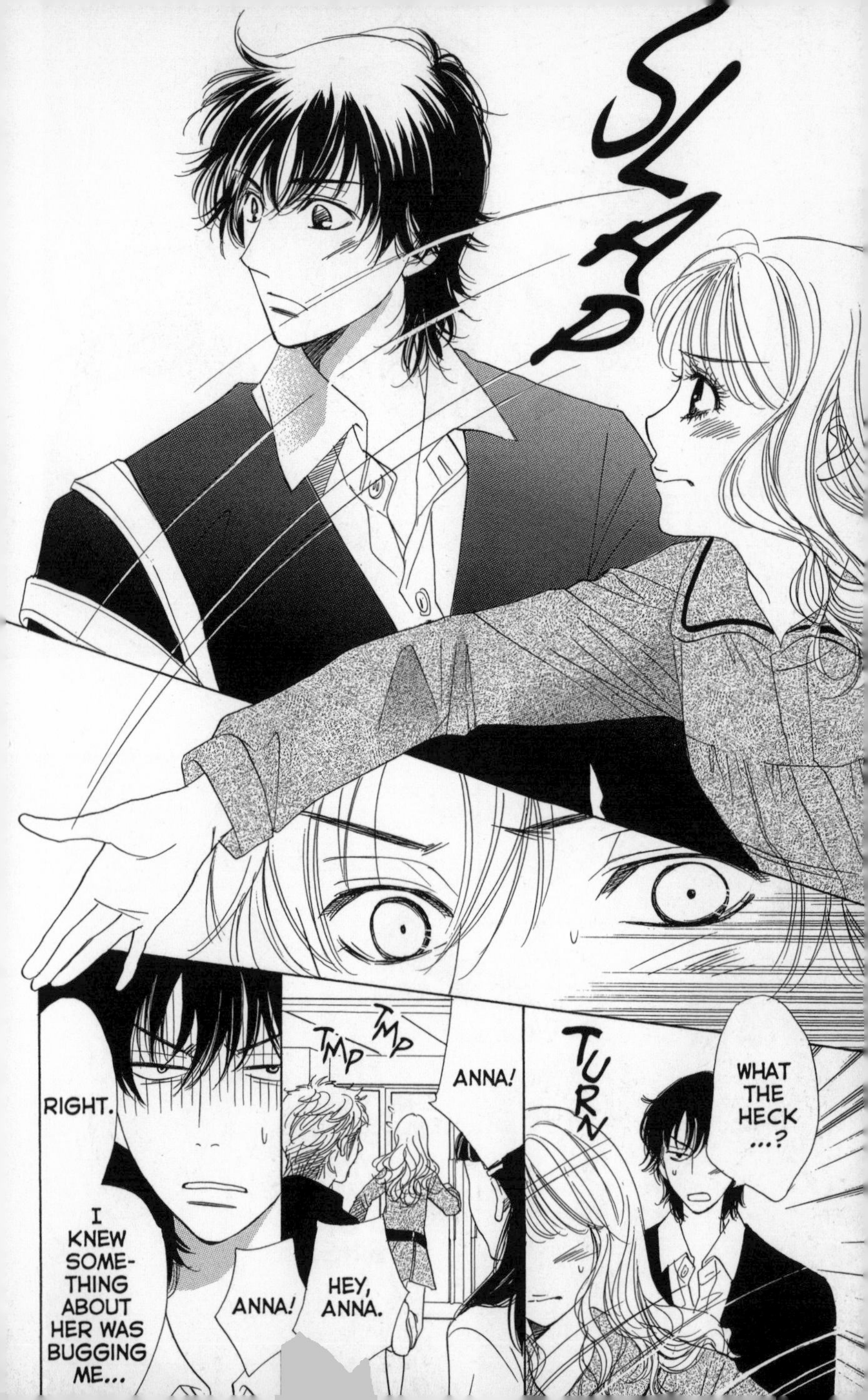
SLAP
WHAT THE HECK...?
TURN
TMP TMP
ANNA!
HEY, ANNA.
ANNA!
RIGHT.
I KNEW SOME-THING ABOUT HER WAS BUGGING ME...

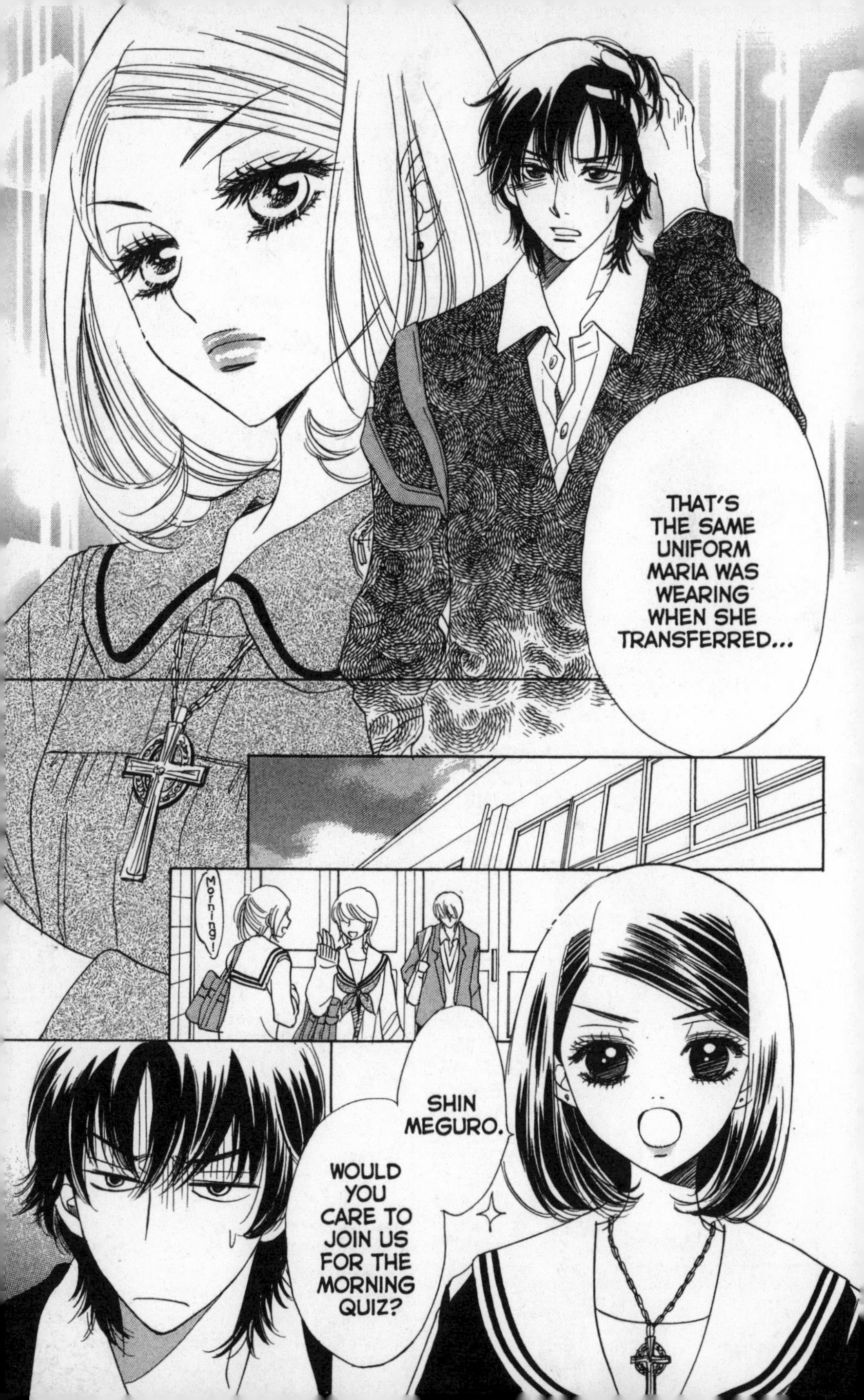
THAT'S THE SAME UNIFORM MARIA WAS WEARING WHEN SHE TRANSFERRED...
Morning!
SHIN MEGURO.
WOULD YOU CARE TO JOIN US FOR THE MORNING QUIZ?

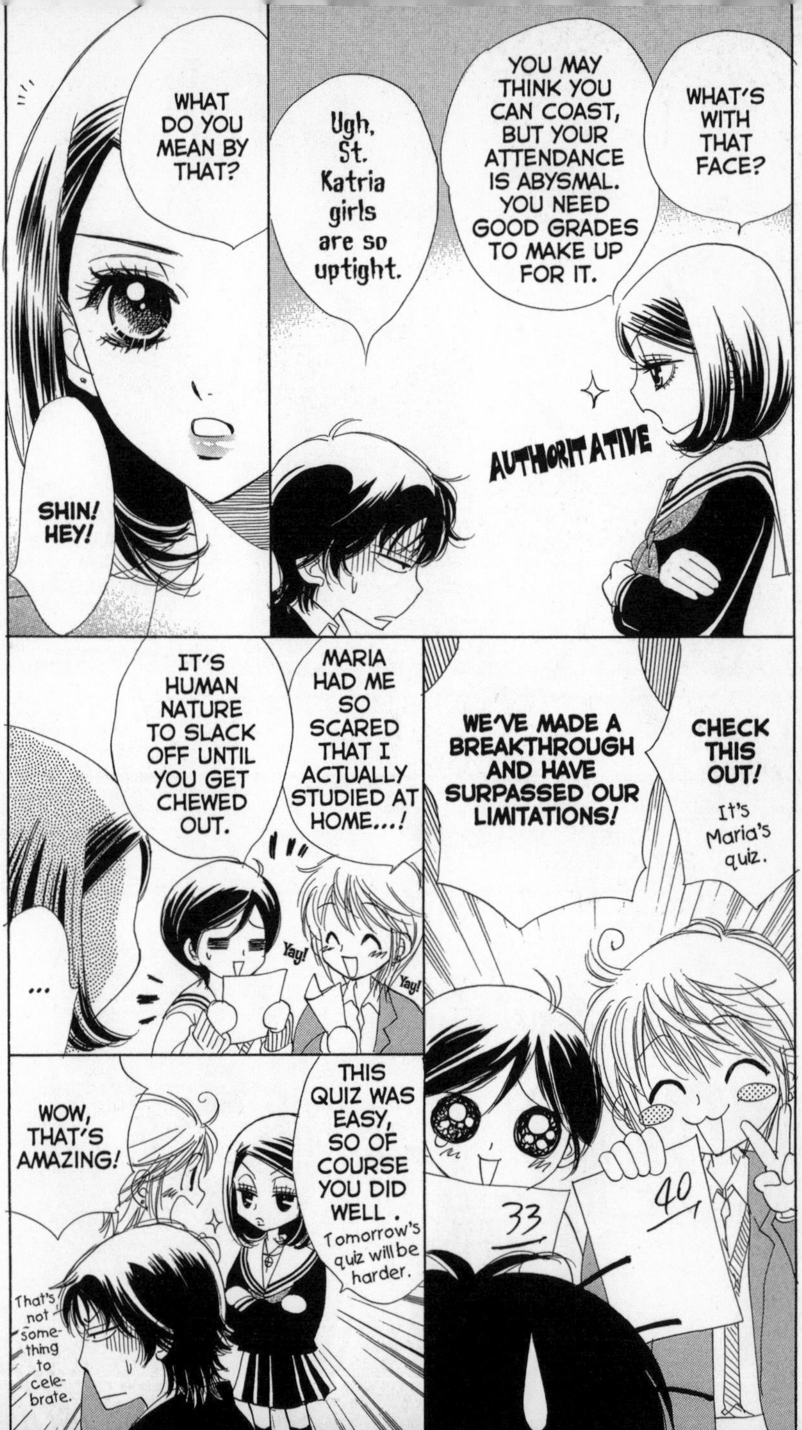
WHAT'S WITH THAT FACE?
YOU MAY THINK YOU CAN COAST, BUT YOUR ATTENDANCE IS ABYSMAL. YOU NEED GOOD GRADES TO MAKE UP FOR IT.
AUTHORITATIVE
Ugh, St. Katria girls are so uptight.
WHAT DO YOU MEAN BY THAT?
SHIN! HEY!
CHECK THIS OUT!
It's Maria's quiz.
WE'VE MADE A BREAKTHROUGH AND HAVE SURPASSED OUR LIMITATIONS!
40
33
MARIA HAD ME SO SCARED THAT I ACTUALLY STUDIED AT HOME...!
IT'S HUMAN NATURE TO SLACK OFF UNTIL YOU GET CHEWED OUT.
Yay!
Yay!
...
THIS QUIZ WAS EASY, SO OF COURSE YOU DID WELL.
Tomorrow's quiz will be harder.
WOW, THAT'S AMAZING!
That's not some-thing to cele-brate.

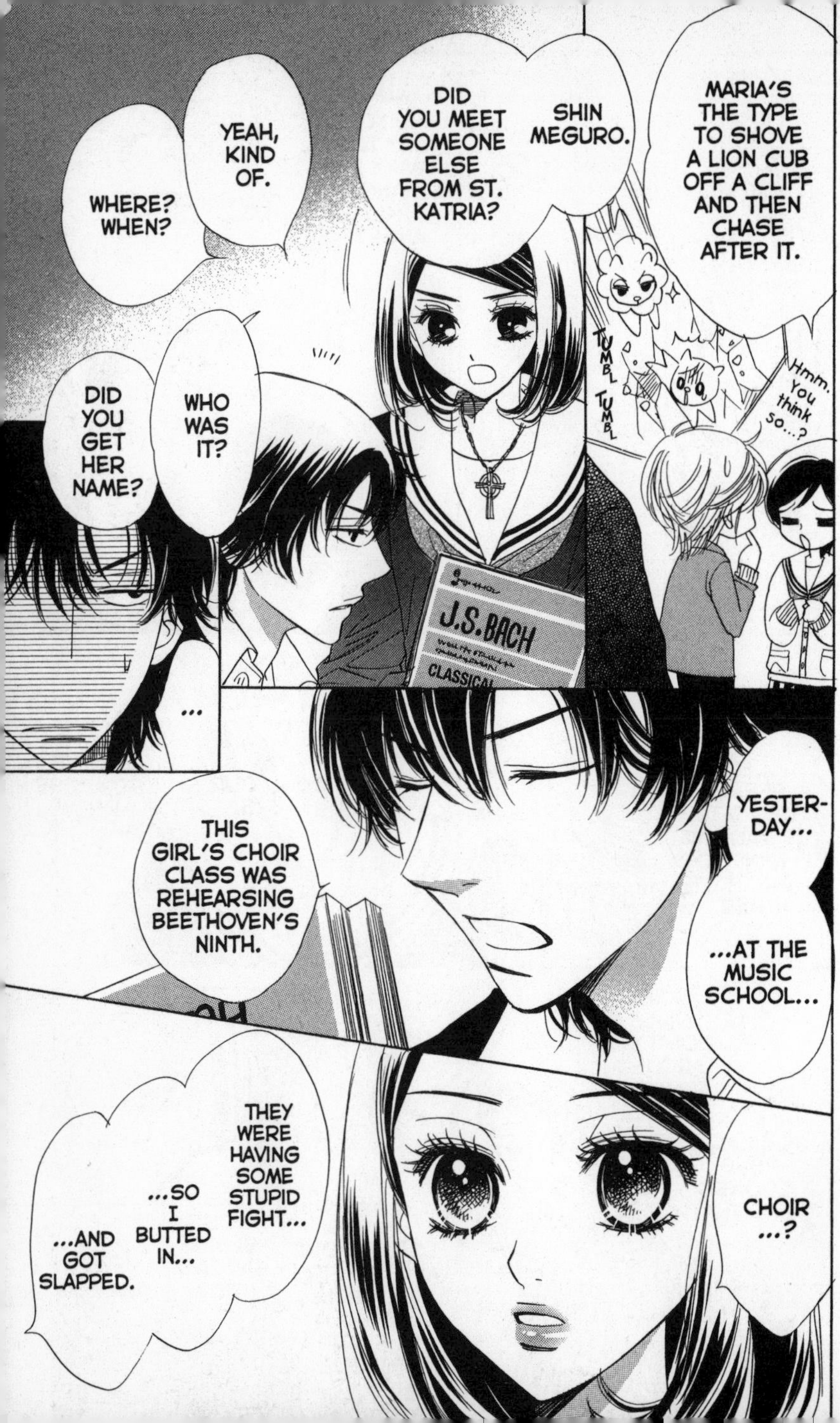
MARIA'S THE TYPE TO SHOVE A LION CUB OFF A CLIFF AND THEN CHASE AFTER IT.
TUMBL TUMBL
Hmm. You think so...?
SHIN MEGURO.
DID YOU MEET SOMEONE ELSE FROM ST. KATRIA?
YEAH, KIND OF.
WHERE? WHEN?
WHO WAS IT?
DID YOU GET HER NAME?
J.S.BACH
CLASSICAL
...
YESTER-DAY...
...AT THE MUSIC SCHOOL...
THIS GIRL'S CHOIR CLASS WAS REHEARSING BEETHOVEN'S NINTH.
CHOIR ...?
THEY WERE HAVING SOME STUPID FIGHT...
...SO I BUTTED IN...
...AND GOT SLAPPED.

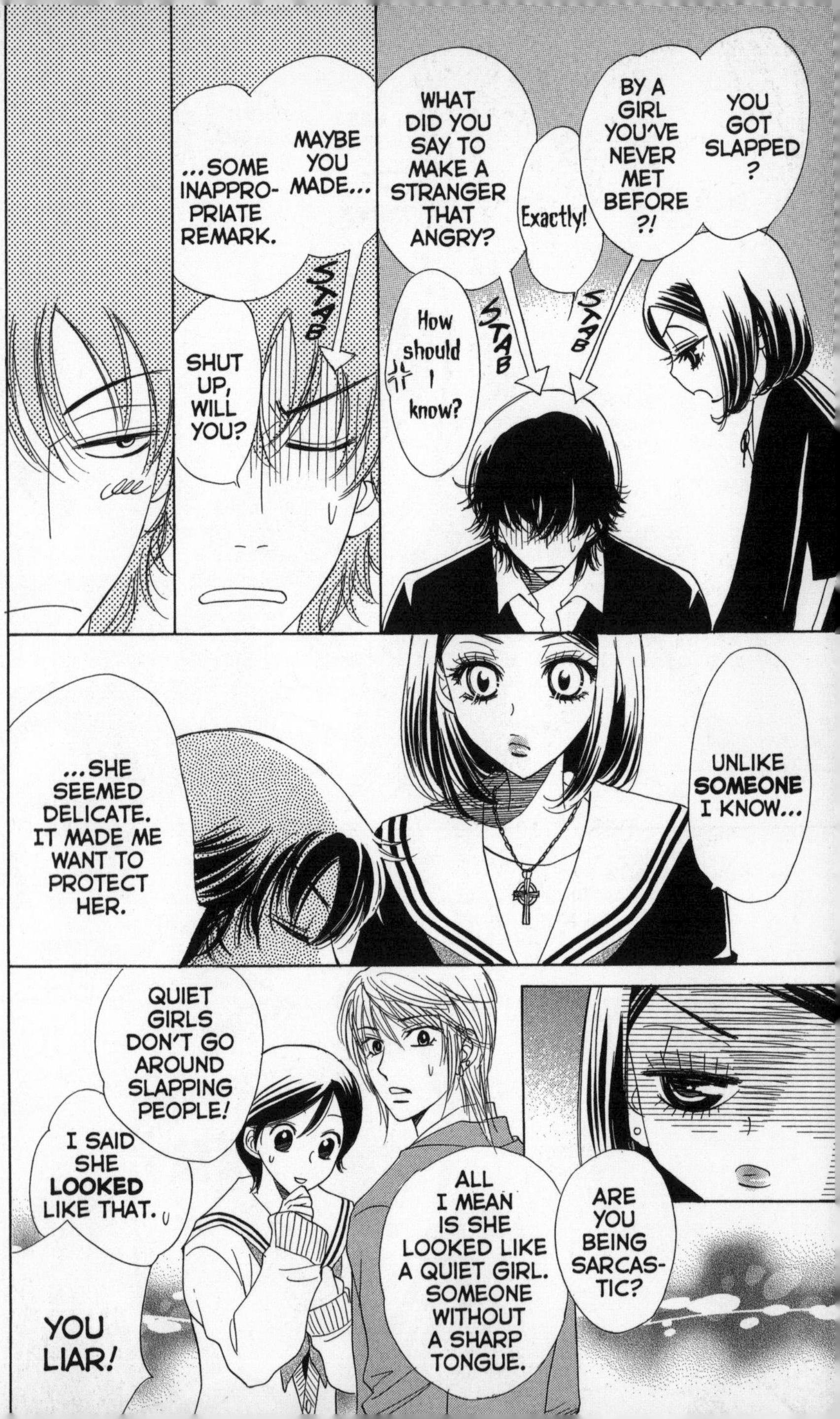
YOU GOT SLAPPED?
BY A GIRL YOU'VE NEVER MET BEFORE?!
Exactly!
WHAT DID YOU SAY TO MAKE A STRANGER THAT ANGRY?
STAB
STAB
How should I know?
MAYBE YOU MADE...
...SOME INAPPROPRIATE REMARK.
STAB
SHUT UP, WILL YOU?
UNLIKE **SOMEONE** I KNOW...
...SHE SEEMED DELICATE. IT MADE ME WANT TO PROTECT HER.
ARE YOU BEING SARCASTIC?
ALL I MEAN IS SHE LOOKED LIKE A QUIET GIRL. SOMEONE WITHOUT A SHARP TONGUE.
QUIET GIRLS DON'T GO AROUND SLAPPING PEOPLE!
I SAID SHE **LOOKED** LIKE THAT.
YOU LIAR!

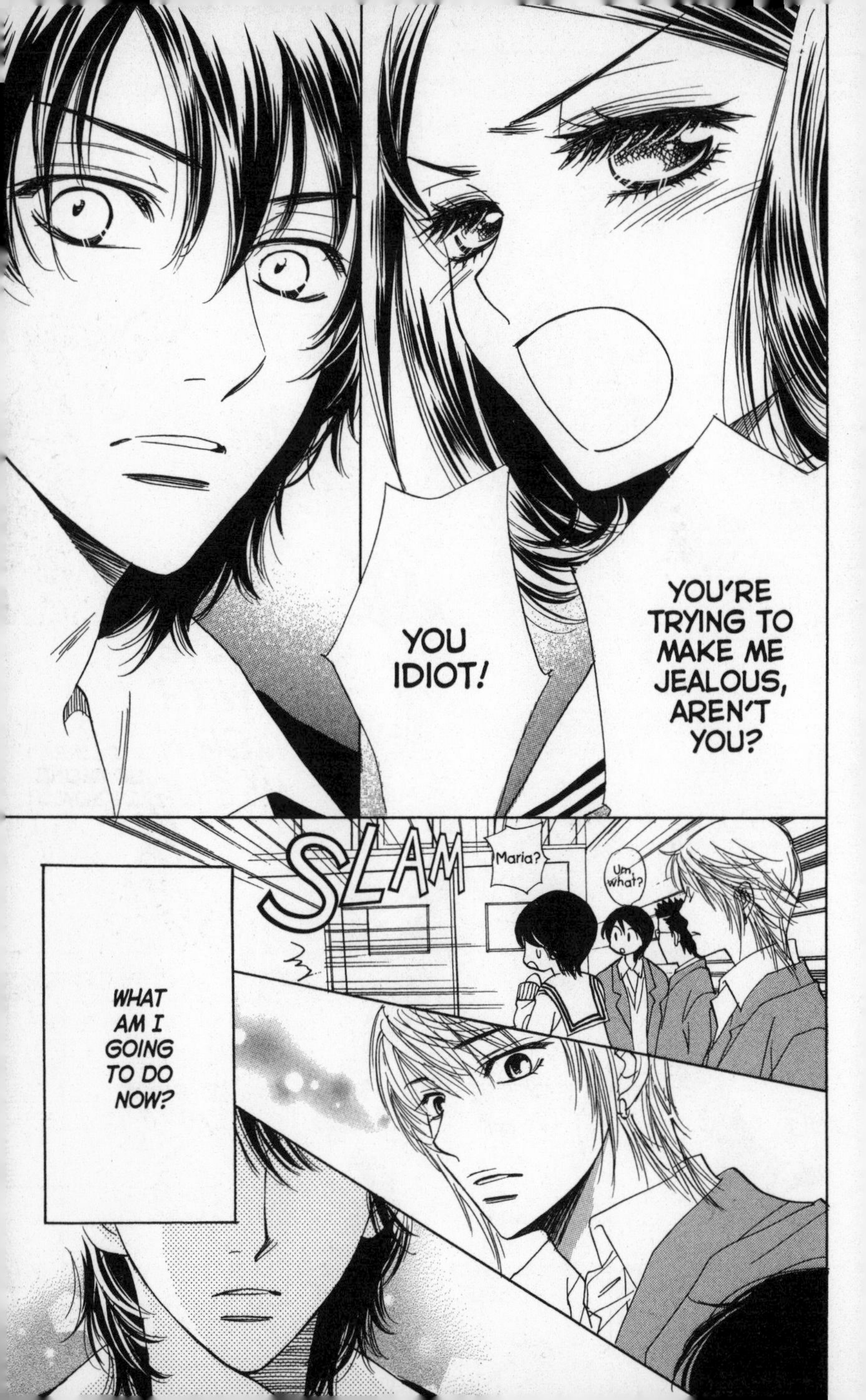
YOU'RE TRYING TO MAKE ME JEALOUS, AREN'T YOU?
YOU IDIOT!
SLAM
Maria?
Um, what?
WHAT AM I GOING TO DO NOW?

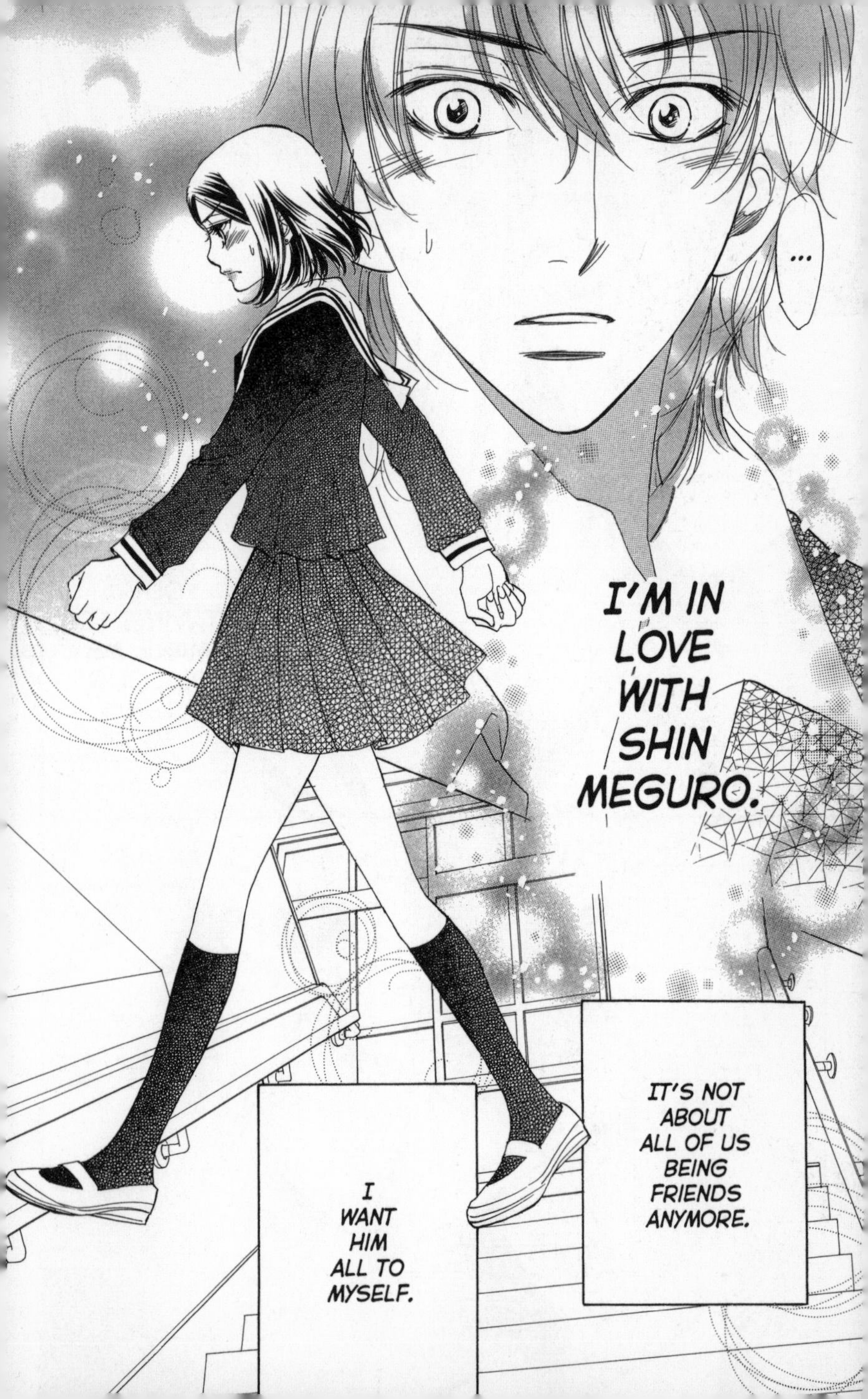
...
I'M IN LOVE WITH SHIN MEGURO.
IT'S NOT ABOUT ALL OF US BEING FRIENDS ANYMORE.
I WANT HIM ALL TO MYSELF.

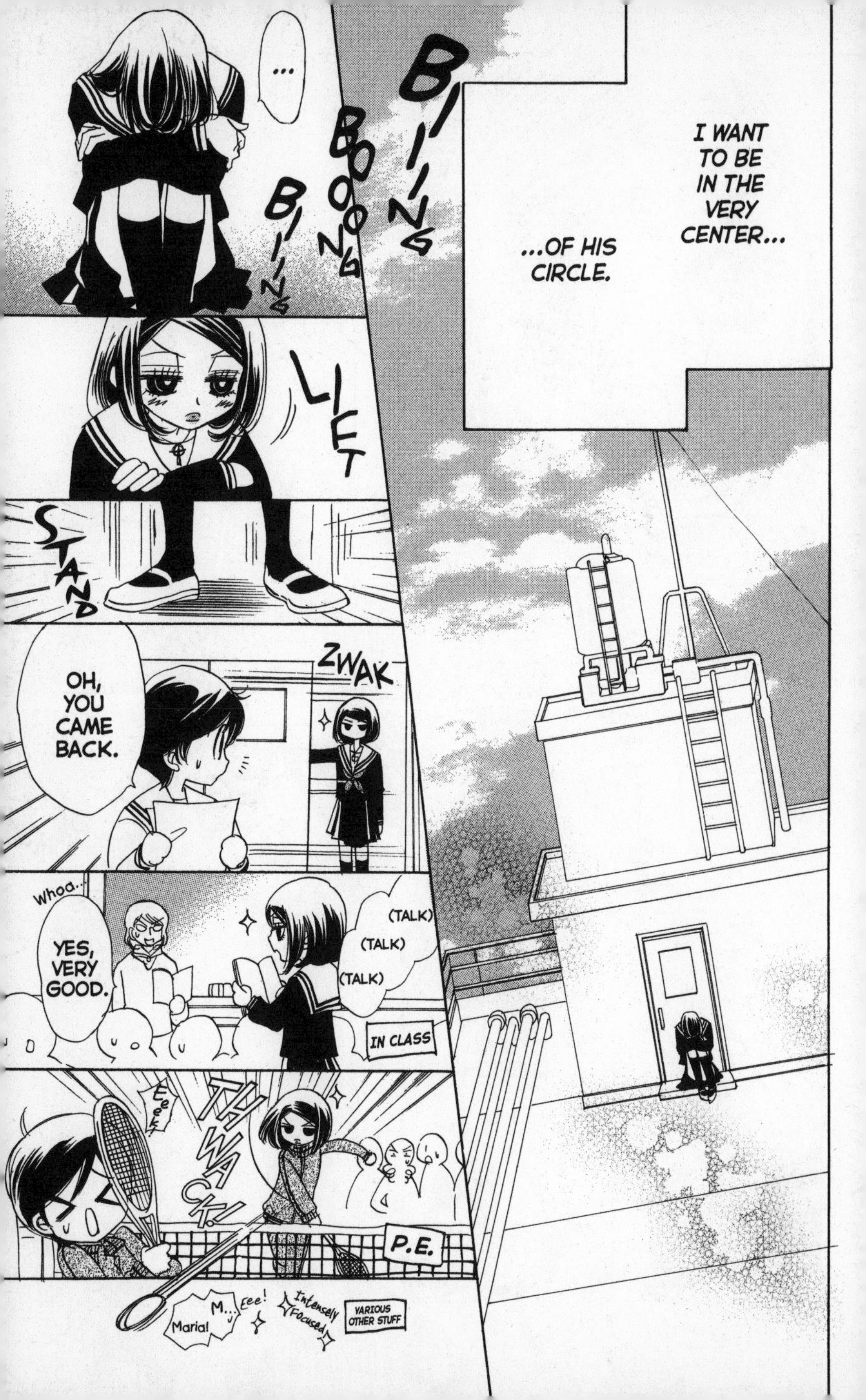
I WANT TO BE IN THE VERY CENTER...
...OF HIS CIRCLE.
BIIING
BOOONG
BIIING
...
LIFT
STAND
ZWAK
OH, YOU CAME BACK.
IN CLASS
(TALK)
(TALK)
(TALK)
Whoa...
YES, VERY GOOD.
P.E.
THWACK!
Eeek!
Intensely Focused
Eee!
M...
Maria!
VARIOUS OTHER STUFF

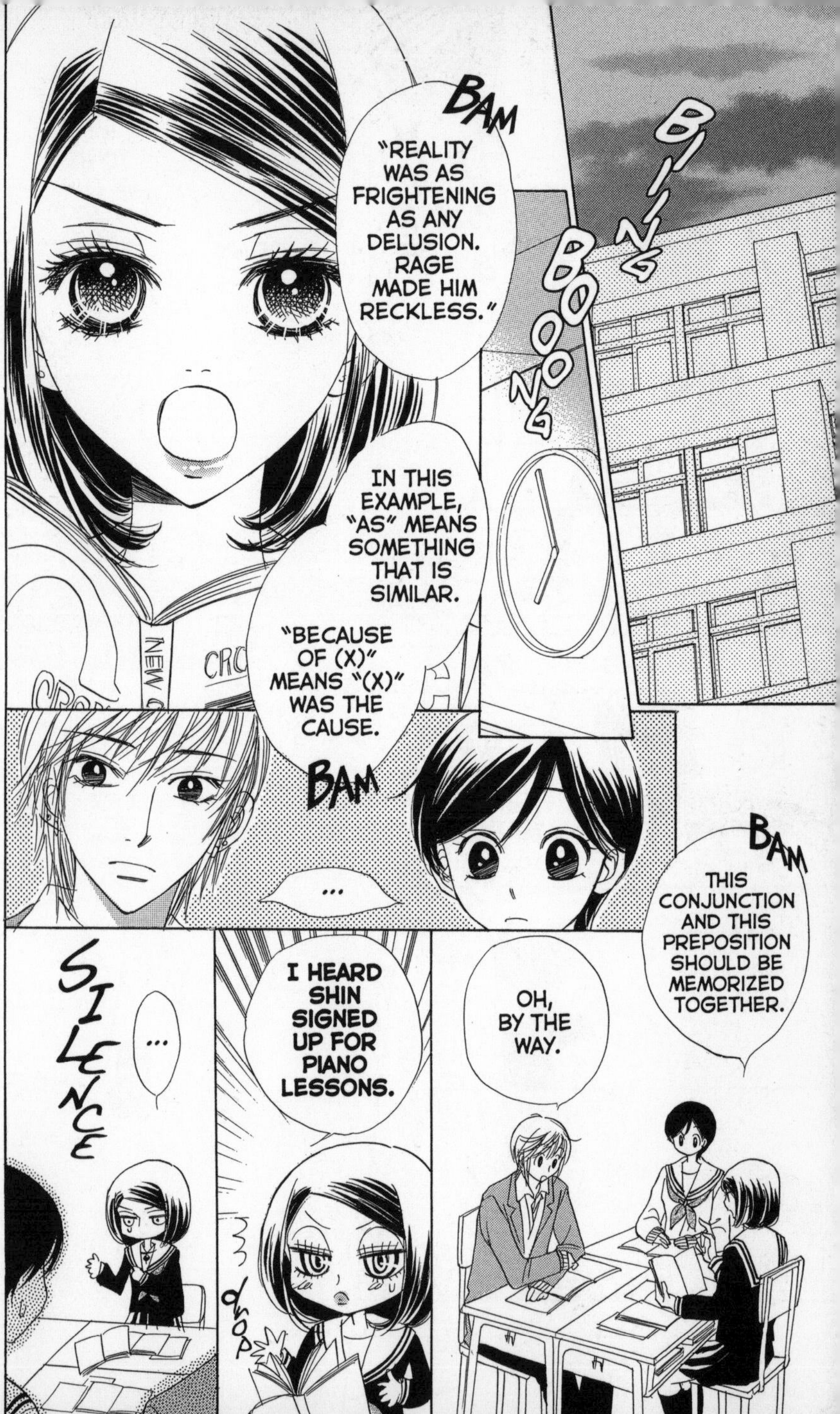
BIIING
BOOONG
BAM
"REALITY WAS AS FRIGHTENING AS ANY DELUSION. RAGE MADE HIM RECKLESS."
IN THIS EXAMPLE, "AS" MEANS SOMETHING THAT IS SIMILAR.
"BECAUSE OF (X)" MEANS "(X)" WAS THE CAUSE.
BAM
THIS CONJUNCTION AND THIS PREPOSITION SHOULD BE MEMORIZED TOGETHER.
...
BAM
OH, BY THE WAY.
I HEARD SHIN SIGNED UP FOR PIANO LESSONS.
DROP
SILENCE
...

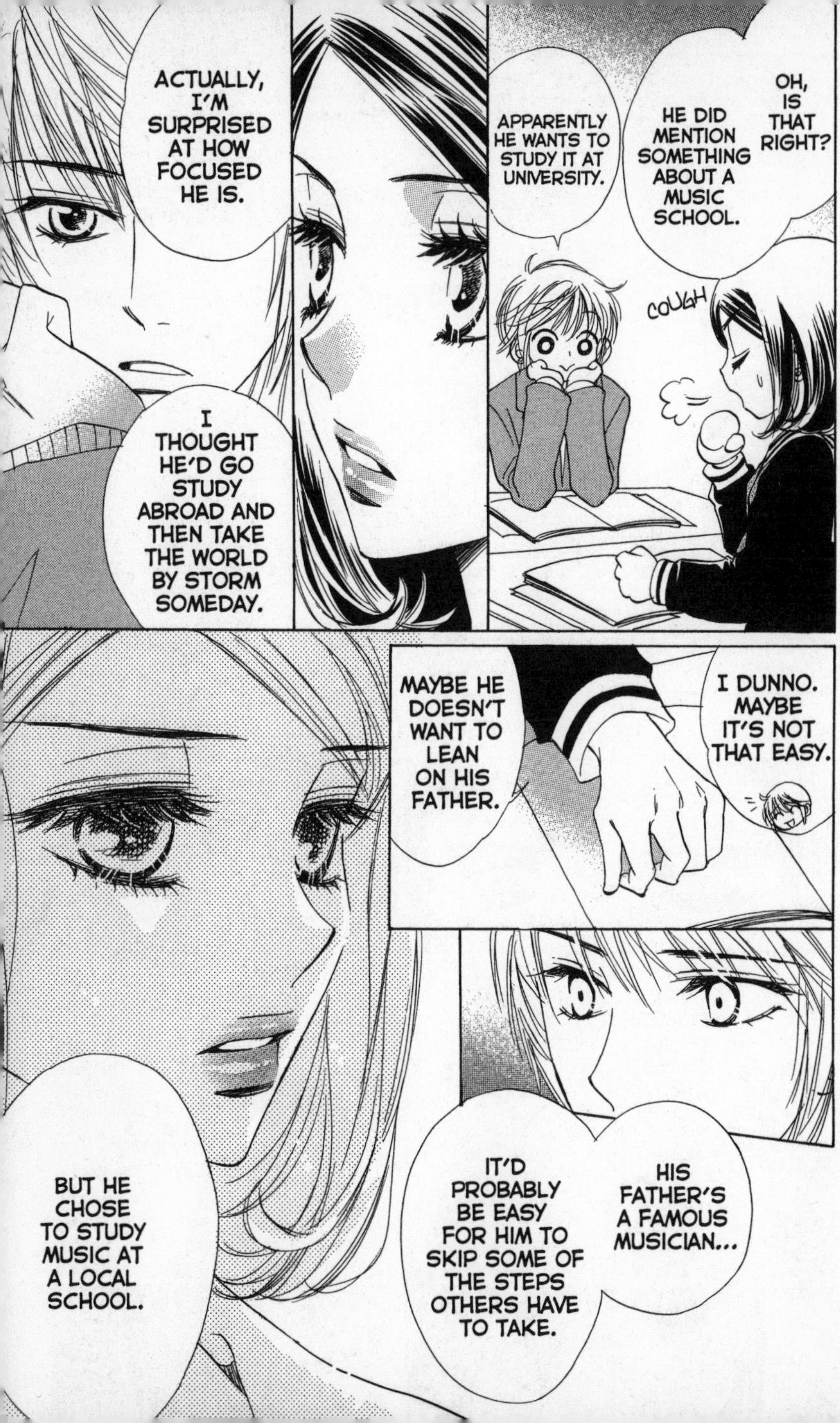
OH, IS THAT RIGHT?
HE DID MENTION SOMETHING ABOUT A MUSIC SCHOOL.
APPARENTLY HE WANTS TO STUDY IT AT UNIVERSITY.
COUGH
ACTUALLY, I'M SURPRISED AT HOW FOCUSED HE IS.
I THOUGHT HE'D GO STUDY ABROAD AND THEN TAKE THE WORLD BY STORM SOMEDAY.
I DUNNO. MAYBE IT'S NOT THAT EASY.
MAYBE HE DOESN'T WANT TO LEAN ON HIS FATHER.
HIS FATHER'S A FAMOUS MUSICIAN...
IT'D PROBABLY BE EASY FOR HIM TO SKIP SOME OF THE STEPS OTHERS HAVE TO TAKE.
BUT HE CHOSE TO STUDY MUSIC AT A LOCAL SCHOOL.

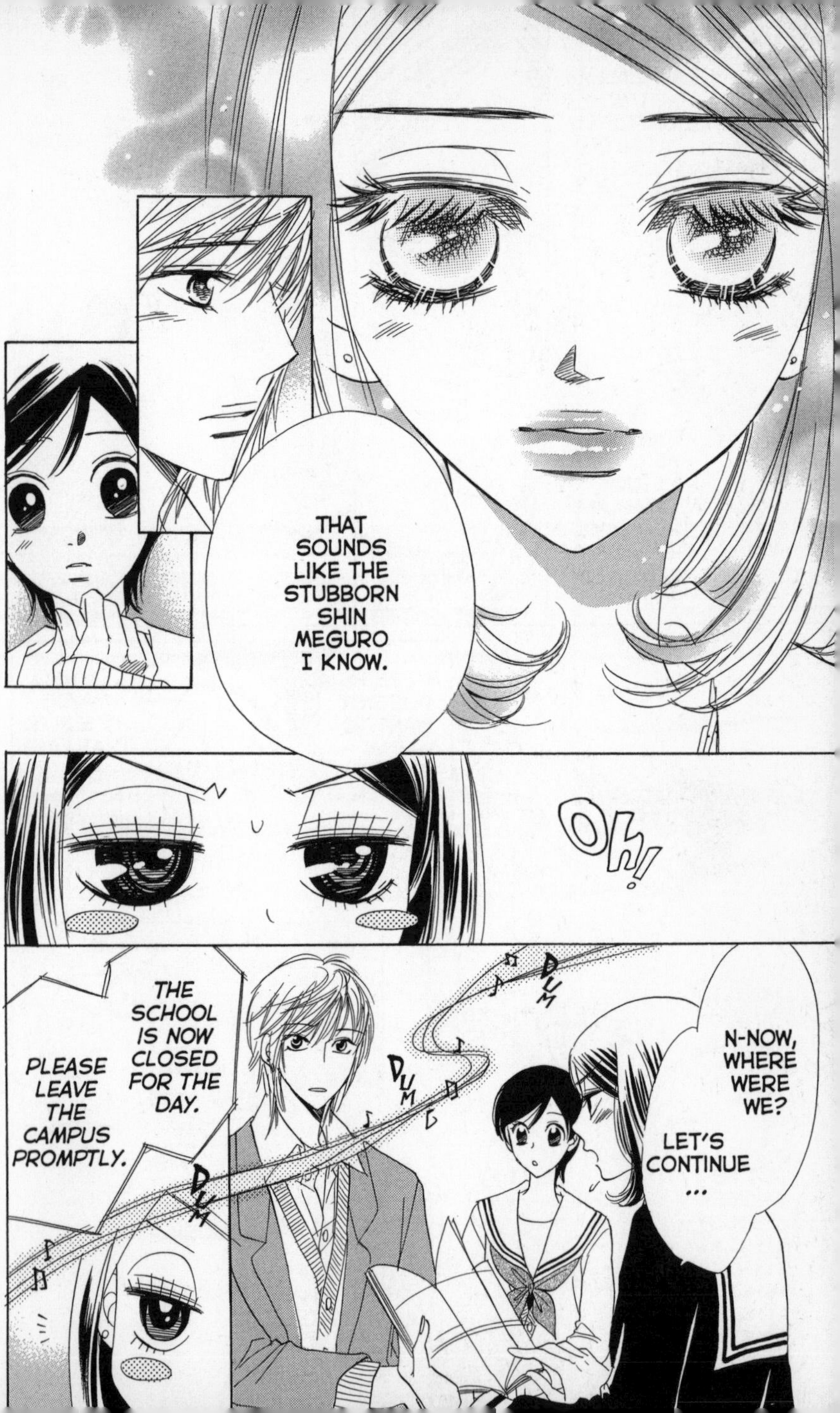
THAT SOUNDS LIKE THE STUBBORN SHIN MEGURO I KNOW.
Oh!
N-NOW, WHERE WERE WE?
LET'S CONTINUE...
DUM
DUM
DUM
THE SCHOOL IS NOW CLOSED FOR THE DAY.
PLEASE LEAVE THE CAMPUS PROMPTLY.

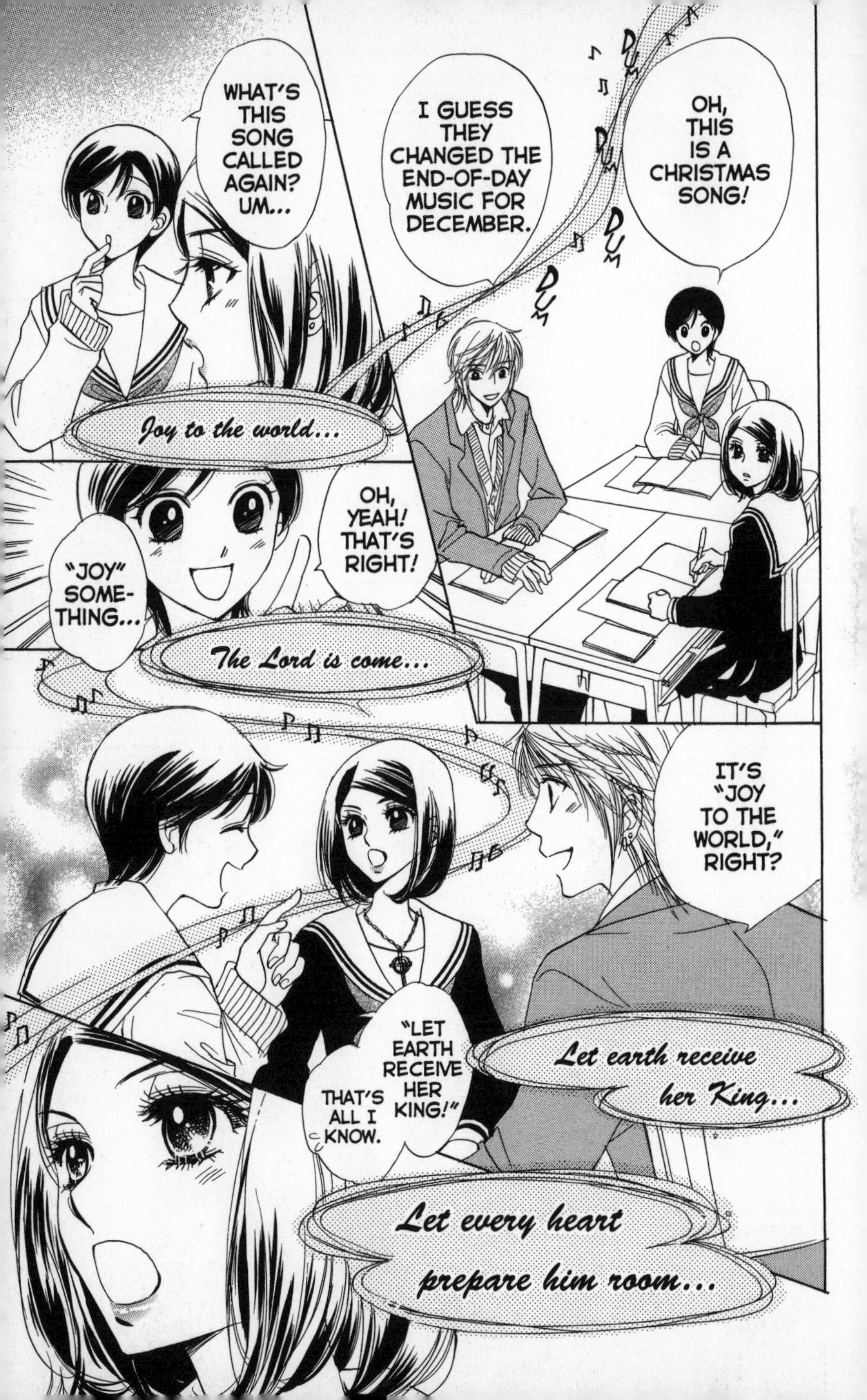
DUM DUM DUM DUM
OH, THIS IS A CHRISTMAS SONG!
I GUESS THEY CHANGED THE END-OF-DAY MUSIC FOR DECEMBER.
WHAT'S THIS SONG CALLED AGAIN? UM...
Joy to the world...
OH, YEAH! THAT'S RIGHT!
"JOY" SOMETHING...
The Lord is come...
IT'S "JOY TO THE WORLD," RIGHT?
Let earth receive her King...
"LET EARTH RECEIVE HER KING!"
THAT'S ALL I KNOW.
Let every heart prepare him room...

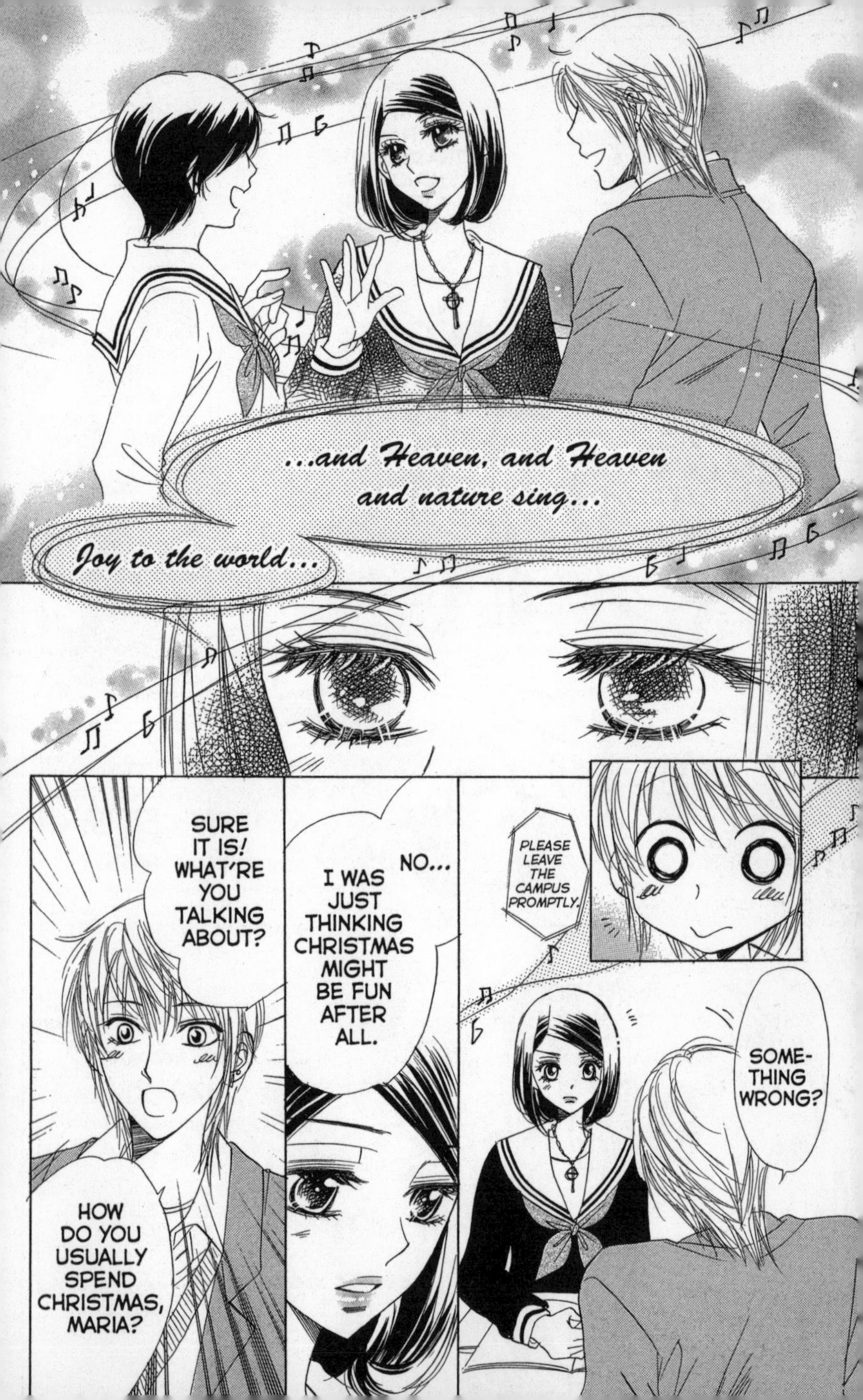
Joy to the world...
...and Heaven, and Heaven and nature sing...
PLEASE LEAVE THE CAMPUS PROMPTLY.
SOME-THING WRONG?
NO...
I WAS JUST THINKING CHRISTMAS MIGHT BE FUN AFTER ALL.
SURE IT IS! WHAT'RE YOU TALKING ABOUT?
HOW DO YOU USUALLY SPEND CHRISTMAS, MARIA?

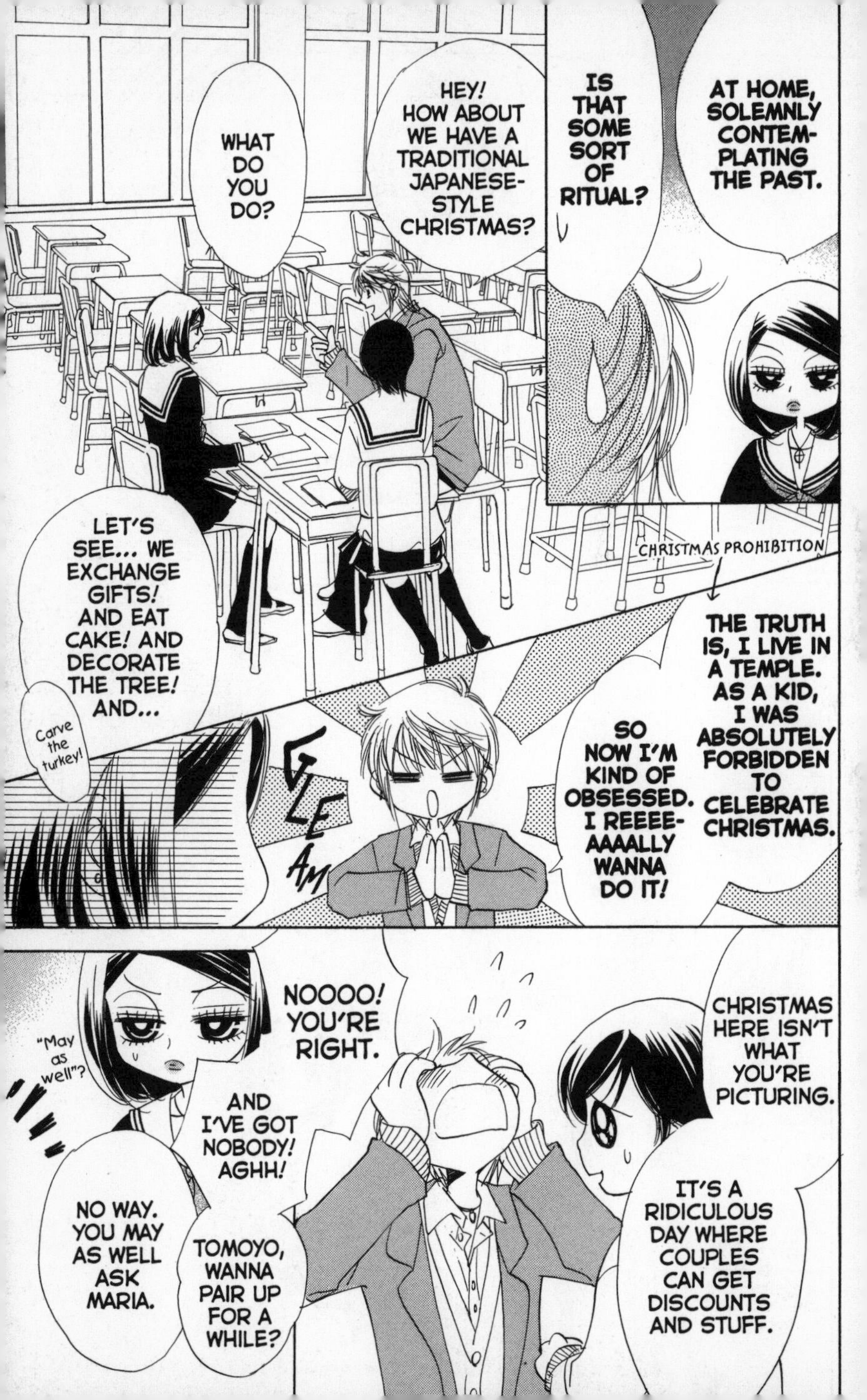
HEY! HOW ABOUT WE HAVE A TRADITIONAL JAPANESE-STYLE CHRISTMAS?
WHAT DO YOU DO?
AT HOME, SOLEMNLY CONTEM-PLATING THE PAST.
IS THAT SOME SORT OF RITUAL?
CHRISTMAS PROHIBITION
THE TRUTH IS, I LIVE IN A TEMPLE. AS A KID, I WAS ABSOLUTELY FORBIDDEN TO CELEBRATE CHRISTMAS.
SO NOW I'M KIND OF OBSESSED. I REEEE-AAAALLY WANNA DO IT!
GLEAM
LET'S SEE... WE EXCHANGE GIFTS! AND EAT CAKE! AND DECORATE THE TREE! AND...
Carve the turkey!
CHRISTMAS HERE ISN'T WHAT YOU'RE PICTURING.
IT'S A RIDICULOUS DAY WHERE COUPLES CAN GET DISCOUNTS AND STUFF.
NOOOO! YOU'RE RIGHT.
AND I'VE GOT NOBODY! AGHH!
TOMOYO, WANNA PAIR UP FOR A WHILE?
NO WAY. YOU MAY AS WELL ASK MARIA.
"May as well"?

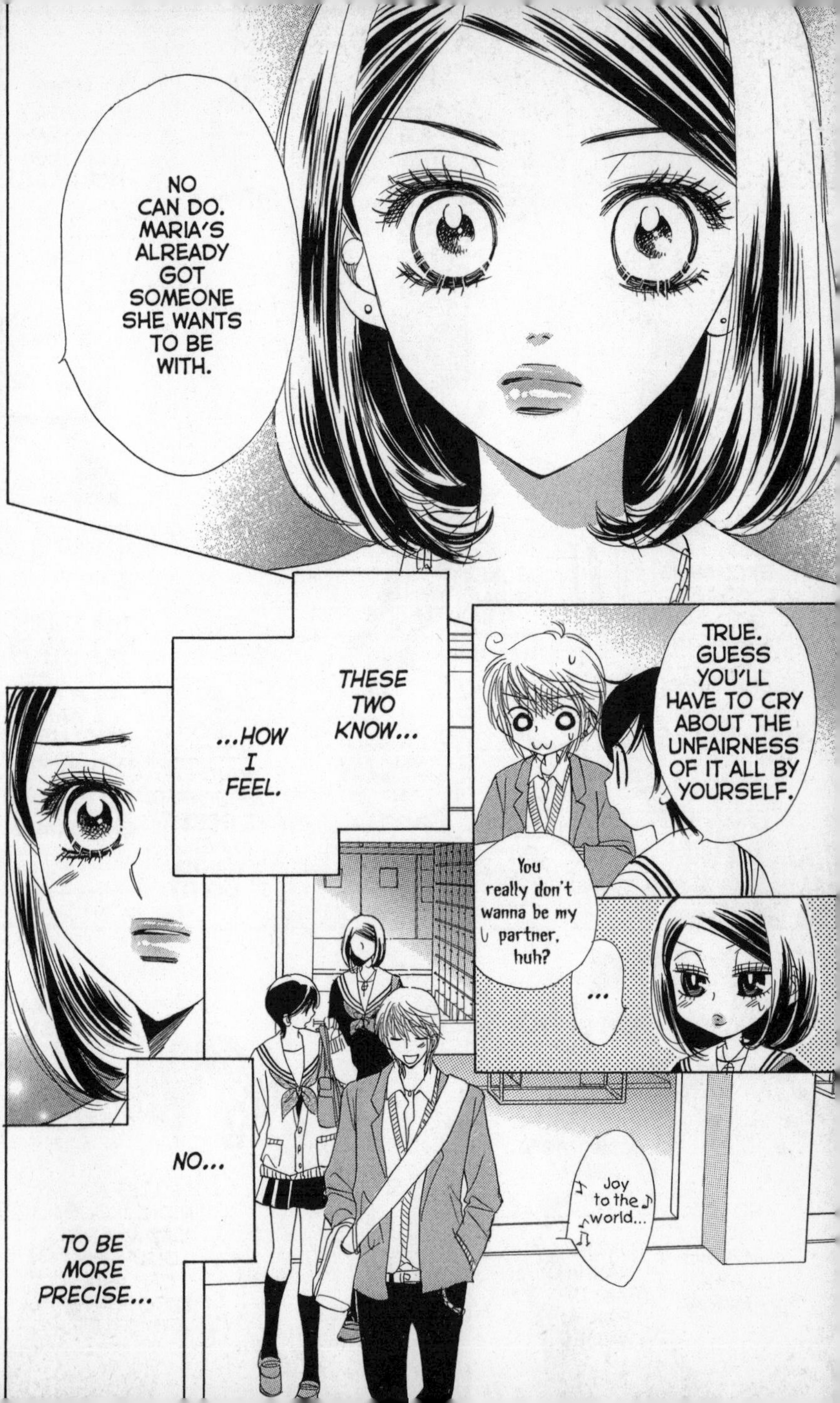
NO CAN DO. MARIA'S ALREADY GOT SOMEONE SHE WANTS TO BE WITH.
TRUE. GUESS YOU'LL HAVE TO CRY ABOUT THE UNFAIRNESS OF IT ALL BY YOURSELF.
You really don't wanna be my partner, huh?
...
THESE TWO KNOW...
...HOW I FEEL.
Joy to the world...
NO...
TO BE MORE PRECISE...

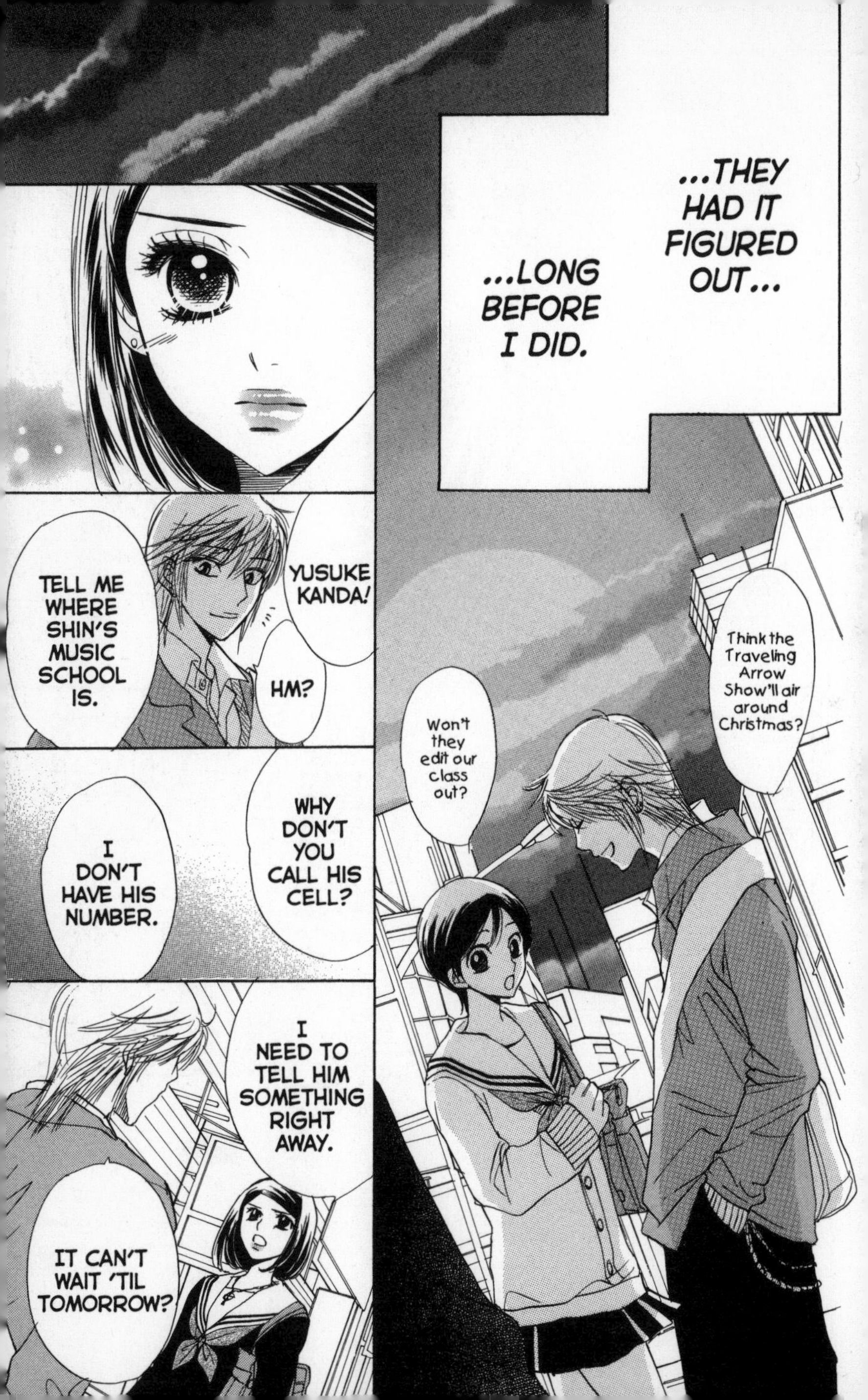
...THEY HAD IT FIGURED OUT...
...LONG BEFORE I DID.
Think the Traveling Arrow Show'll air around Christmas?
Won't they edit our class out?
YUSUKE KANDA!
HM?
TELL ME WHERE SHIN'S MUSIC SCHOOL IS.
WHY DON'T YOU CALL HIS CELL?
I DON'T HAVE HIS NUMBER.
I NEED TO TELL HIM SOMETHING RIGHT AWAY.
IT CAN'T WAIT 'TIL TOMORROW?

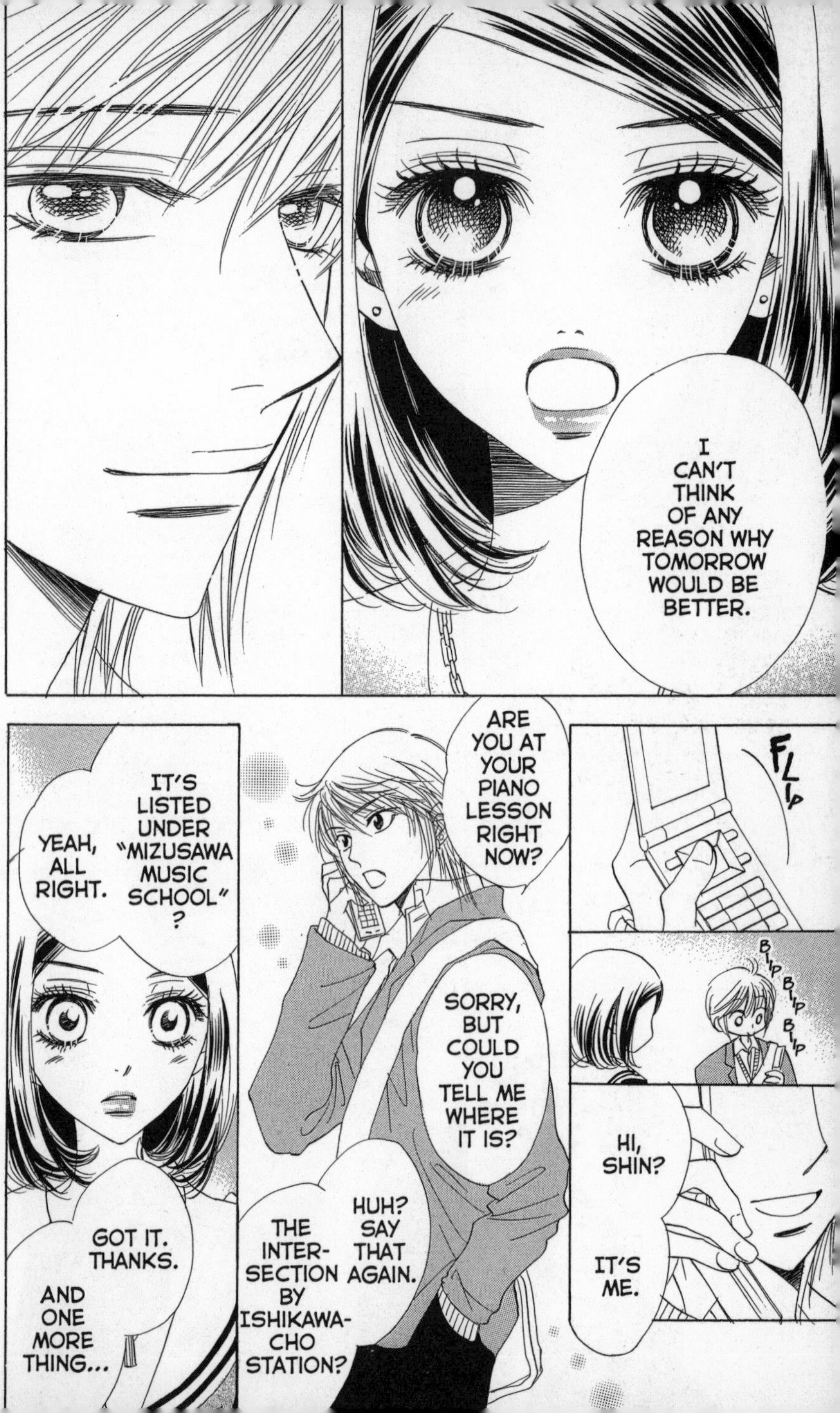
I CAN'T THINK OF ANY REASON WHY TOMORROW WOULD BE BETTER.
FLIP
BLIP BLIP BLIP
HI, SHIN? IT'S ME.
ARE YOU AT YOUR PIANO LESSON RIGHT NOW?
SORRY, BUT COULD YOU TELL ME WHERE IT IS?
HUH? SAY THAT AGAIN.
THE INTER-SECTION BY ISHIKAWA-CHO STATION?
IT'S LISTED UNDER "MIZUSAWA MUSIC SCHOOL"?
YEAH, ALL RIGHT.
GOT IT. THANKS.
AND ONE MORE THING...

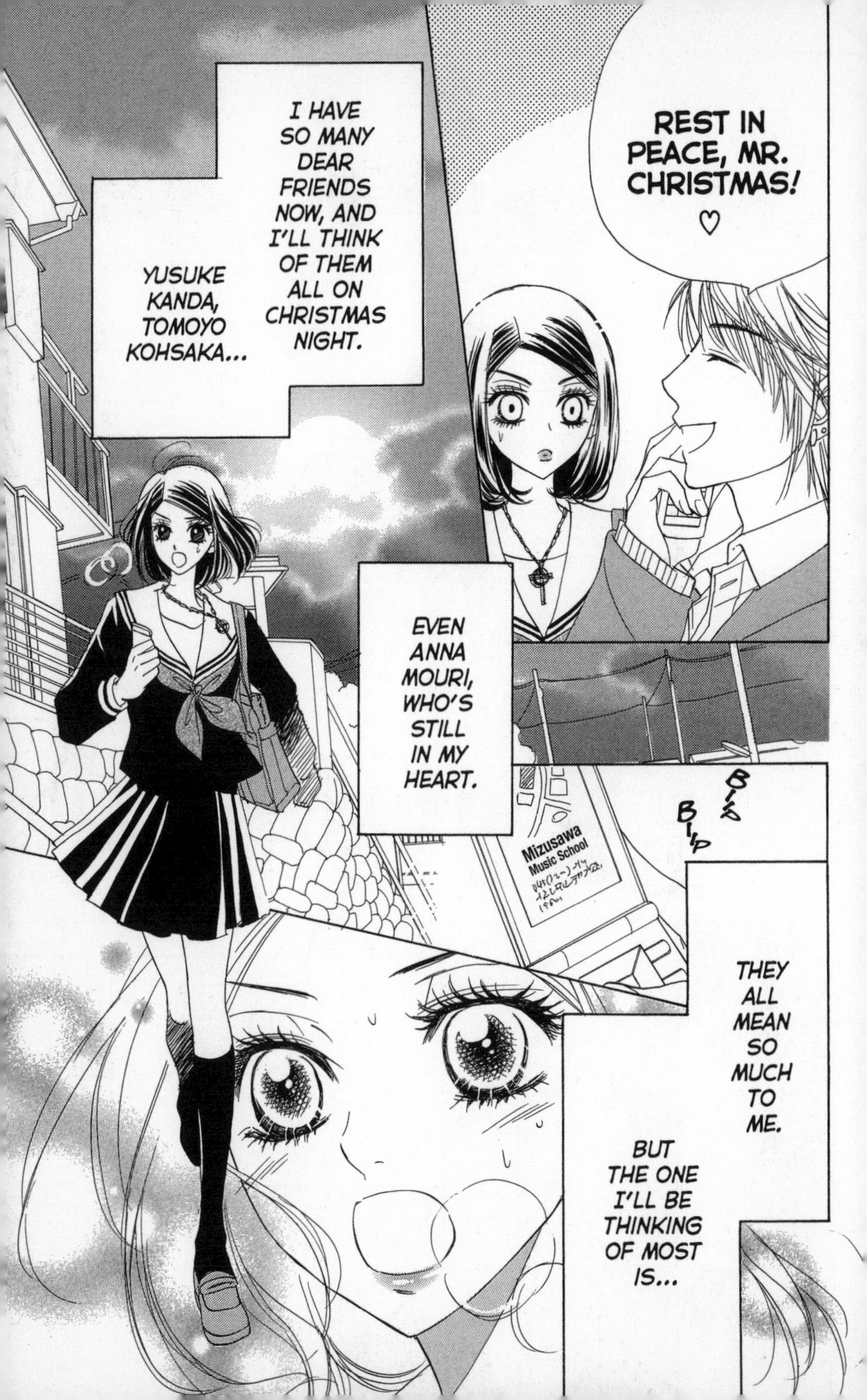
REST IN PEACE, MR. CHRISTMAS! ♡
I HAVE SO MANY DEAR FRIENDS NOW, AND I'LL THINK OF THEM ALL ON CHRISTMAS NIGHT.
YUSUKE KANDA, TOMOYO KOHSAKA...
EVEN ANNA MOURI, WHO'S STILL IN MY HEART.
BIP BIP
Mizusawa Music School
THEY ALL MEAN SO MUCH TO ME.
BUT THE ONE I'LL BE THINKING OF MOST IS...

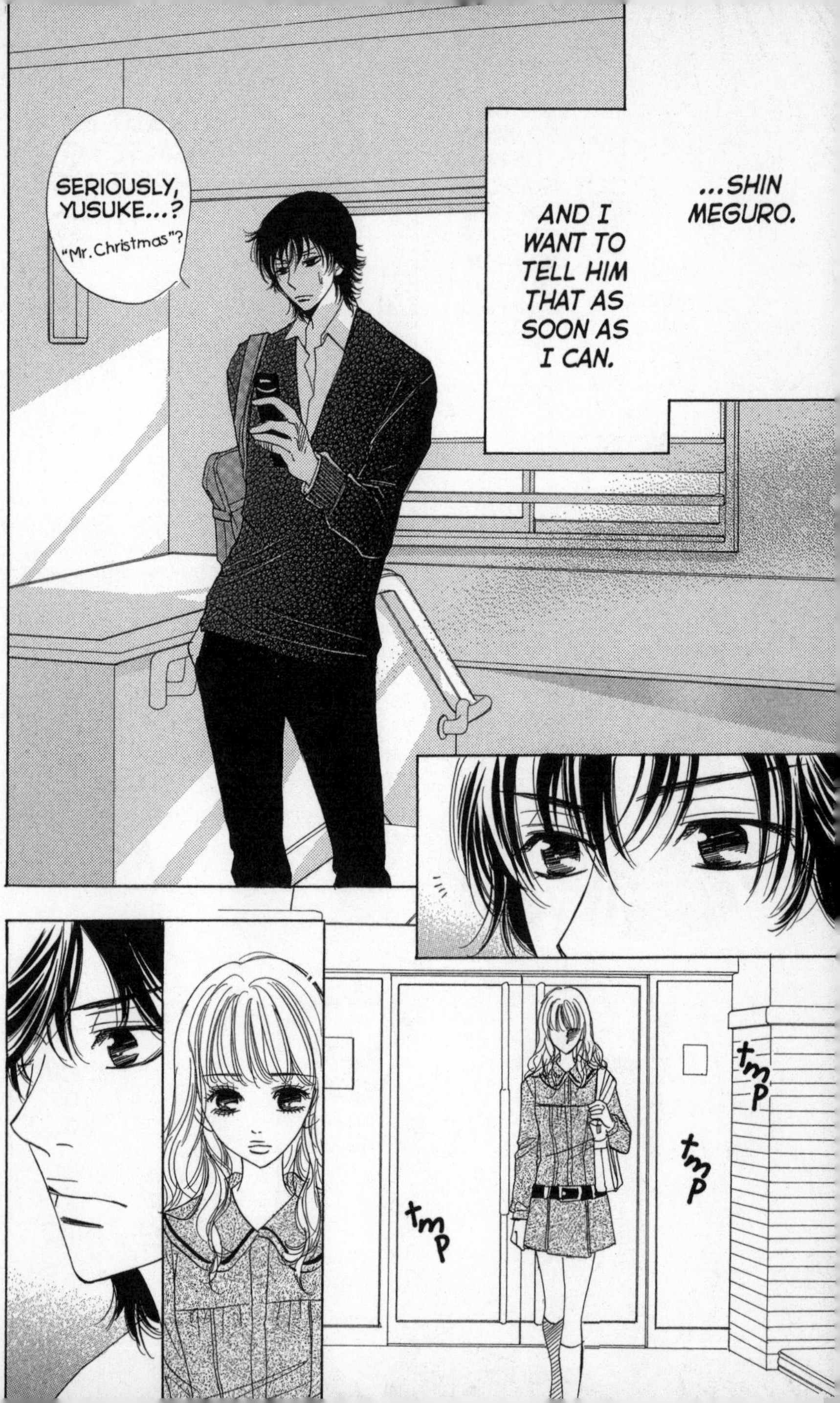
...SHIN MEGURO.
AND I WANT TO TELL HIM THAT AS SOON AS I CAN.
SERIOUSLY, YUSUKE...?
"Mr. Christmas"?
tmp
tmp
tmp

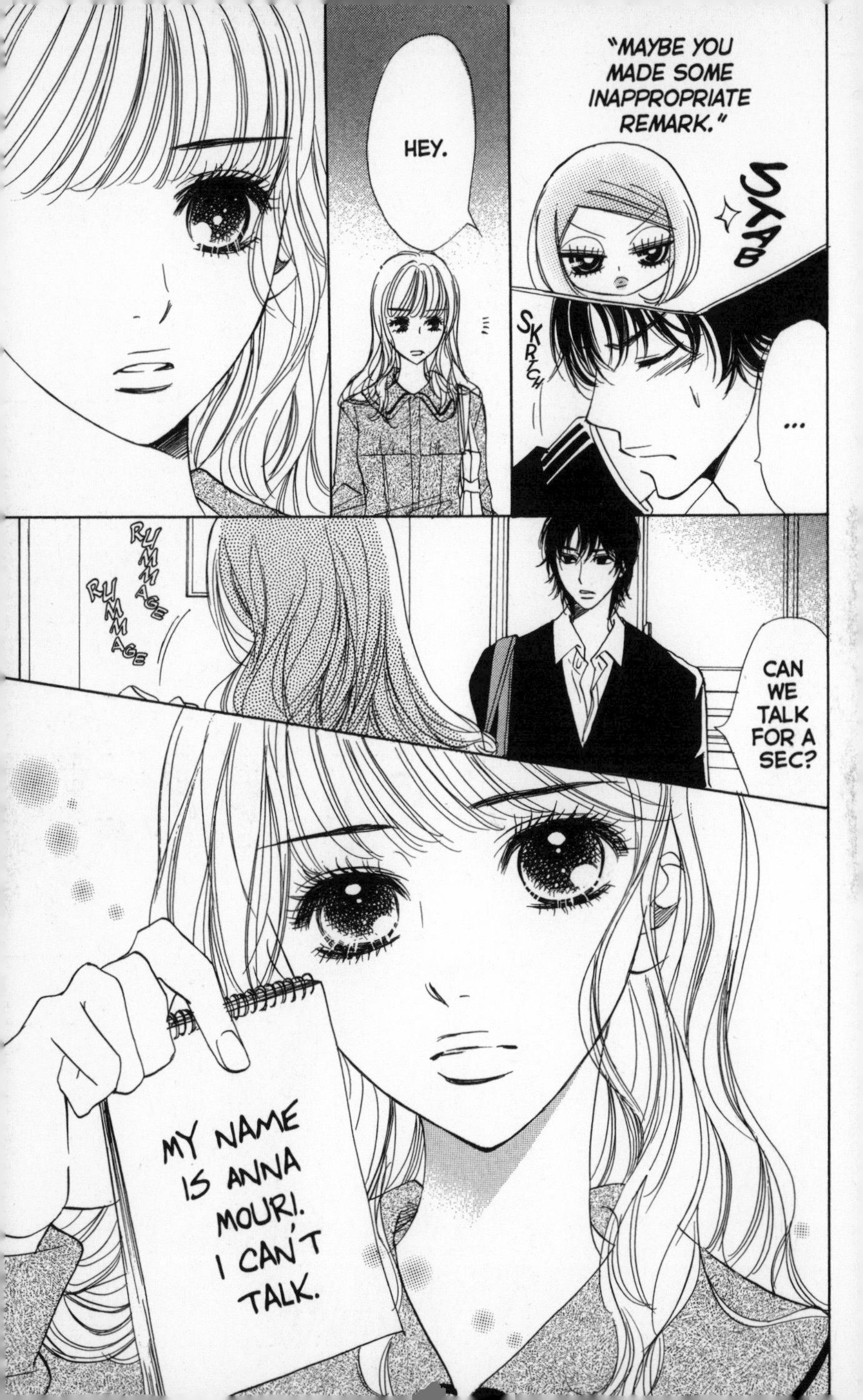
"MAYBE YOU MADE SOME INAPPROPRIATE REMARK."
STAB
SKRCH
...
HEY.
CAN WE TALK FOR A SEC?
RUMMAGE RUMMAGE
MY NAME IS ANNA MOURI. I CAN'T TALK.

A Devil and
Her Love Song

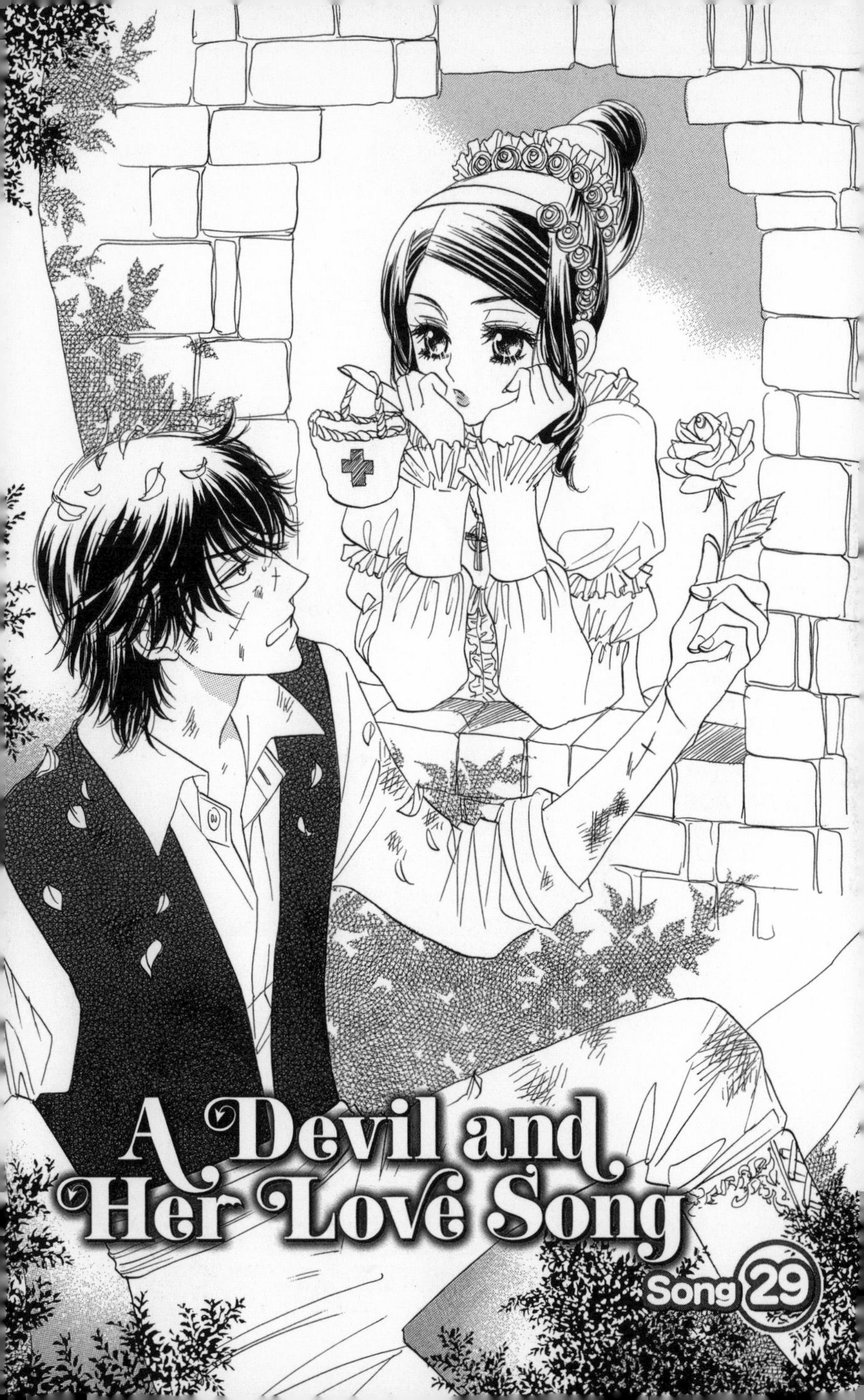
A Devil and
Her Love Song
Song 29

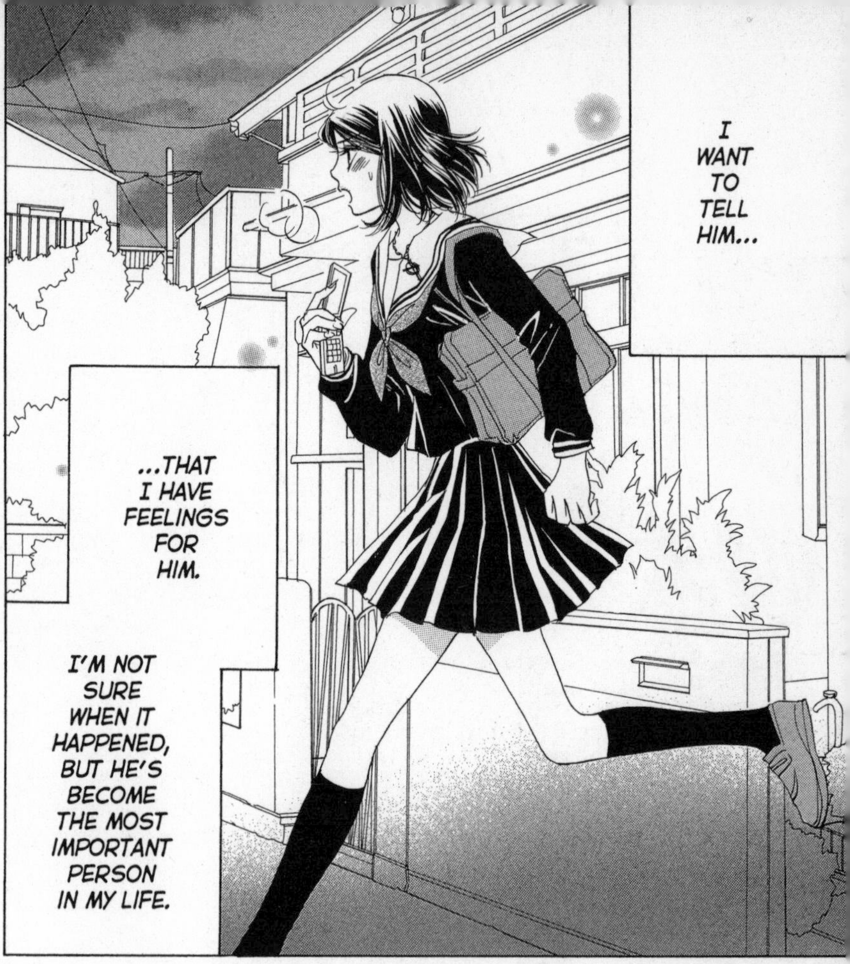
I WANT TO TELL HIM...
...THAT I HAVE FEELINGS FOR HIM.
I'M NOT SURE WHEN IT HAPPENED, BUT HE'S BECOME THE MOST IMPORTANT PERSON IN MY LIFE.

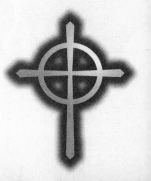

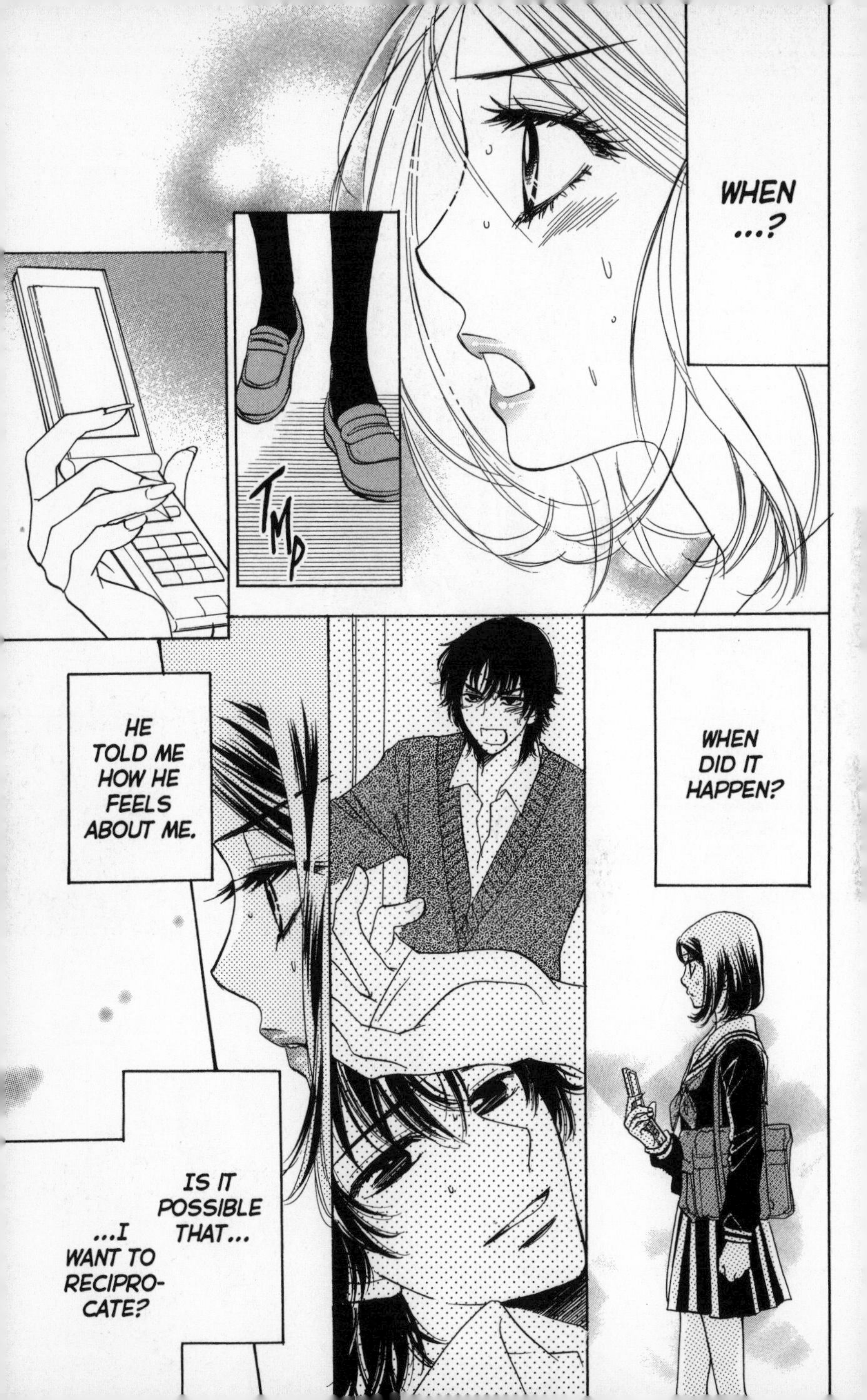
WHEN ...?
TMP
WHEN DID IT HAPPEN?
HE TOLD ME HOW HE FEELS ABOUT ME.
IS IT POSSIBLE THAT...
...I WANT TO RECIPRO-CATE?

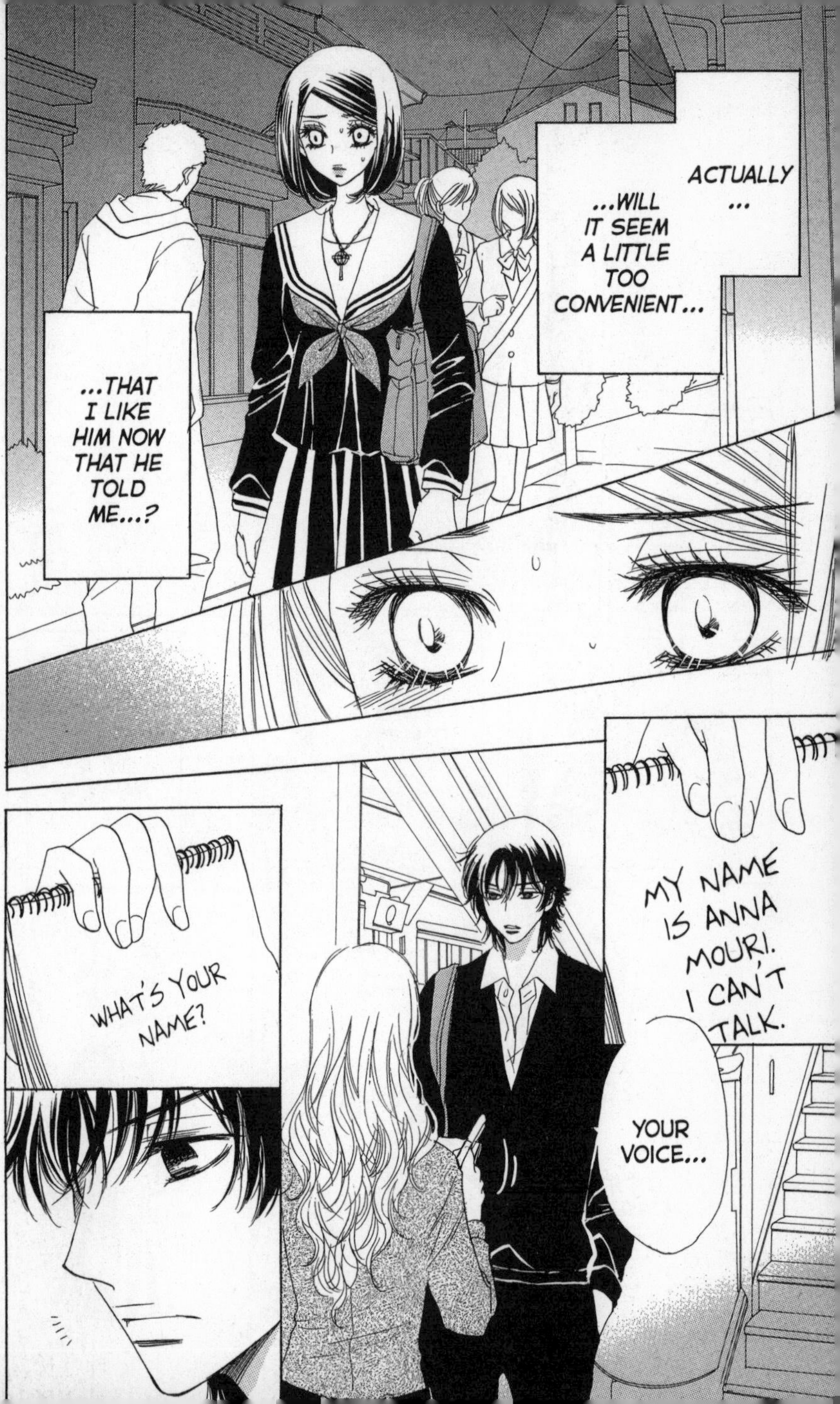
ACTUALLY ...
...WILL IT SEEM A LITTLE TOO CONVENIENT...
...THAT I LIKE HIM NOW THAT HE TOLD ME...?
MY NAME IS ANNA MOURI. I CAN'T TALK.
WHAT'S YOUR NAME?
YOUR VOICE...

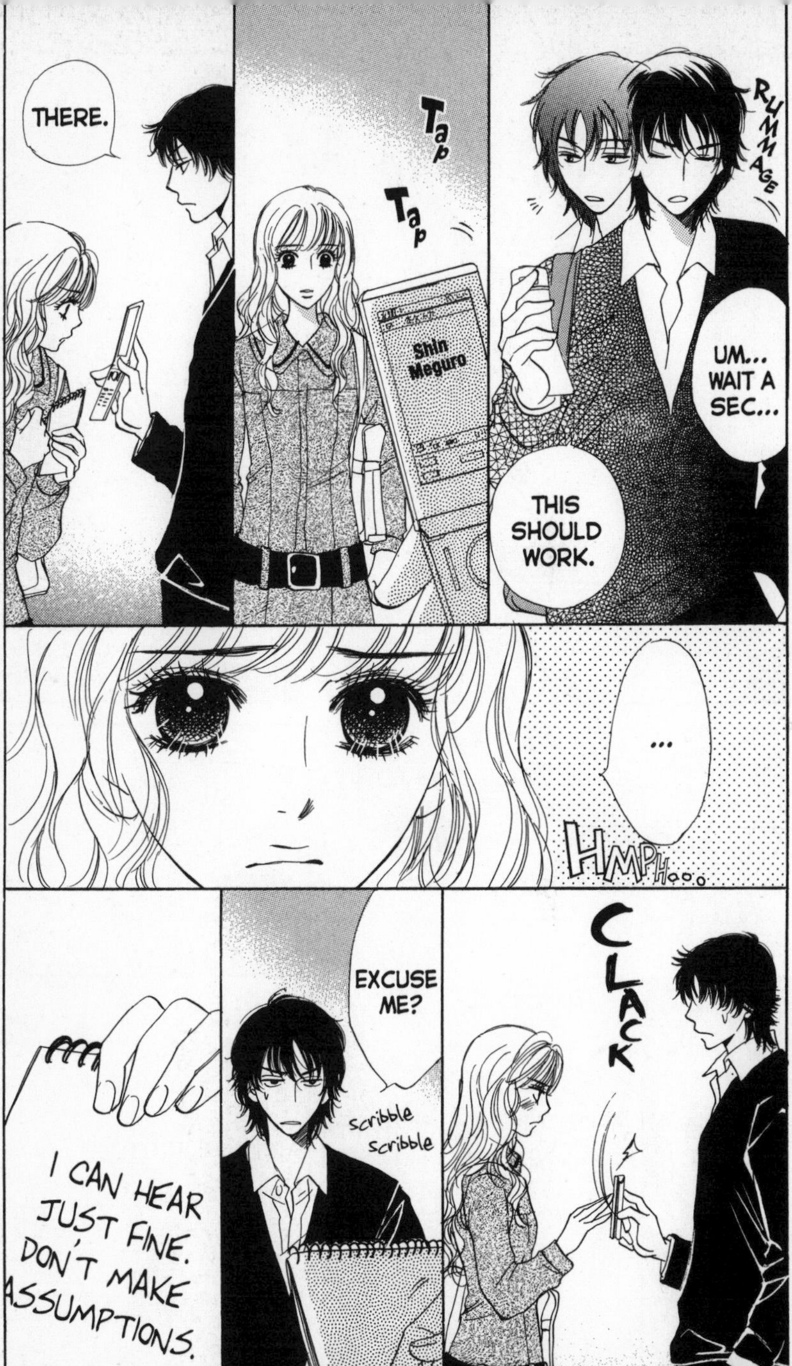
RUMMAGE
UM... WAIT A SEC...
THIS SHOULD WORK.
Tap
Tap
Shin Meguro
THERE.
...
HMPH...
CLACK
EXCUSE ME?
scribble scribble
I CAN HEAR JUST FINE. DON'T MAKE ASSUMPTIONS.

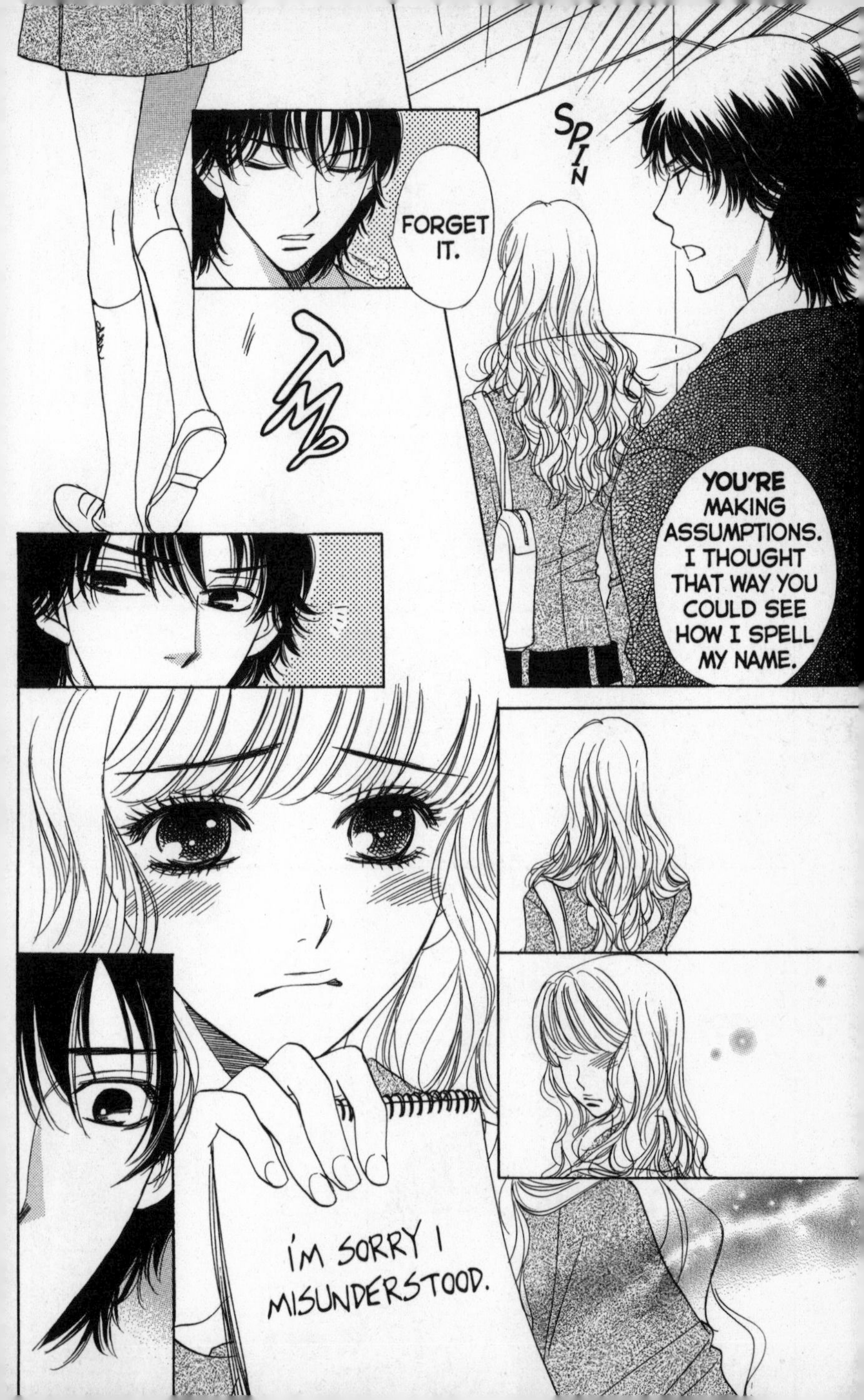
SPIN
YOU'RE MAKING ASSUMPTIONS. I THOUGHT THAT WAY YOU COULD SEE HOW I SPELL MY NAME.
FORGET IT.
TMP
I'M SORRY I MISUNDERSTOOD.

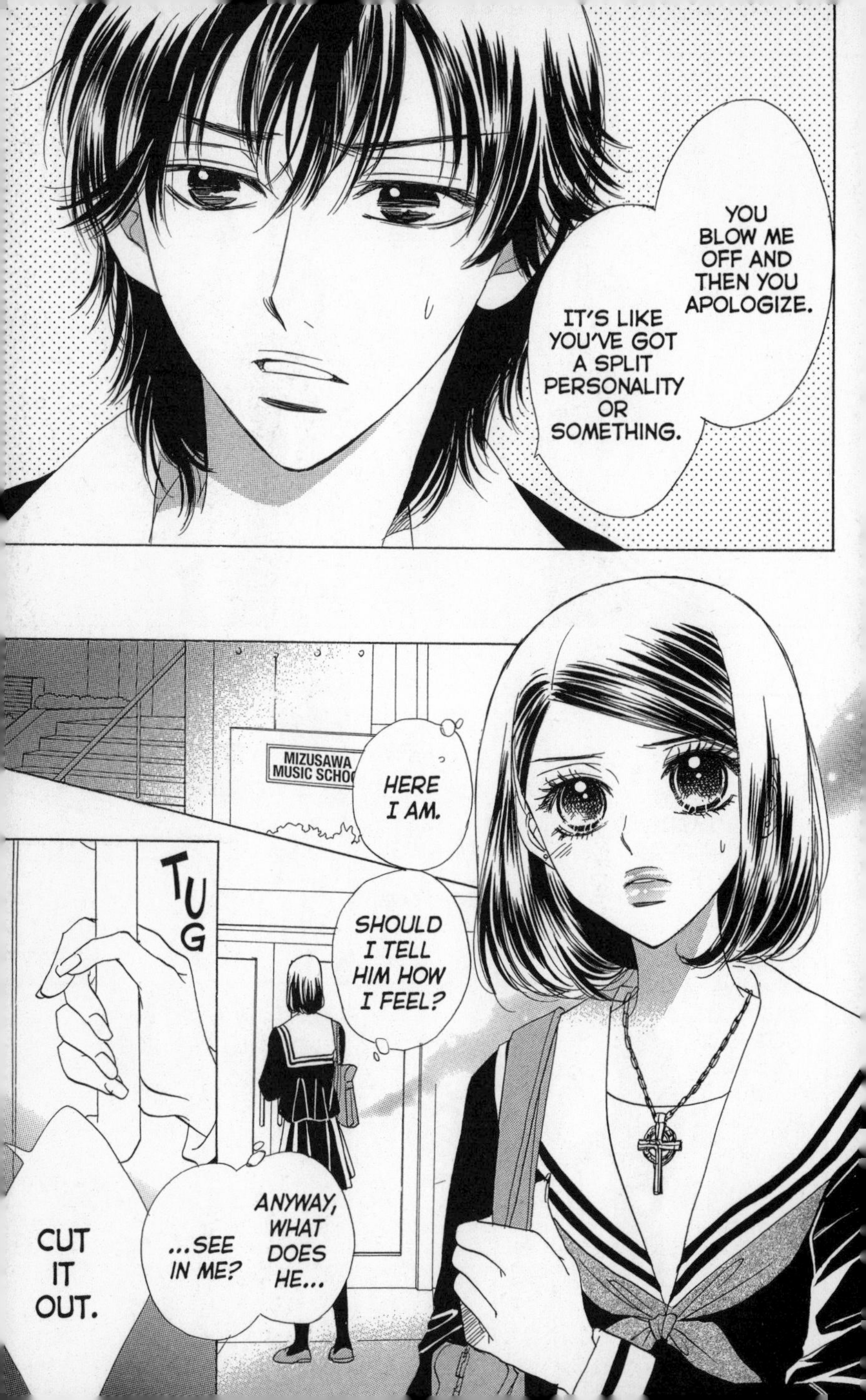
YOU BLOW ME OFF AND THEN YOU APOLOGIZE.
IT'S LIKE YOU'VE GOT A SPLIT PERSONALITY OR SOMETHING.
MIZUSAWA MUSIC SCHOO
HERE I AM.
SHOULD I TELL HIM HOW I FEEL?
TUG
ANYWAY, WHAT DOES HE...
...SEE IN ME?
CUT IT OUT.

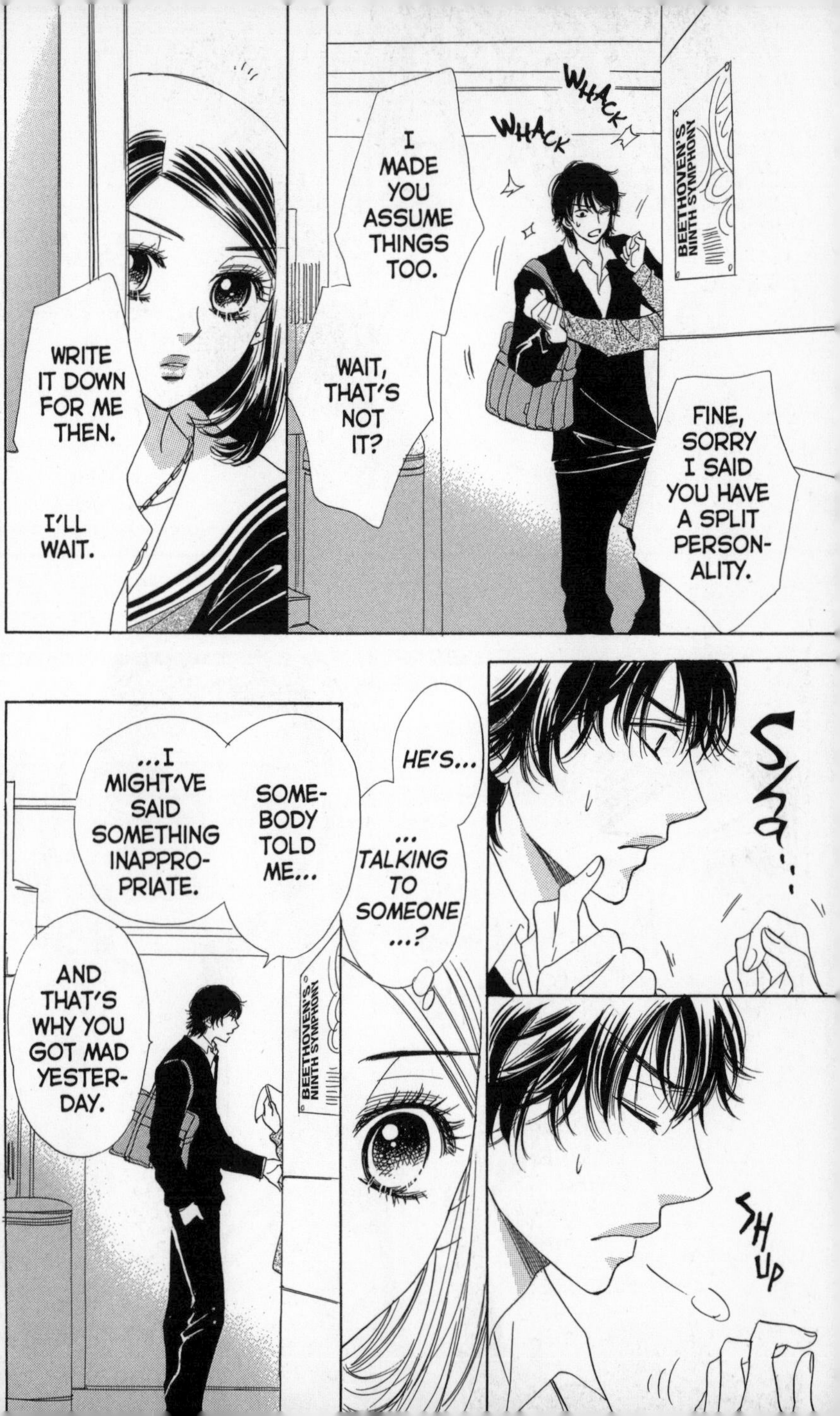
WHACK
WHACK
BEETHOVEN'S NINTH SYMPHONY
FINE, SORRY I SAID YOU HAVE A SPLIT PERSON-ALITY.
I MADE YOU ASSUME THINGS TOO.
WAIT, THAT'S NOT IT?
WRITE IT DOWN FOR ME THEN.
I'LL WAIT.
Sha..
SHUP
HE'S...
...TALKING TO SOMEONE...?
SOME-BODY TOLD ME...
...I MIGHT'VE SAID SOMETHING INAPPRO-PRIATE.
BEETHOVEN'S NINTH SYMPHONY
AND THAT'S WHY YOU GOT MAD YESTER-DAY.

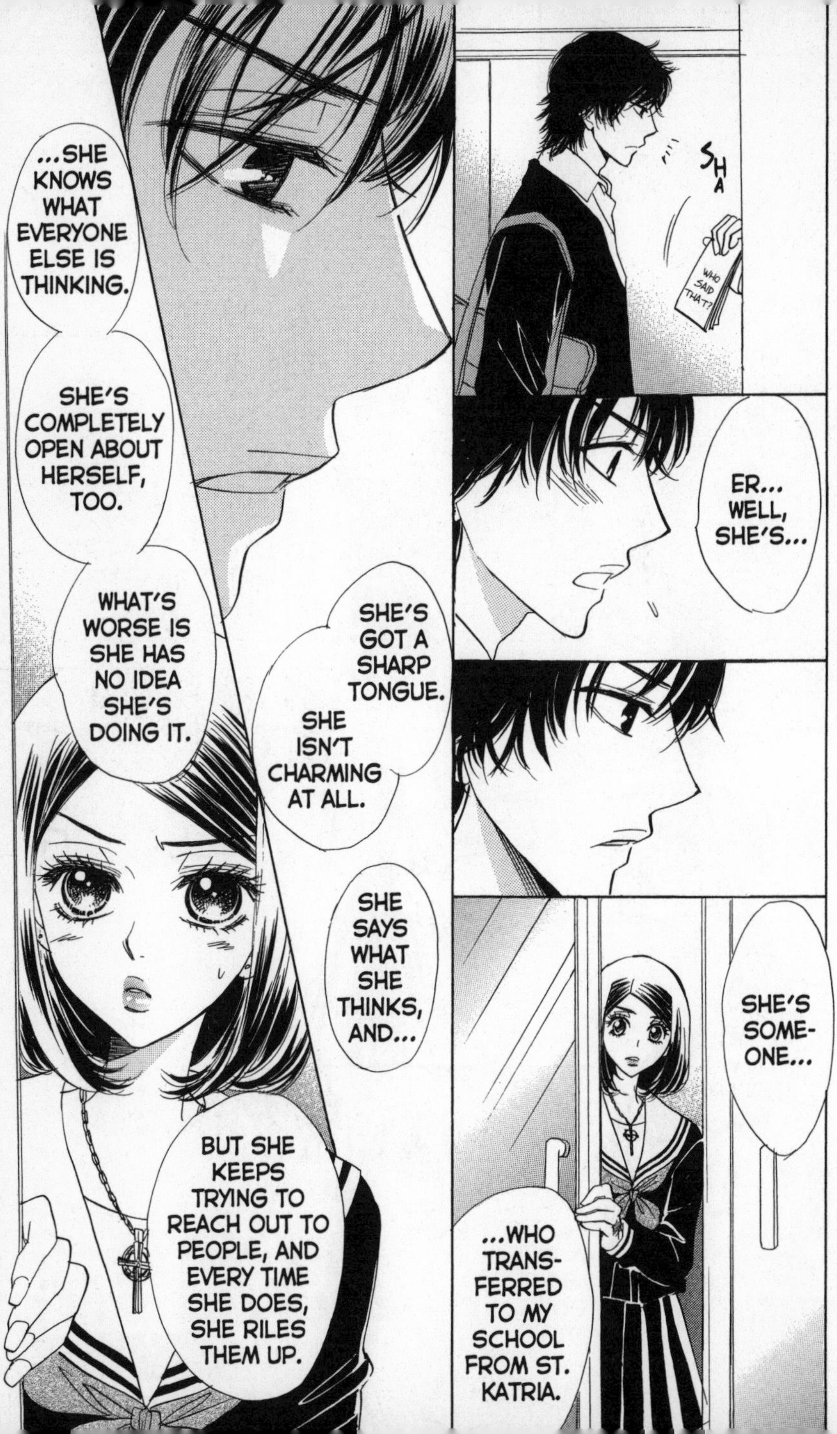
SHA
WHO SAID THAT?
ER... WELL, SHE'S...
SHE'S SOME-ONE...
...WHO TRANS-FERRED TO MY SCHOOL FROM ST. KATRIA.
SHE'S GOT A SHARP TONGUE.
SHE ISN'T CHARMING AT ALL.
SHE SAYS WHAT SHE THINKS, AND...
...SHE KNOWS WHAT EVERYONE ELSE IS THINKING.
SHE'S COMPLETELY OPEN ABOUT HERSELF, TOO.
WHAT'S WORSE IS SHE HAS NO IDEA SHE'S DOING IT.
BUT SHE KEEPS TRYING TO REACH OUT TO PEOPLE, AND EVERY TIME SHE DOES, SHE RILES THEM UP.

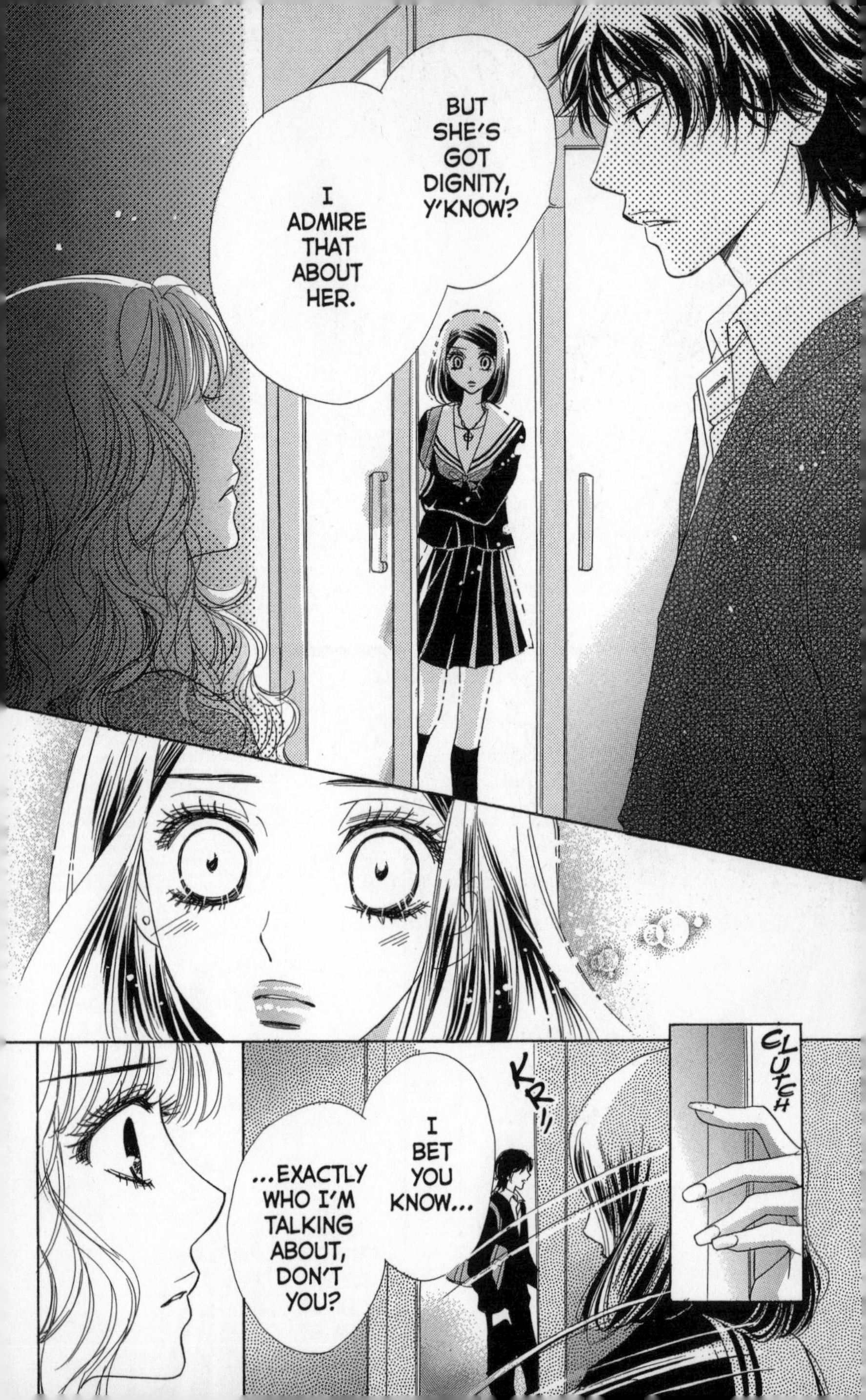
BUT SHE'S GOT DIGNITY, Y'KNOW?
I ADMIRE THAT ABOUT HER.
CLUTCH
KRI
I BET YOU KNOW...
...EXACTLY WHO I'M TALKING ABOUT, DON'T YOU?

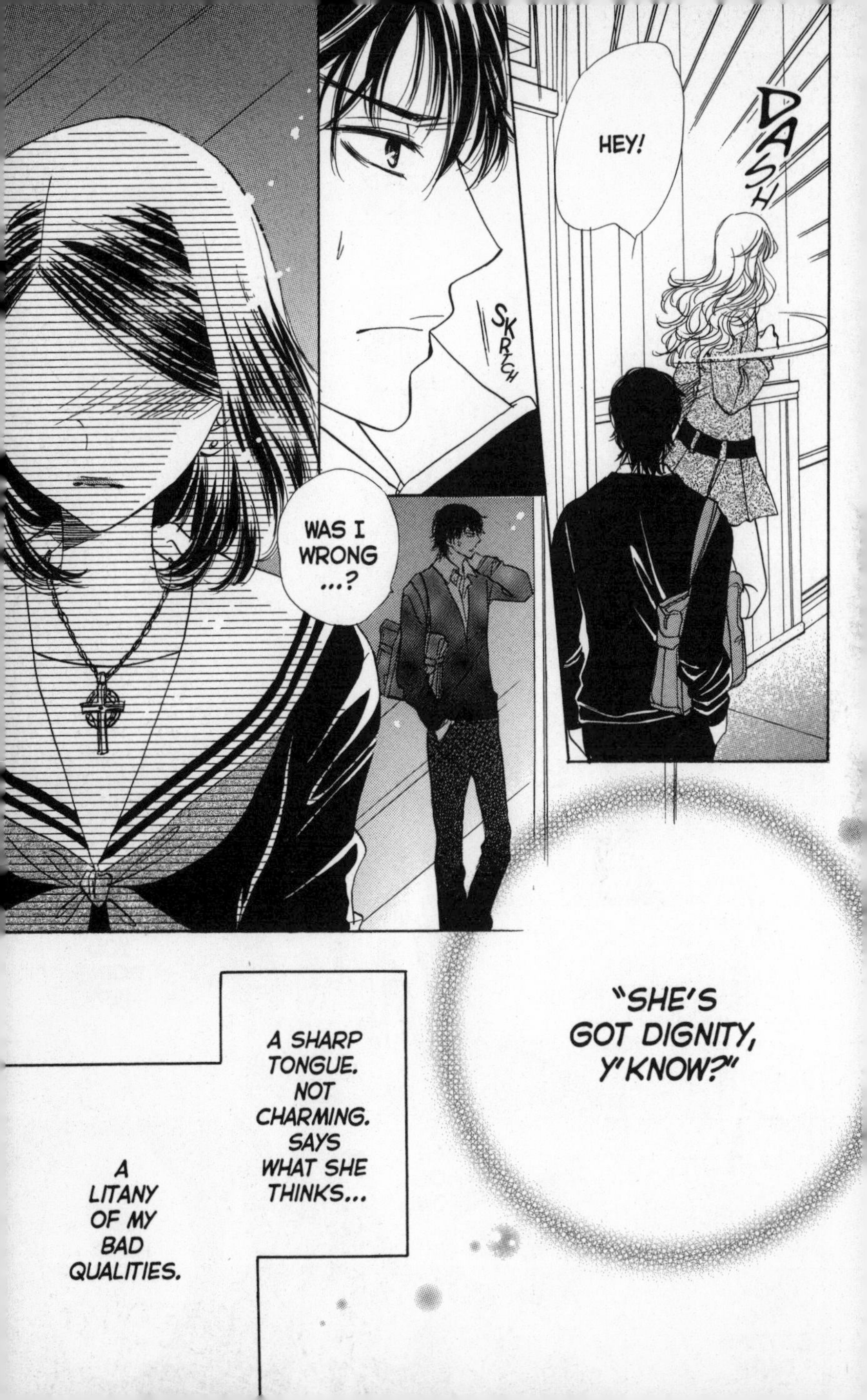
DASH
HEY!
SKRTCH
WAS I WRONG ...?
"SHE'S GOT DIGNITY, Y'KNOW?"
A SHARP TONGUE. NOT CHARMING. SAYS WHAT SHE THINKS...
A LITANY OF MY BAD QUALITIES.

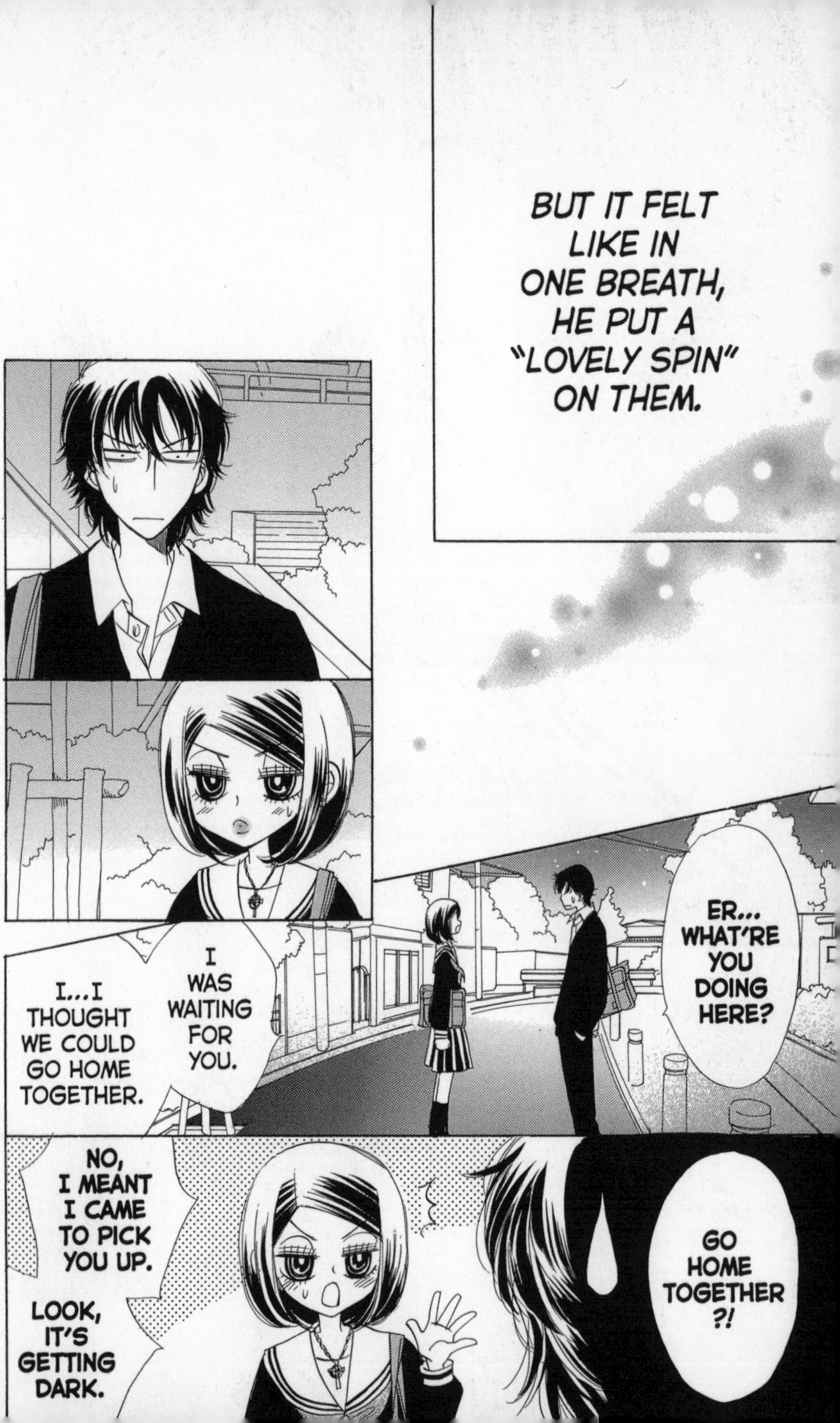
BUT IT FELT LIKE IN ONE BREATH, HE PUT A "LOVELY SPIN" ON THEM.
ER... WHAT'RE YOU DOING HERE?
I WAS WAITING FOR YOU.
I...I THOUGHT WE COULD GO HOME TOGETHER.
GO HOME TOGETHER ?!
NO, I MEANT I CAME TO PICK YOU UP.
LOOK, IT'S GETTING DARK.

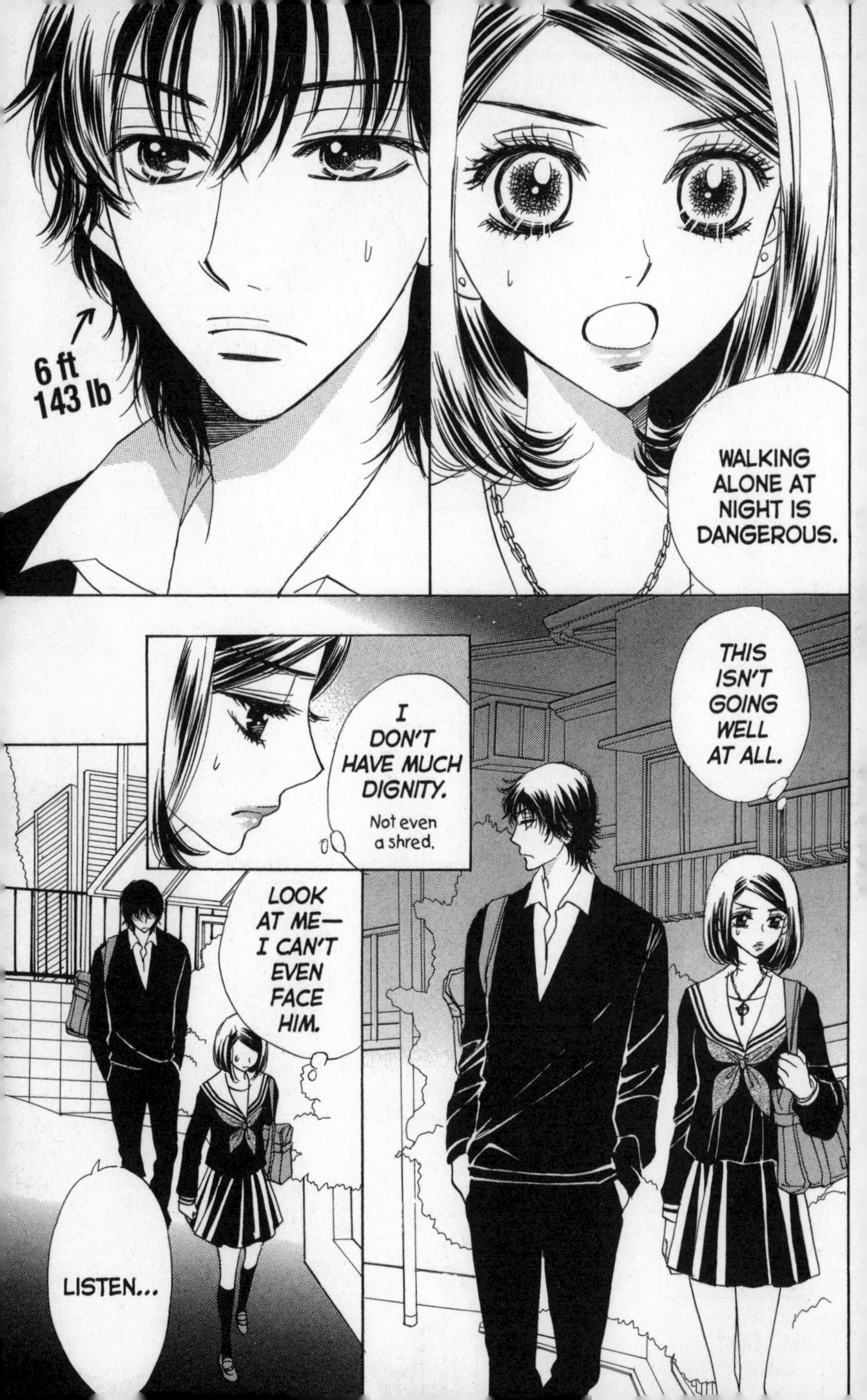
WALKING ALONE AT NIGHT IS DANGEROUS.
6 ft 143 lb
THIS ISN'T GOING WELL AT ALL.
I DON'T HAVE MUCH DIGNITY.
Not even a shred.
LOOK AT ME— I CAN'T EVEN FACE HIM.
LISTEN...

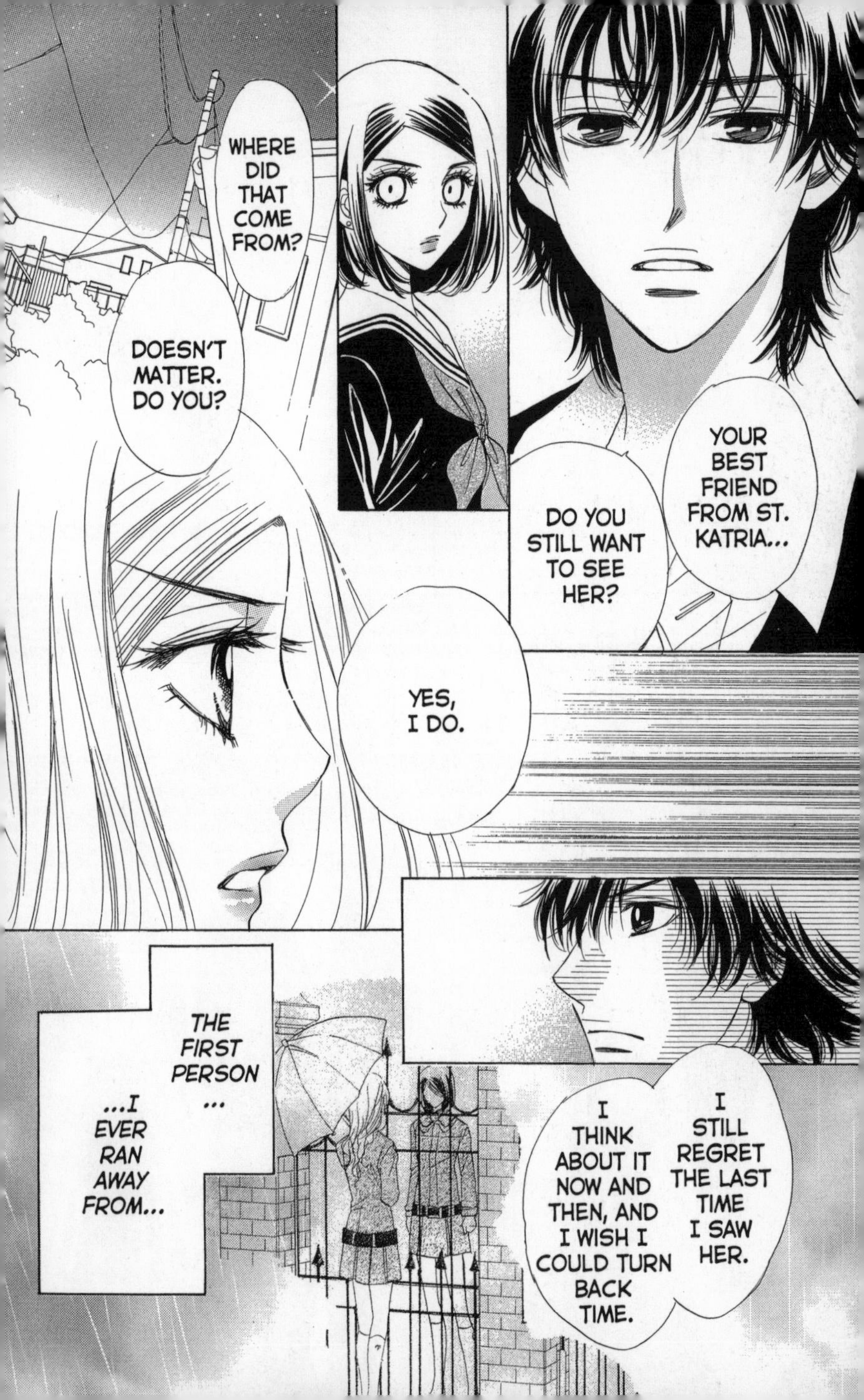
YOUR BEST FRIEND FROM ST. KATRIA...
DO YOU STILL WANT TO SEE HER?
WHERE DID THAT COME FROM?
DOESN'T MATTER. DO YOU?
YES, I DO.
I STILL REGRET THE LAST TIME I SAW HER.
I THINK ABOUT IT NOW AND THEN, AND I WISH I COULD TURN BACK TIME.
THE FIRST PERSON...
...I EVER RAN AWAY FROM...

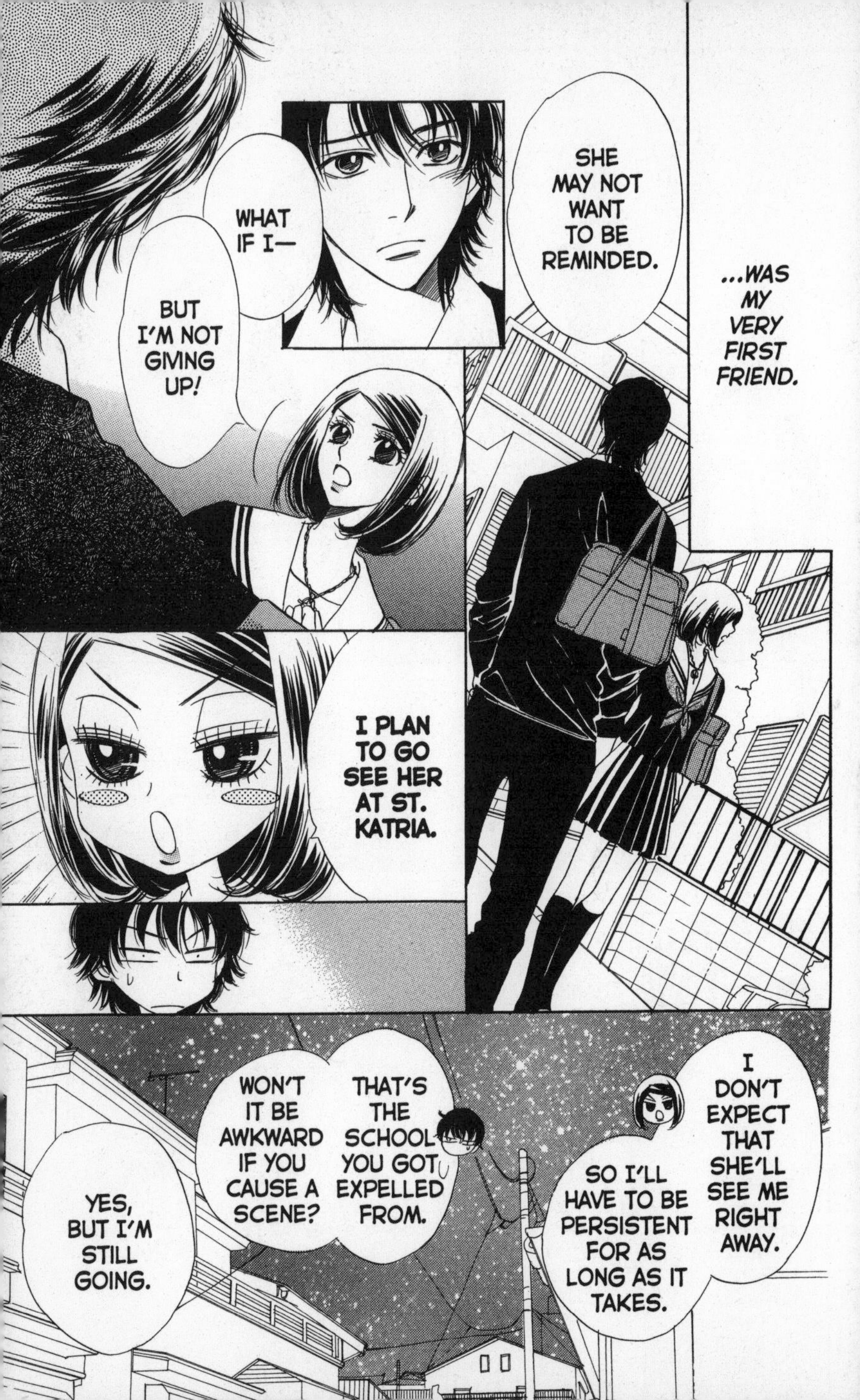
...WAS MY VERY FIRST FRIEND.
SHE MAY NOT WANT TO BE REMINDED.
WHAT IF I—
BUT I'M NOT GIVING UP!
I PLAN TO GO SEE HER AT ST. KATRIA.
I DON'T EXPECT THAT SHE'LL SEE ME RIGHT AWAY.
SO I'LL HAVE TO BE PERSISTENT FOR AS LONG AS IT TAKES.
THAT'S THE SCHOOL YOU GOT EXPELLED FROM.
WON'T IT BE AWKWARD IF YOU CAUSE A SCENE?
YES, BUT I'M STILL GOING.

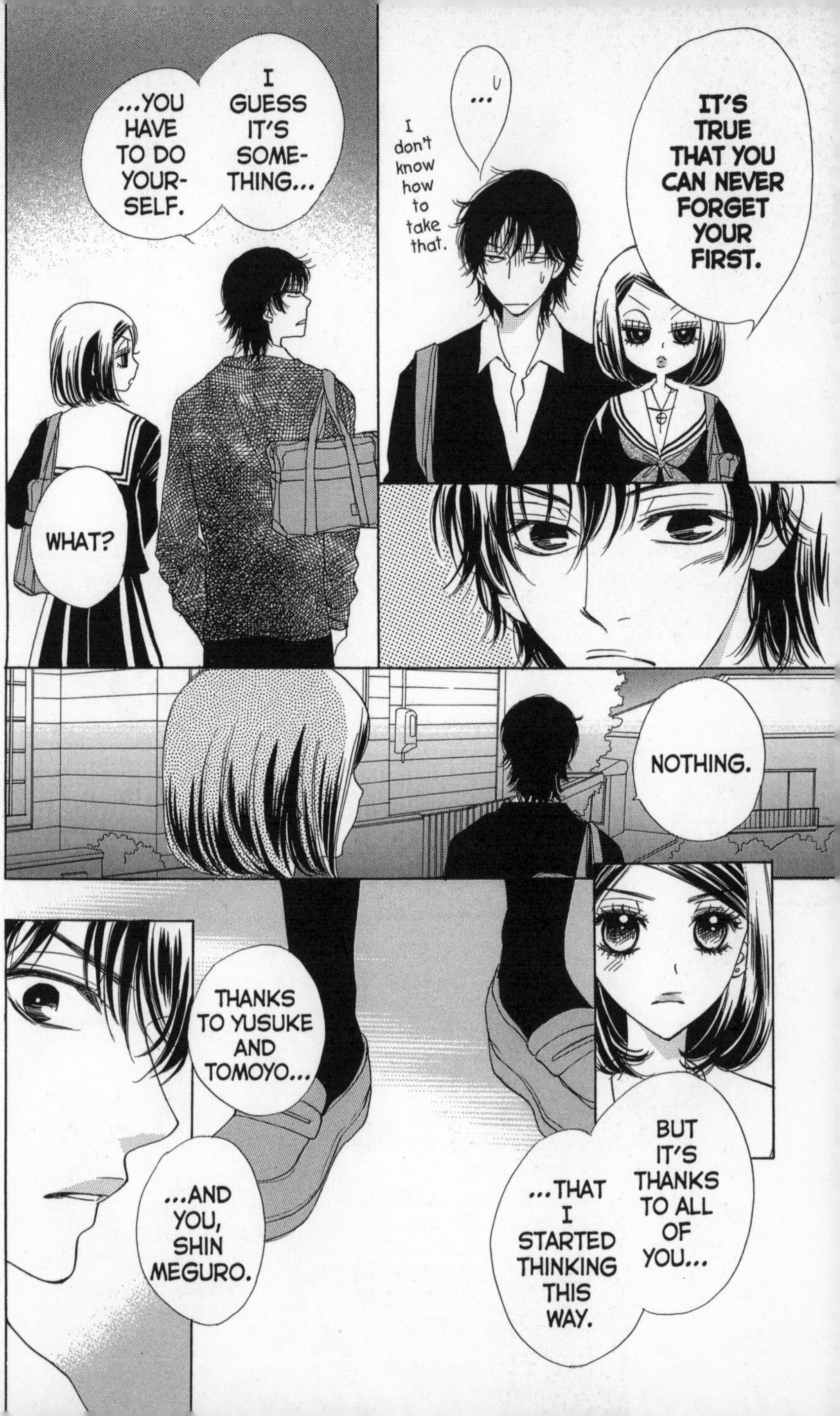
IT'S TRUE THAT YOU CAN NEVER FORGET YOUR FIRST.
...
I don't know how to take that.
I GUESS IT'S SOMETHING...
...YOU HAVE TO DO YOURSELF.
WHAT?
NOTHING.
BUT IT'S THANKS TO ALL OF YOU...
...THAT I STARTED THINKING THIS WAY.
THANKS TO YUSUKE AND TOMOYO...
...AND YOU, SHIN MEGURO.

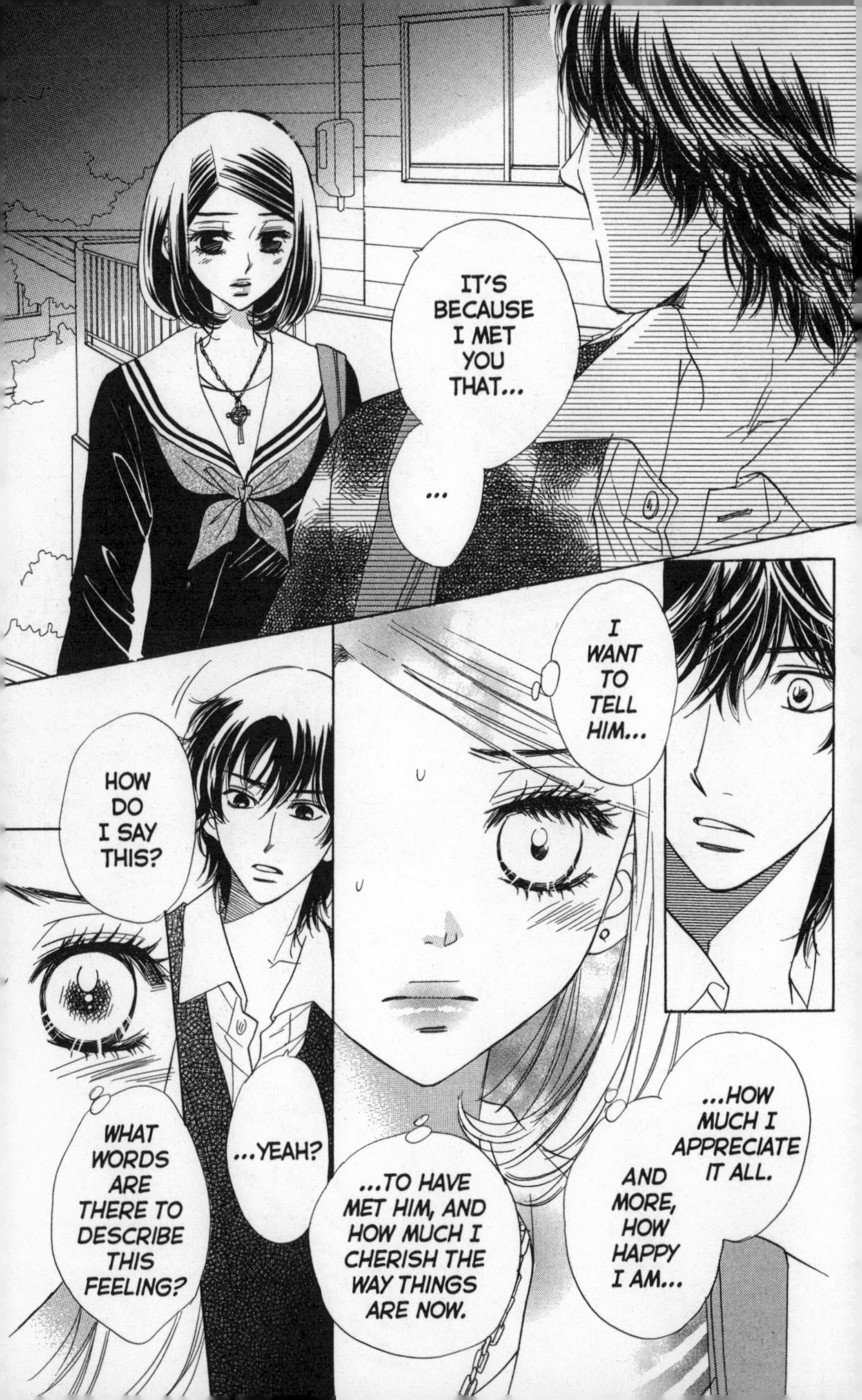
IT'S BECAUSE I MET YOU THAT...
...
I WANT TO TELL HIM...
...HOW MUCH I APPRECIATE IT ALL.
AND MORE, HOW HAPPY I AM...
...TO HAVE MET HIM, AND HOW MUCH I CHERISH THE WAY THINGS ARE NOW.
HOW DO I SAY THIS?
...YEAH?
WHAT WORDS ARE THERE TO DESCRIBE THIS FEELING?

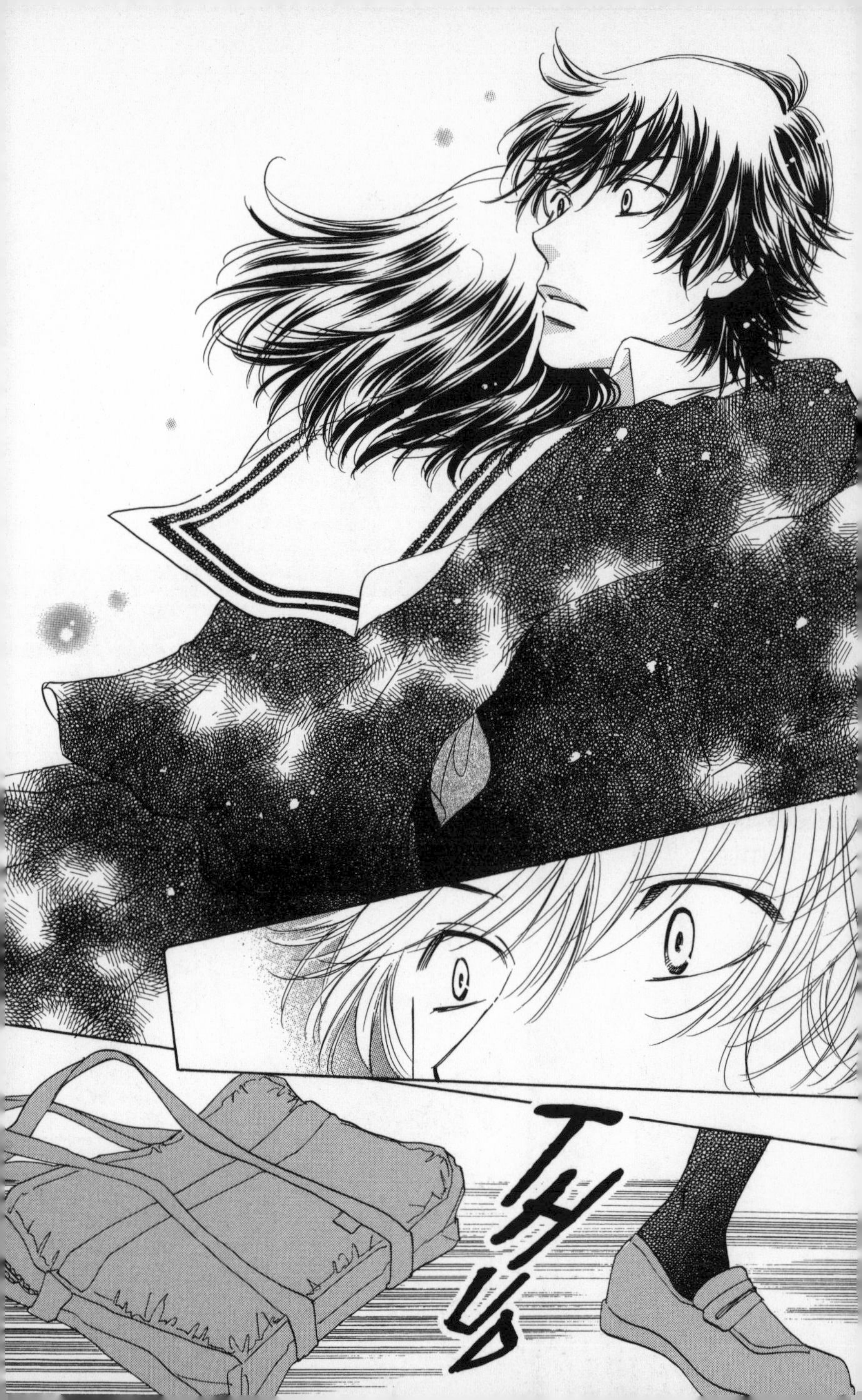
THUD

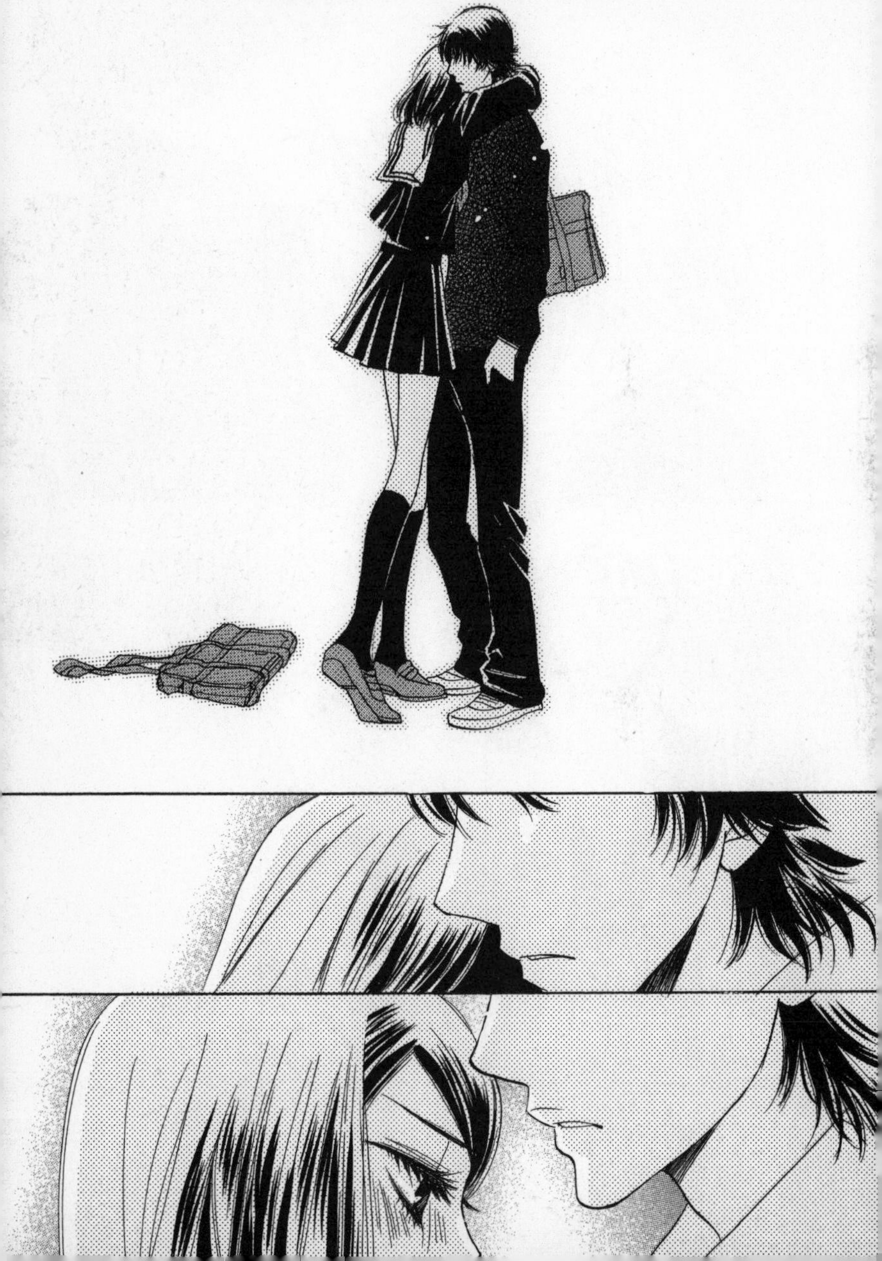

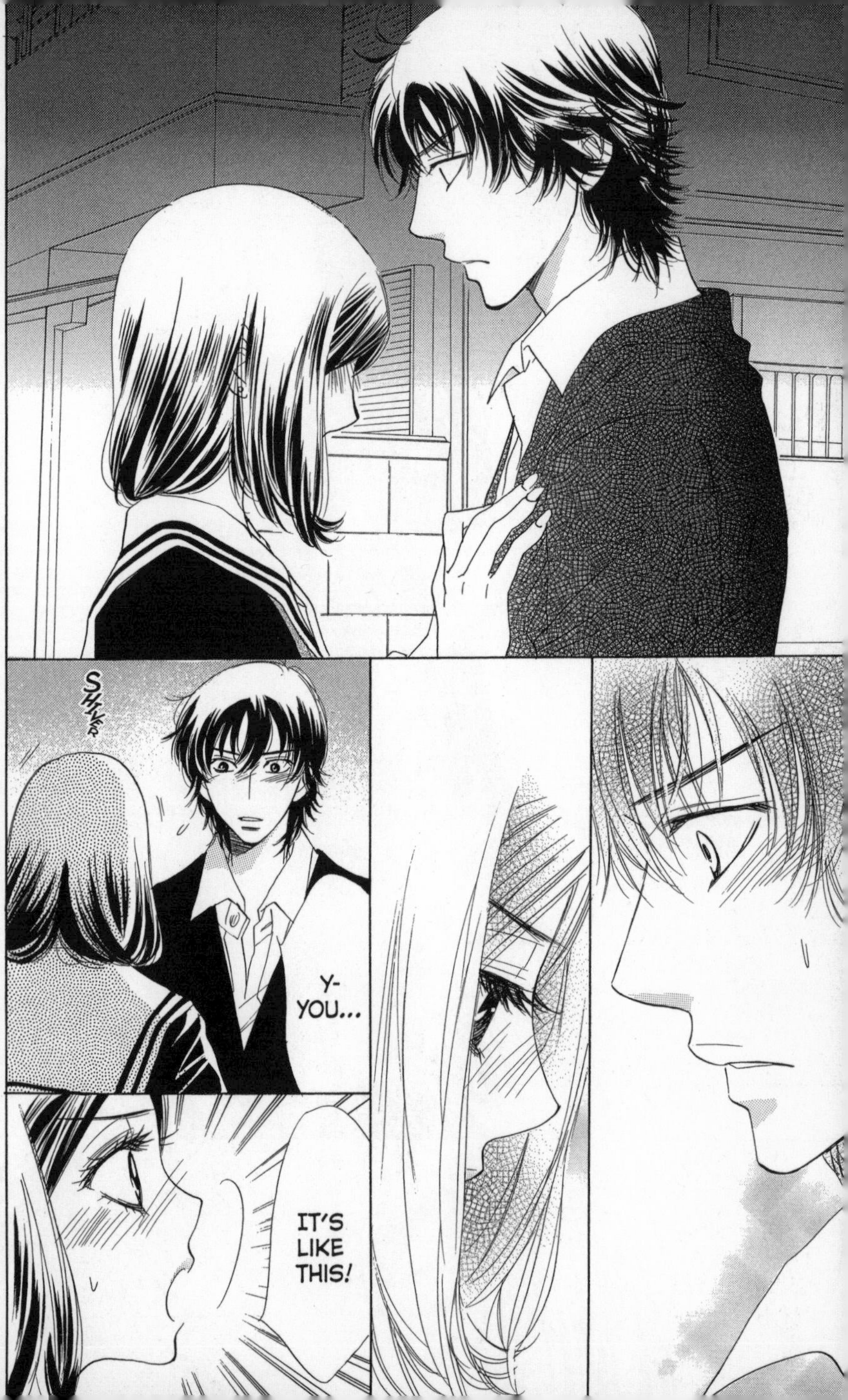
SHIVER
Y-YOU...
IT'S LIKE THIS!

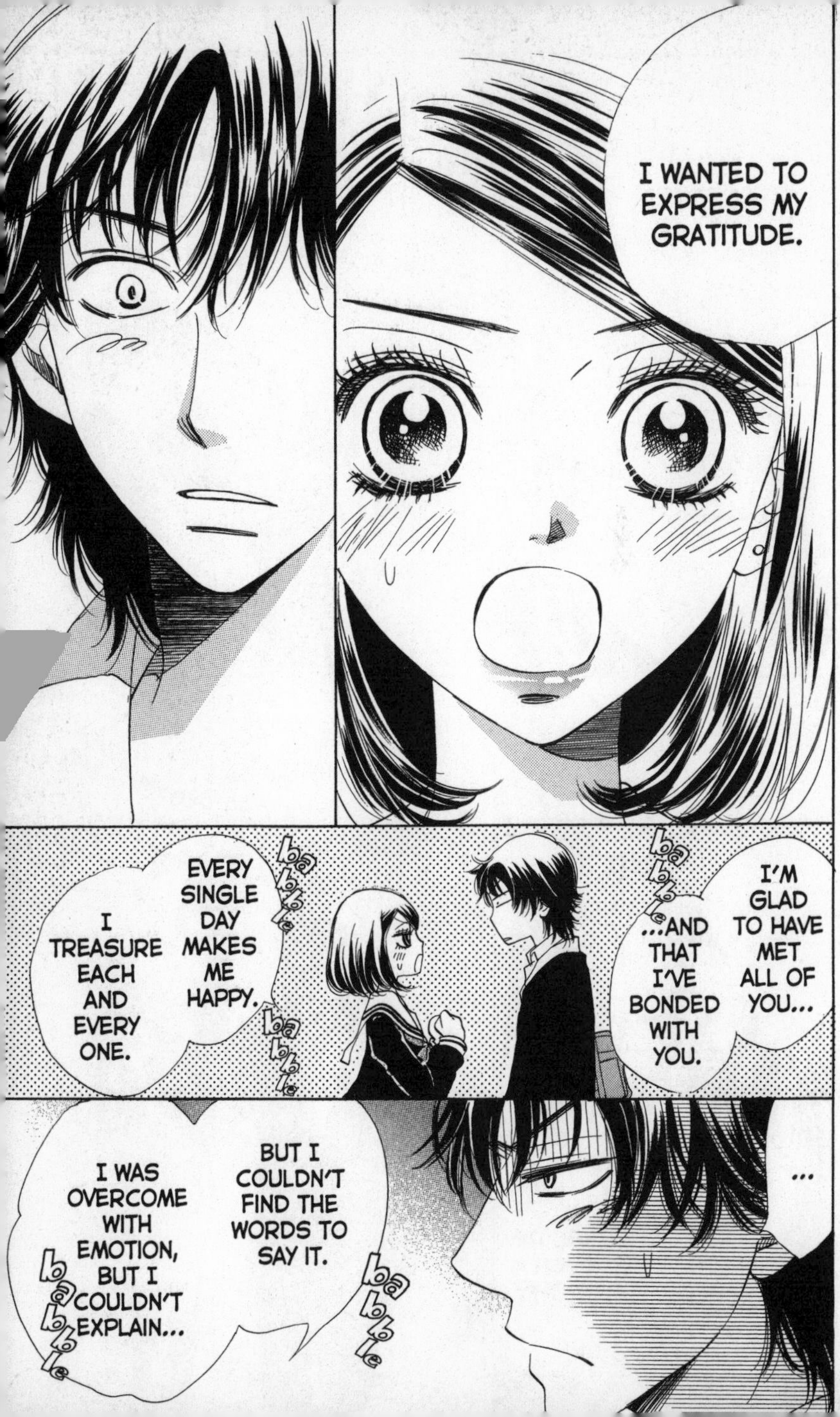
I WANTED TO EXPRESS MY GRATITUDE.
babble
I'M GLAD TO HAVE MET ALL OF YOU...
...AND THAT I'VE BONDED WITH YOU.
babble
EVERY SINGLE DAY MAKES ME HAPPY.
I TREASURE EACH AND EVERY ONE.
babble
...
babble
BUT I COULDN'T FIND THE WORDS TO SAY IT.
I WAS OVERCOME WITH EMOTION, BUT I COULDN'T EXPLAIN...
babble

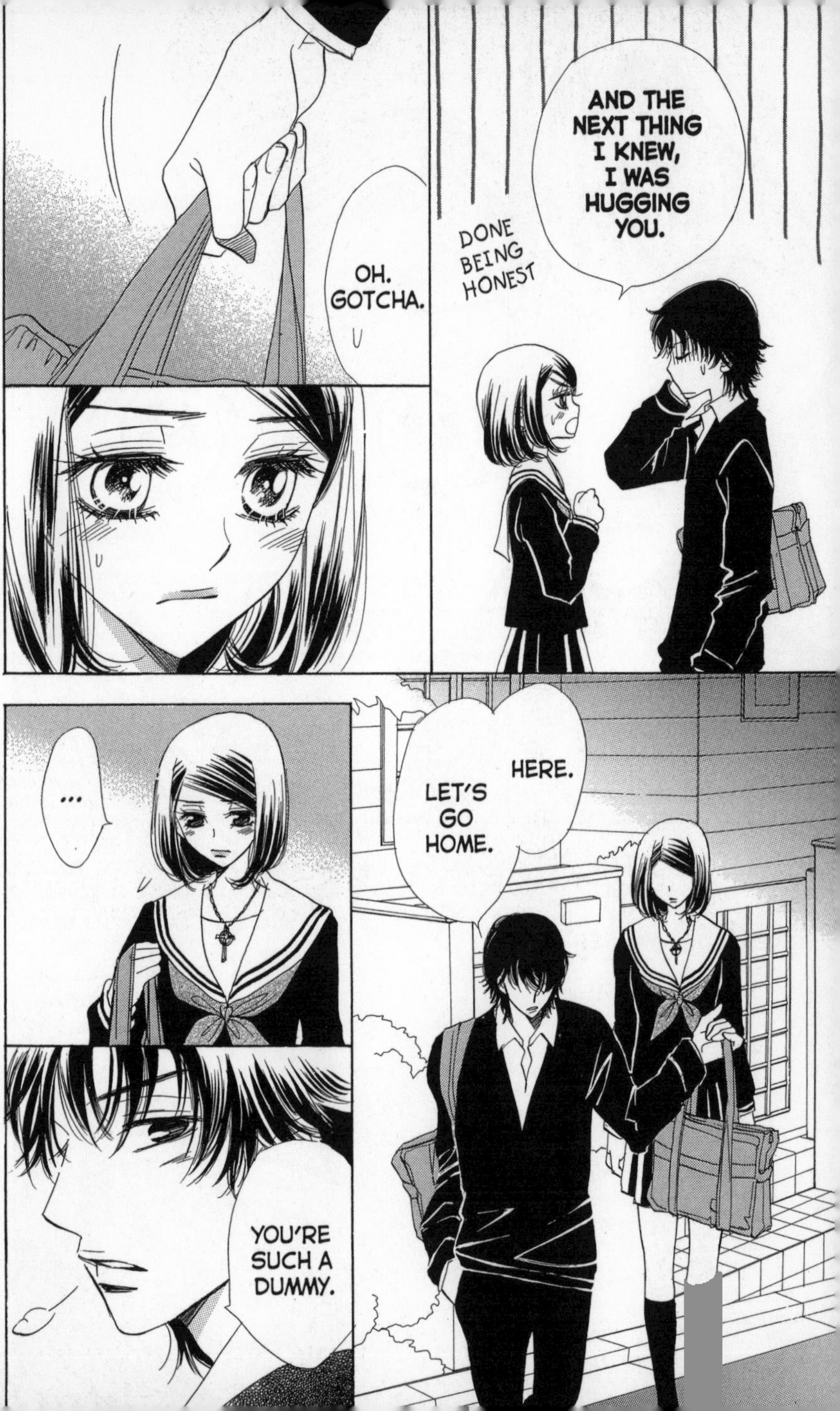
AND THE NEXT THING I KNEW, I WAS HUGGING YOU.
DONE BEING HONEST
OH. GOTCHA.
HERE.
LET'S GO HOME.
...
YOU'RE SUCH A DUMMY.

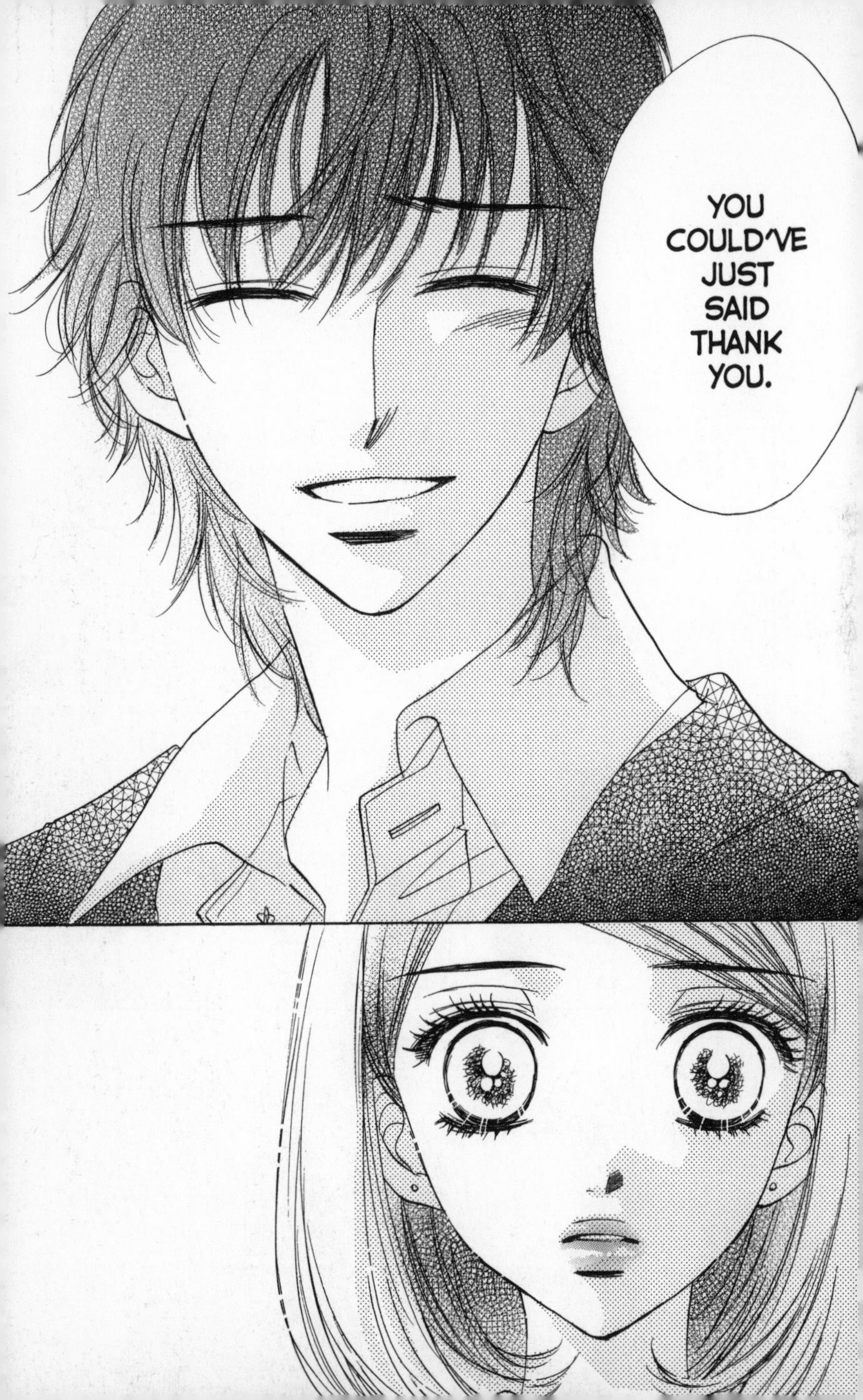
YOU COULD'VE JUST SAID THANK YOU.

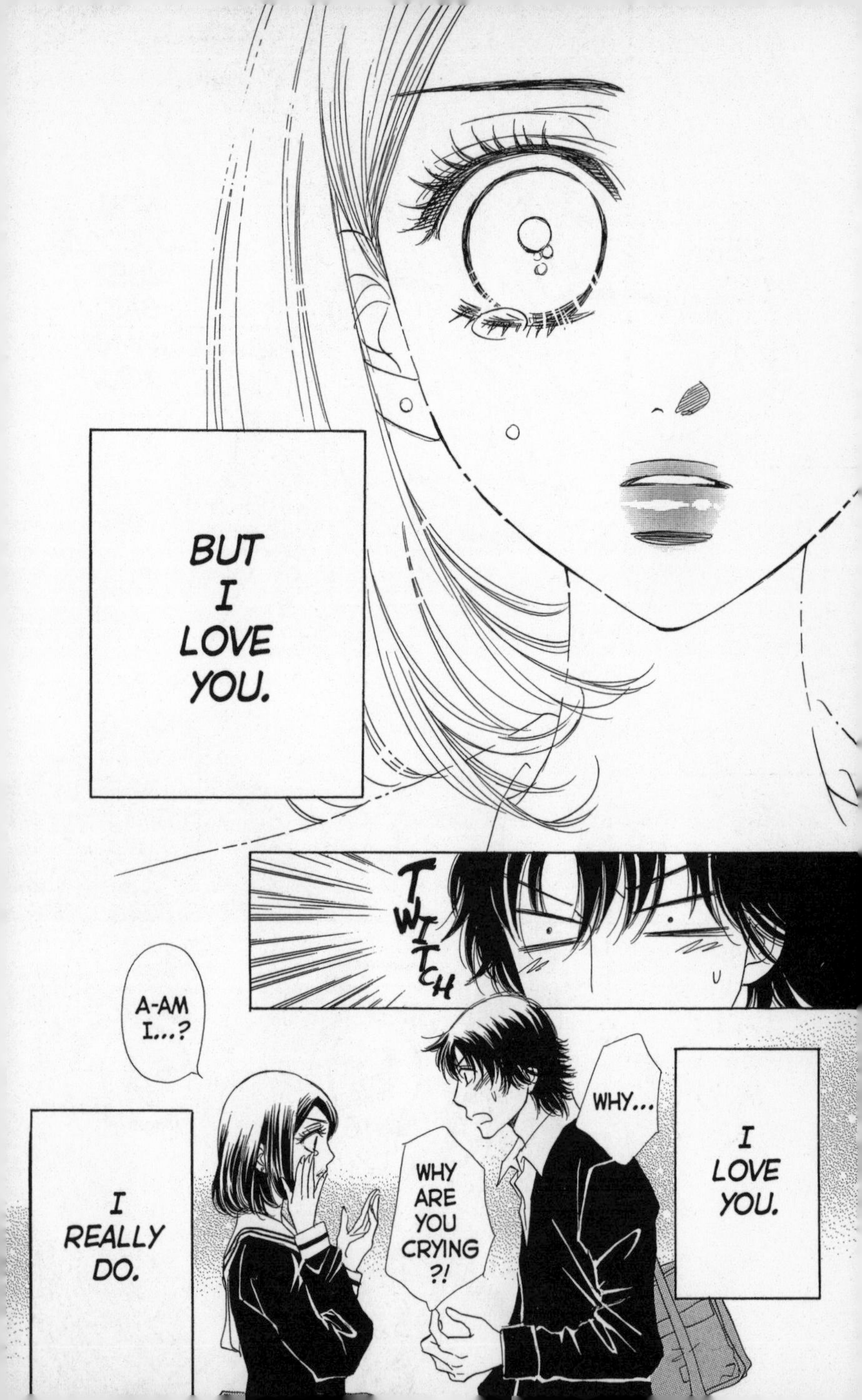
BUT I LOVE YOU.
TWITCH
I LOVE YOU.
WHY...
WHY ARE YOU CRYING?!
A-AM I...?
I REALLY DO.

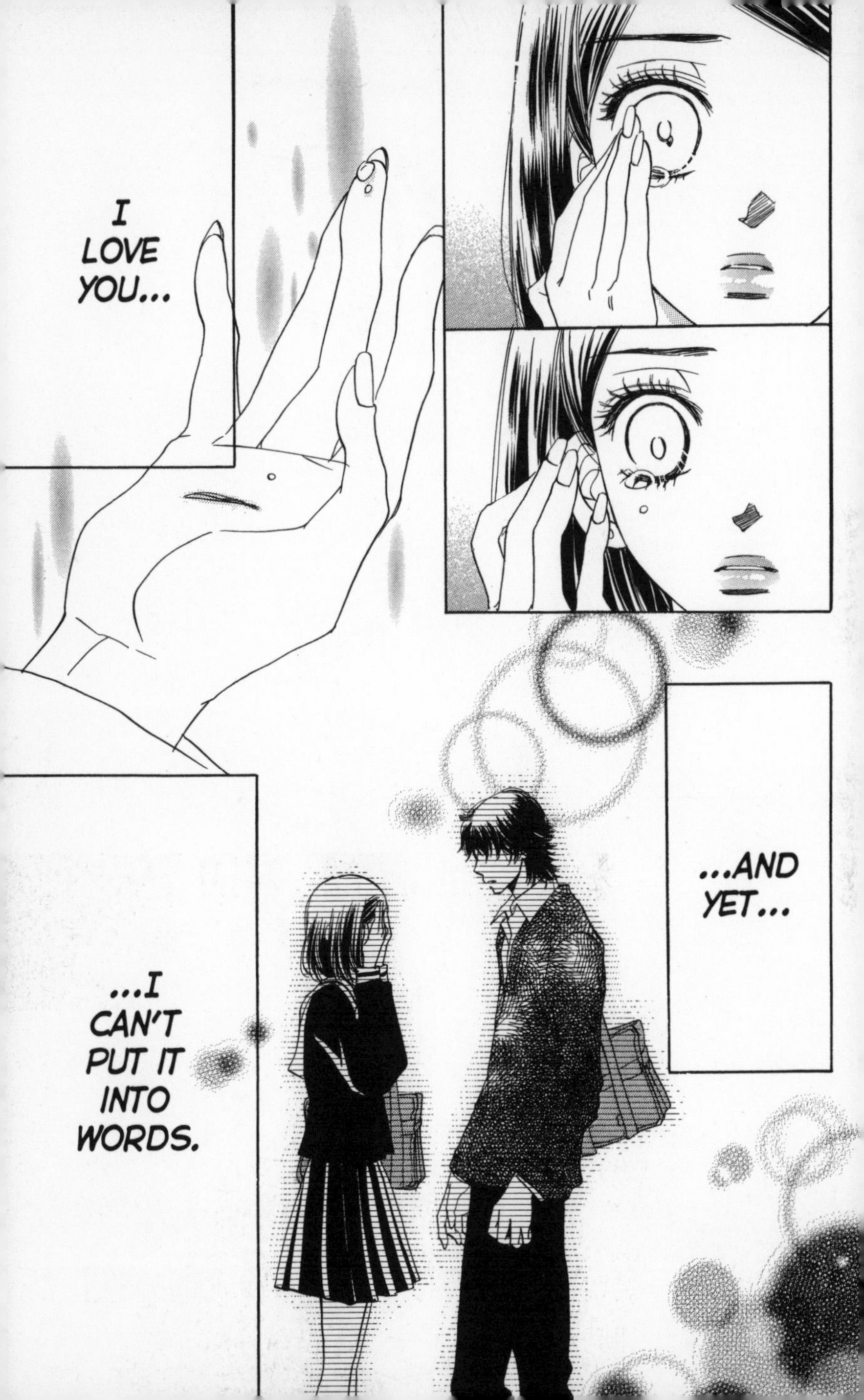
I LOVE YOU...
...AND YET...
...I CAN'T PUT IT INTO WORDS.

A Devil and
Her Love Song

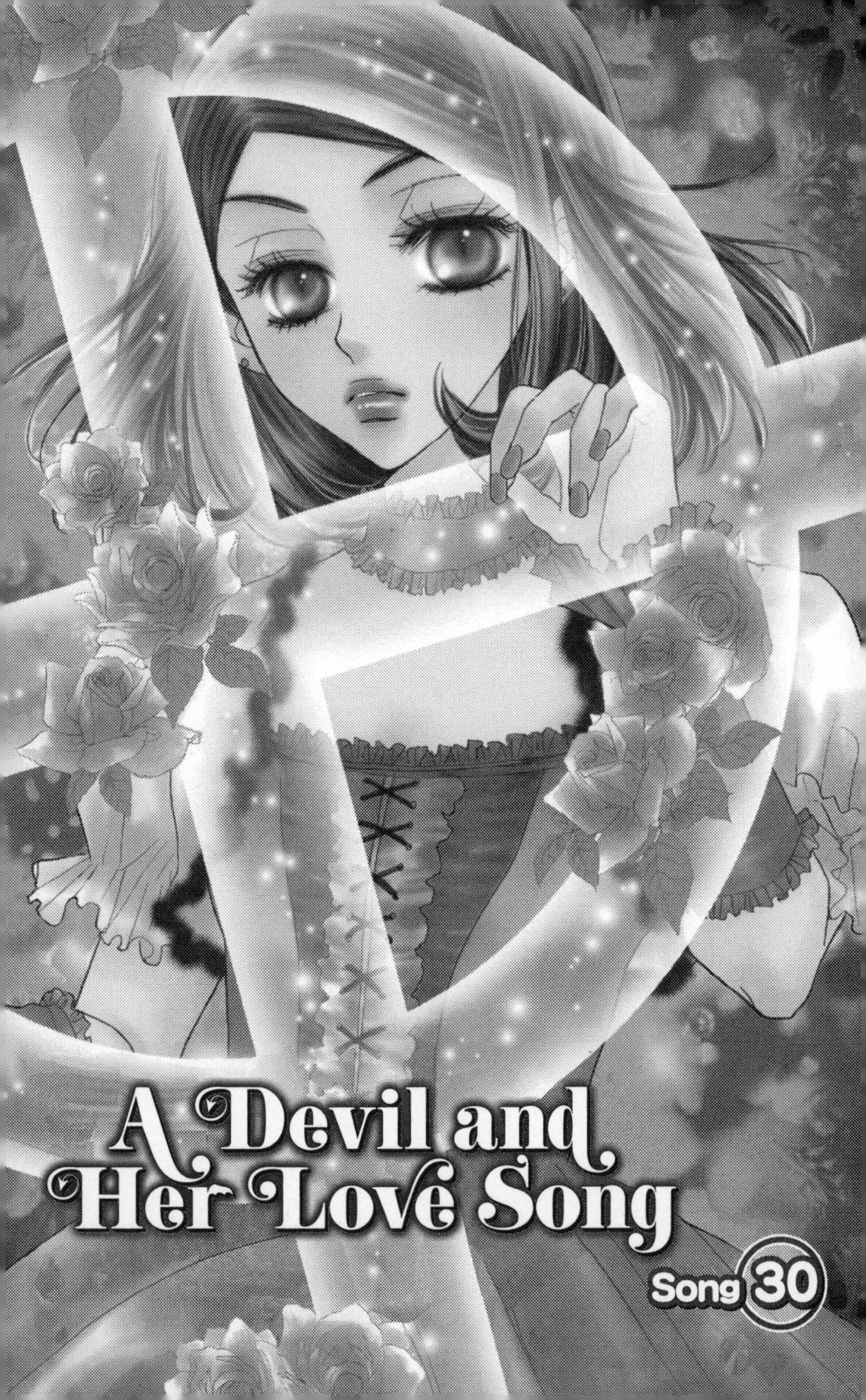
A Devil and Her Love Song
Song 30

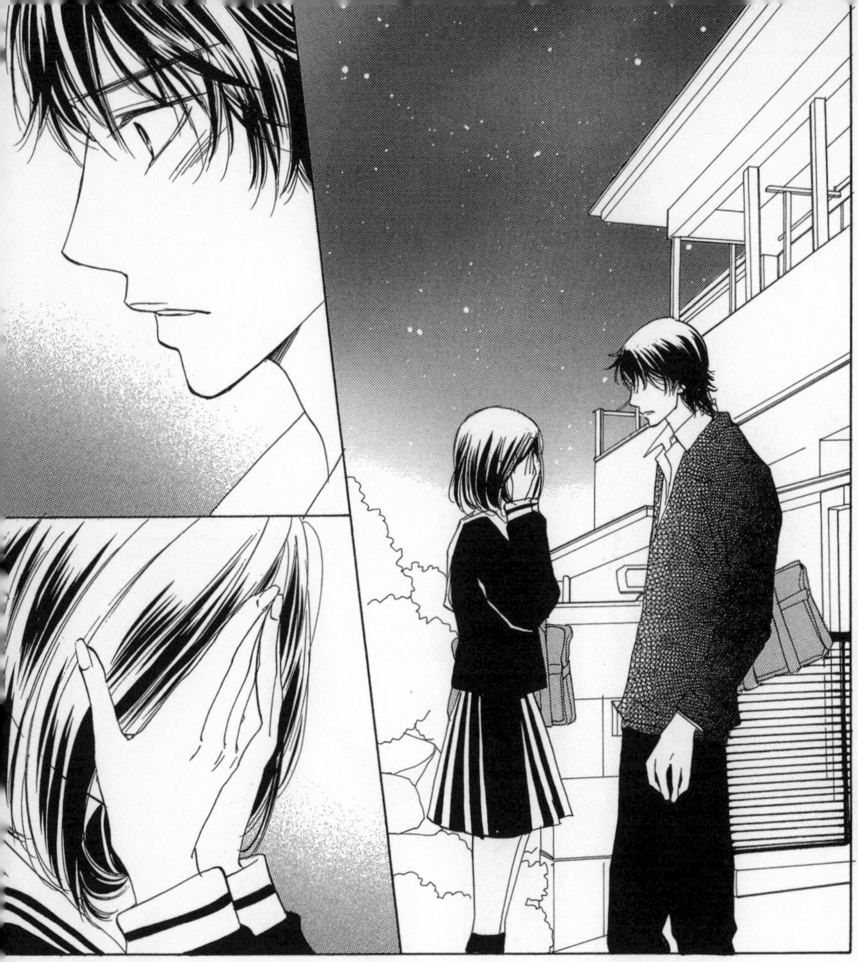

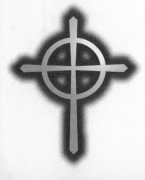

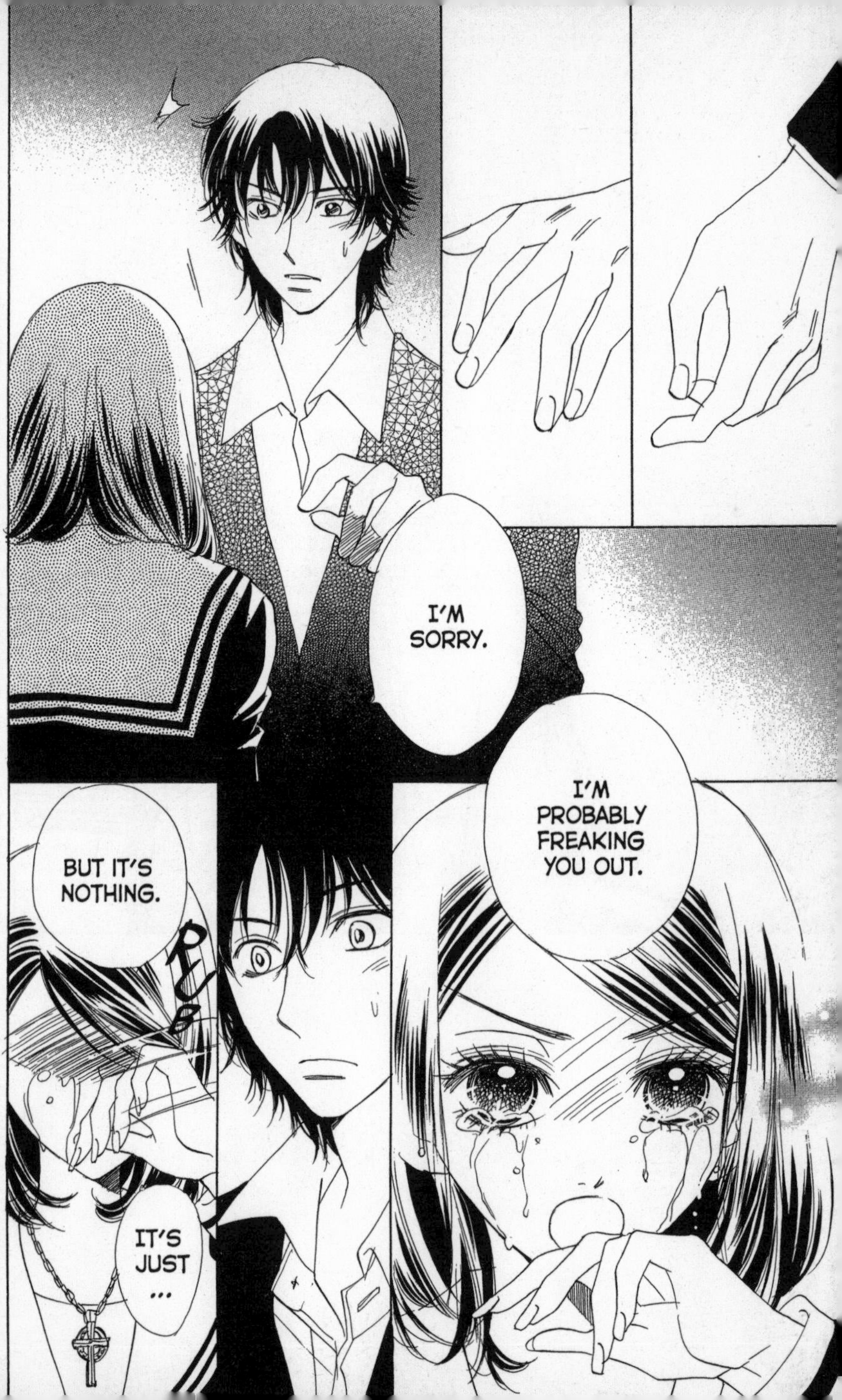
I'M SORRY.
I'M PROBABLY FREAKING YOU OUT.
BUT IT'S NOTHING.
RUB
IT'S JUST ...

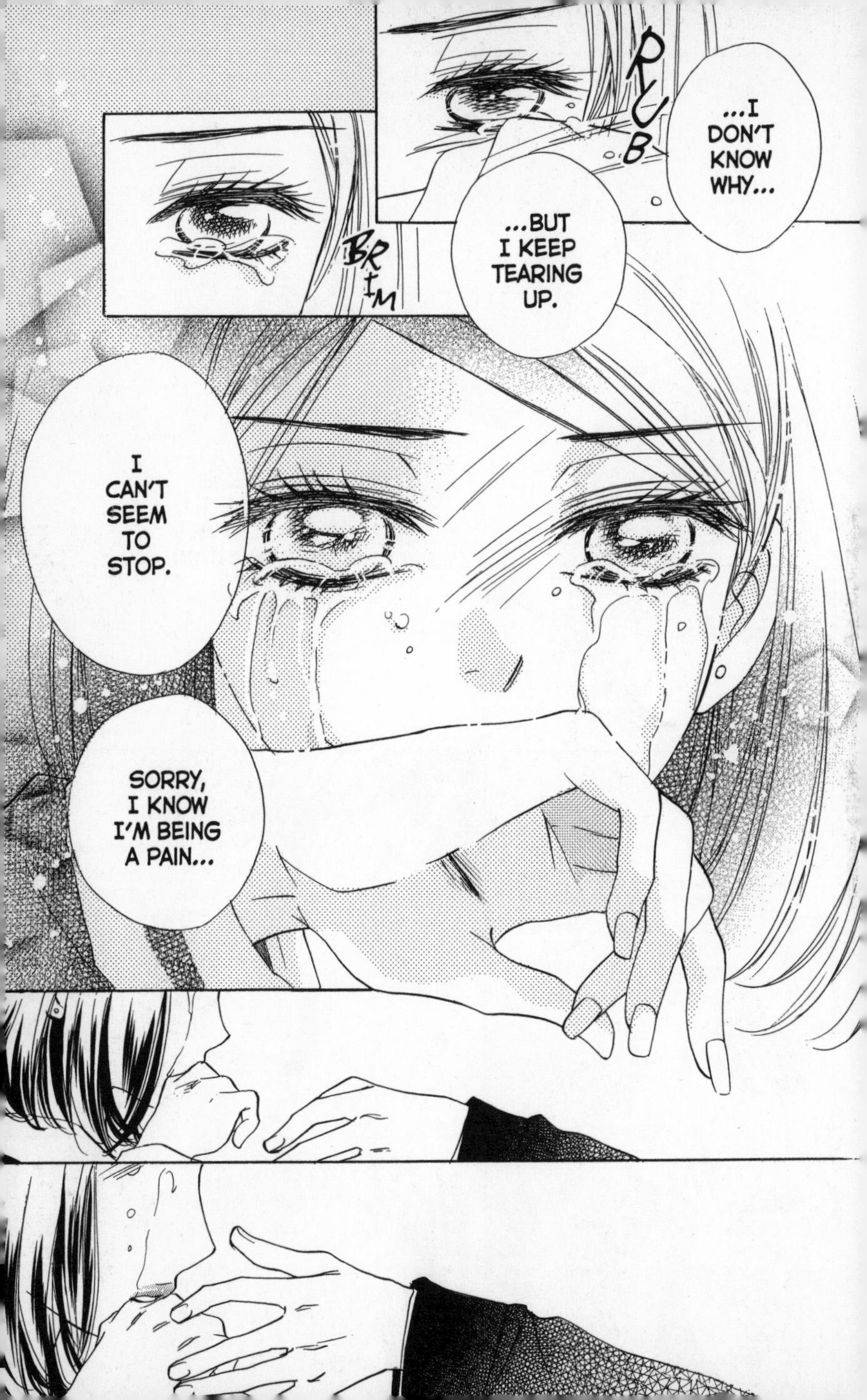

RUB
...I DON'T KNOW WHY...
BRIM
...BUT I KEEP TEARING UP.
I CAN'T SEEM TO STOP.
SORRY, I KNOW I'M BEING A PAIN...

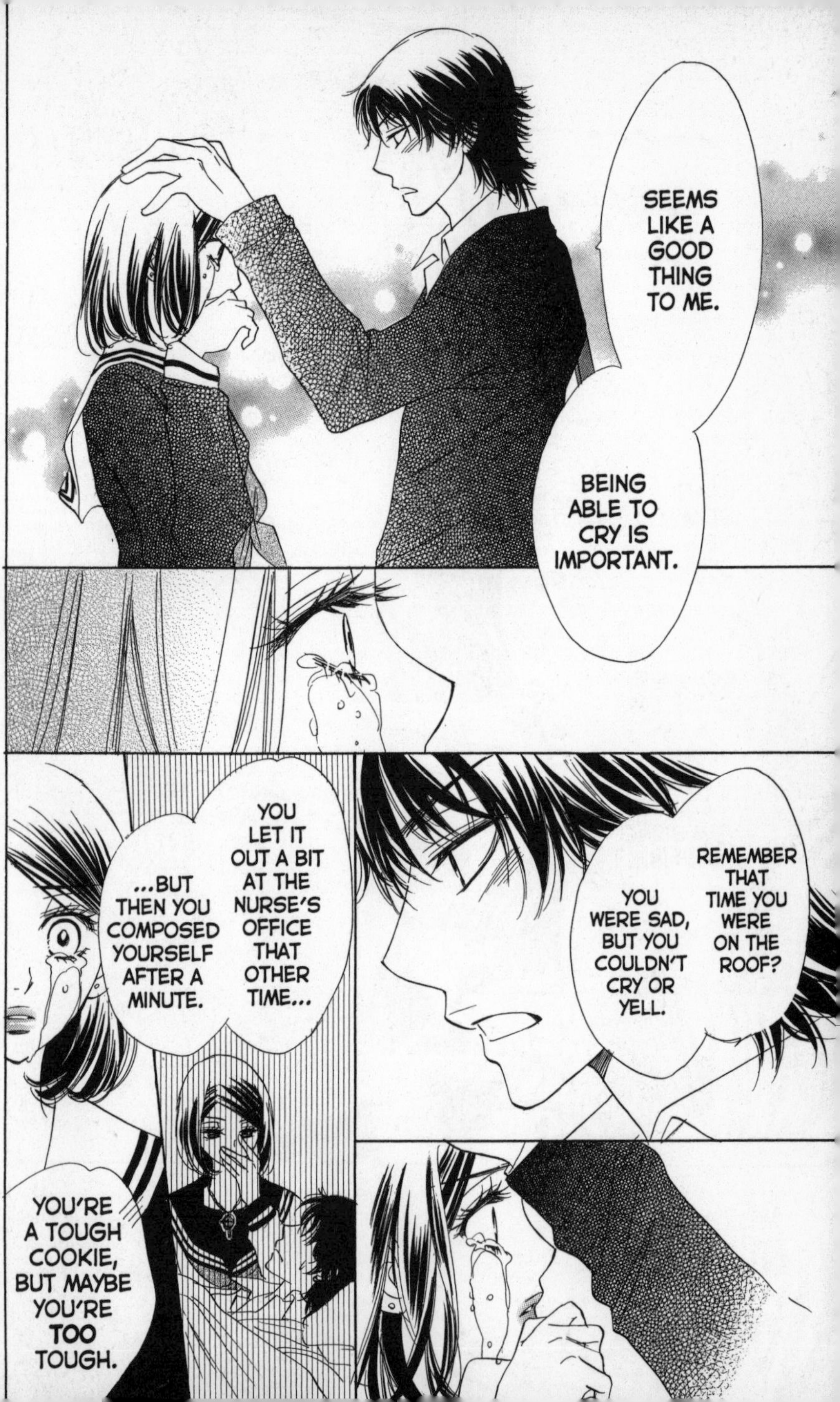
SEEMS LIKE A GOOD THING TO ME.
BEING ABLE TO CRY IS IMPORTANT.
REMEMBER THAT TIME YOU WERE ON THE ROOF?
YOU WERE SAD, BUT YOU COULDN'T CRY OR YELL.
YOU LET IT OUT A BIT AT THE NURSE'S OFFICE THAT OTHER TIME...
...BUT THEN YOU COMPOSED YOURSELF AFTER A MINUTE.
YOU'RE A TOUGH COOKIE, BUT MAYBE YOU'RE TOO TOUGH.

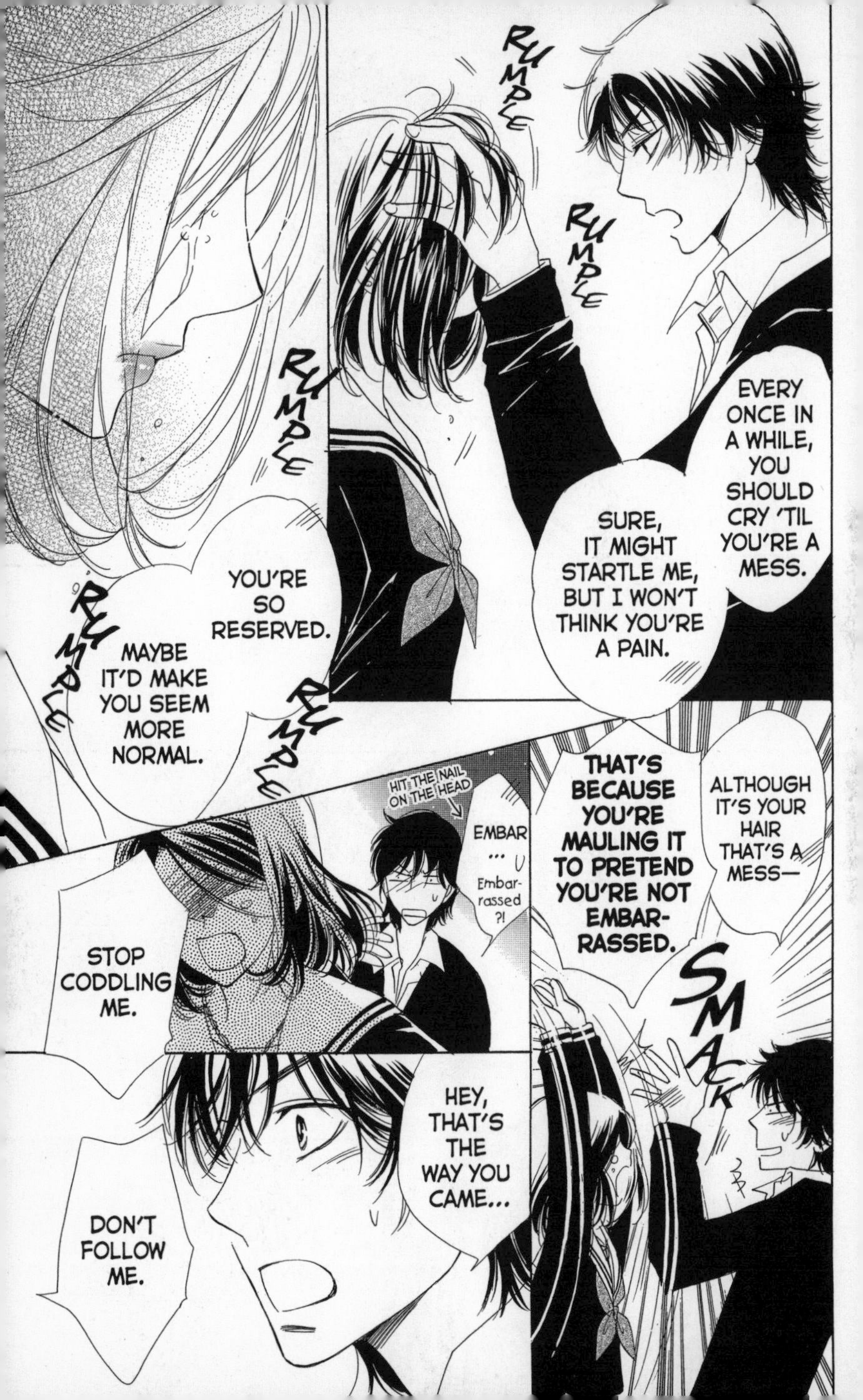
RUMPLE
RUMPLE
EVERY ONCE IN A WHILE, YOU SHOULD CRY 'TIL YOU'RE A MESS.
SURE, IT MIGHT STARTLE ME, BUT I WON'T THINK YOU'RE A PAIN.
RUMPLE
YOU'RE SO RESERVED.
MAYBE IT'D MAKE YOU SEEM MORE NORMAL.
RUMPLE
RUMPLE
ALTHOUGH IT'S YOUR HAIR THAT'S A MESS—
THAT'S BECAUSE YOU'RE MAULING IT TO PRETEND YOU'RE NOT EMBARRASSED.
SMACK
HIT THE NAIL ON THE HEAD
EMBAR...
Embarrassed?!
STOP CODDLING ME.
HEY, THAT'S THE WAY YOU CAME...
DON'T FOLLOW ME.

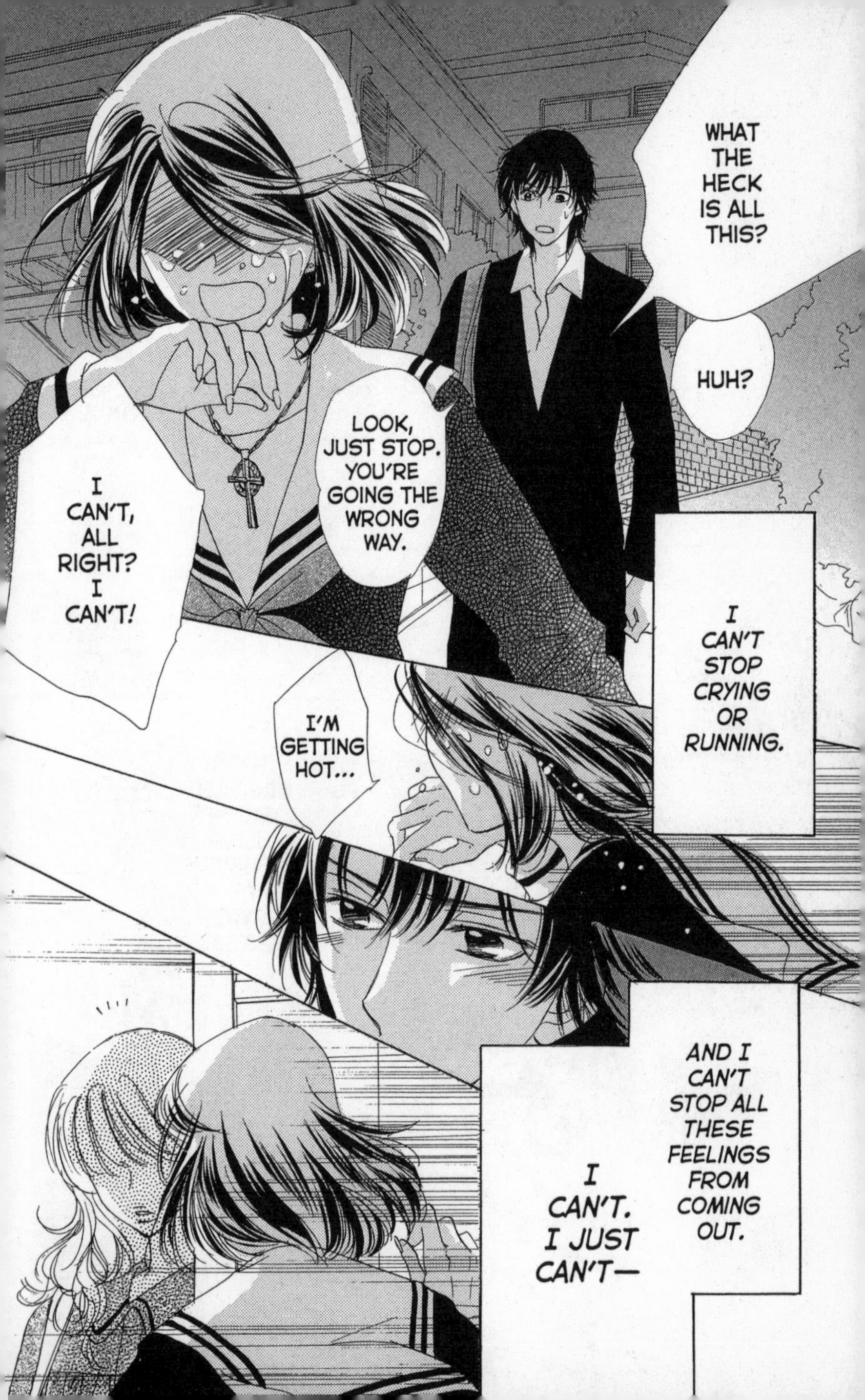
WHAT THE HECK IS ALL THIS?
HUH?
LOOK, JUST STOP. YOU'RE GOING THE WRONG WAY.
I CAN'T, ALL RIGHT? I CAN'T!
I CAN'T STOP CRYING OR RUNNING.
I'M GETTING HOT...
AND I CAN'T STOP ALL THESE FEELINGS FROM COMING OUT.
I CAN'T. I JUST CAN'T—

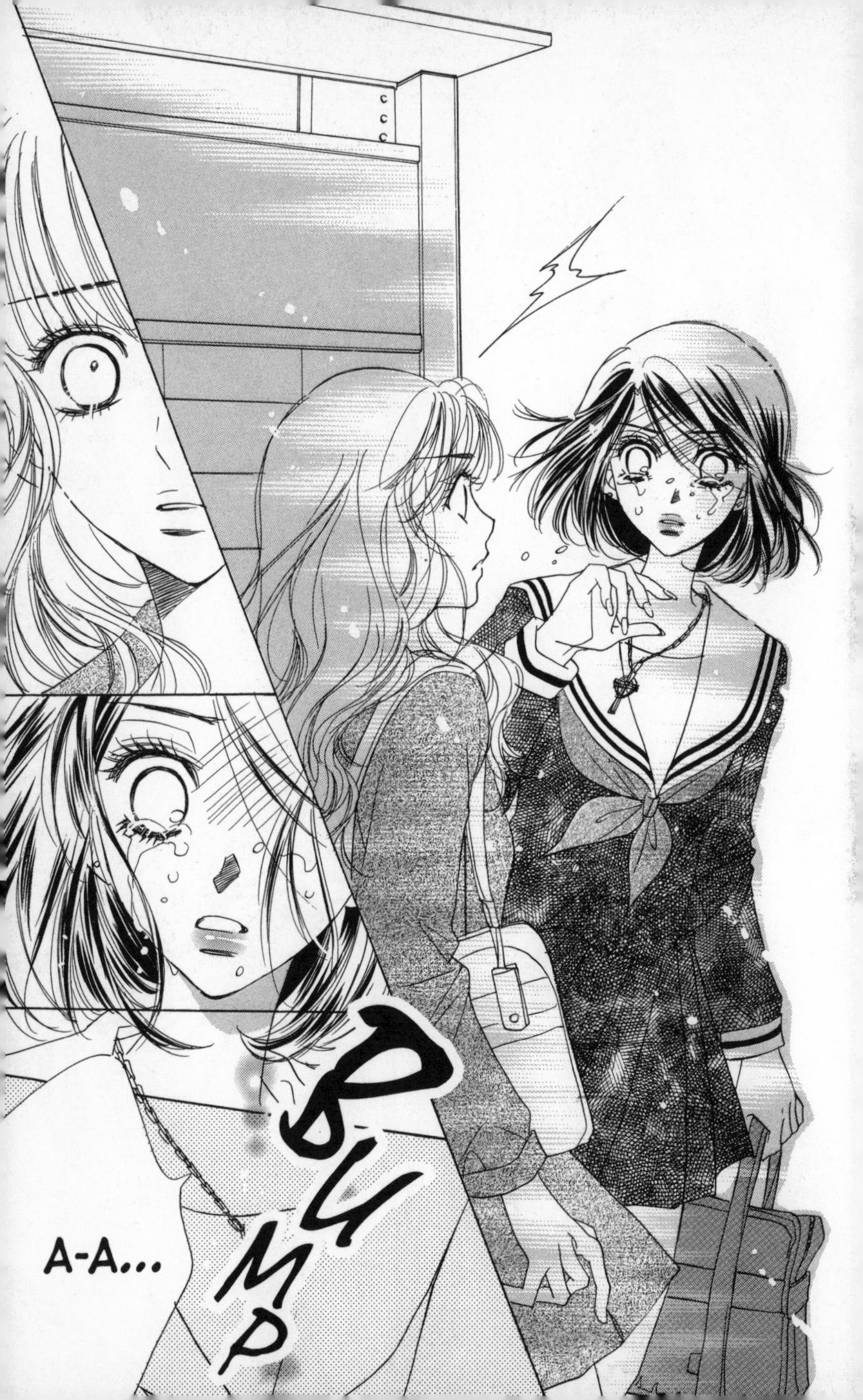
BUMP
A-A...

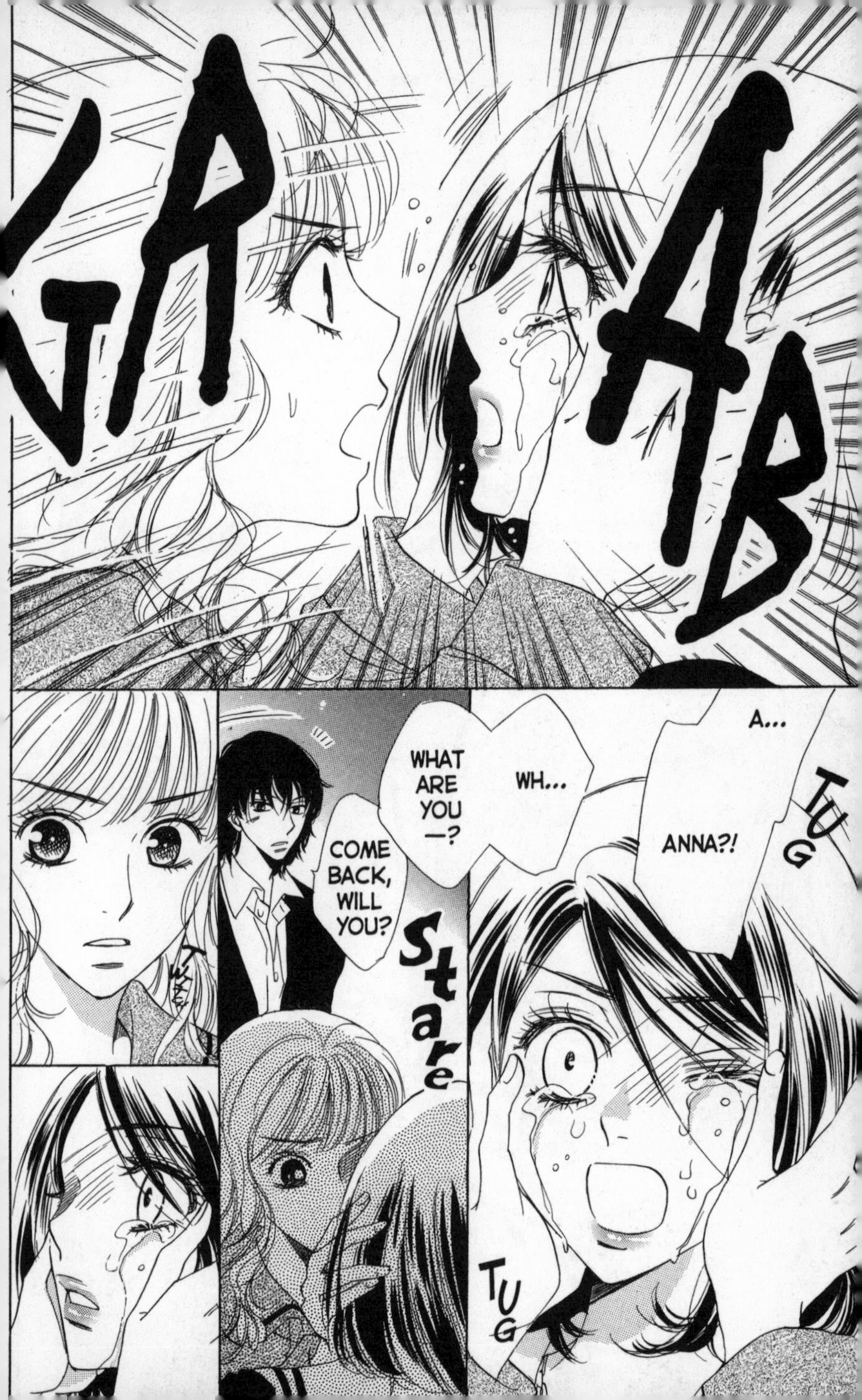

GRAB
A...
ANNA?!
TUG
TUG
WH...
WHAT ARE YOU—?
COME BACK, WILL YOU?
Stare

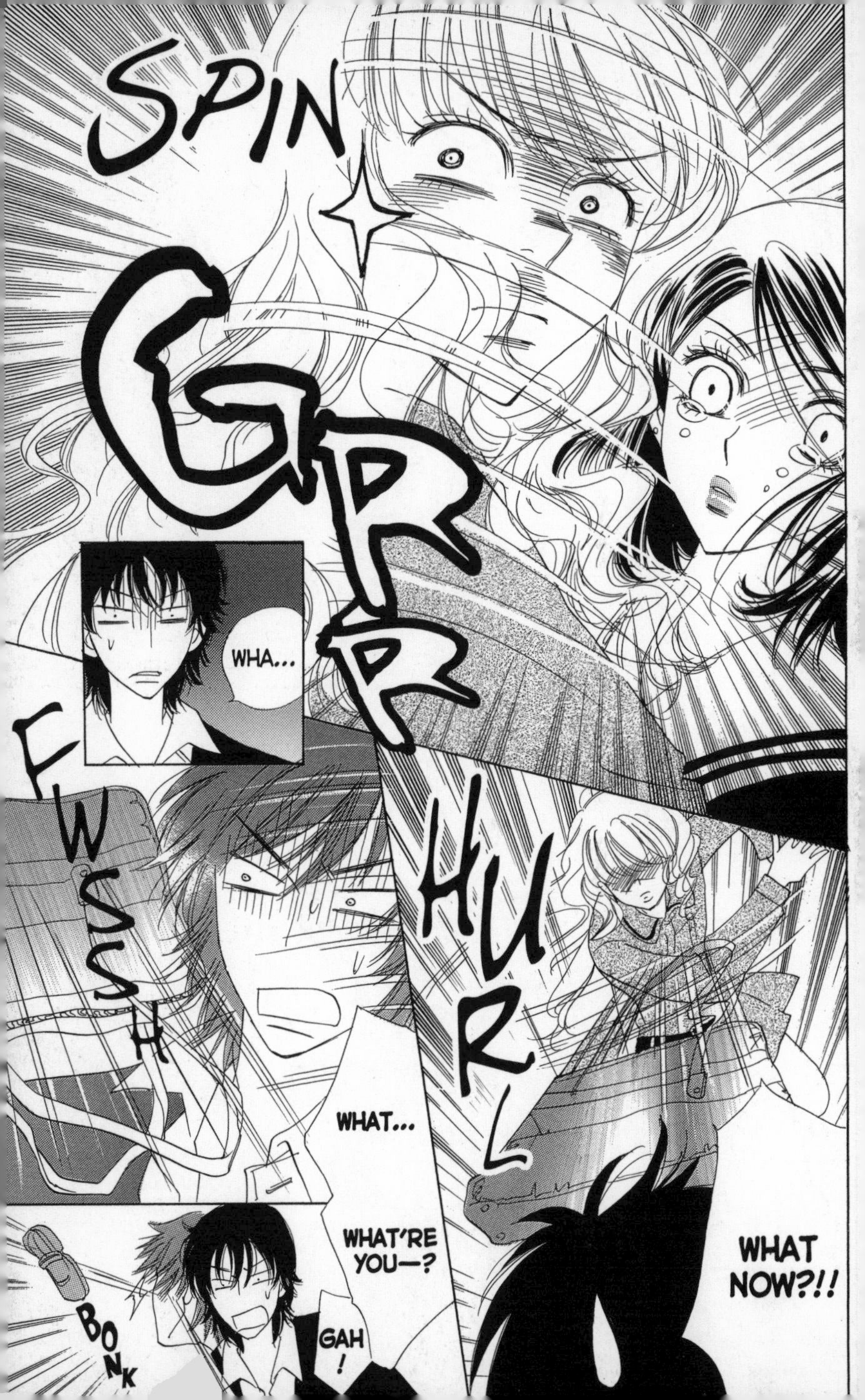
SPIN
GRRR
WHA...
HURL
FWSSH
WHAT...
WHAT NOW?!!
WHAT'RE YOU—?
GAH!
BONK

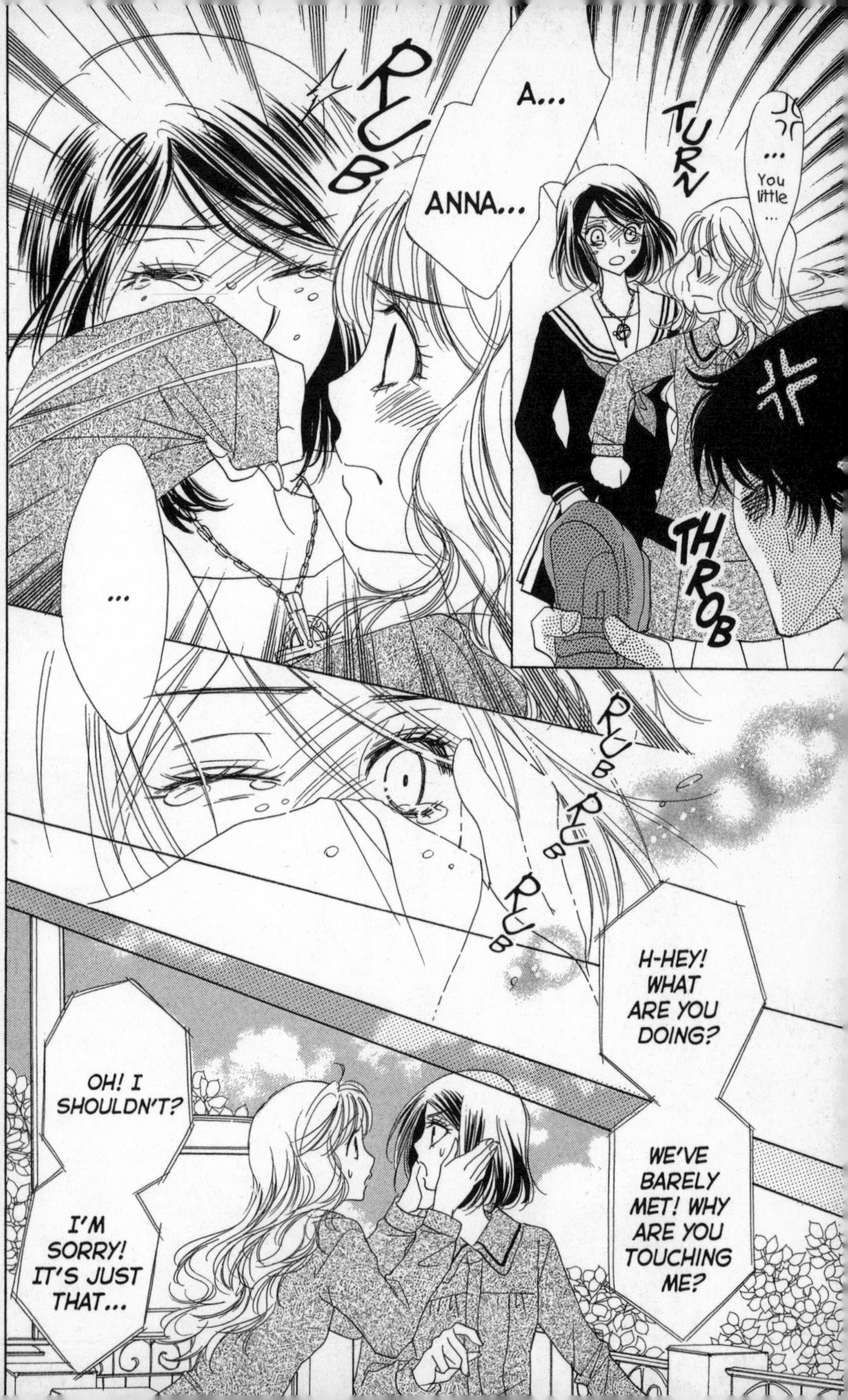
TURN
... You little ...
THROB
RUB
A...
ANNA...
...
RUB RUB RUB
H-HEY! WHAT ARE YOU DOING?
WE'VE BARELY MET! WHY ARE YOU TOUCHING ME?
OH! I SHOULDN'T?
I'M SORRY! IT'S JUST THAT...

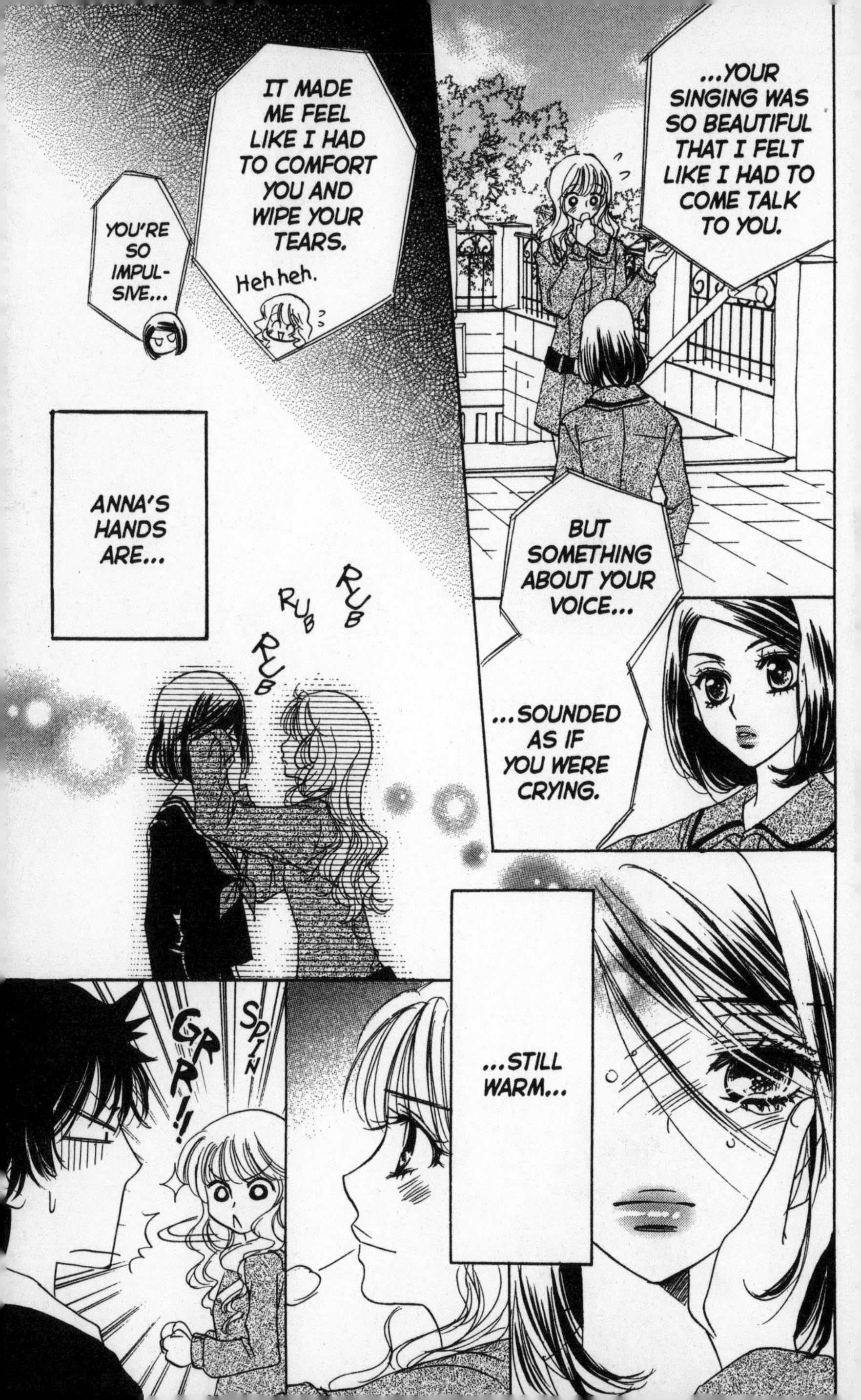
...YOUR SINGING WAS SO BEAUTIFUL THAT I FELT LIKE I HAD TO COME TALK TO YOU.
BUT SOMETHING ABOUT YOUR VOICE...
...SOUNDED AS IF YOU WERE CRYING.
IT MADE ME FEEL LIKE I HAD TO COMFORT YOU AND WIPE YOUR TEARS.
Heh heh.
YOU'RE SO IMPUL-SIVE...
ANNA'S HANDS ARE...
RUB
RUB
RUB
...STILL WARM...
SPIN
GRR!!

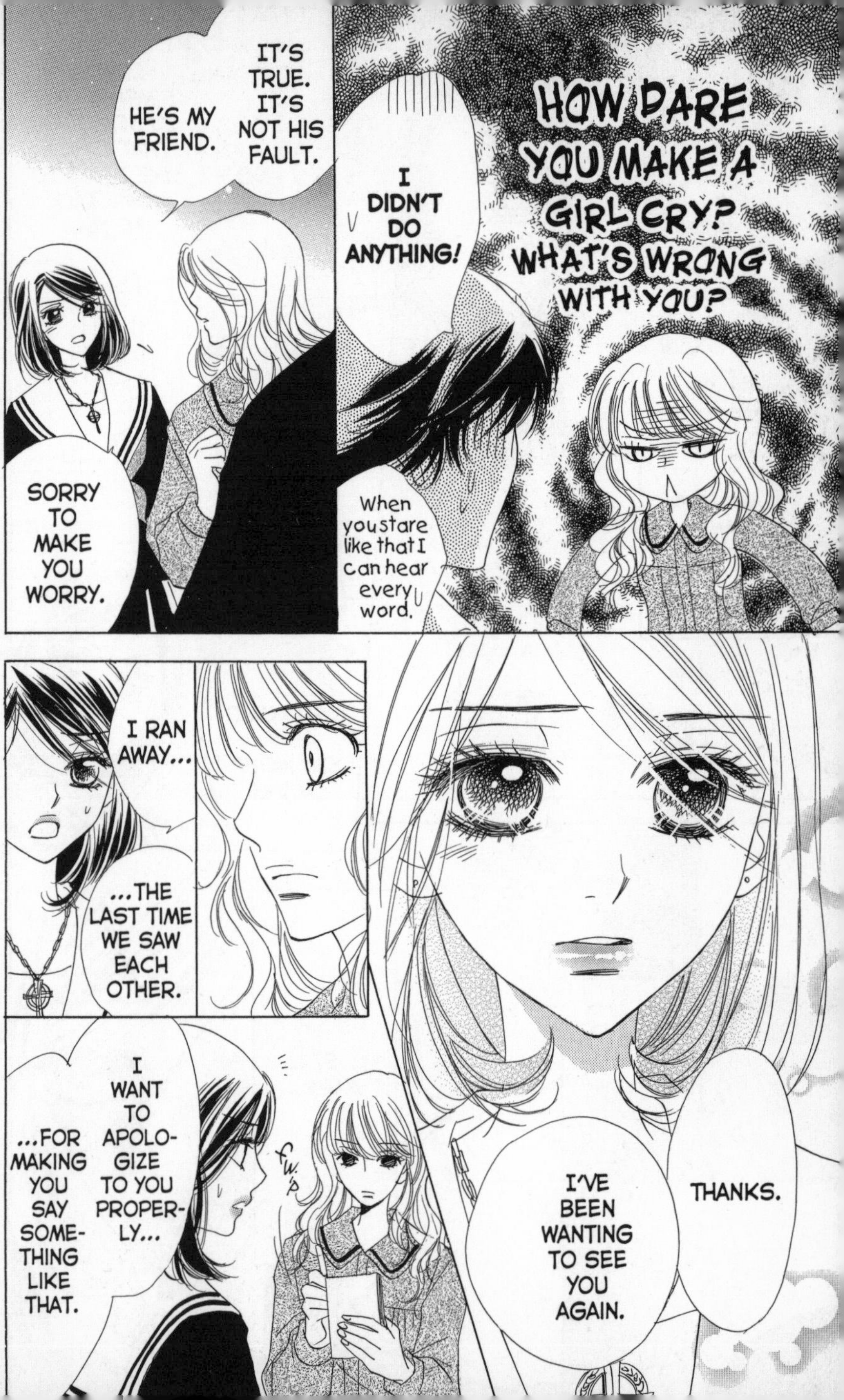
HOW DARE YOU MAKE A GIRL CRY? WHAT'S WRONG WITH YOU?
I DIDN'T DO ANYTHING!
When you stare like that I can hear every word.
IT'S TRUE. IT'S NOT HIS FAULT.
HE'S MY FRIEND.
SORRY TO MAKE YOU WORRY.
THANKS.
I'VE BEEN WANTING TO SEE YOU AGAIN.
I RAN AWAY...
...THE LAST TIME WE SAW EACH OTHER.
I WANT TO APOLOGIZE TO YOU PROPERLY...
...FOR MAKING YOU SAY SOMETHING LIKE THAT.
FWIP

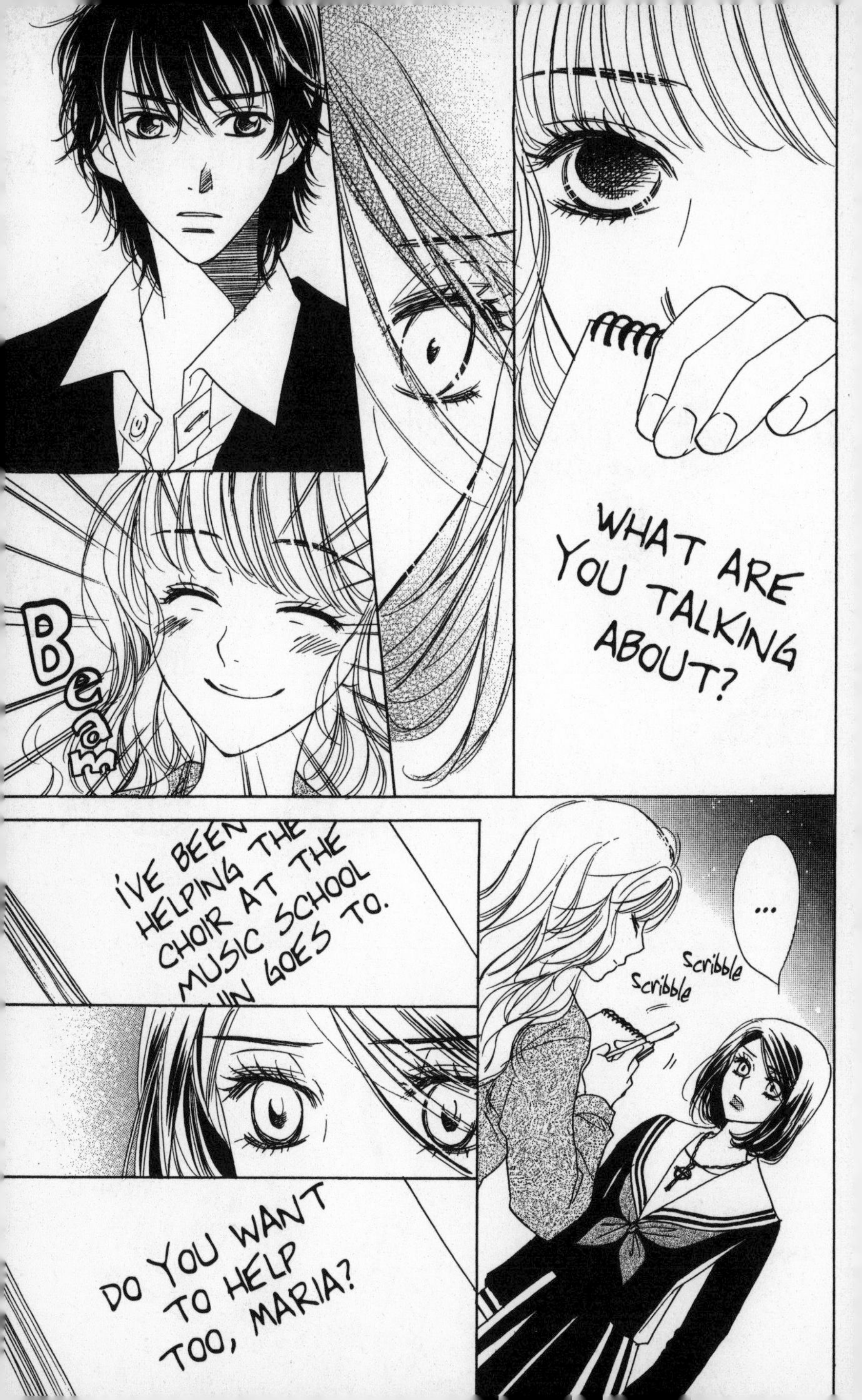
WHAT ARE YOU TALKING ABOUT?
Beam
...
Scribble
Scribble
I'VE BEEN HELPING THE CHOIR AT THE MUSIC SCHOOL
GOES TO.
DO YOU WANT TO HELP TOO, MARIA?

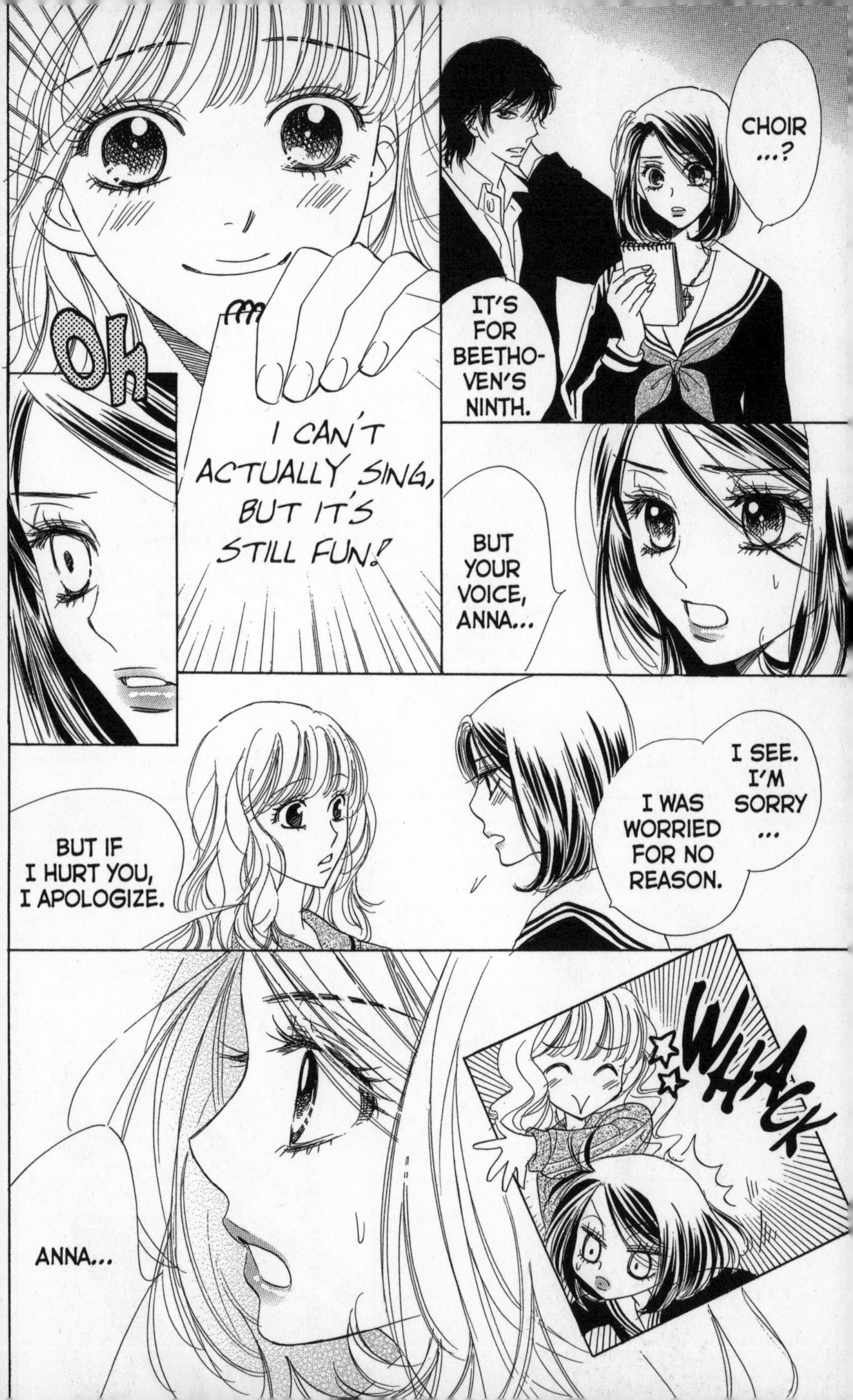
CHOIR ...?
IT'S FOR BEETHOVEN'S NINTH.
I CAN'T ACTUALLY SING, BUT IT'S STILL FUN!
Oh
BUT YOUR VOICE, ANNA...
I SEE. I'M SORRY ...
I WAS WORRIED FOR NO REASON.
BUT IF I HURT YOU, I APOLOGIZE.
WHACK
ANNA...

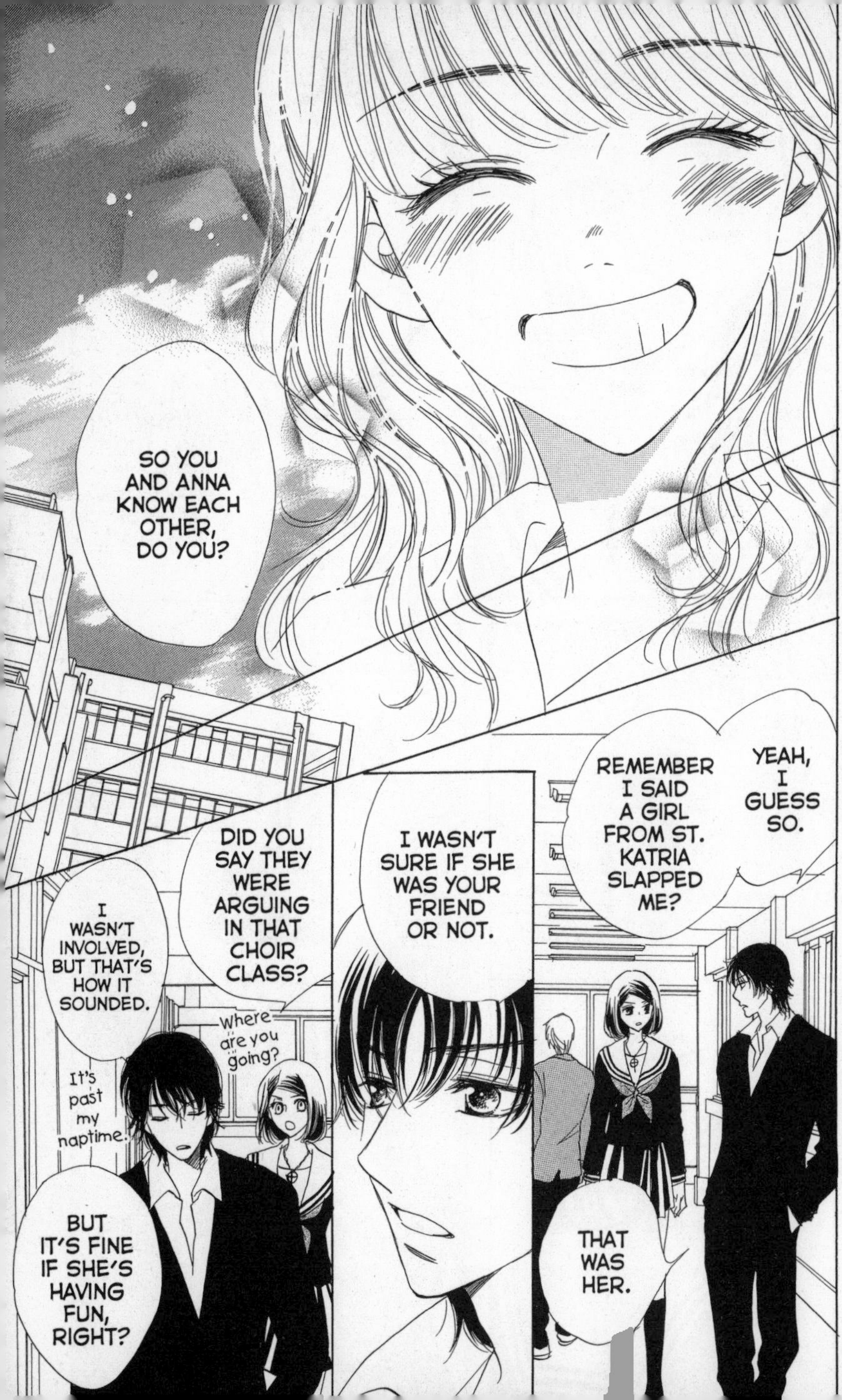
SO YOU AND ANNA KNOW EACH OTHER, DO YOU?
YEAH, I GUESS SO.
REMEMBER I SAID A GIRL FROM ST. KATRIA SLAPPED ME?
THAT WAS HER.
I WASN'T SURE IF SHE WAS YOUR FRIEND OR NOT.
DID YOU SAY THEY WERE ARGUING IN THAT CHOIR CLASS?
I WASN'T INVOLVED, BUT THAT'S HOW IT SOUNDED.
Where are you going?
It's past my naptime.
BUT IT'S FINE IF SHE'S HAVING FUN, RIGHT?

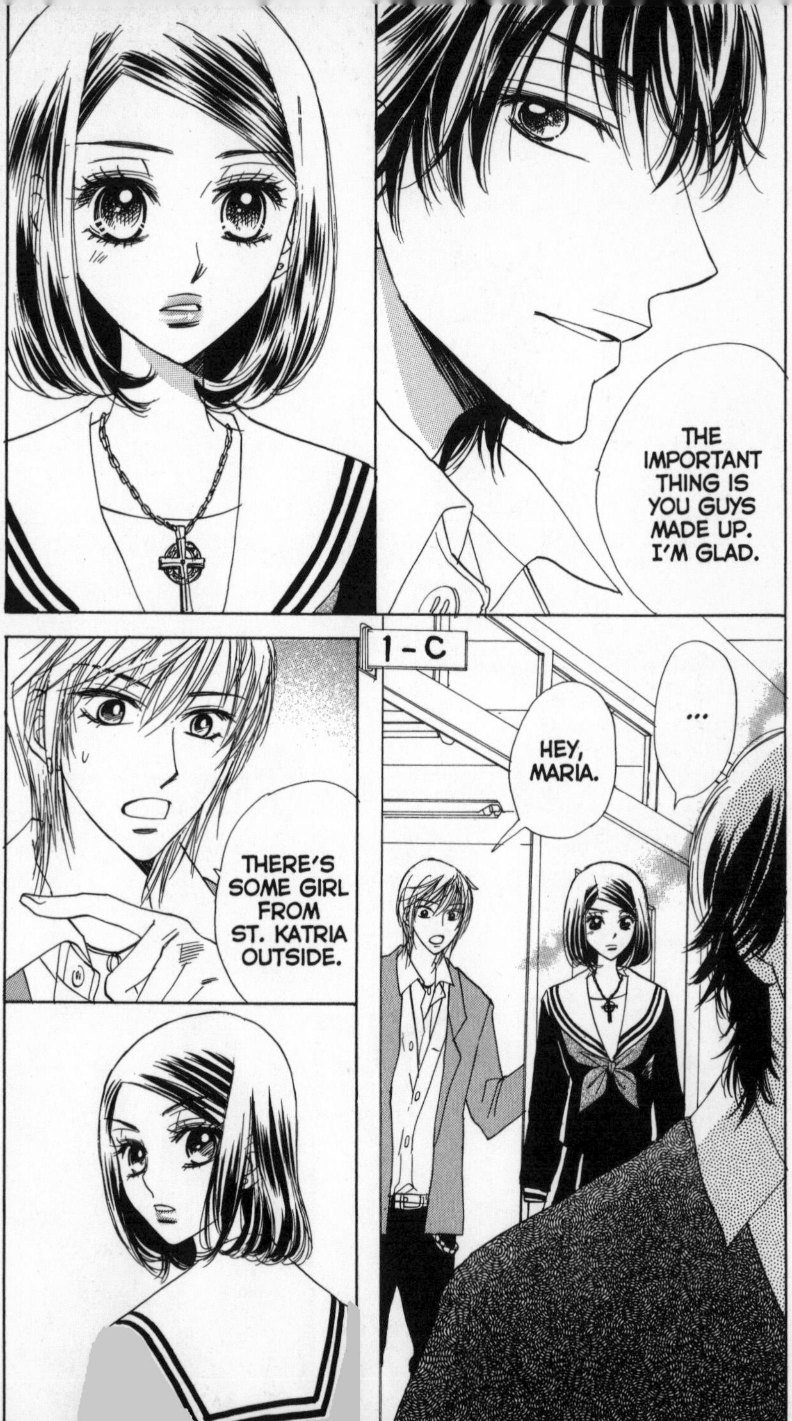

THE IMPORTANT THING IS YOU GUYS MADE UP. I'M GLAD.
1-C
...
HEY, MARIA.
THERE'S SOME GIRL FROM ST. KATRIA OUTSIDE.

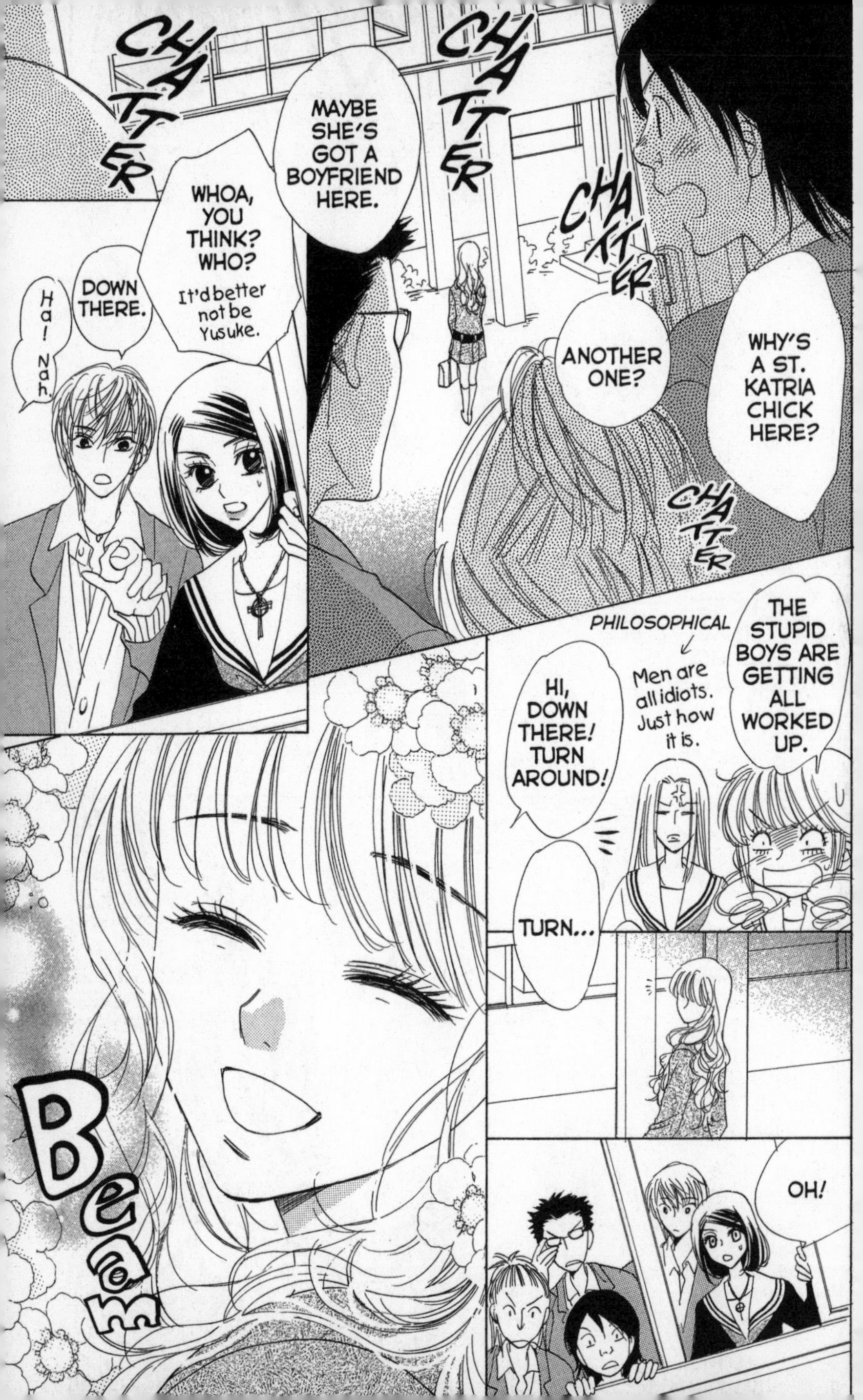
CHATTER
CHATTER
WHY'S A ST. KATRIA CHICK HERE?
CHATTER
ANOTHER ONE?
CHATTER
MAYBE SHE'S GOT A BOYFRIEND HERE.
CHATTER
WHOA, YOU THINK? WHO?
It'd better not be Yusuke.
DOWN THERE.
Ha! Nah.
THE STUPID BOYS ARE GETTING ALL WORKED UP.
PHILOSOPHICAL
Men are all idiots. Just how it is.
HI, DOWN THERE! TURN AROUND!
TURN...
OH!
Beam

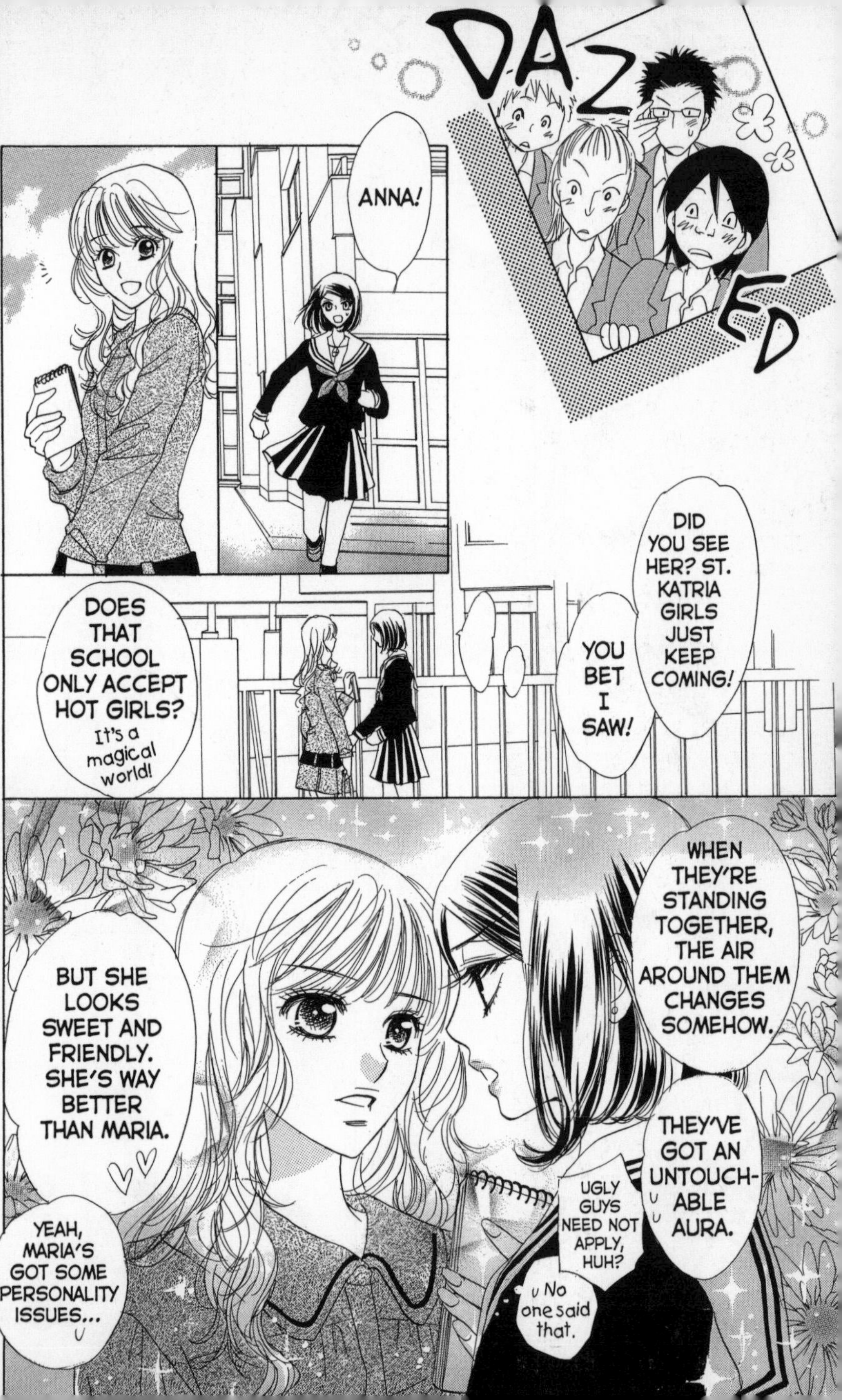
DAZED
ANNA!
DID YOU SEE HER? ST. KATRIA GIRLS JUST KEEP COMING!
YOU BET I SAW!
DOES THAT SCHOOL ONLY ACCEPT HOT GIRLS?
It's a magical world!
WHEN THEY'RE STANDING TOGETHER, THE AIR AROUND THEM CHANGES SOMEHOW.
THEY'VE GOT AN UNTOUCH-ABLE AURA.
UGLY GUYS NEED NOT APPLY, HUH?
No one said that.
BUT SHE LOOKS SWEET AND FRIENDLY. SHE'S WAY BETTER THAN MARIA.
YEAH, MARIA'S GOT SOME PERSONALITY ISSUES...

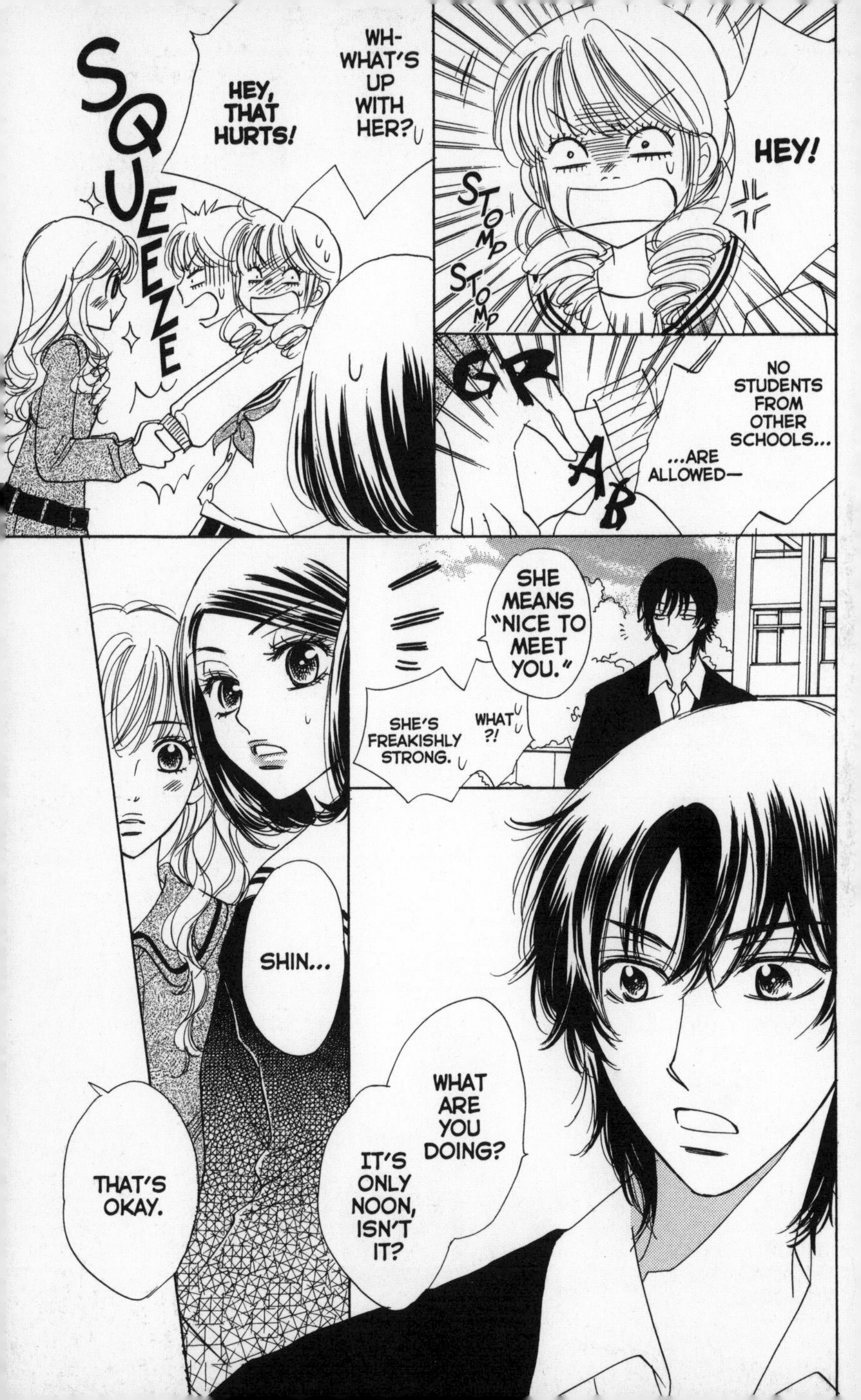
HEY!
STOMP STOMP
NO STUDENTS FROM OTHER SCHOOLS...
...ARE ALLOWED—
GRAB
WH-WHAT'S UP WITH HER?
HEY, THAT HURTS!
SQUEEZE
SHE MEANS "NICE TO MEET YOU."
WHAT?!
SHE'S FREAKISHLY STRONG.
WHAT ARE YOU DOING?
IT'S ONLY NOON, ISN'T IT?
SHIN...
THAT'S OKAY.

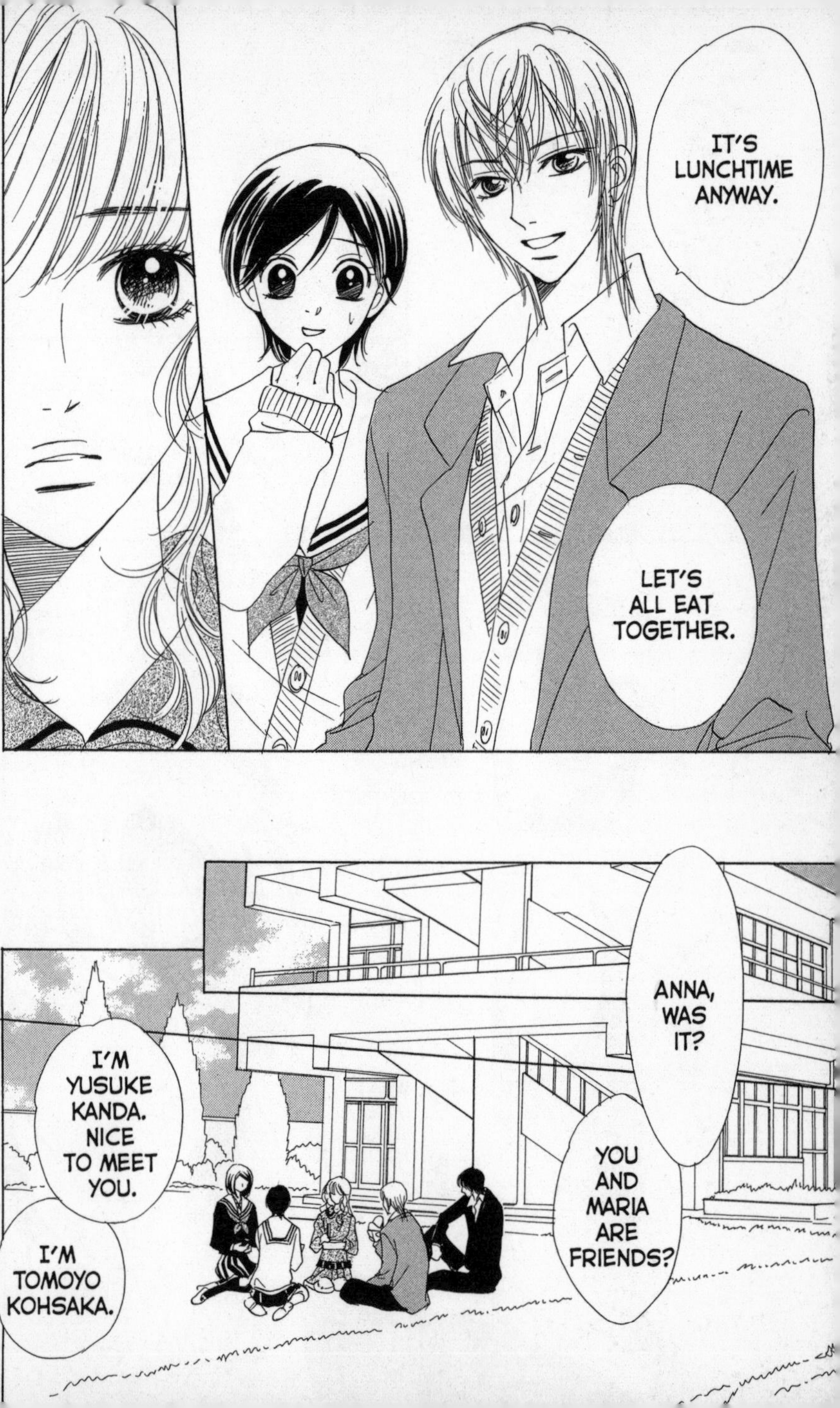
IT'S LUNCHTIME ANYWAY.
LET'S ALL EAT TOGETHER.
ANNA, WAS IT?
YOU AND MARIA ARE FRIENDS?
I'M YUSUKE KANDA. NICE TO MEET YOU.
I'M TOMOYO KOHSAKA.

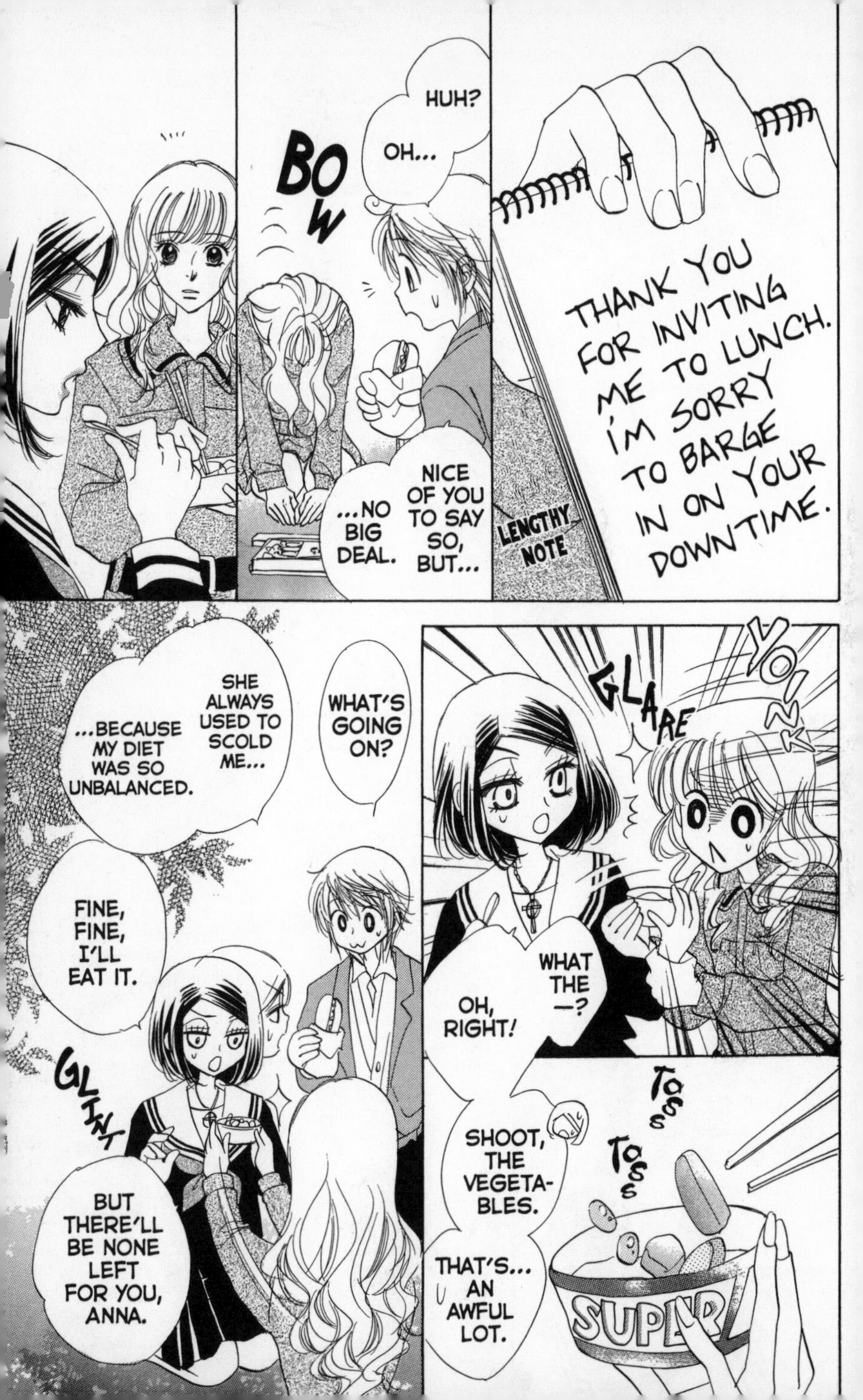
THANK YOU FOR INVITING ME TO LUNCH. I'M SORRY TO BARGE IN ON YOUR DOWNTIME.
LENGTHY NOTE
HUH?
OH...
BOW
NICE OF YOU TO SAY SO, BUT...
...NO BIG DEAL.
YOINK
GLARE
WHAT THE—?
OH, RIGHT!
TOSS
TOSS
SHOOT, THE VEGETA-BLES.
THAT'S... AN AWFUL LOT.
SUPER
WHAT'S GOING ON?
SHE ALWAYS USED TO SCOLD ME...
...BECAUSE MY DIET WAS SO UNBALANCED.
FINE, FINE, I'LL EAT IT.
GLINK
BUT THERE'LL BE NONE LEFT FOR YOU, ANNA.

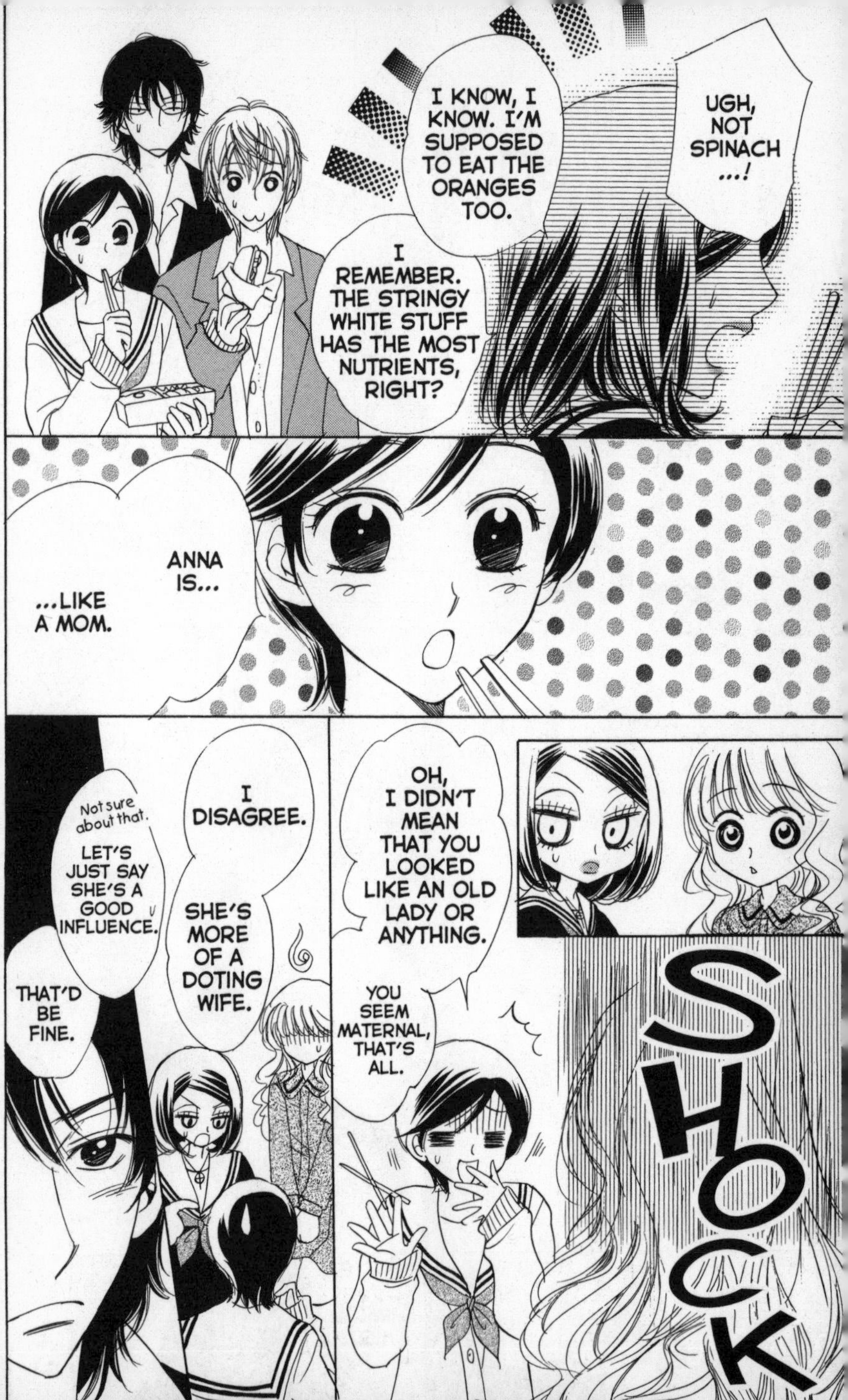
UGH, NOT SPINACH ...!
I KNOW, I KNOW. I'M SUPPOSED TO EAT THE ORANGES TOO.
I REMEMBER. THE STRINGY WHITE STUFF HAS THE MOST NUTRIENTS, RIGHT?
ANNA IS...
...LIKE A MOM.
SHOCK
OH, I DIDN'T MEAN THAT YOU LOOKED LIKE AN OLD LADY OR ANYTHING.
YOU SEEM MATERNAL, THAT'S ALL.
I DISAGREE.
SHE'S MORE OF A DOTING WIFE.
Not sure about that.
LET'S JUST SAY SHE'S A GOOD INFLUENCE.
THAT'D BE FINE.

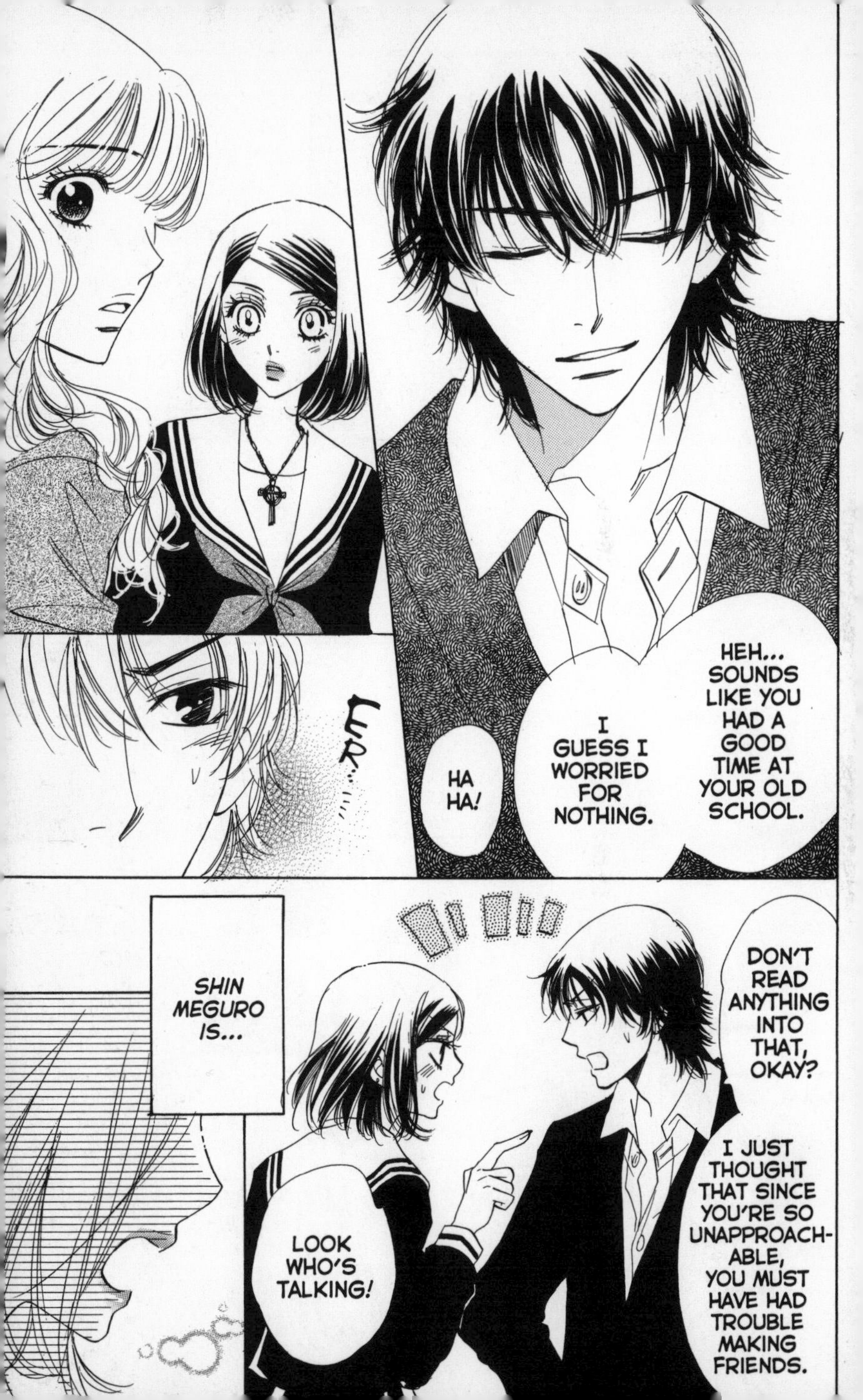
HEH... SOUNDS LIKE YOU HAD A GOOD TIME AT YOUR OLD SCHOOL.
I GUESS I WORRIED FOR NOTHING.
HA HA!
ER...
DON'T READ ANYTHING INTO THAT, OKAY?
I JUST THOUGHT THAT SINCE YOU'RE SO UNAPPROACH-ABLE, YOU MUST HAVE HAD TROUBLE MAKING FRIENDS.
LOOK WHO'S TALKING!
SHIN MEGURO IS...

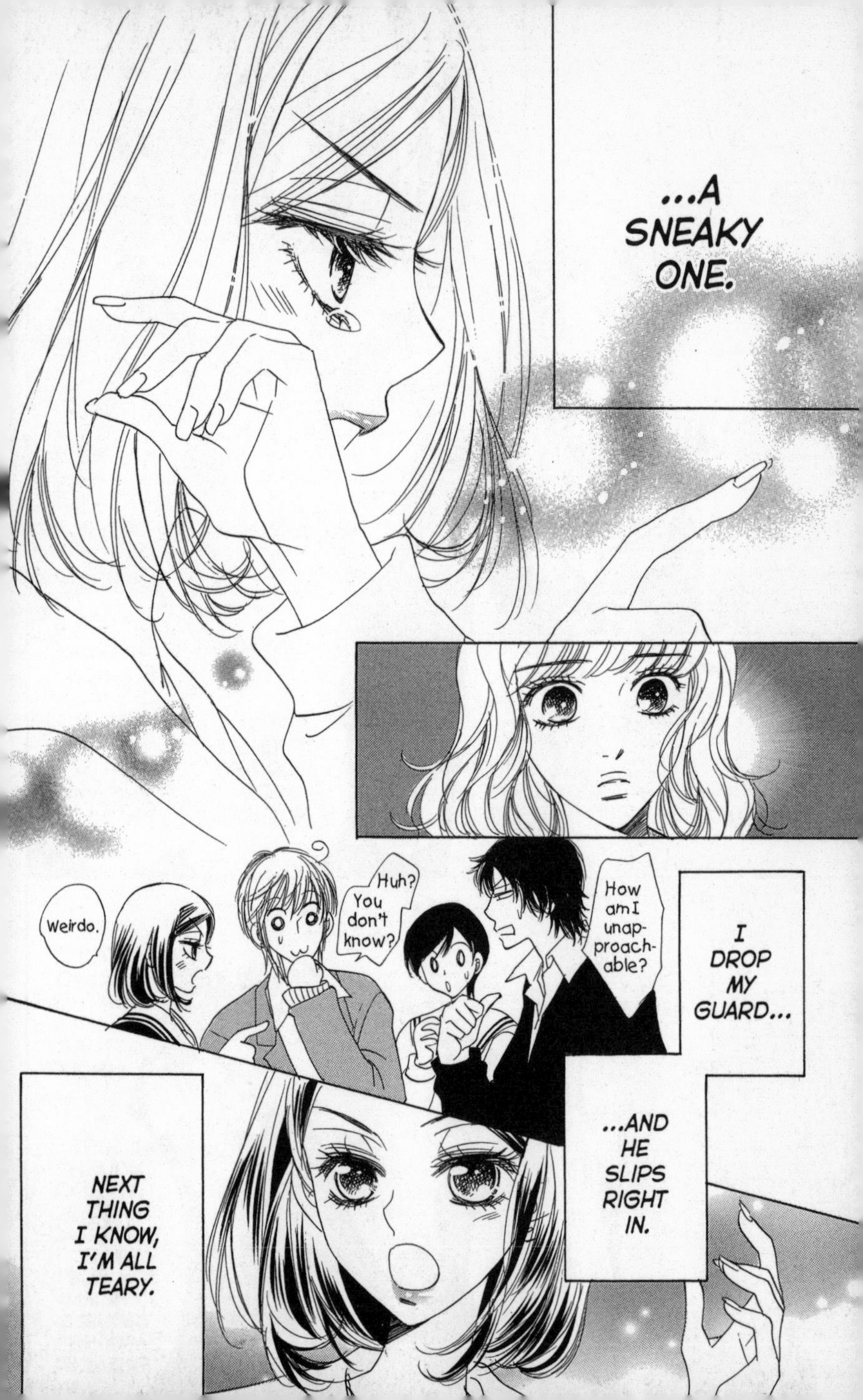
...A SNEAKY ONE.
I DROP MY GUARD...
How am I unapproachable?
Huh? You don't know?
Weirdo.
...AND HE SLIPS RIGHT IN.
NEXT THING I KNOW, I'M ALL TEARY.

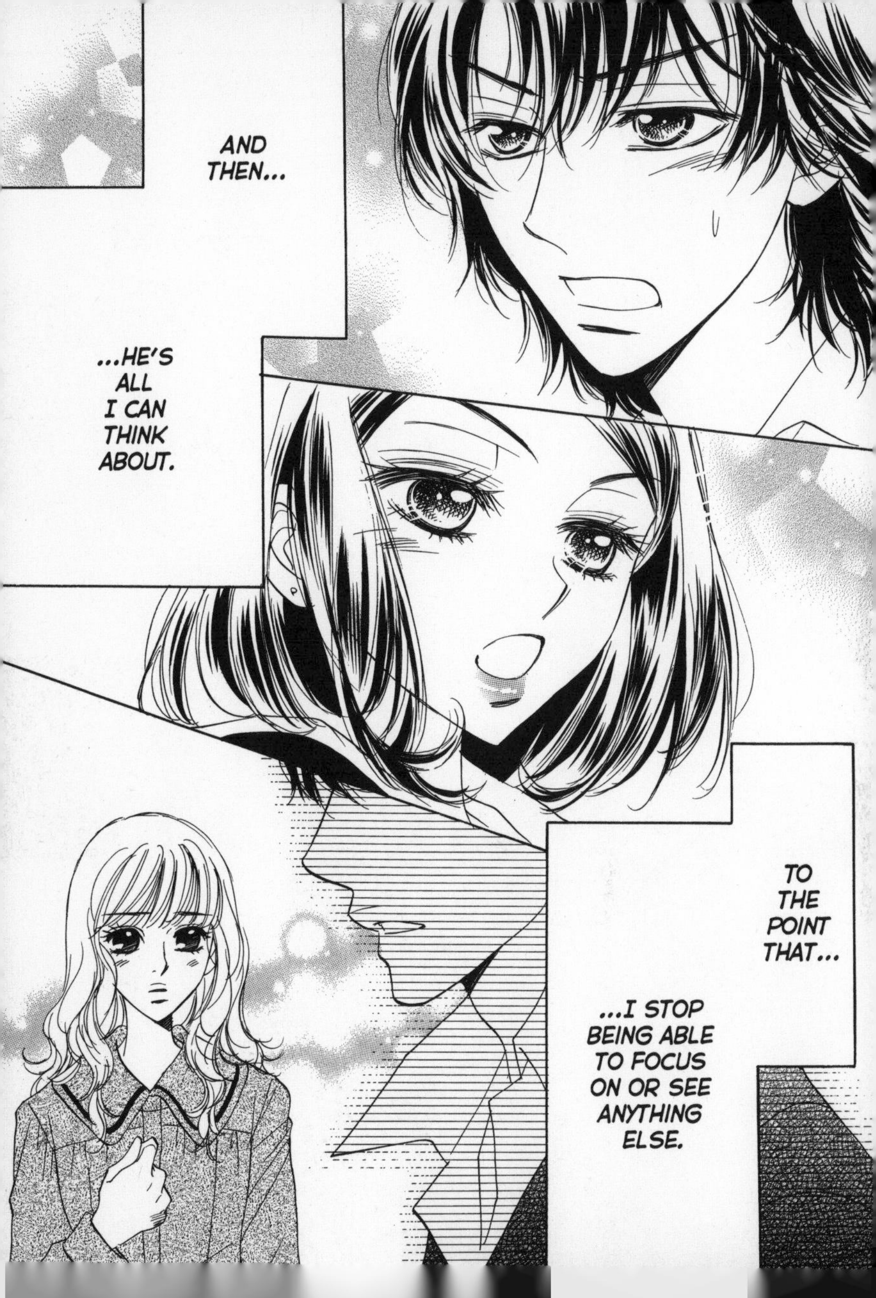
AND THEN...
...HE'S ALL I CAN THINK ABOUT.
TO THE POINT THAT...
...I STOP BEING ABLE TO FOCUS ON OR SEE ANYTHING ELSE.

A Devil and
Her Love Song

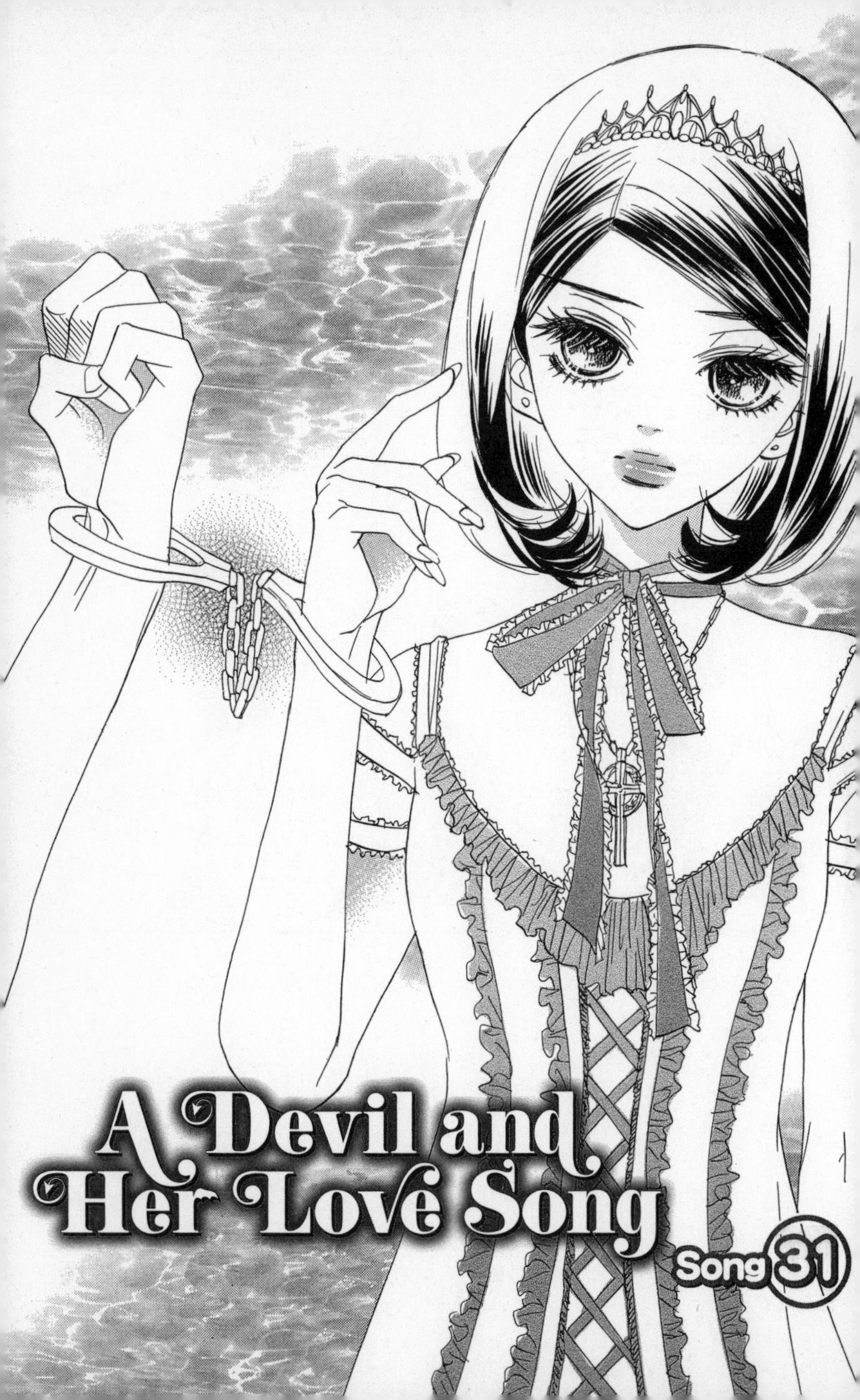
A Devil and Her Love Song
Song 31

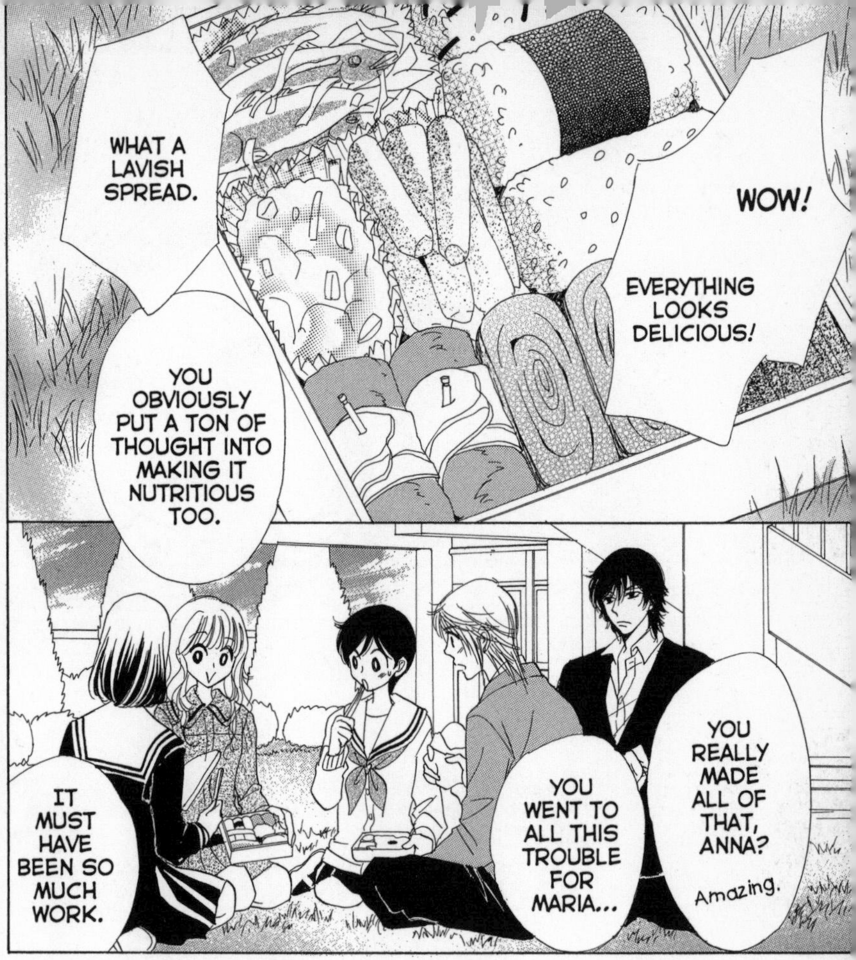
WOW!
EVERYTHING LOOKS DELICIOUS!
WHAT A LAVISH SPREAD.
YOU OBVIOUSLY PUT A TON OF THOUGHT INTO MAKING IT NUTRITIOUS TOO.
YOU REALLY MADE ALL OF THAT, ANNA?
Amazing.
YOU WENT TO ALL THIS TROUBLE FOR MARIA...
IT MUST HAVE BEEN SO MUCH WORK.

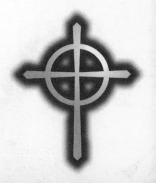

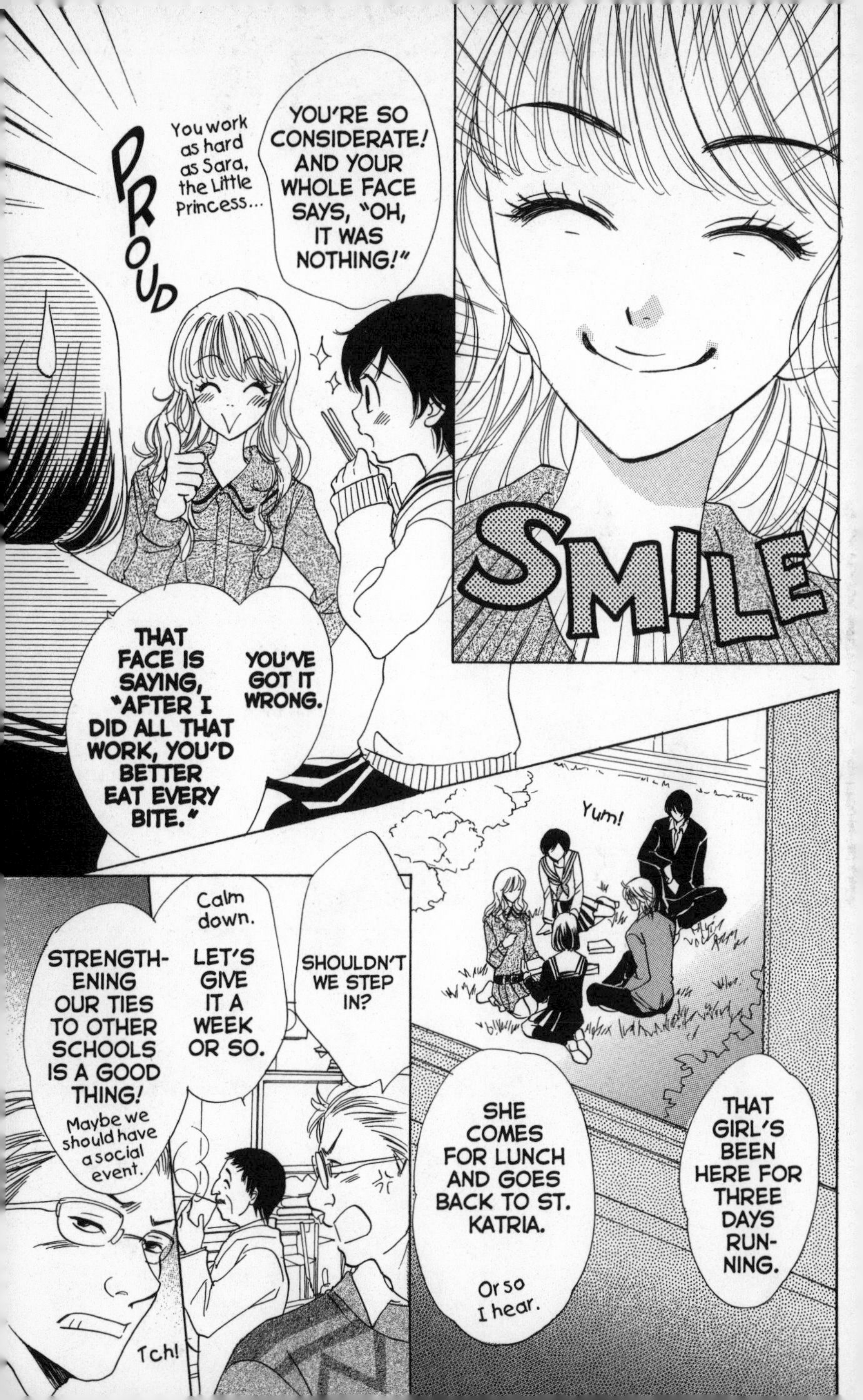
SMILE
YOU'RE SO CONSIDERATE! AND YOUR WHOLE FACE SAYS, "OH, IT WAS NOTHING!"
You work as hard as Sara, the Little Princess...
PROUD
YOU'VE GOT IT WRONG.
THAT FACE IS SAYING, "AFTER I DID ALL THAT WORK, YOU'D BETTER EAT EVERY BITE."
Yum!
THAT GIRL'S BEEN HERE FOR THREE DAYS RUNNING.
SHE COMES FOR LUNCH AND GOES BACK TO ST. KATRIA.
Or so I hear.
SHOULDN'T WE STEP IN?
Calm down.
LET'S GIVE IT A WEEK OR SO.
STRENGTHENING OUR TIES TO OTHER SCHOOLS IS A GOOD THING!
Maybe we should have a social event.
Tch!

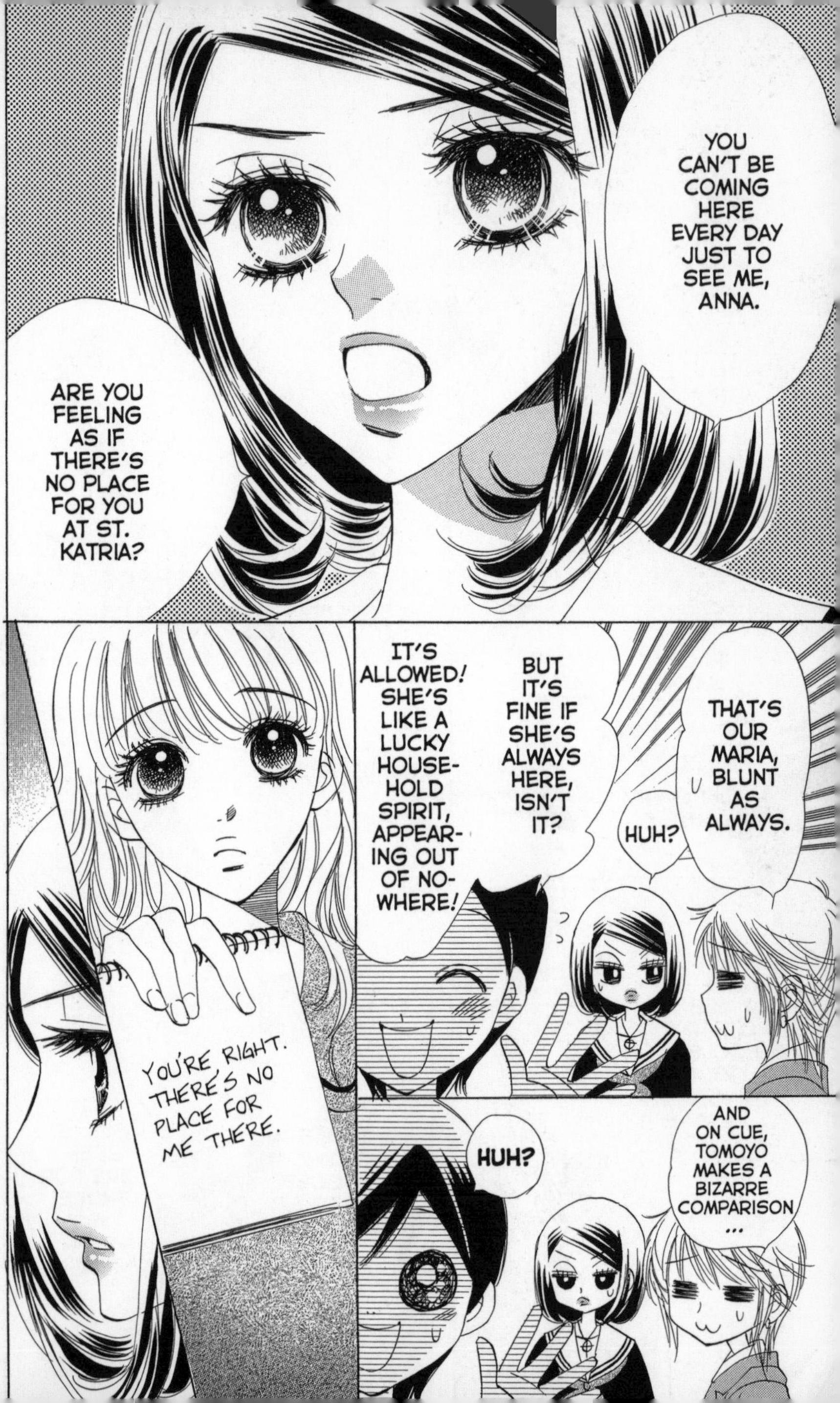
YOU CAN'T BE COMING HERE EVERY DAY JUST TO SEE ME, ANNA.
ARE YOU FEELING AS IF THERE'S NO PLACE FOR YOU AT ST. KATRIA?
THAT'S OUR MARIA, BLUNT AS ALWAYS.
HUH?
BUT IT'S FINE IF SHE'S ALWAYS HERE, ISN'T IT?
IT'S ALLOWED! SHE'S LIKE A LUCKY HOUSE-HOLD SPIRIT, APPEAR-ING OUT OF NO-WHERE!
AND ON CUE, TOMOYO MAKES A BIZARRE COMPARISON ...
HUH?
YOU'RE RIGHT. THERE'S NO PLACE FOR ME THERE.

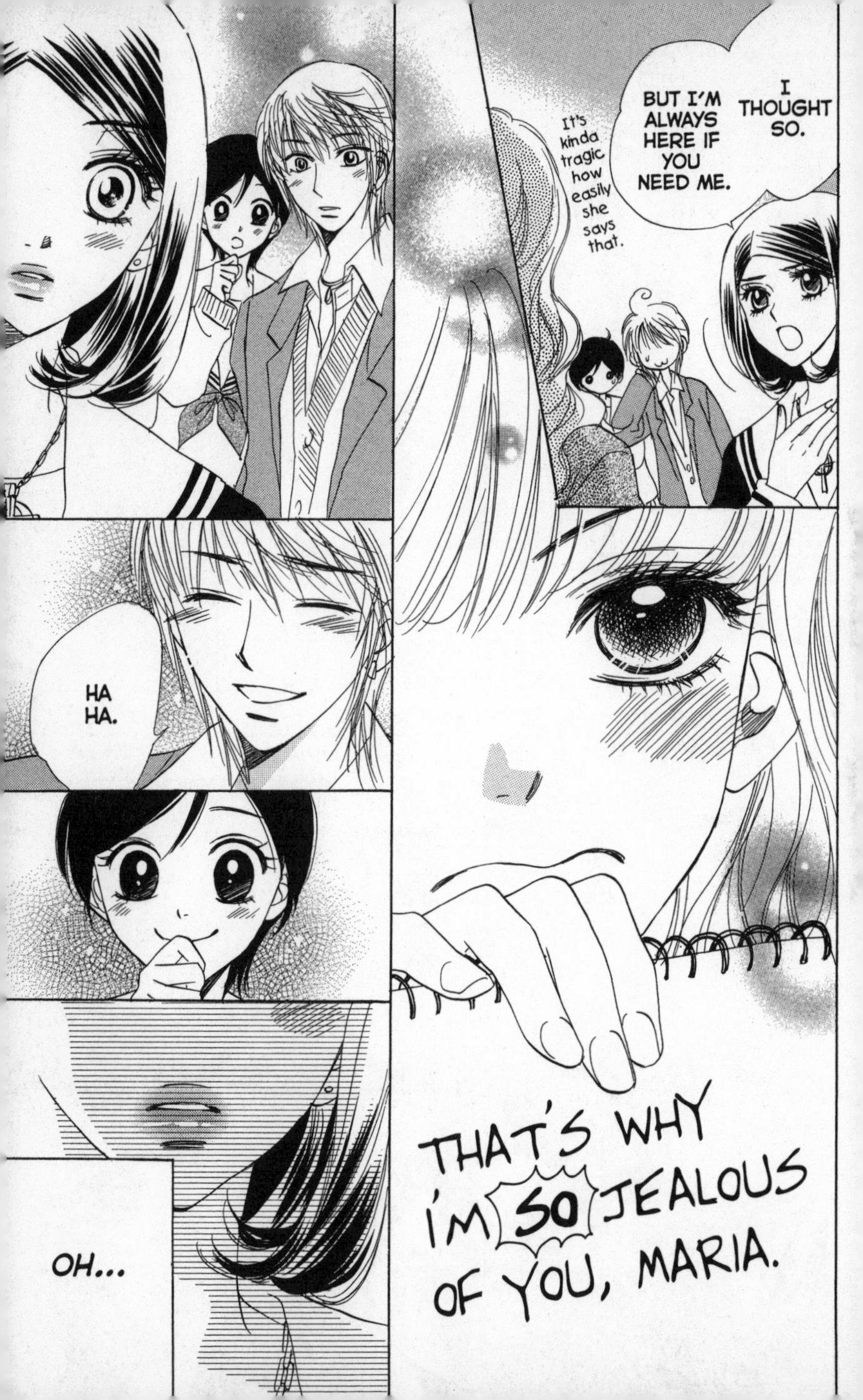
I THOUGHT SO.
BUT I'M ALWAYS HERE IF YOU NEED ME.
It's kinda tragic how easily she says that.
THAT'S WHY I'M SO JEALOUS OF YOU, MARIA.
HA HA.
OH...

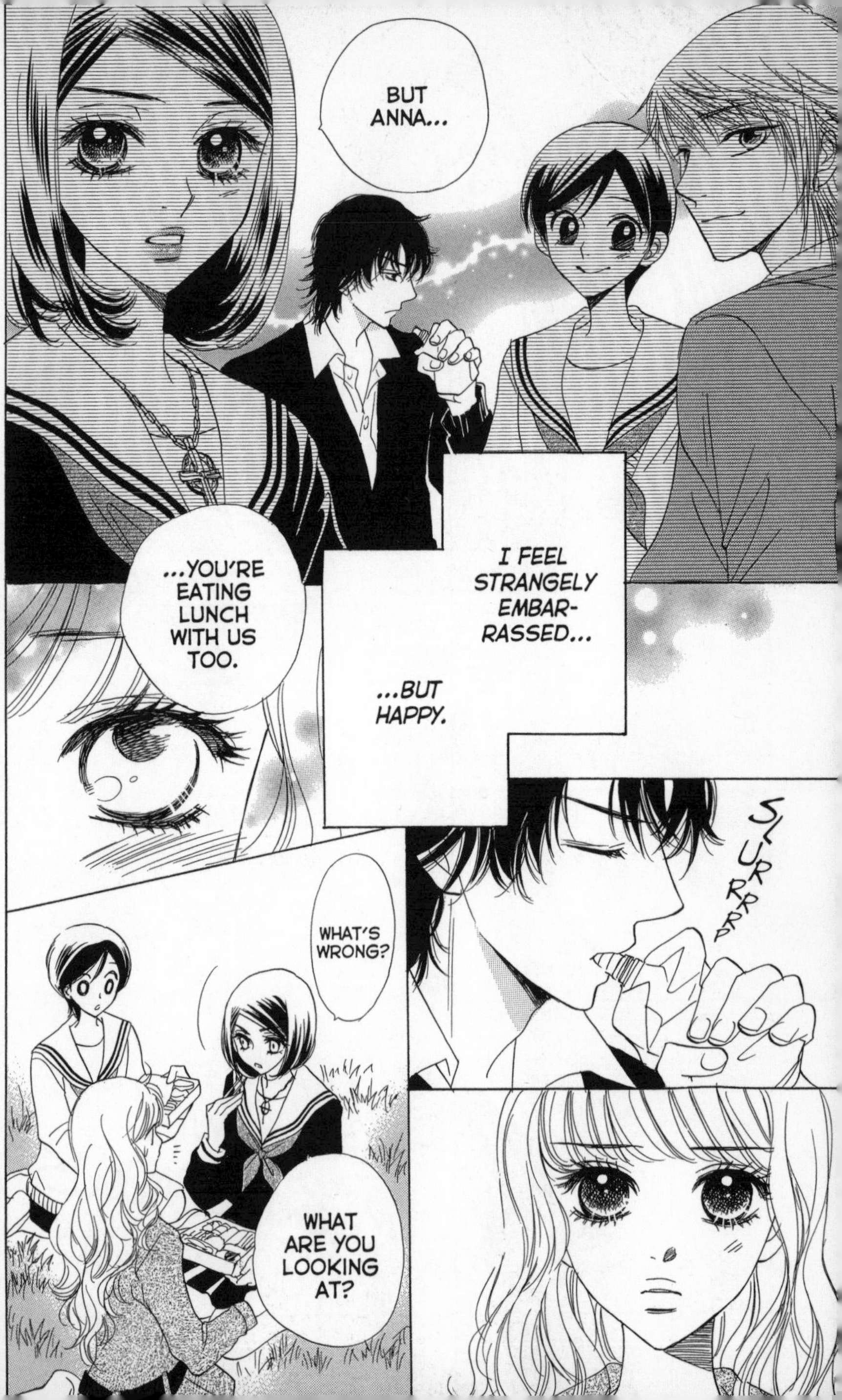
BUT ANNA...
...YOU'RE EATING LUNCH WITH US TOO.
I FEEL STRANGELY EMBAR-RASSED...
...BUT HAPPY.
SLURRRP
WHAT'S WRONG?
WHAT ARE YOU LOOKING AT?

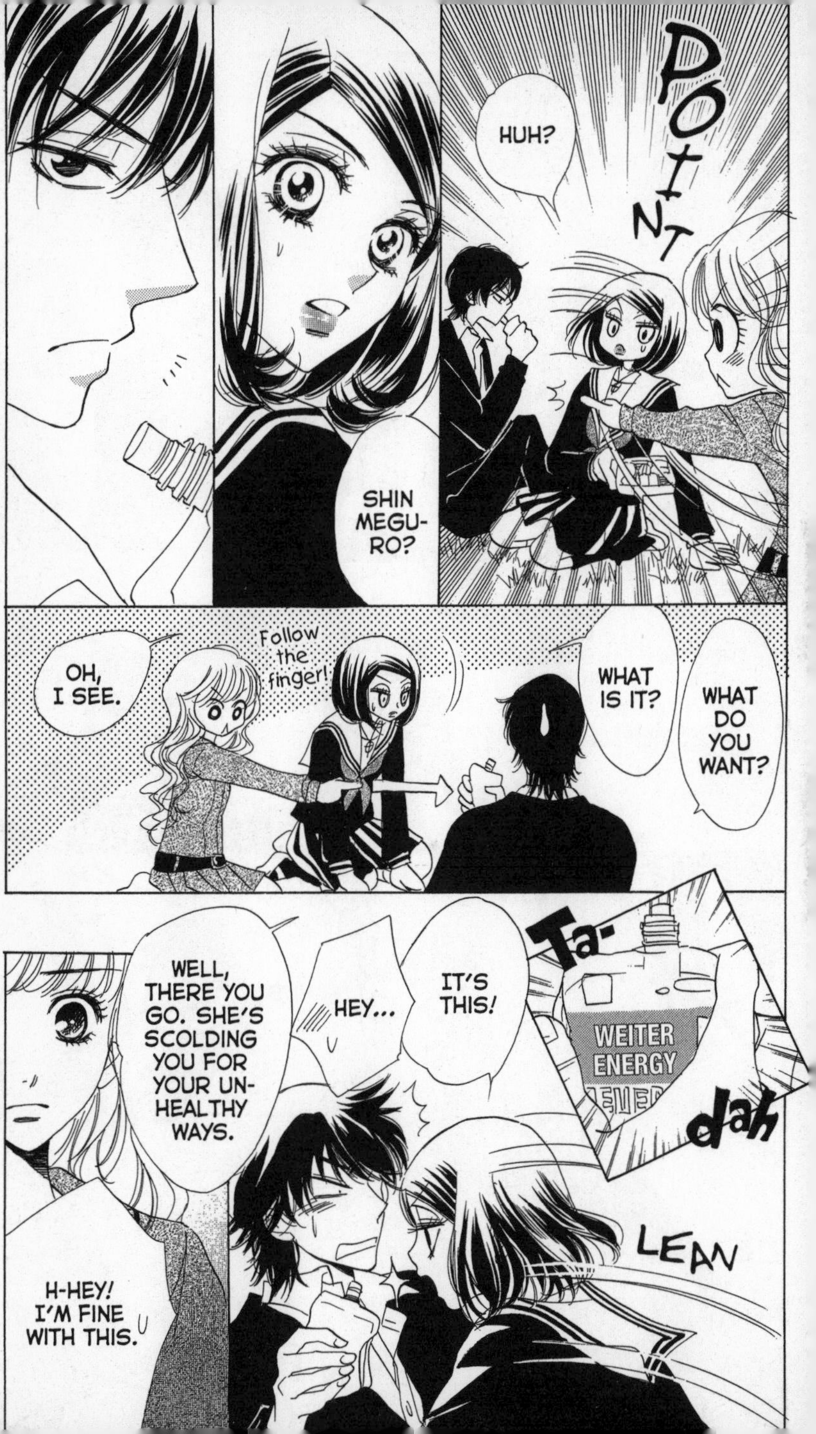
POINT
HUH?
SHIN MEGURO?
WHAT DO YOU WANT?
WHAT IS IT?
Follow the finger!
OH, I SEE.
Ta-dah
WEITER ENERGY
IT'S THIS!
HEY...
WELL, THERE YOU GO. SHE'S SCOLDING YOU FOR YOUR UN-HEALTHY WAYS.
LEAN
H-HEY! I'M FINE WITH THIS.

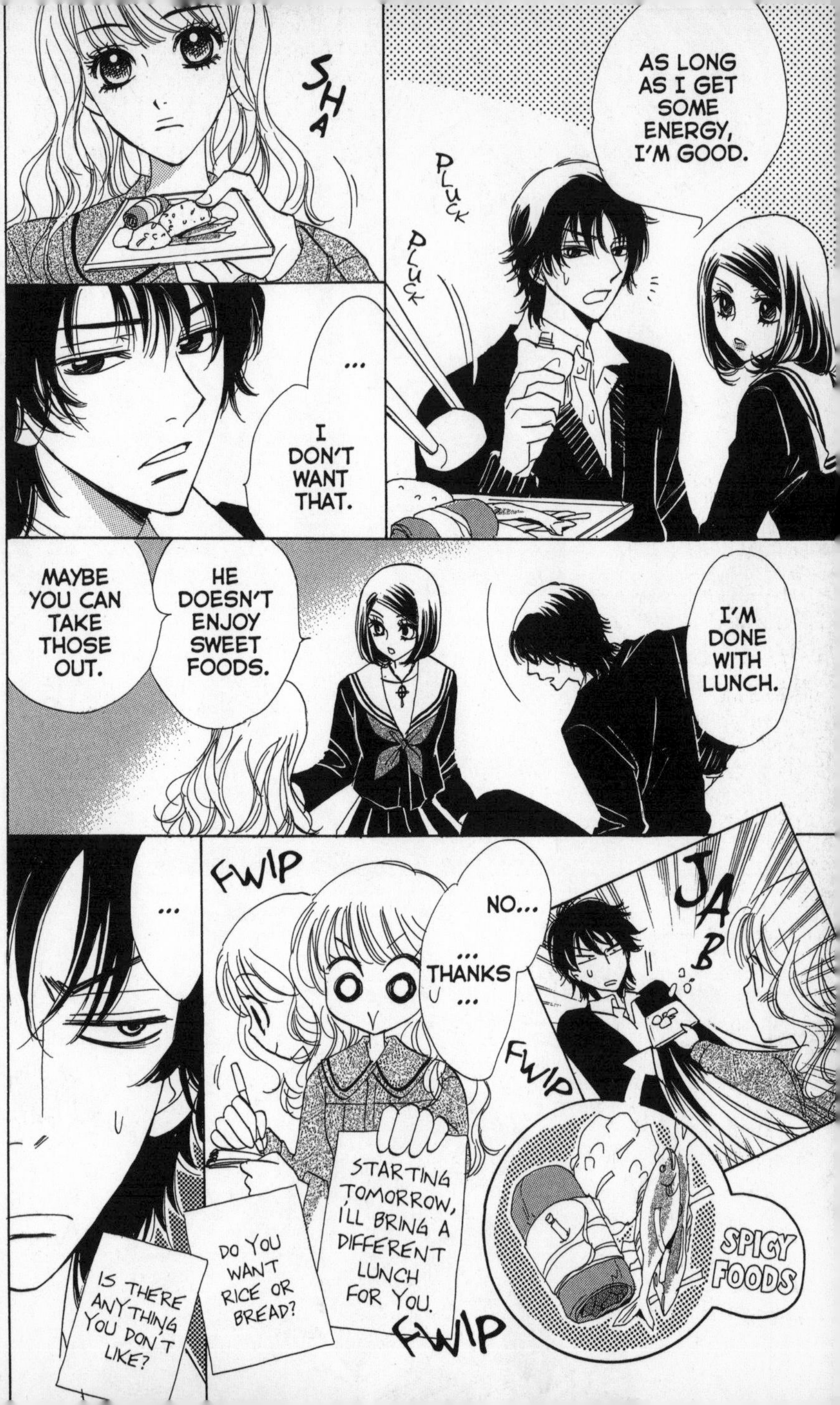
AS LONG AS I GET SOME ENERGY, I'M GOOD.
PLUCK
PLUCK
SHA
...
I DON'T WANT THAT.
I'M DONE WITH LUNCH.
HE DOESN'T ENJOY SWEET FOODS.
MAYBE YOU CAN TAKE THOSE OUT.
JAB
SPICY FOODS
NO...
... THANKS ...
FWIP
FWIP
STARTING TOMORROW, I'LL BRING A DIFFERENT LUNCH FOR YOU.
DO YOU WANT RICE OR BREAD?
IS THERE ANYTHING YOU DON'T LIKE?
FWIP
...

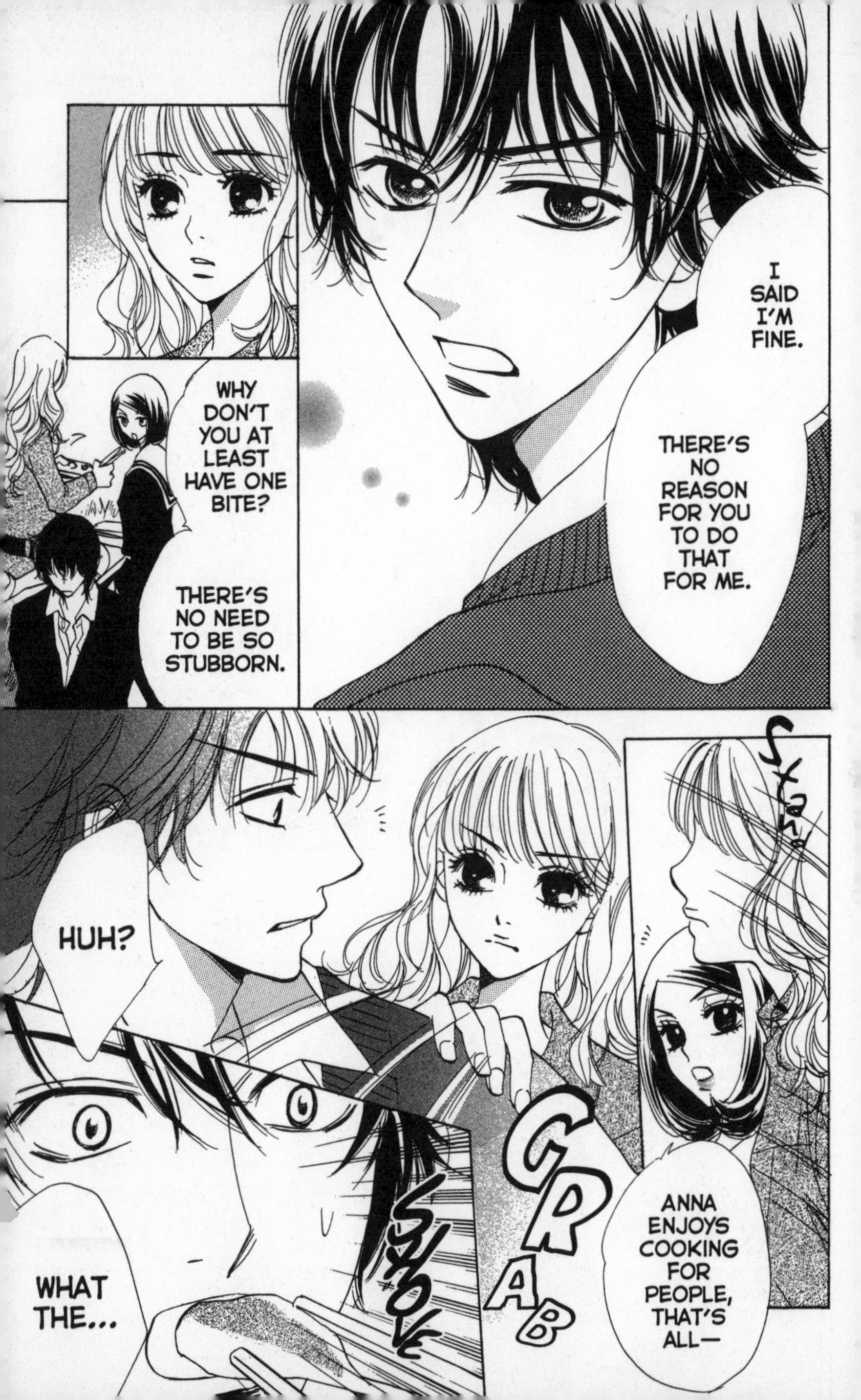
I SAID I'M FINE.
THERE'S NO REASON FOR YOU TO DO THAT FOR ME.
WHY DON'T YOU AT LEAST HAVE ONE BITE?
THERE'S NO NEED TO BE SO STUBBORN.
Stand
ANNA ENJOYS COOKING FOR PEOPLE, THAT'S ALL—
HUH?
GRAB
SHOVE
WHAT THE...

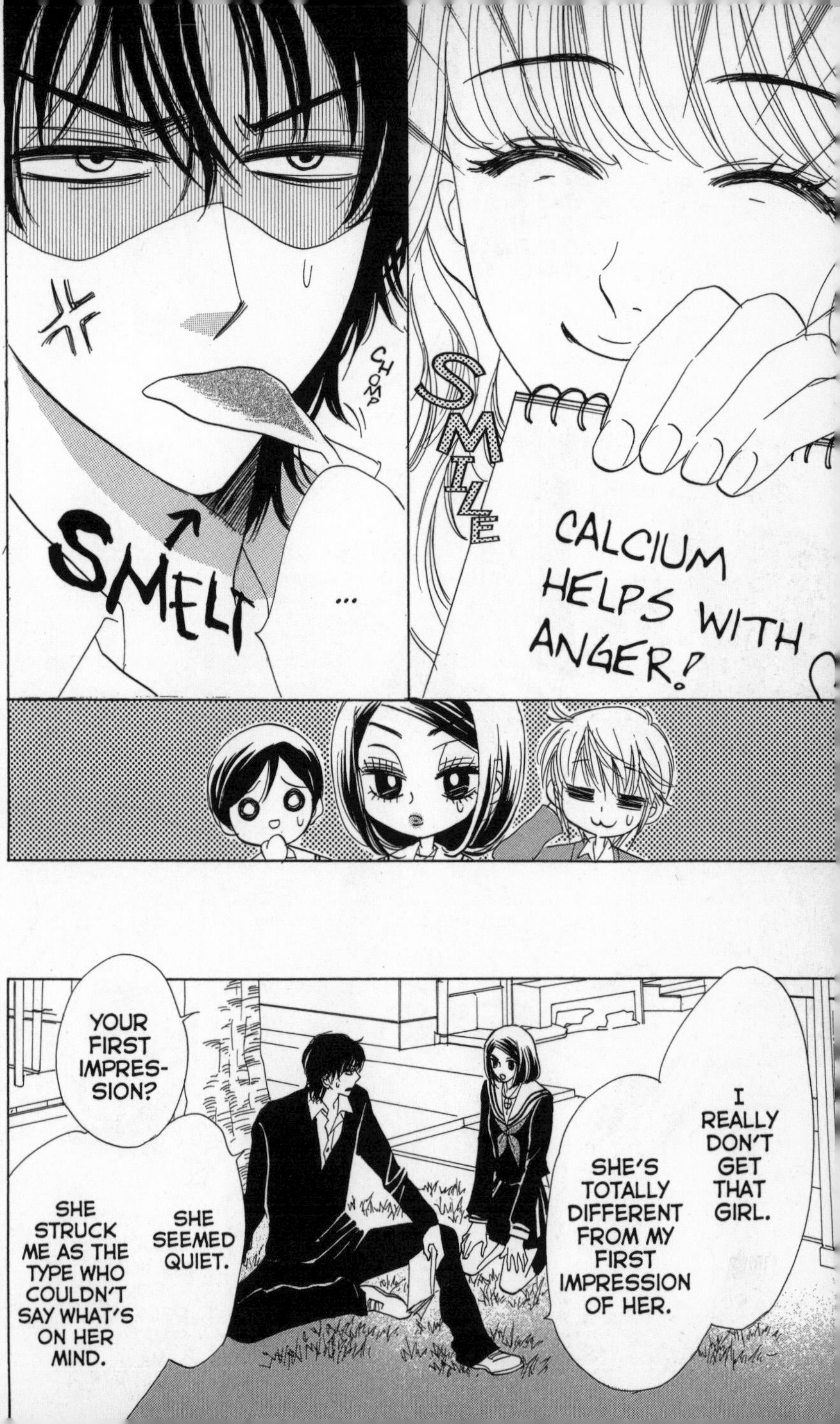
SMILE
CALCIUM HELPS WITH ANGER!
CHOMP
SMELT
...
I REALLY DON'T GET THAT GIRL.
SHE'S TOTALLY DIFFERENT FROM MY FIRST IMPRESSION OF HER.
YOUR FIRST IMPRES-SION?
SHE SEEMED QUIET.
SHE STRUCK ME AS THE TYPE WHO COULDN'T SAY WHAT'S ON HER MIND.

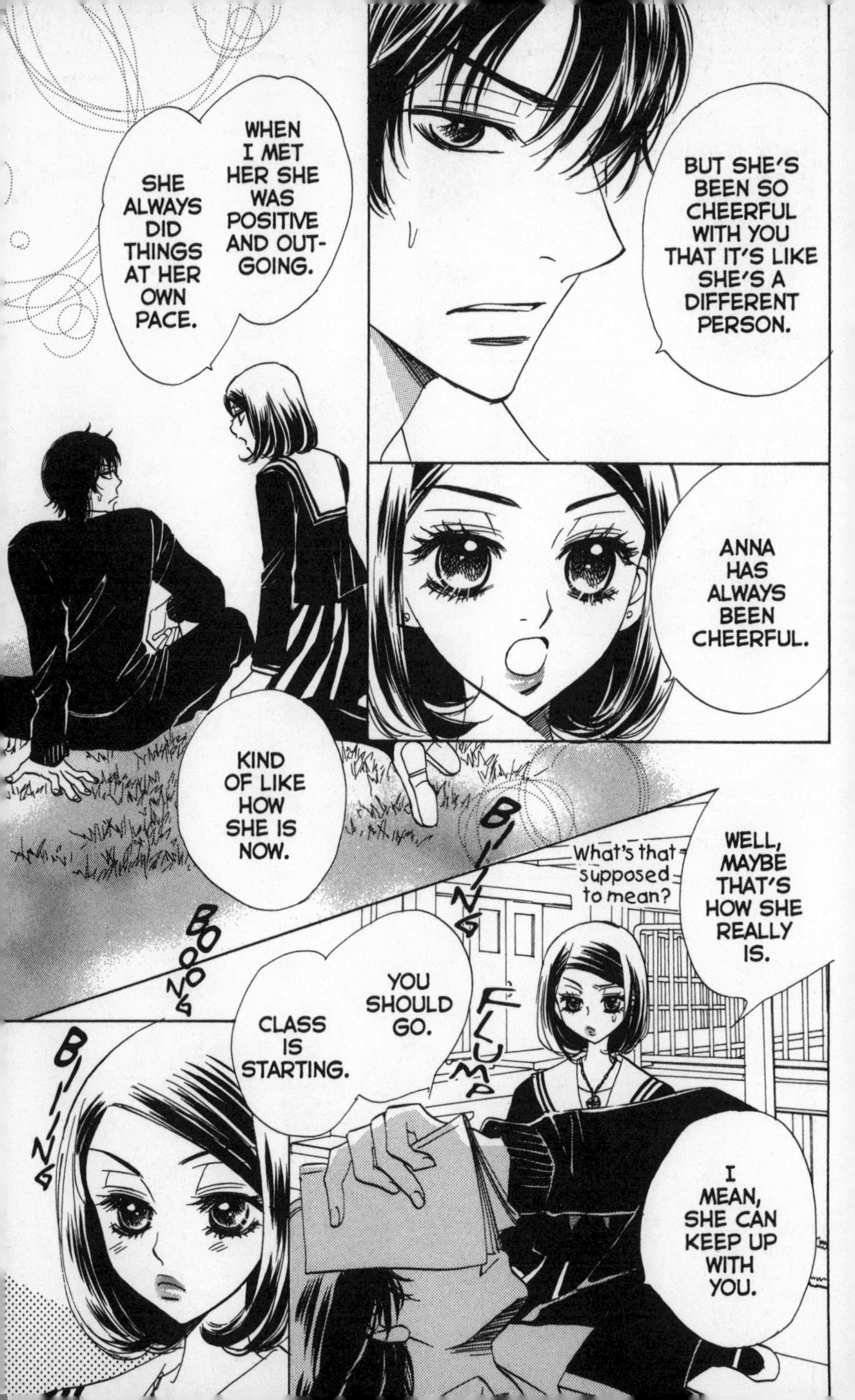
BUT SHE'S BEEN SO CHEERFUL WITH YOU THAT IT'S LIKE SHE'S A DIFFERENT PERSON.
ANNA HAS ALWAYS BEEN CHEERFUL.
WHEN I MET HER SHE WAS POSITIVE AND OUT-GOING.
SHE ALWAYS DID THINGS AT HER OWN PACE.
KIND OF LIKE HOW SHE IS NOW.
BIIING
WELL, MAYBE THAT'S HOW SHE REALLY IS.
What's that supposed to mean?
BOOOONG
I MEAN, SHE CAN KEEP UP WITH YOU.
FLUMP
YOU SHOULD GO.
CLASS IS STARTING.
BIIING

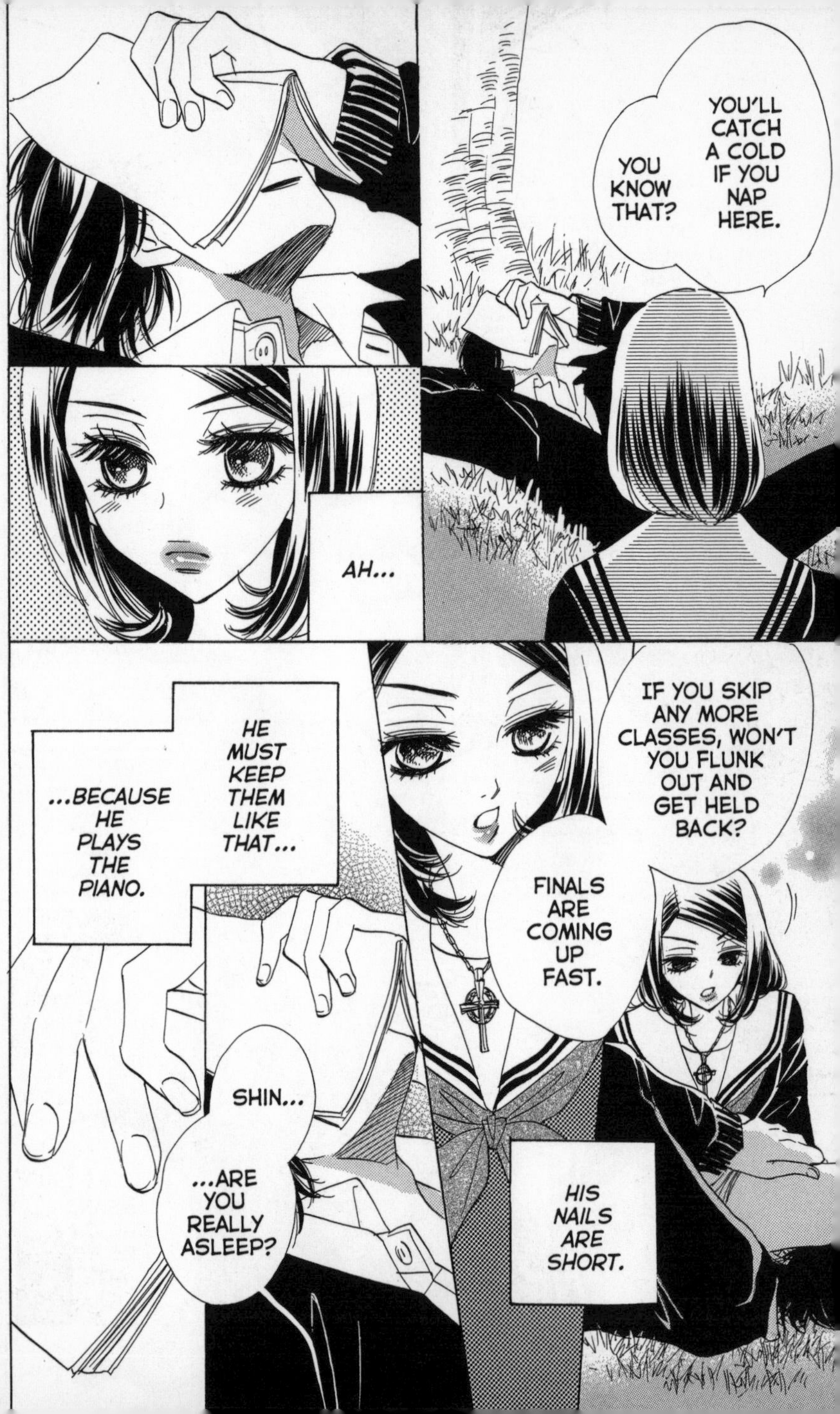
YOU'LL CATCH A COLD IF YOU NAP HERE.
YOU KNOW THAT?
AH...
IF YOU SKIP ANY MORE CLASSES, WON'T YOU FLUNK OUT AND GET HELD BACK?
FINALS ARE COMING UP FAST.
HIS NAILS ARE SHORT.
HE MUST KEEP THEM LIKE THAT...
...BECAUSE HE PLAYS THE PIANO.
SHIN...
...ARE YOU REALLY ASLEEP?

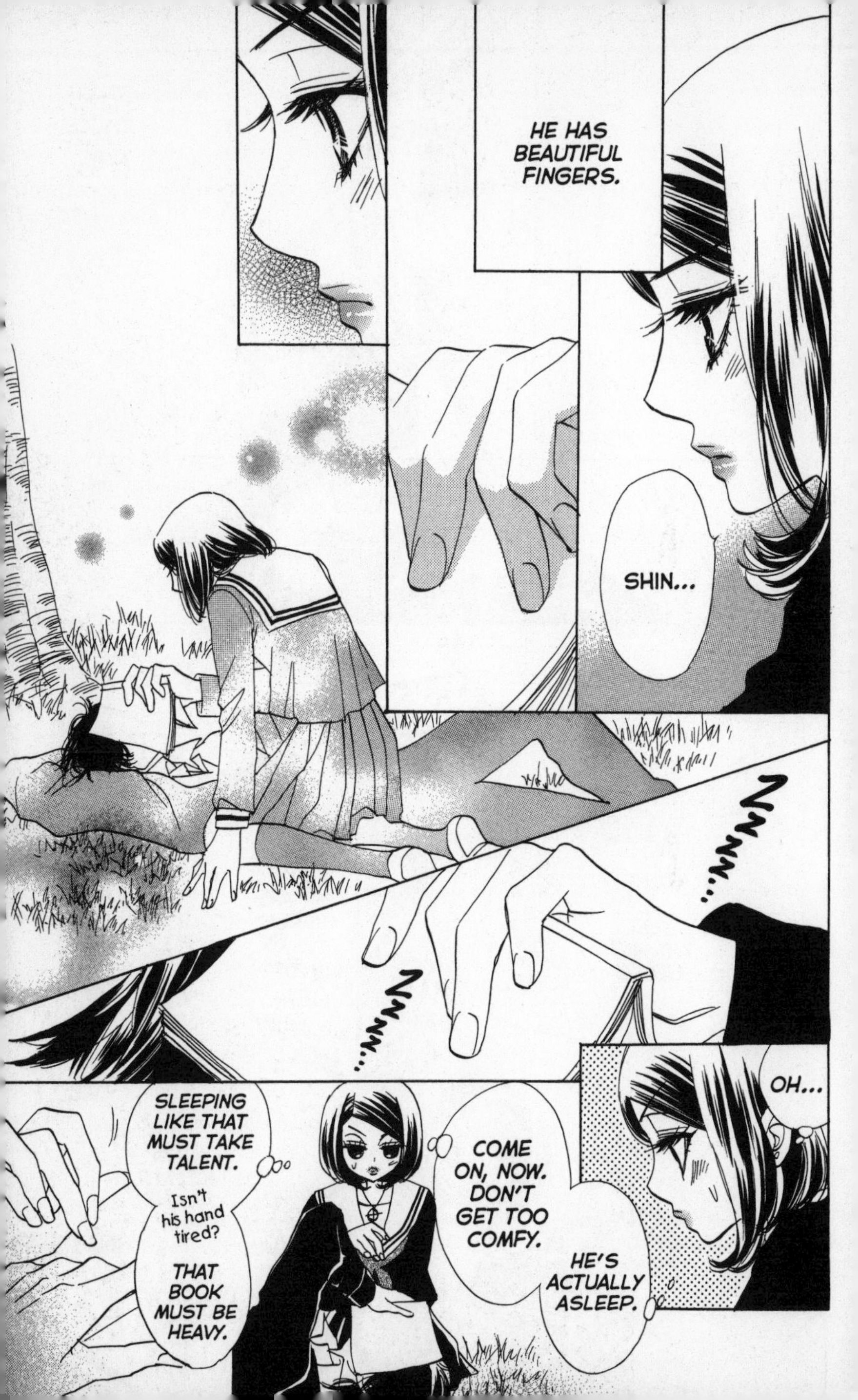
HE HAS BEAUTIFUL FINGERS.
SHIN...
ZNNNN...
ZNNNN...
OH...
COME ON, NOW. DON'T GET TOO COMFY.
HE'S ACTUALLY ASLEEP.
SLEEPING LIKE THAT MUST TAKE TALENT.
Isn't his hand tired?
THAT BOOK MUST BE HEAVY.

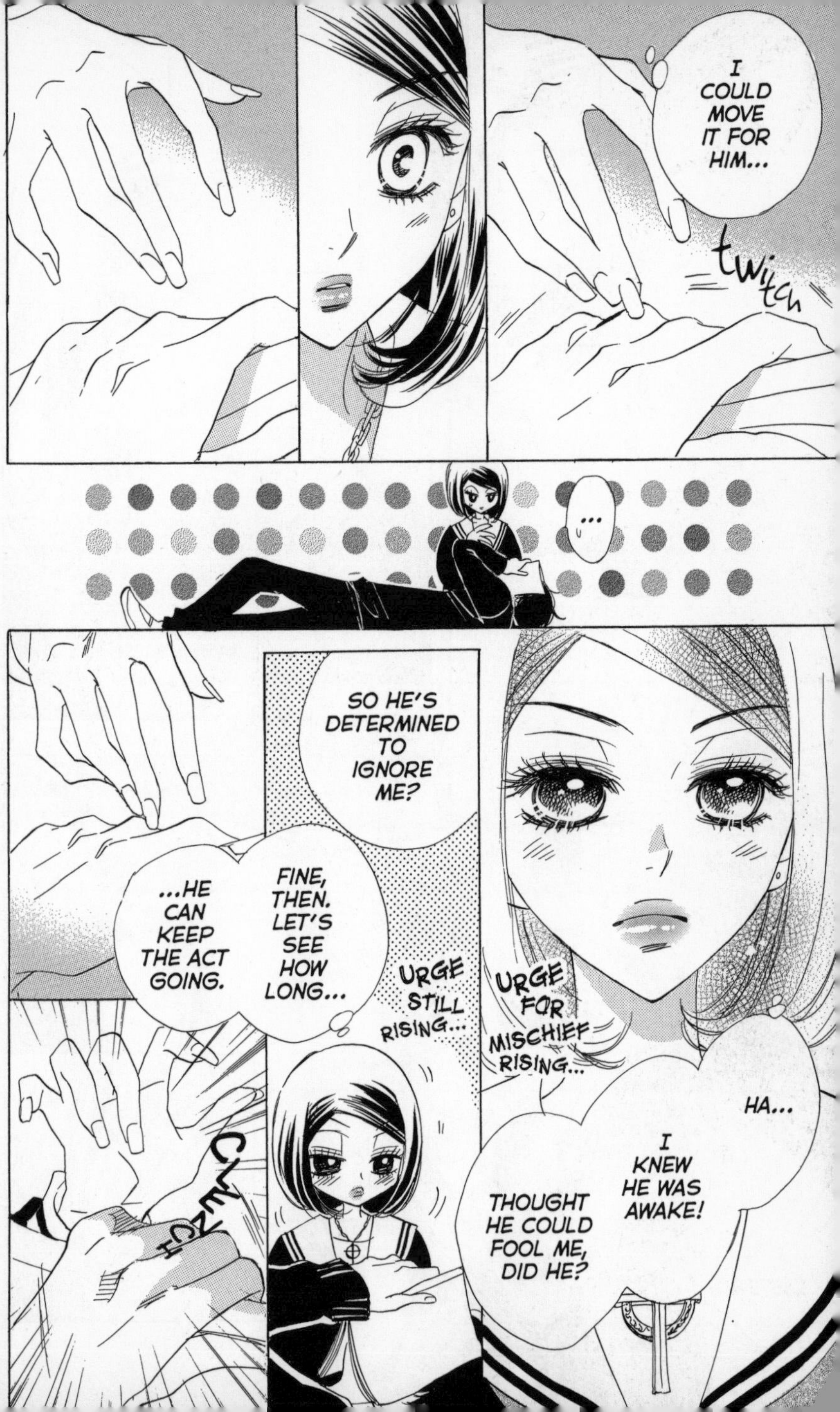
I COULD MOVE IT FOR HIM...
twitch
...
HA...
I KNEW HE WAS AWAKE!
THOUGHT HE COULD FOOL ME, DID HE?
SO HE'S DETERMINED TO IGNORE ME?
URGE FOR MISCHIEF RISING...
URGE STILL RISING...
FINE, THEN. LET'S SEE HOW LONG...
...HE CAN KEEP THE ACT GOING.
CLENCH

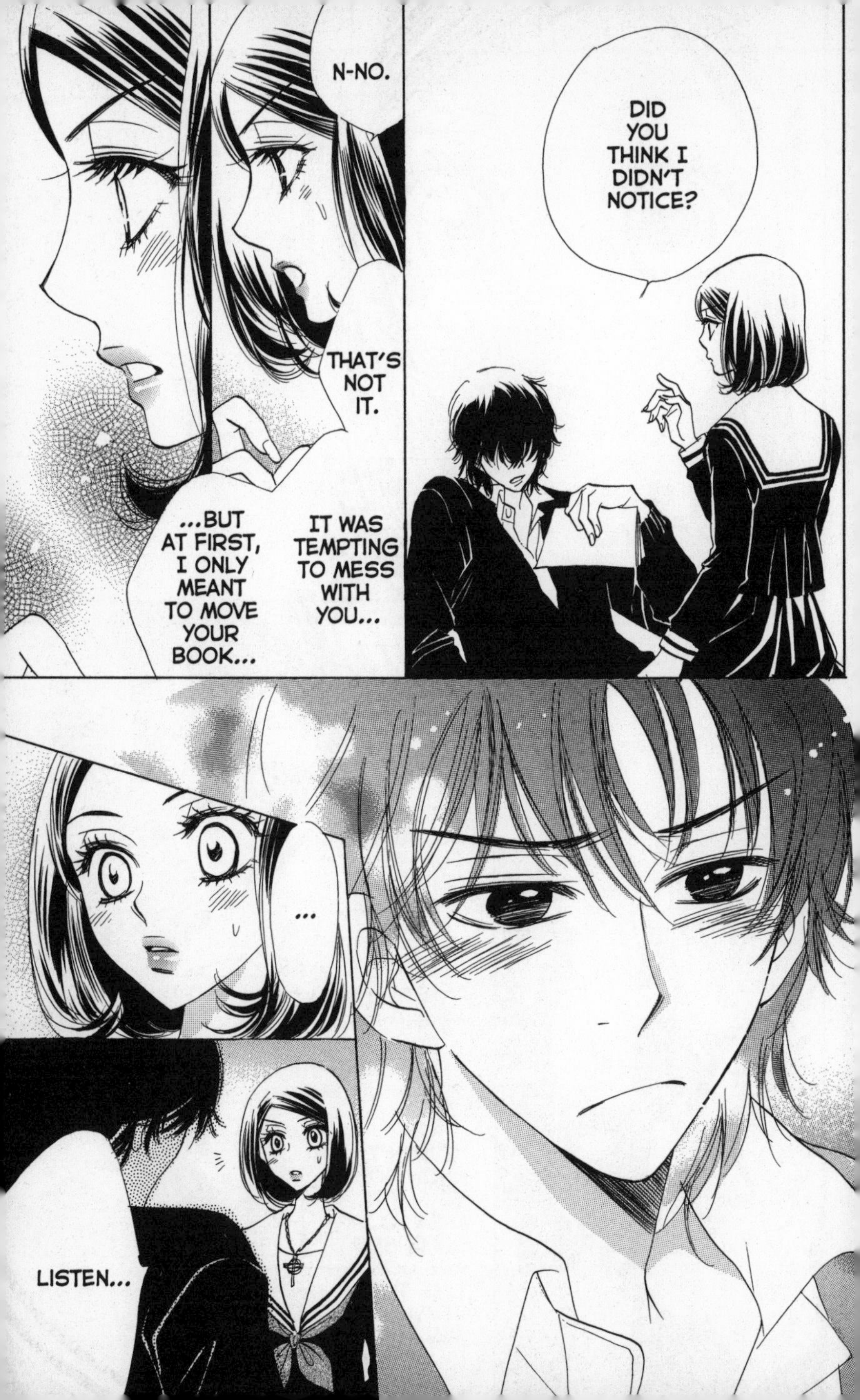
DID YOU THINK I DIDN'T NOTICE?
N-NO.
THAT'S NOT IT.
IT WAS TEMPTING TO MESS WITH YOU...
...BUT AT FIRST, I ONLY MEANT TO MOVE YOUR BOOK...
...
LISTEN...

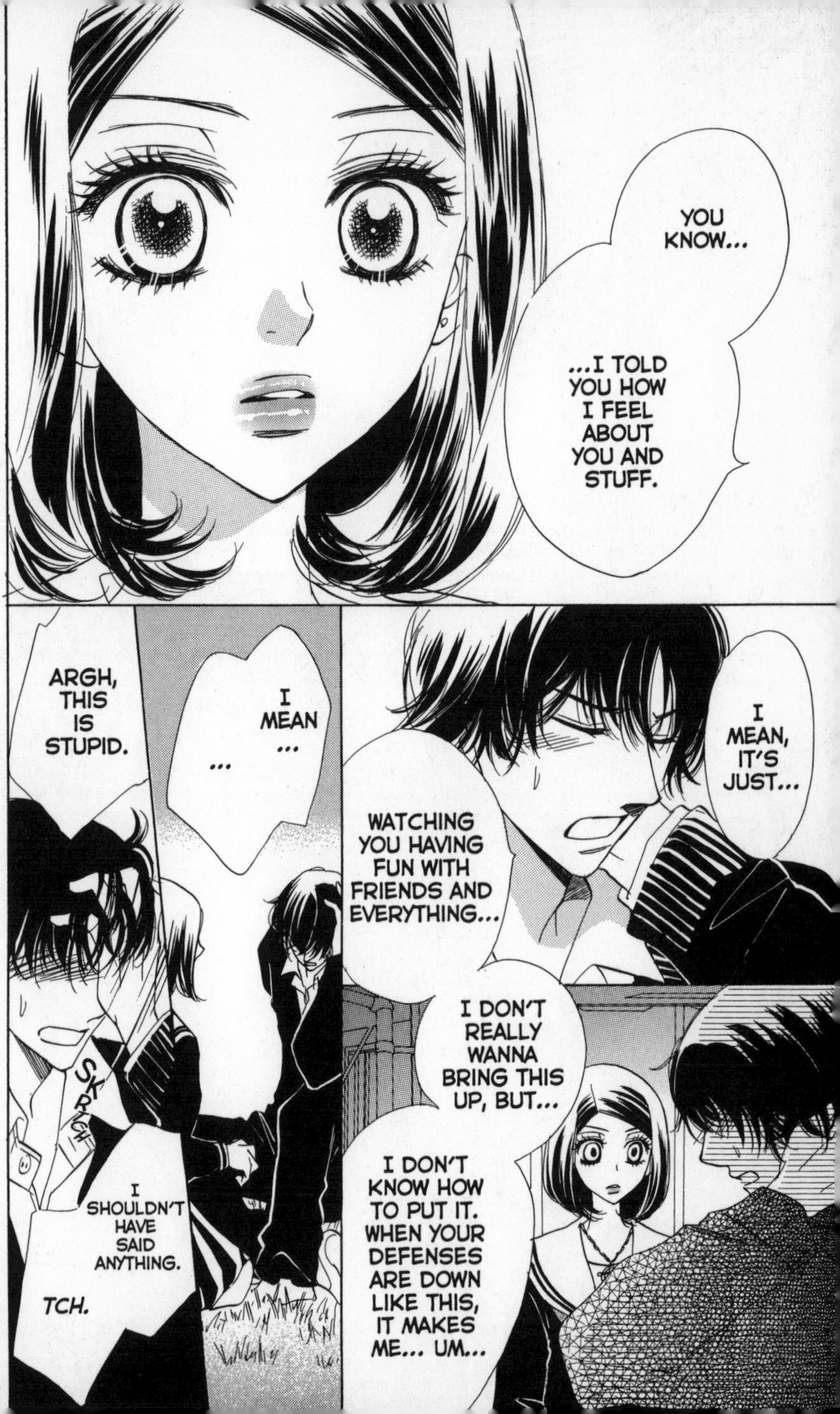
YOU KNOW...
...I TOLD YOU HOW I FEEL ABOUT YOU AND STUFF.
I MEAN, IT'S JUST...
WATCHING YOU HAVING FUN WITH FRIENDS AND EVERYTHING...
I DON'T REALLY WANNA BRING THIS UP, BUT...
I DON'T KNOW HOW TO PUT IT. WHEN YOUR DEFENSES ARE DOWN LIKE THIS, IT MAKES ME... UM...
I MEAN ...
...
ARGH, THIS IS STUPID.
SKRTCH
I SHOULDN'T HAVE SAID ANYTHING.
TCH.

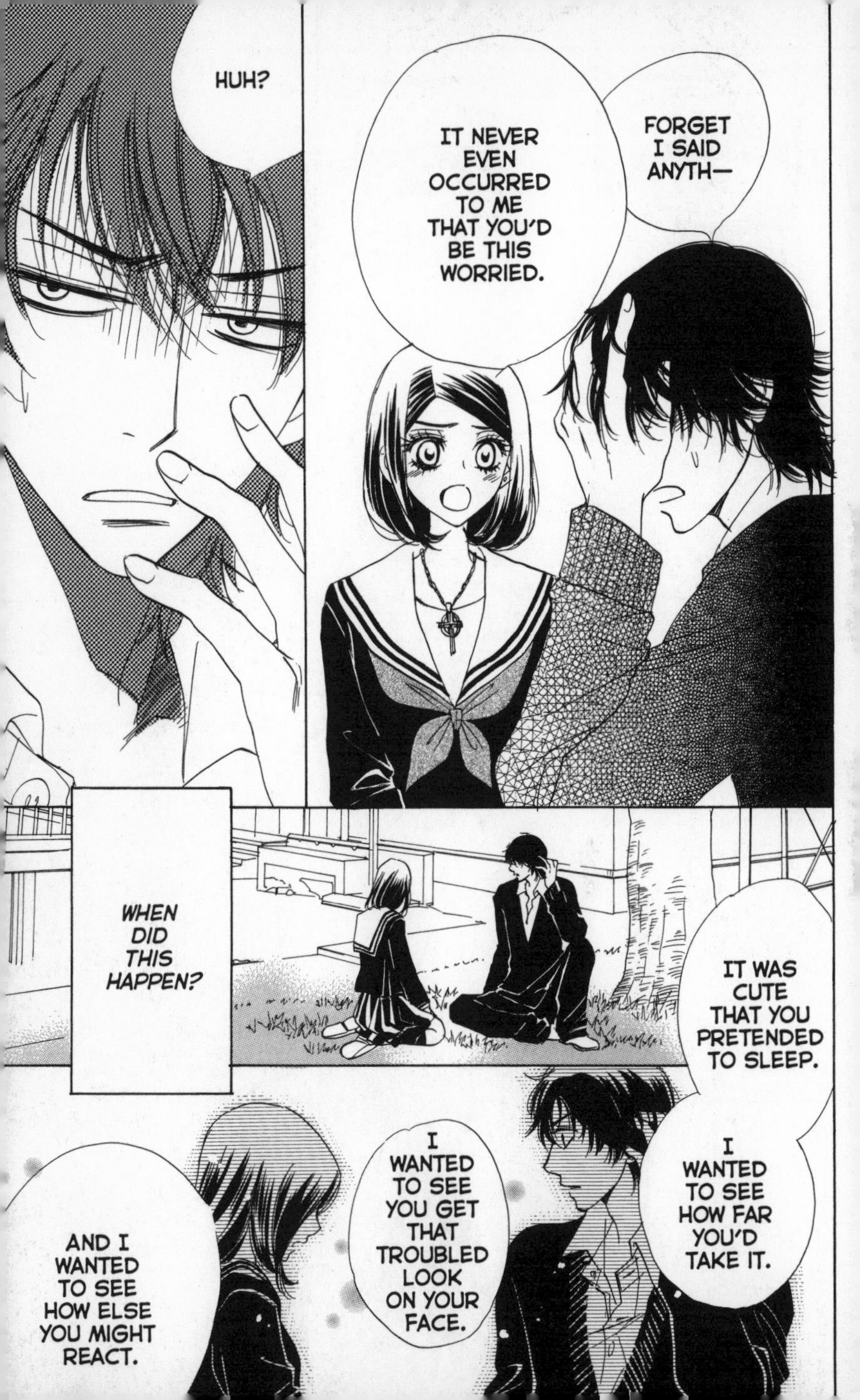
FORGET I SAID ANYTH—
IT NEVER EVEN OCCURRED TO ME THAT YOU'D BE THIS WORRIED.
HUH?
IT WAS CUTE THAT YOU PRETENDED TO SLEEP.
WHEN DID THIS HAPPEN?
I WANTED TO SEE HOW FAR YOU'D TAKE IT.
I WANTED TO SEE YOU GET THAT TROUBLED LOOK ON YOUR FACE.
AND I WANTED TO SEE HOW ELSE YOU MIGHT REACT.

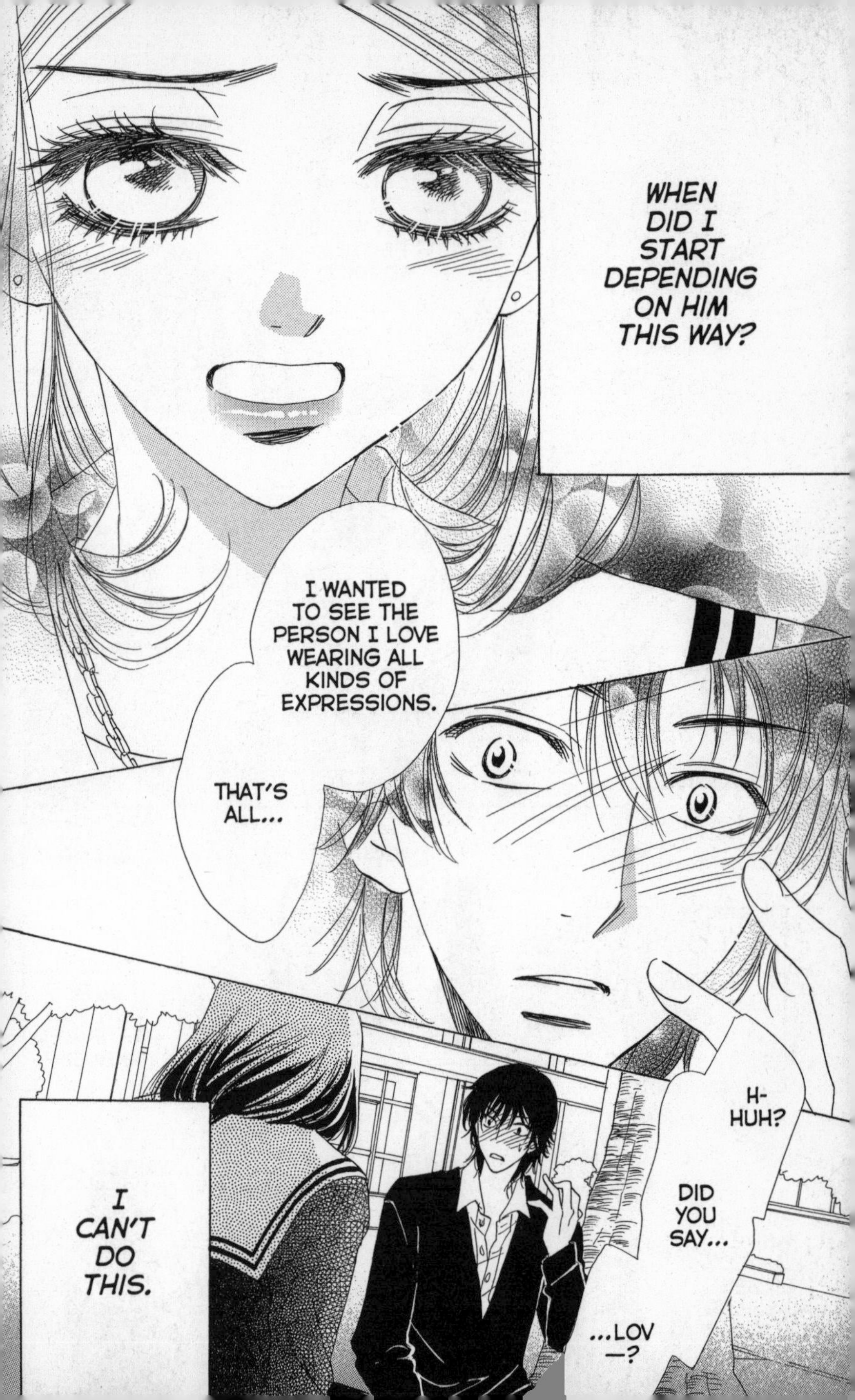
WHEN DID I START DEPENDING ON HIM THIS WAY?
I WANTED TO SEE THE PERSON I LOVE WEARING ALL KINDS OF EXPRESSIONS.
THAT'S ALL...
H- HUH?
DID YOU SAY...
...LOV—?
I CAN'T DO THIS.

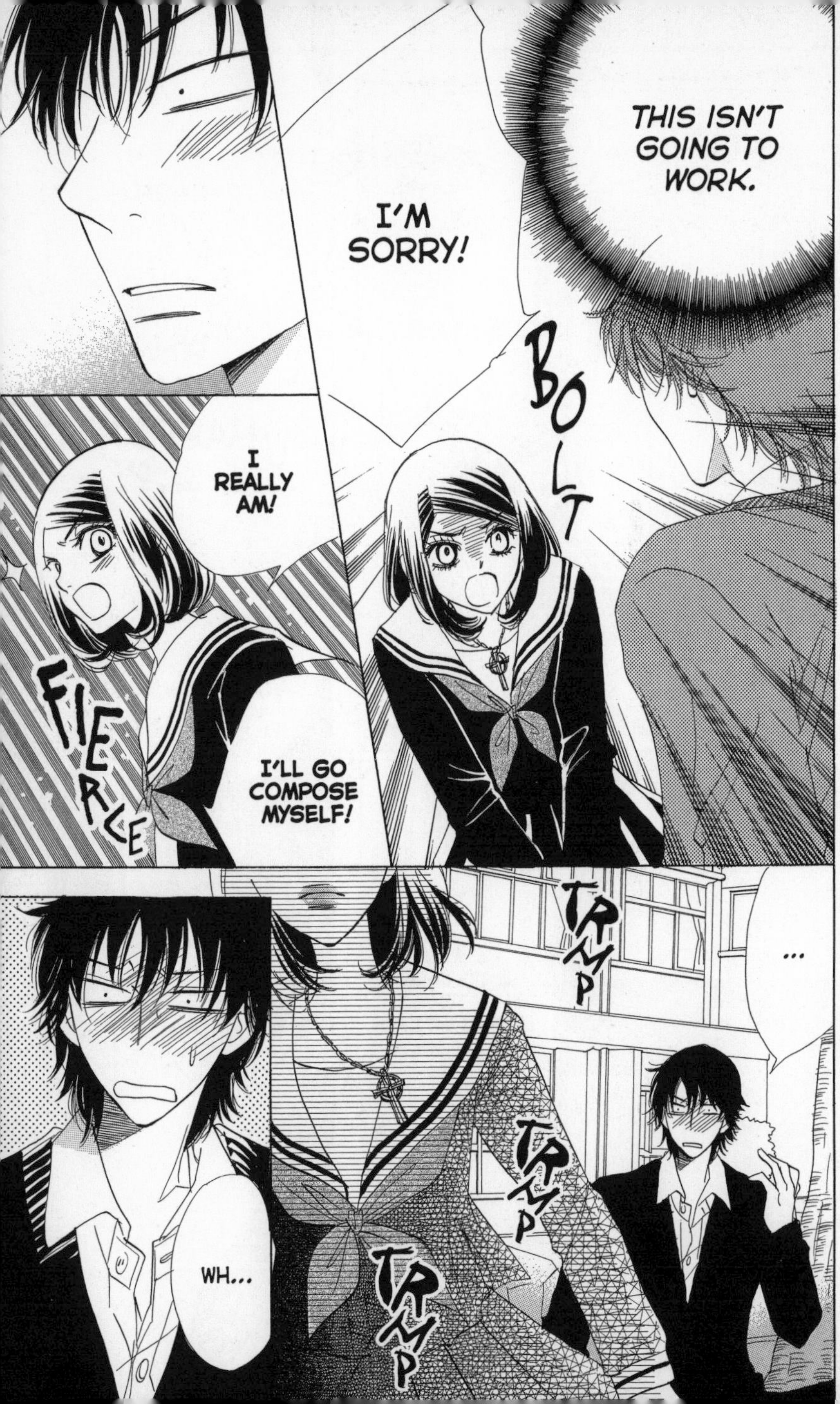
THIS ISN'T GOING TO WORK.
I'M SORRY!
BOLT
I REALLY AM!
FIERCE
I'LL GO COMPOSE MYSELF!
...
TRMP
TRMP
TRMP
WH...

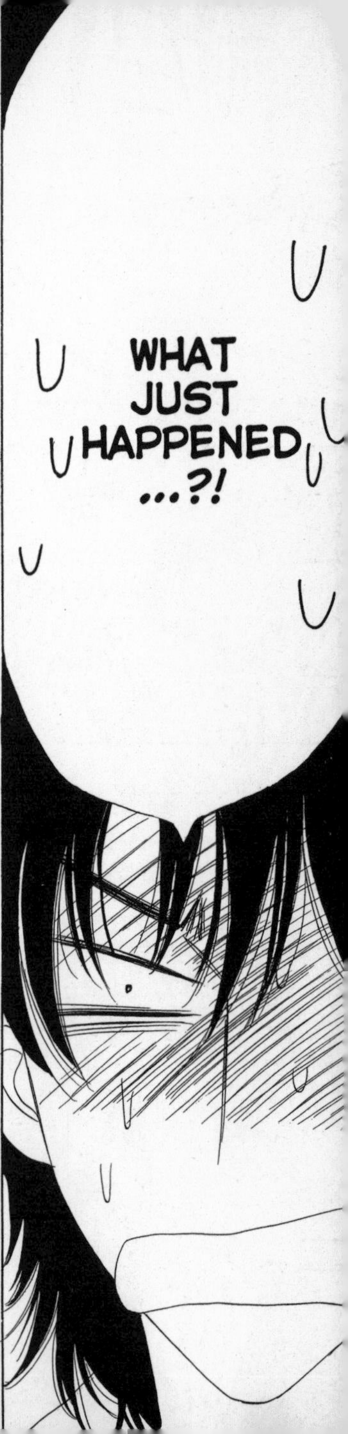
WHAT JUST HAPPENED ...?!

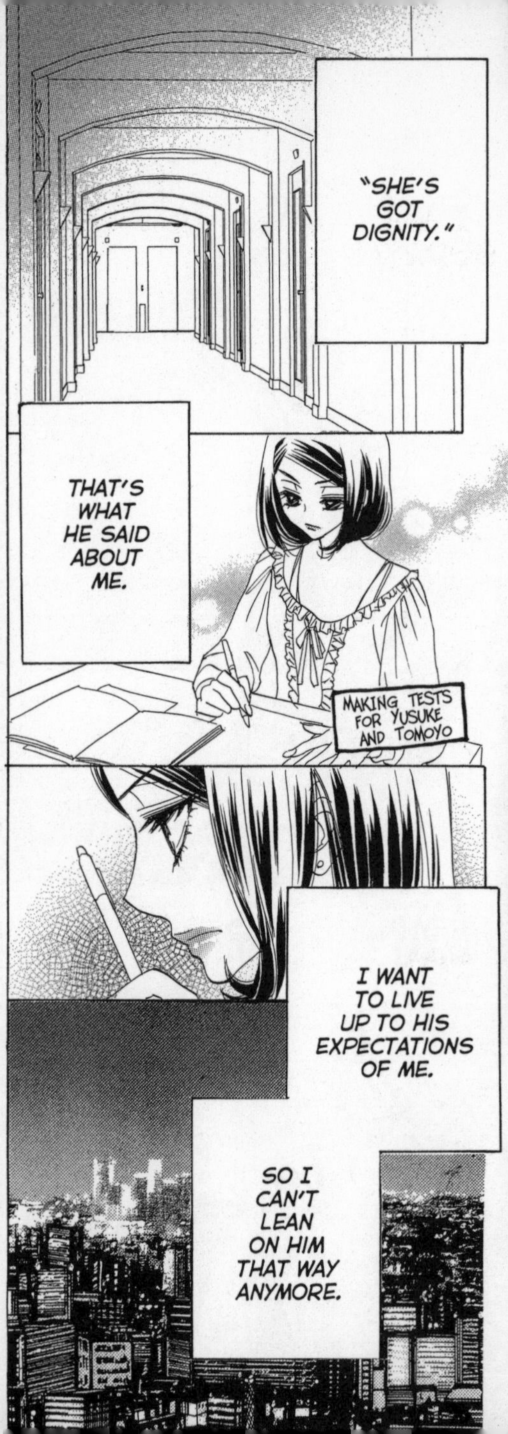
"SHE'S GOT DIGNITY."
THAT'S WHAT HE SAID ABOUT ME.
MAKING TESTS FOR YUSUKE AND TOMOYO
I WANT TO LIVE UP TO HIS EXPECTATIONS OF ME.
SO I CAN'T LEAN ON HIM THAT WAY ANYMORE.

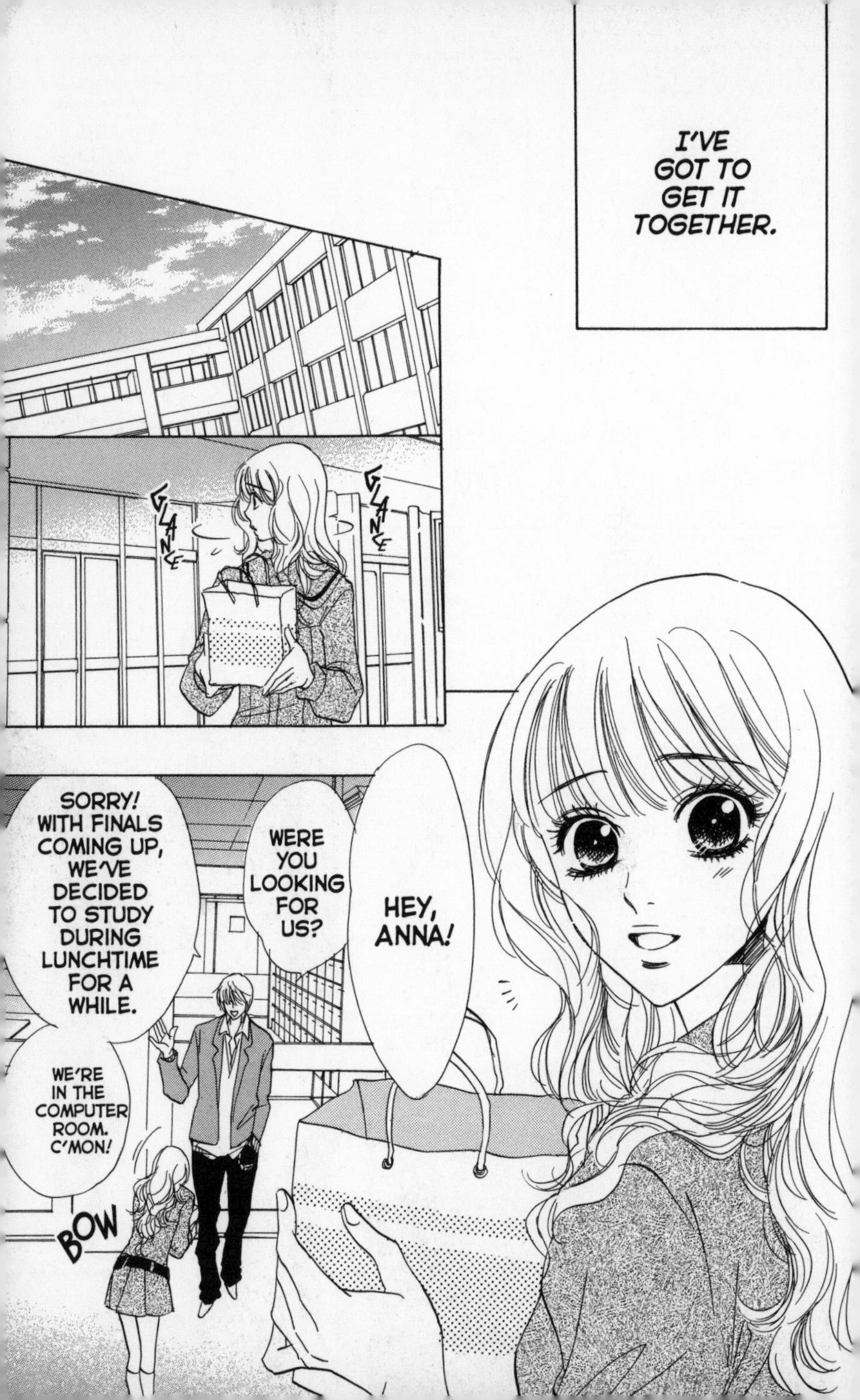
I'VE GOT TO GET IT TOGETHER.
GLANCE
GLANCE
HEY, ANNA!
WERE YOU LOOKING FOR US?
SORRY! WITH FINALS COMING UP, WE'VE DECIDED TO STUDY DURING LUNCHTIME FOR A WHILE.
WE'RE IN THE COMPUTER ROOM. C'MON!
BOW

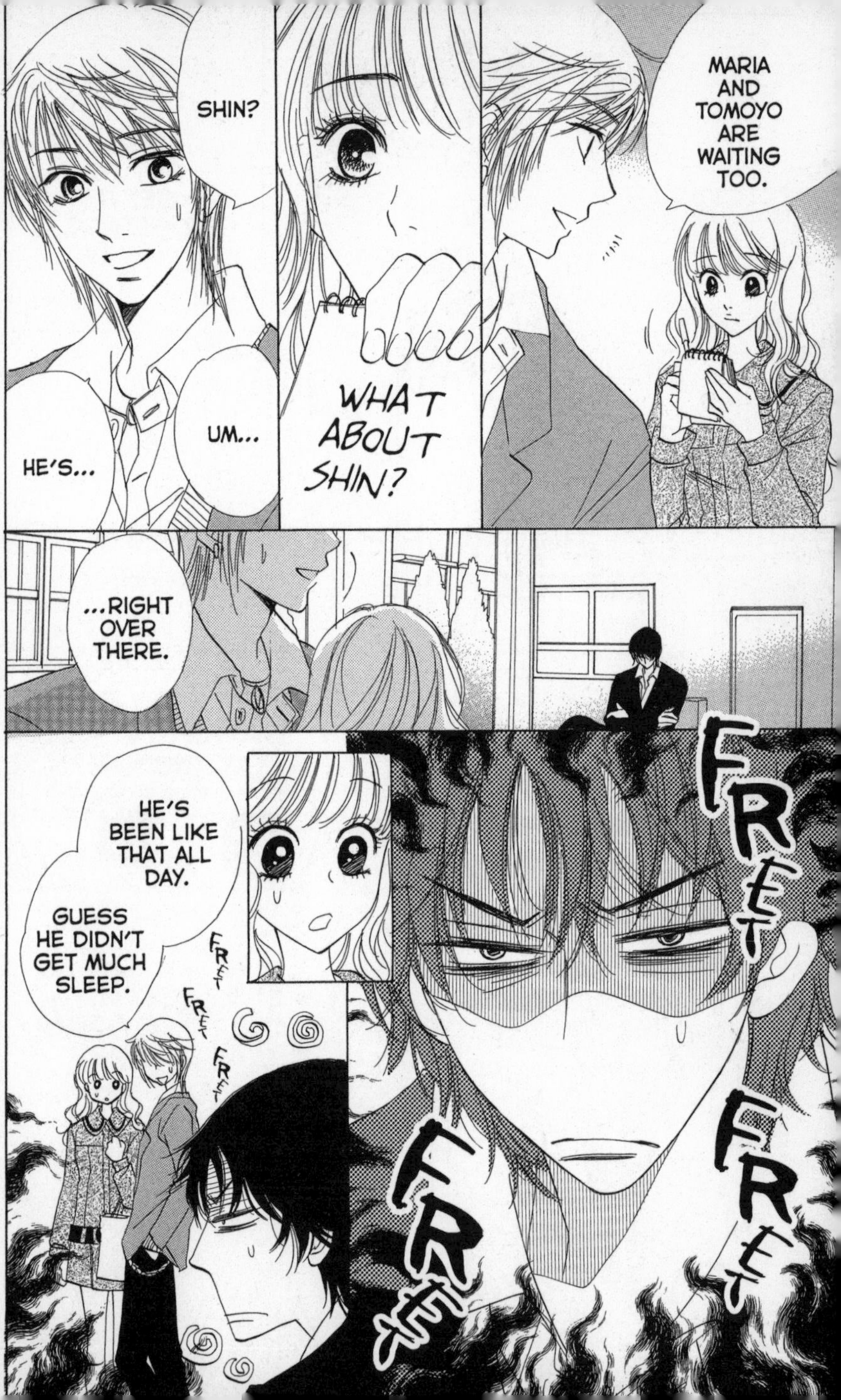
MARIA AND TOMOYO ARE WAITING TOO.
WHAT ABOUT SHIN?
SHIN?
UM...
HE'S...
...RIGHT OVER THERE.
FRET
FRET
FRET
HE'S BEEN LIKE THAT ALL DAY.
GUESS HE DIDN'T GET MUCH SLEEP.
FRET
FRET
FRET

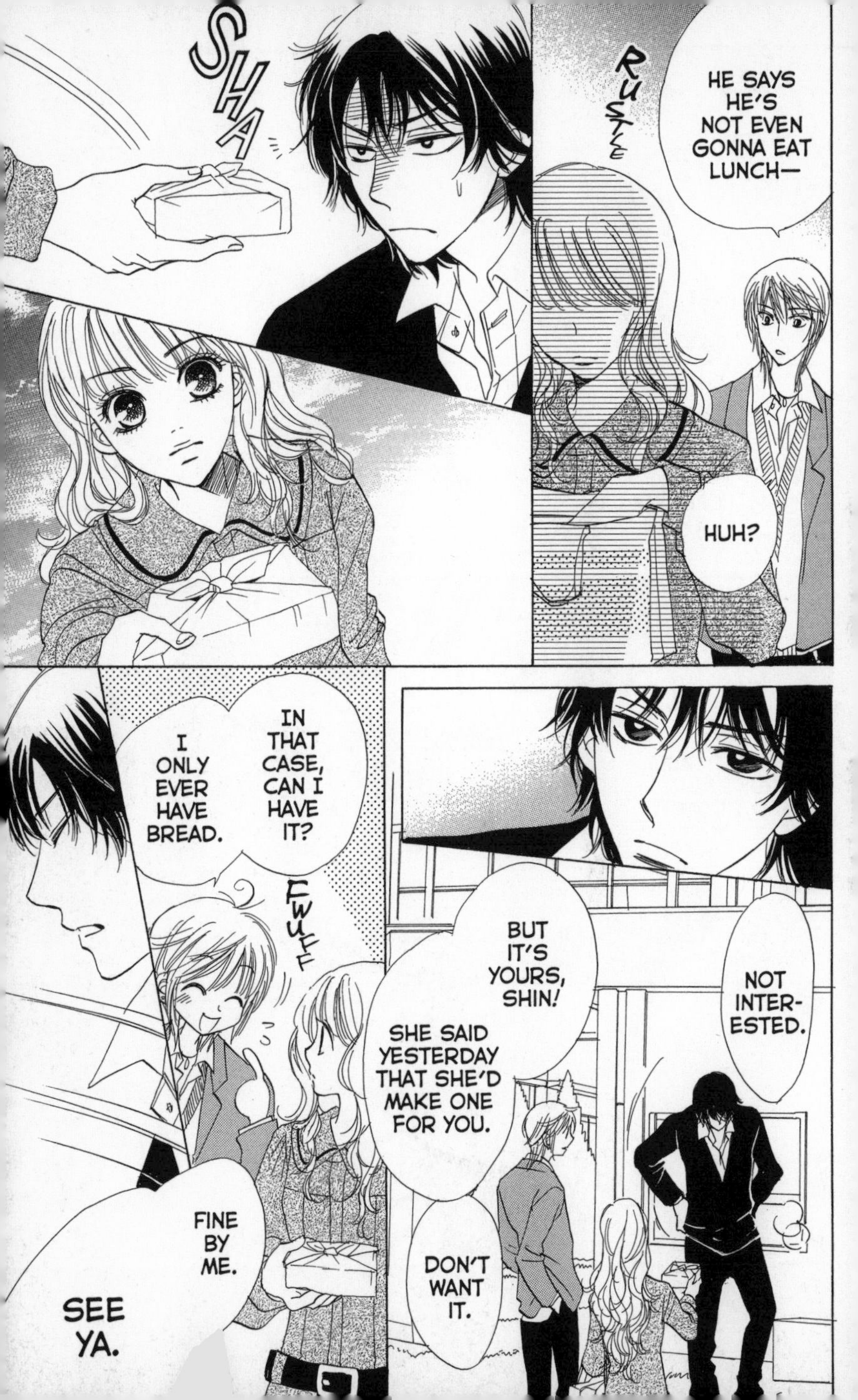
HE SAYS HE'S NOT EVEN GONNA EAT LUNCH—
RUSTLE
HUH?
SHA
NOT INTER-ESTED.
BUT IT'S YOURS, SHIN!
SHE SAID YESTERDAY THAT SHE'D MAKE ONE FOR YOU.
DON'T WANT IT.
IN THAT CASE, CAN I HAVE IT?
I ONLY EVER HAVE BREAD.
FWUFF
FINE BY ME.
SEE YA.

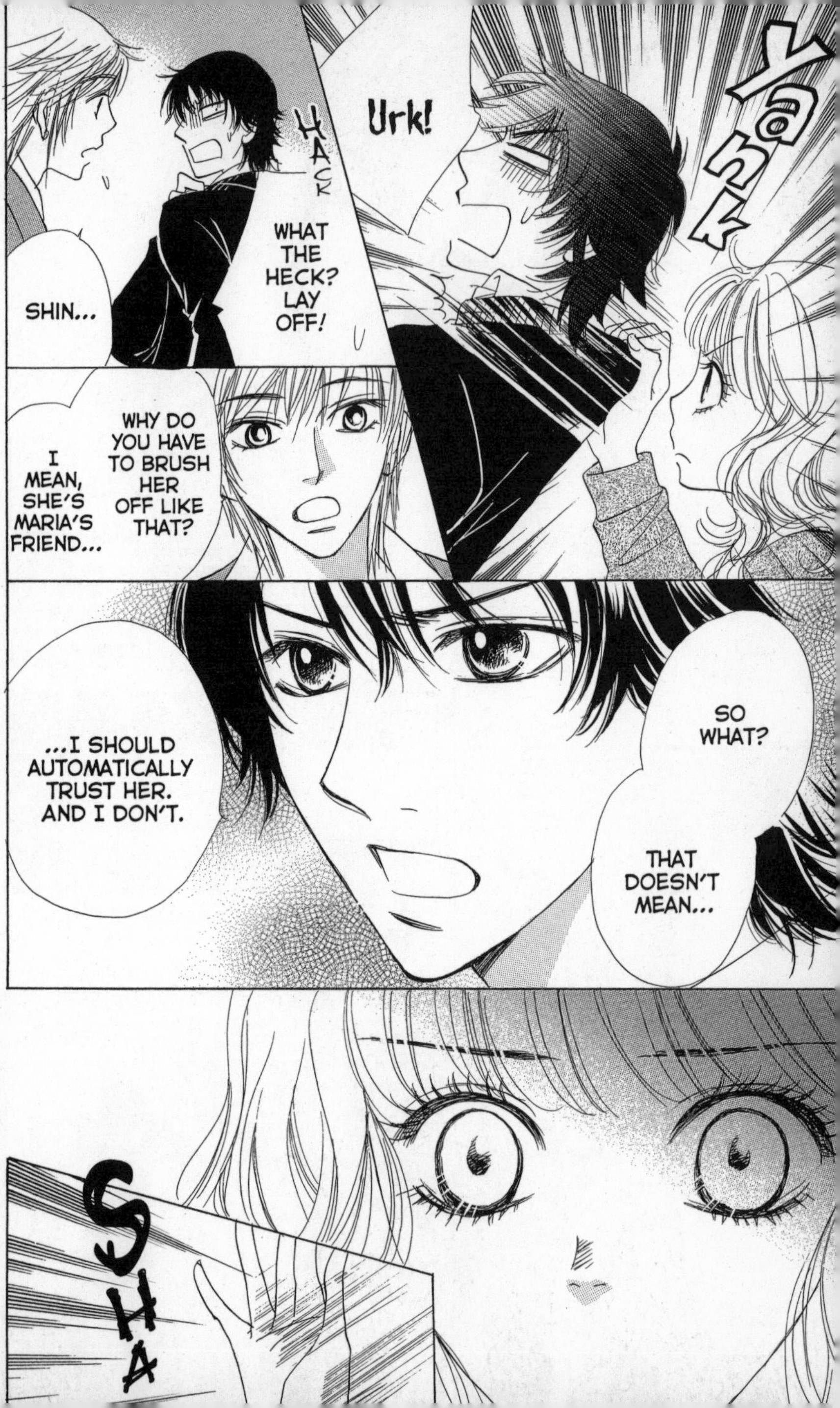
Yank
Urk!
HACK
WHAT THE HECK? LAY OFF!
SHIN...
WHY DO YOU HAVE TO BRUSH HER OFF LIKE THAT?
I MEAN, SHE'S MARIA'S FRIEND...
SO WHAT?
THAT DOESN'T MEAN...
...I SHOULD AUTOMATICALLY TRUST HER. AND I DON'T.
SHA

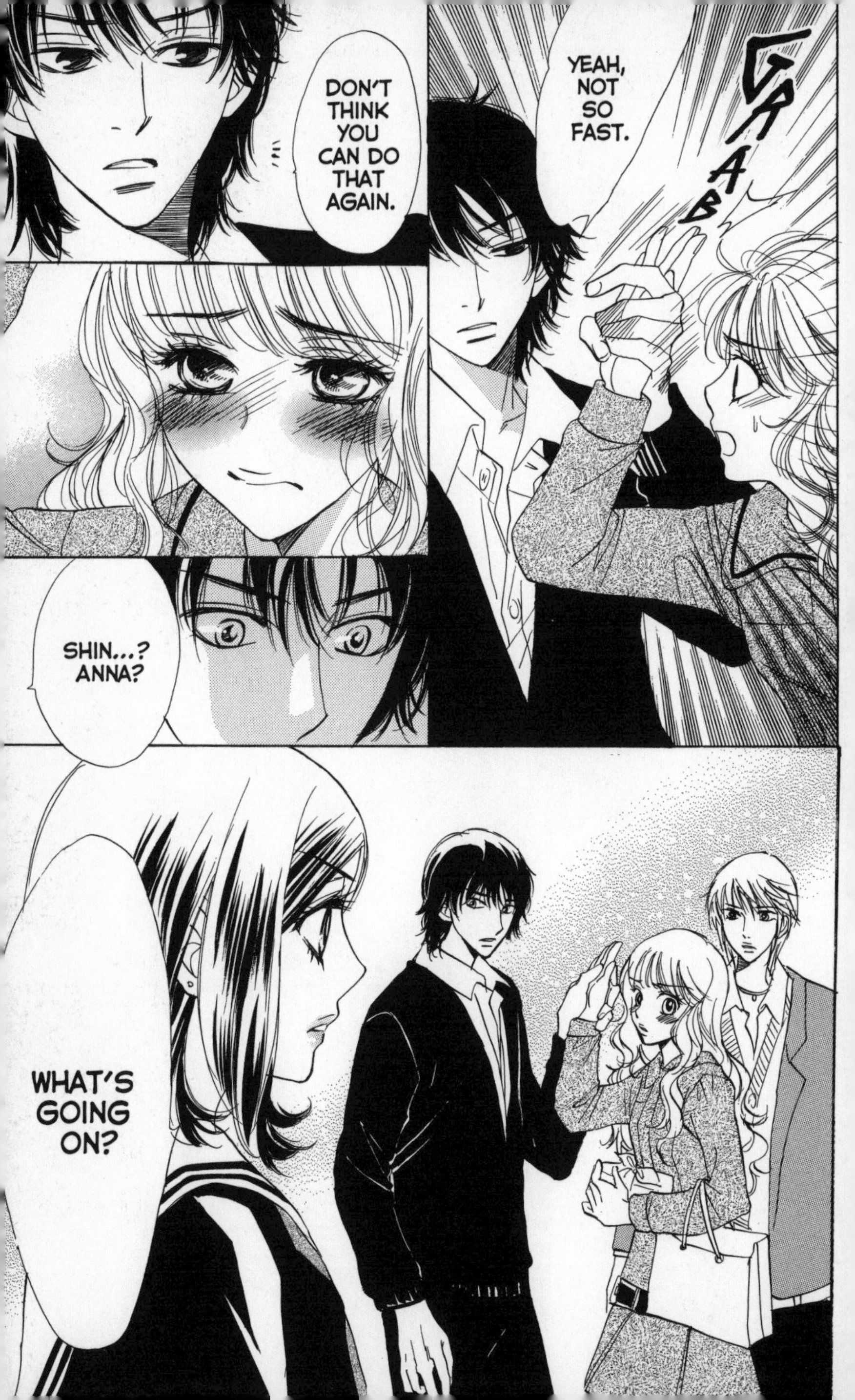
GRAB
YEAH, NOT SO FAST.
DON'T THINK YOU CAN DO THAT AGAIN.
SHIN...? ANNA?
WHAT'S GOING ON?

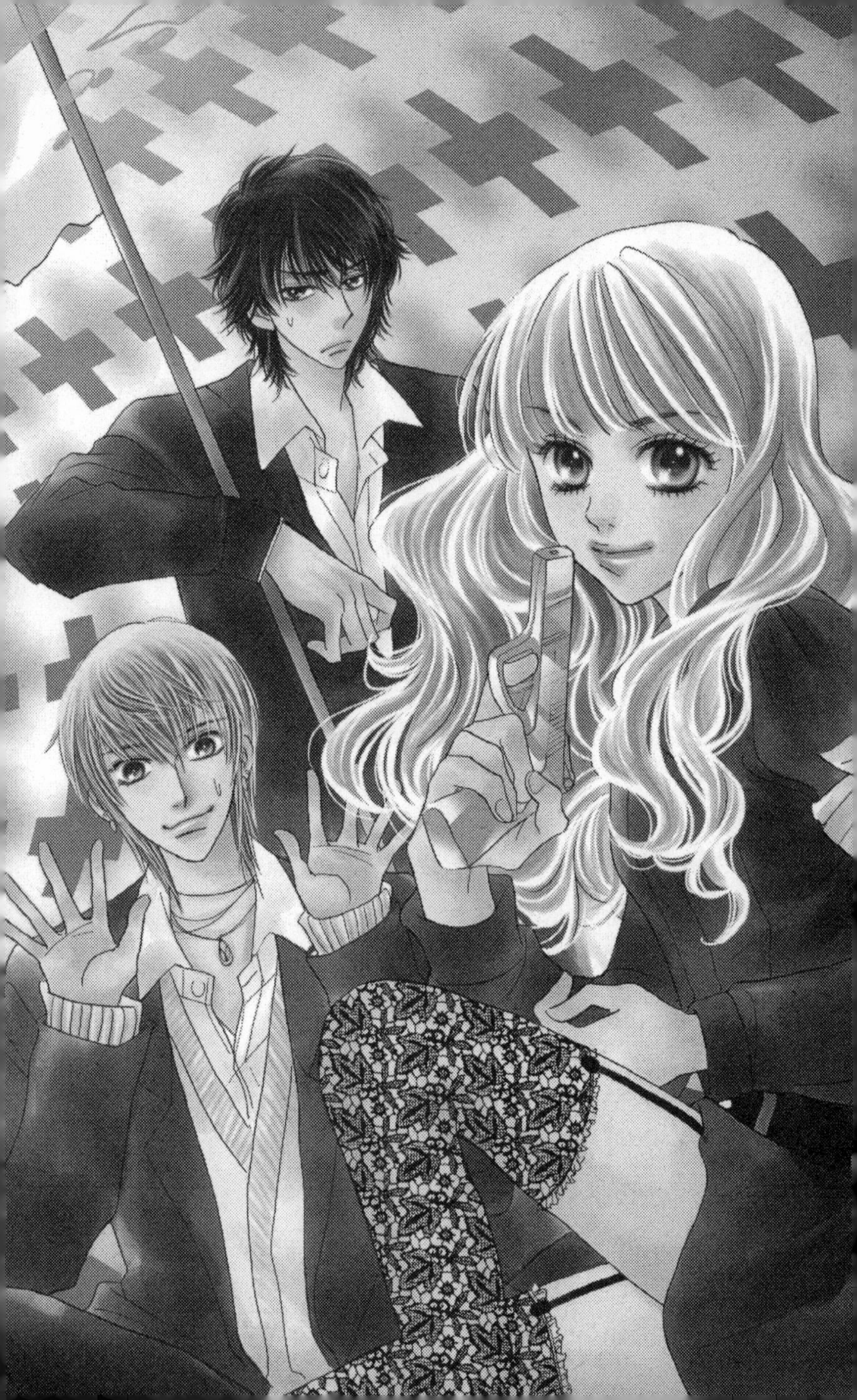

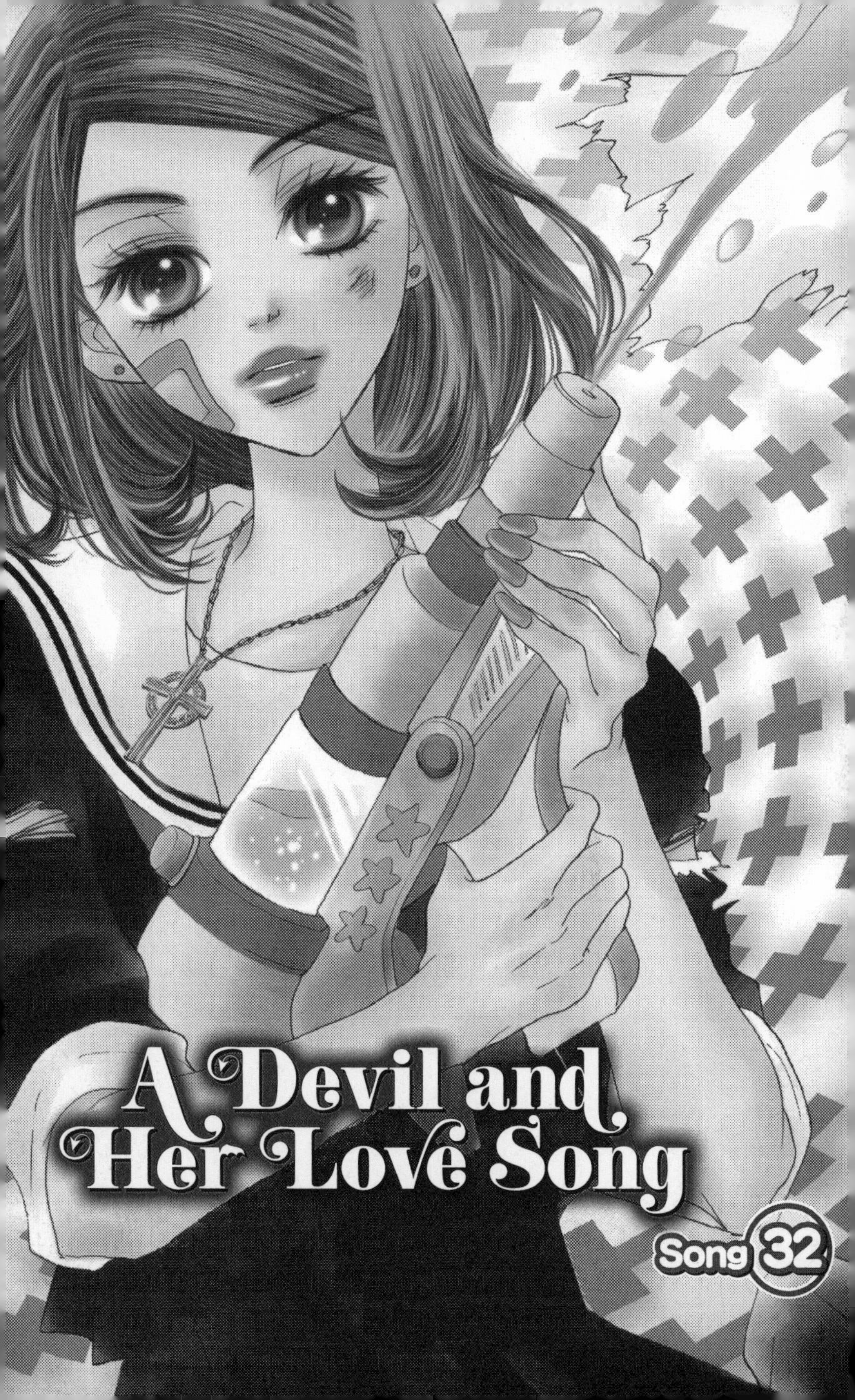
A Devil and Her Love Song
Song 32

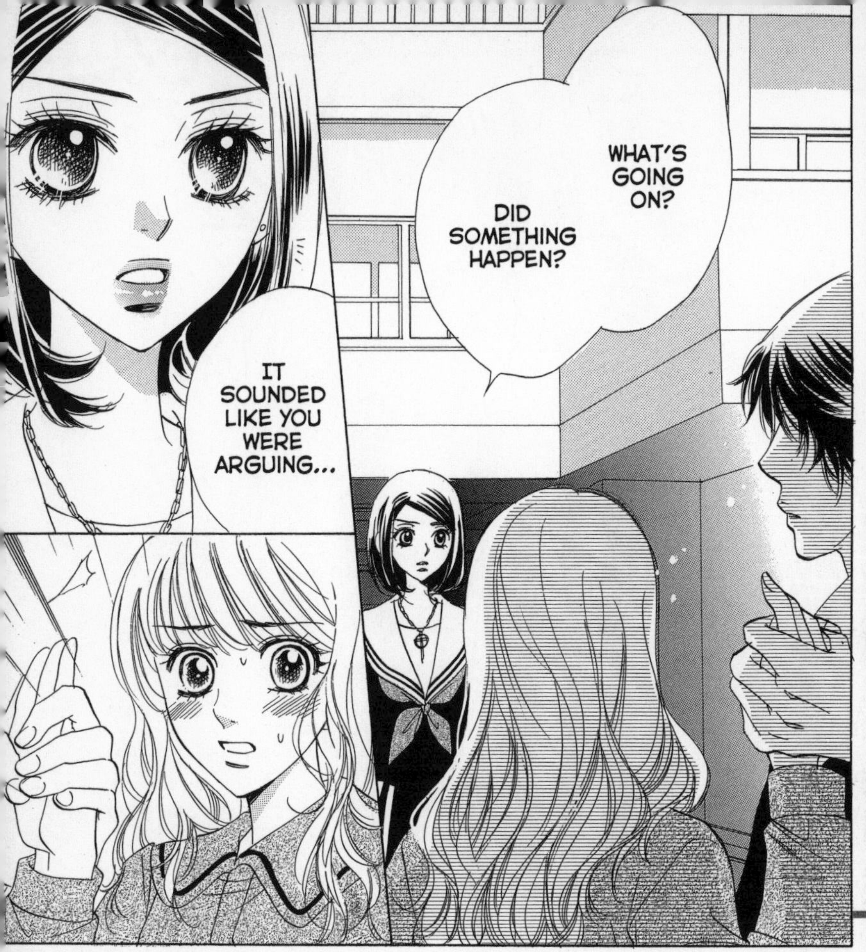
WHAT'S GOING ON?
DID SOMETHING HAPPEN?
IT SOUNDED LIKE YOU WERE ARGUING...

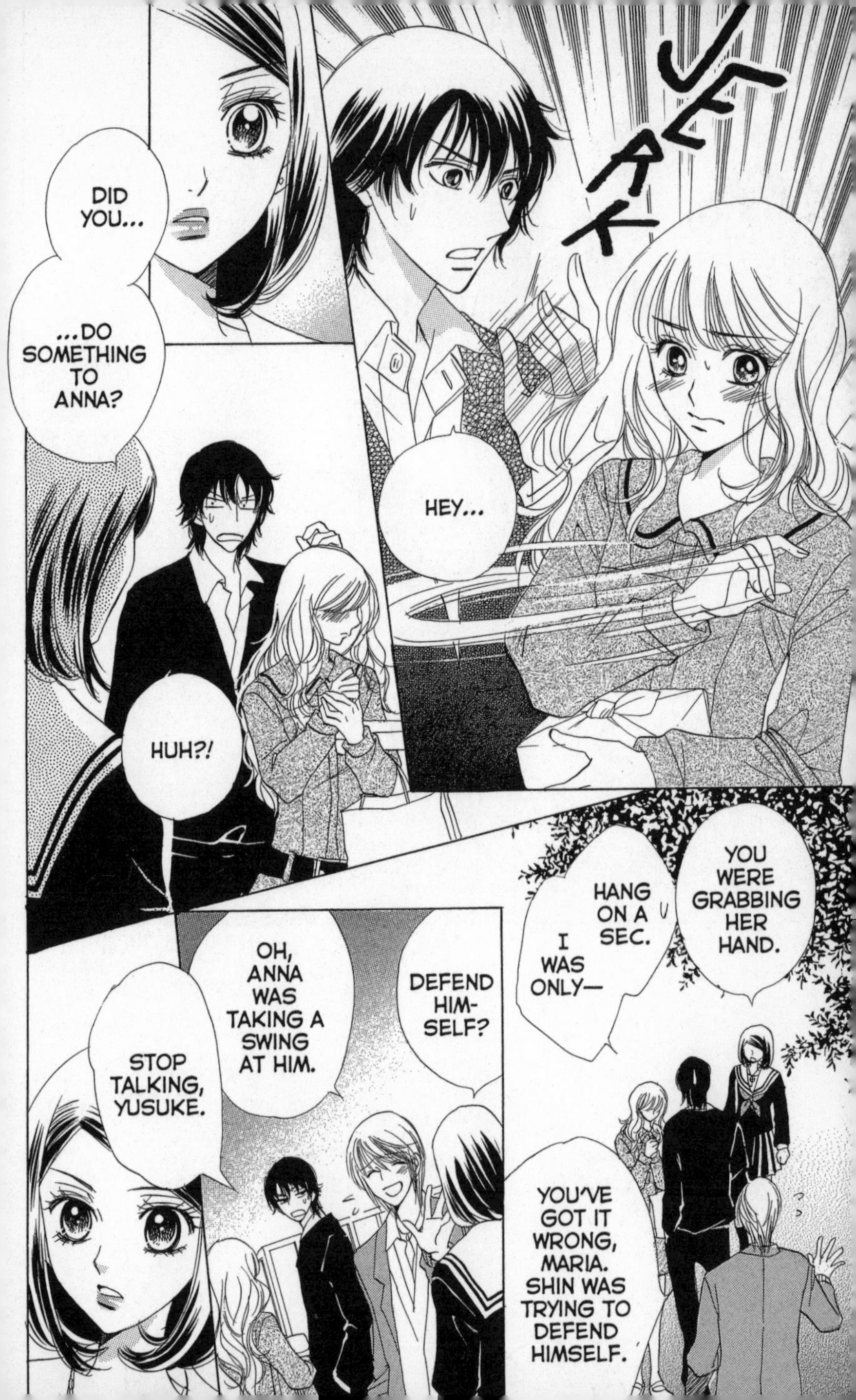
JERK
HEY...
DID YOU...
...DO SOMETHING TO ANNA?
HUH?!
YOU WERE GRABBING HER HAND.
HANG ON A SEC.
I WAS ONLY—
YOU'VE GOT IT WRONG, MARIA. SHIN WAS TRYING TO DEFEND HIMSELF.
DEFEND HIMSELF?
OH, ANNA WAS TAKING A SWING AT HIM.
STOP TALKING, YUSUKE.

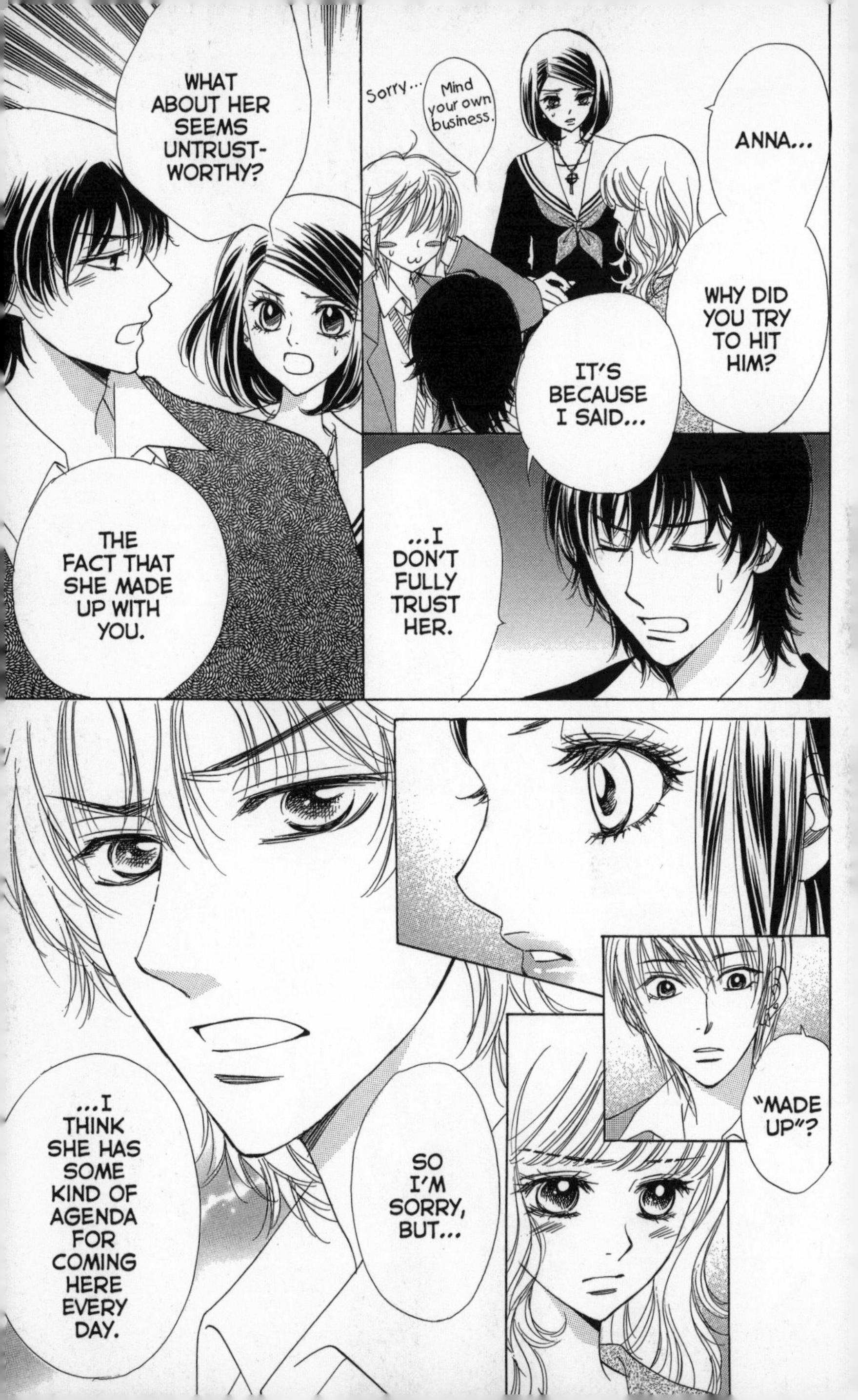
ANNA...
WHY DID YOU TRY TO HIT HIM?
Mind your own business.
Sorry...
IT'S BECAUSE I SAID...
...I DON'T FULLY TRUST HER.
WHAT ABOUT HER SEEMS UNTRUST-WORTHY?
THE FACT THAT SHE MADE UP WITH YOU.
"MADE UP"?
SO I'M SORRY, BUT...
...I THINK SHE HAS SOME KIND OF AGENDA FOR COMING HERE EVERY DAY.

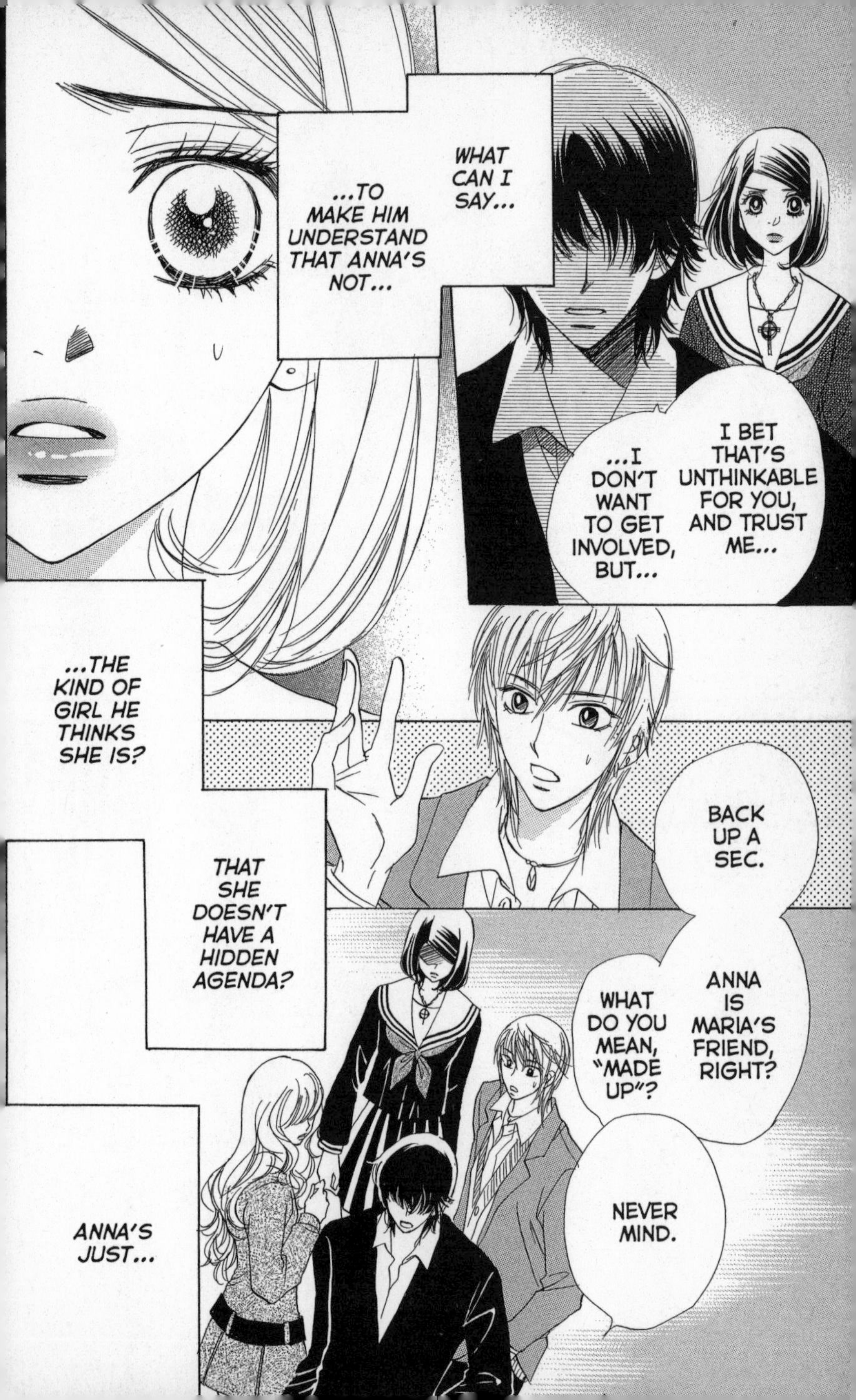
I BET THAT'S UNTHINKABLE FOR YOU, AND TRUST ME...
...I DON'T WANT TO GET INVOLVED, BUT...
WHAT CAN I SAY...
...TO MAKE HIM UNDERSTAND THAT ANNA'S NOT...
...THE KIND OF GIRL HE THINKS SHE IS?
BACK UP A SEC.
THAT SHE DOESN'T HAVE A HIDDEN AGENDA?
ANNA IS MARIA'S FRIEND, RIGHT?
WHAT DO YOU MEAN, "MADE UP"?
NEVER MIND.
ANNA'S JUST...

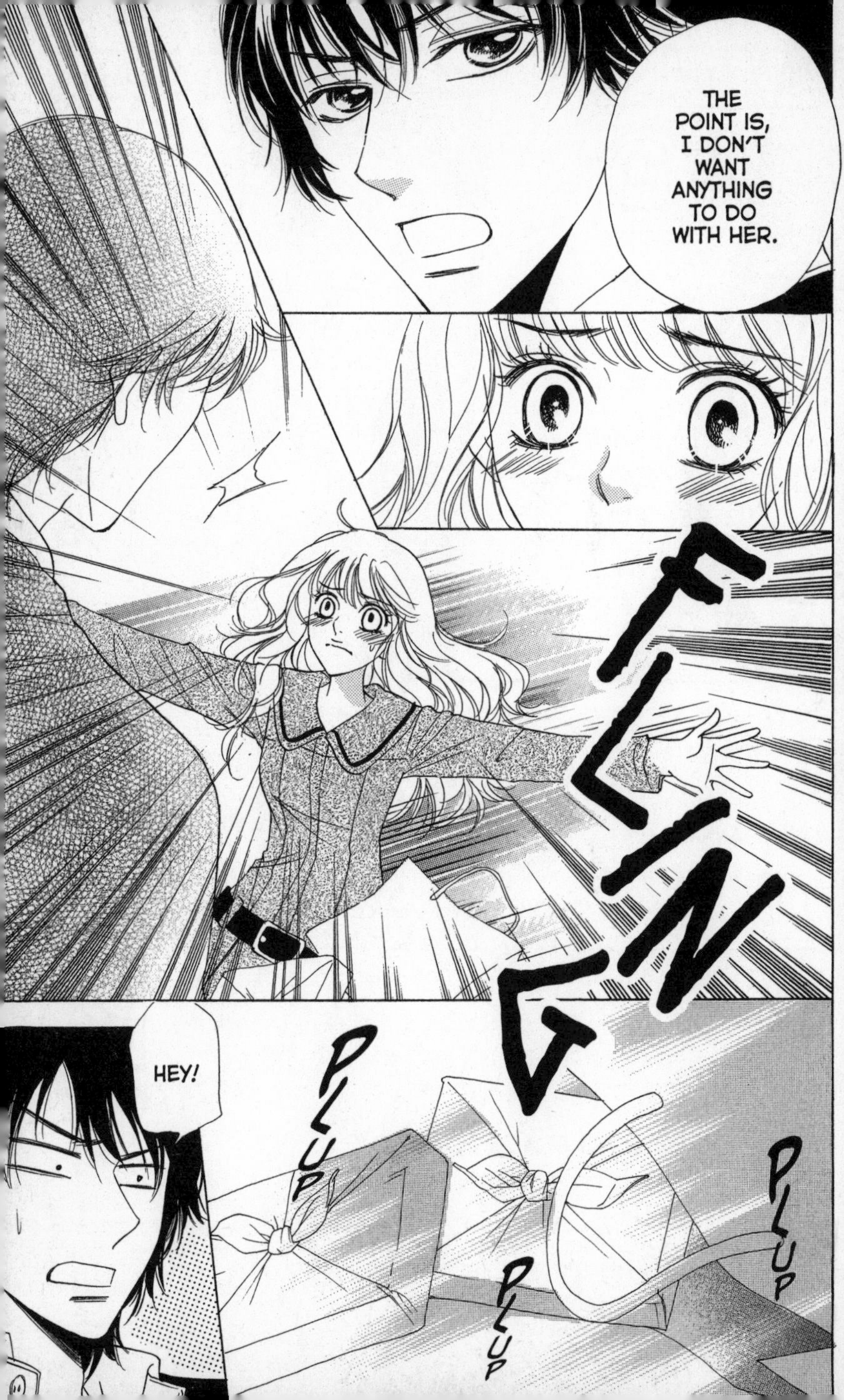
THE POINT IS, I DON'T WANT ANYTHING TO DO WITH HER.
FLING
PLUP
PLUP
PLUP
PLUP
HEY!

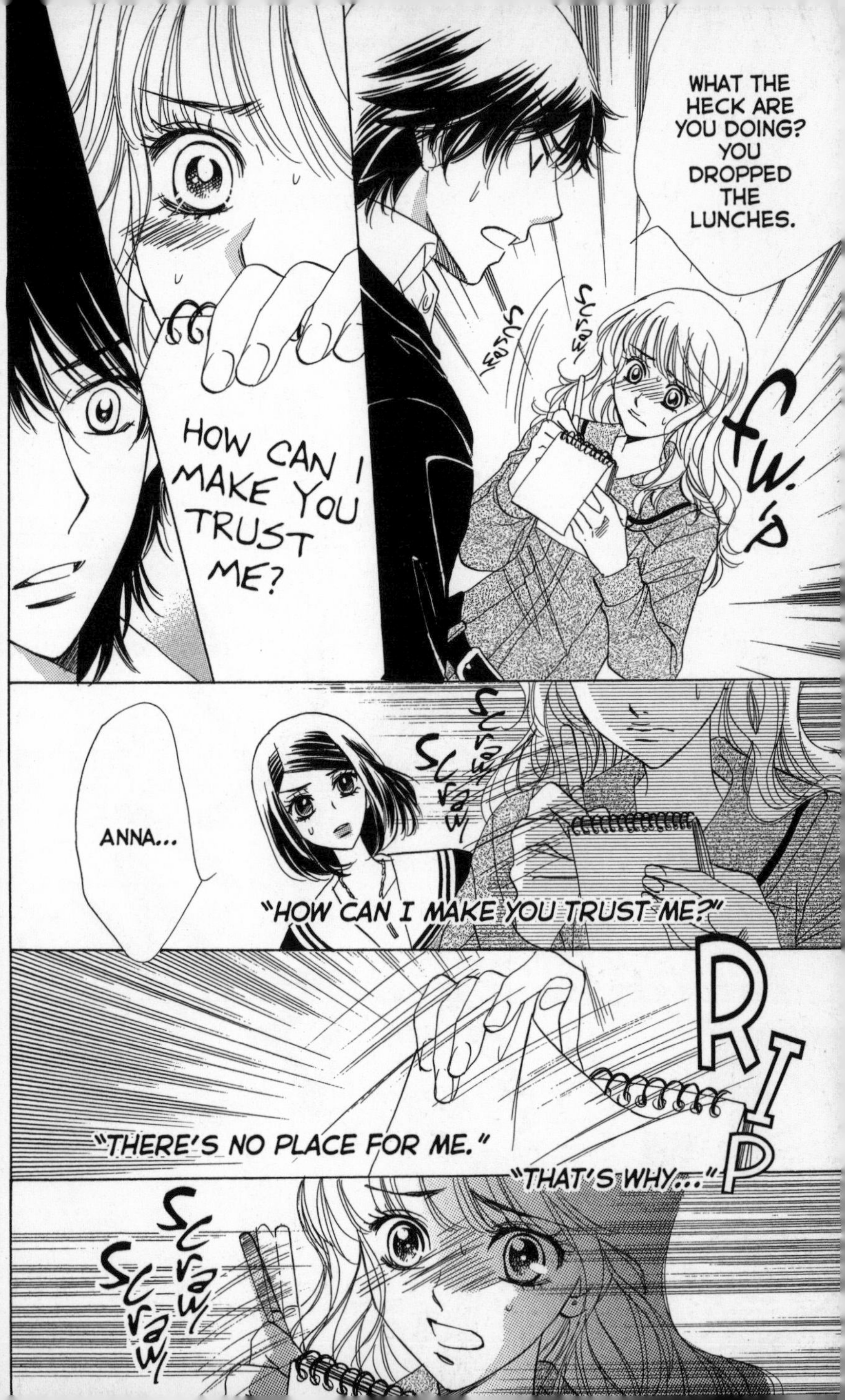
WHAT THE HECK ARE YOU DOING? YOU DROPPED THE LUNCHES.
FWIP
SCRAW SCRAW
HOW CAN I MAKE YOU TRUST ME?
SCRAW SCRAW
ANNA...
"HOW CAN I MAKE YOU TRUST ME?"
RIP
"THERE'S NO PLACE FOR ME."
"THAT'S WHY..."
SCRAW SCRAW

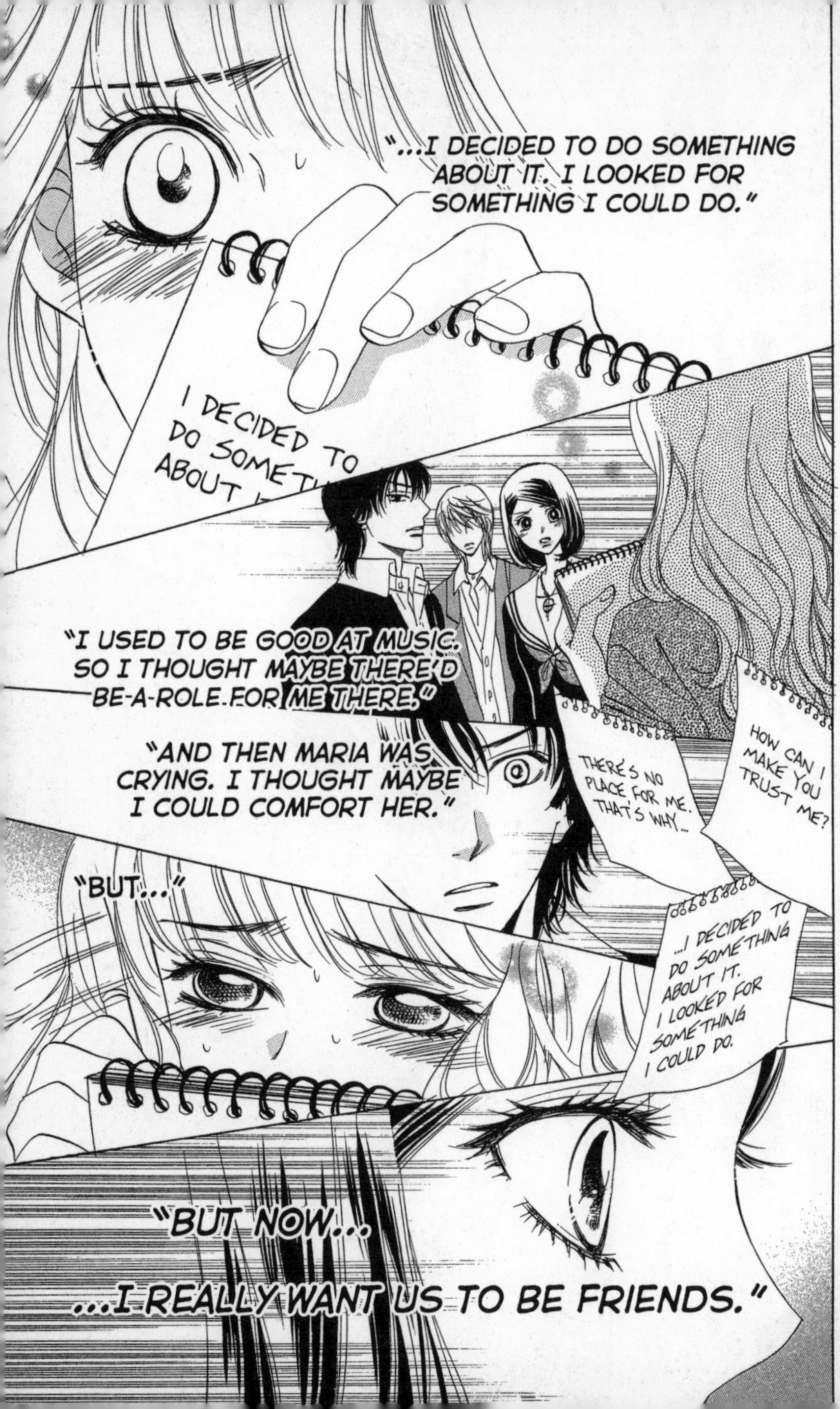
"...I DECIDED TO DO SOMETHING ABOUT IT. I LOOKED FOR SOMETHING I COULD DO."
I DECIDED TO DO SOMET ABOUT
"I USED TO BE GOOD AT MUSIC. SO I THOUGHT MAYBE THERE'D BE A ROLE FOR ME THERE."
HOW CAN I MAKE YOU TRUST ME?
THERE'S NO PLACE FOR ME. THAT'S WHY...
"AND THEN MARIA WAS CRYING. I THOUGHT MAYBE I COULD COMFORT HER."
...I DECIDED TO DO SOMETHING ABOUT IT. I LOOKED FOR SOMETHING I COULD DO.
"BUT..."
"BUT NOW...
...I REALLY WANT US TO BE FRIENDS."

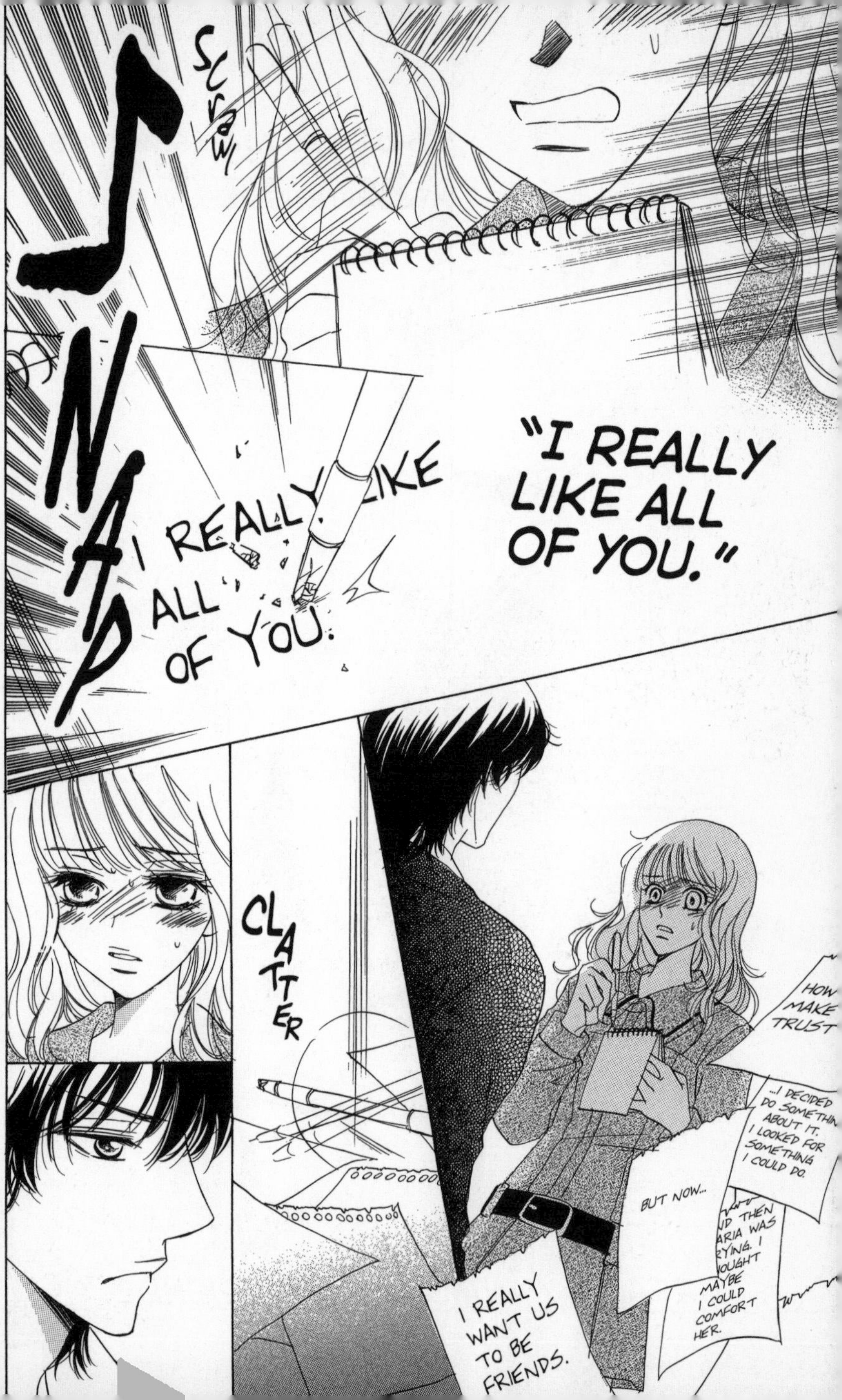
SCRAW
"I REALLY LIKE ALL OF YOU."
I REALLY LIKE ALL OF YOU.
SNAP
CLATTER
HOW MAKE TRUST
...I DECIDED DO SOMETHIN ABOUT IT. I LOOKED FOR SOMETHING I COULD DO.
ND THEN ARIA WAS RYING. I HOUGHT MAYBE I COULD COMFORT HER.
BUT NOW...
I REALLY WANT US TO BE FRIENDS.

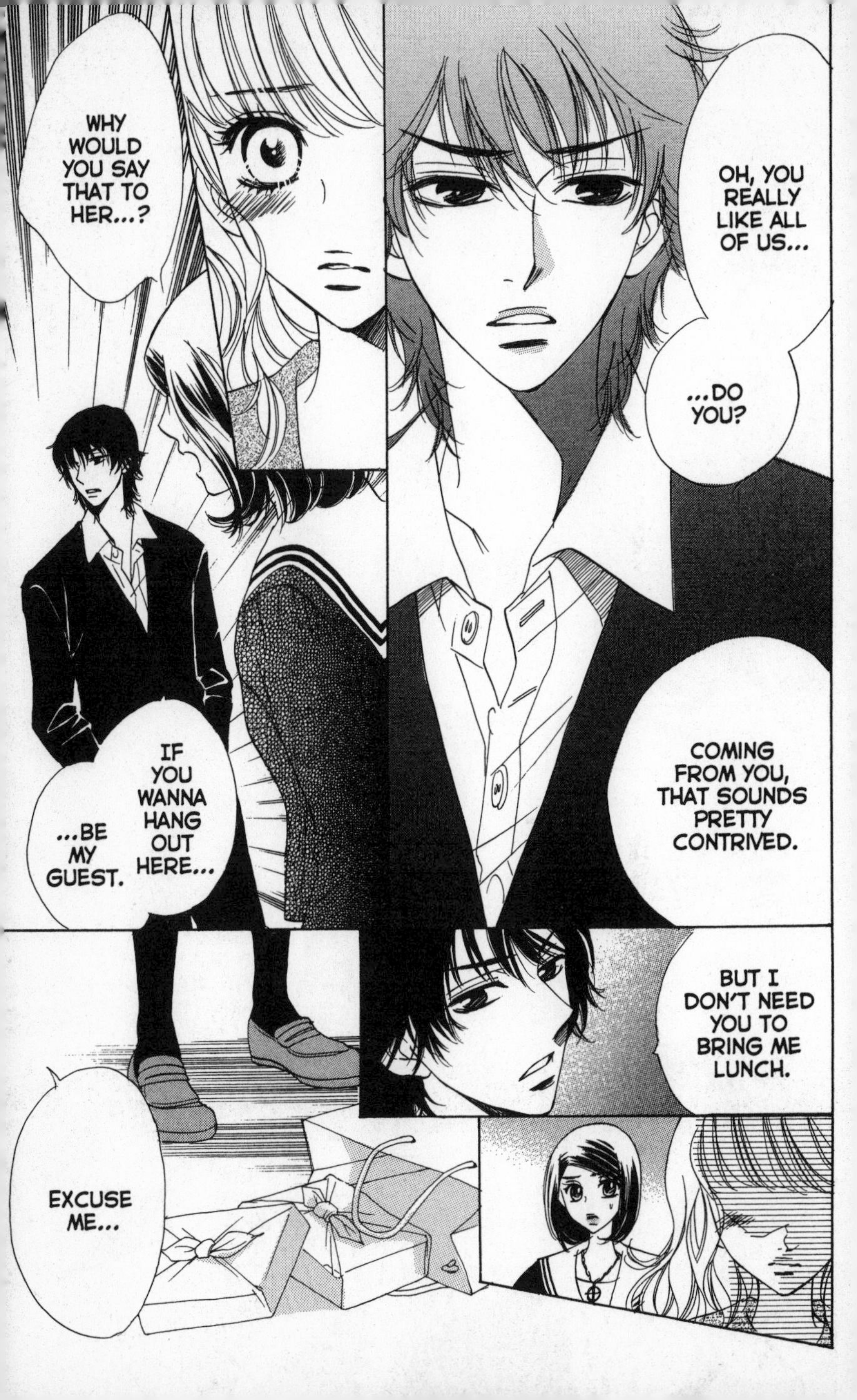
OH, YOU REALLY LIKE ALL OF US...
...DO YOU?
COMING FROM YOU, THAT SOUNDS PRETTY CONTRIVED.
WHY WOULD YOU SAY THAT TO HER...?
IF YOU WANNA HANG OUT HERE...
...BE MY GUEST.
BUT I DON'T NEED YOU TO BRING ME LUNCH.
EXCUSE ME...

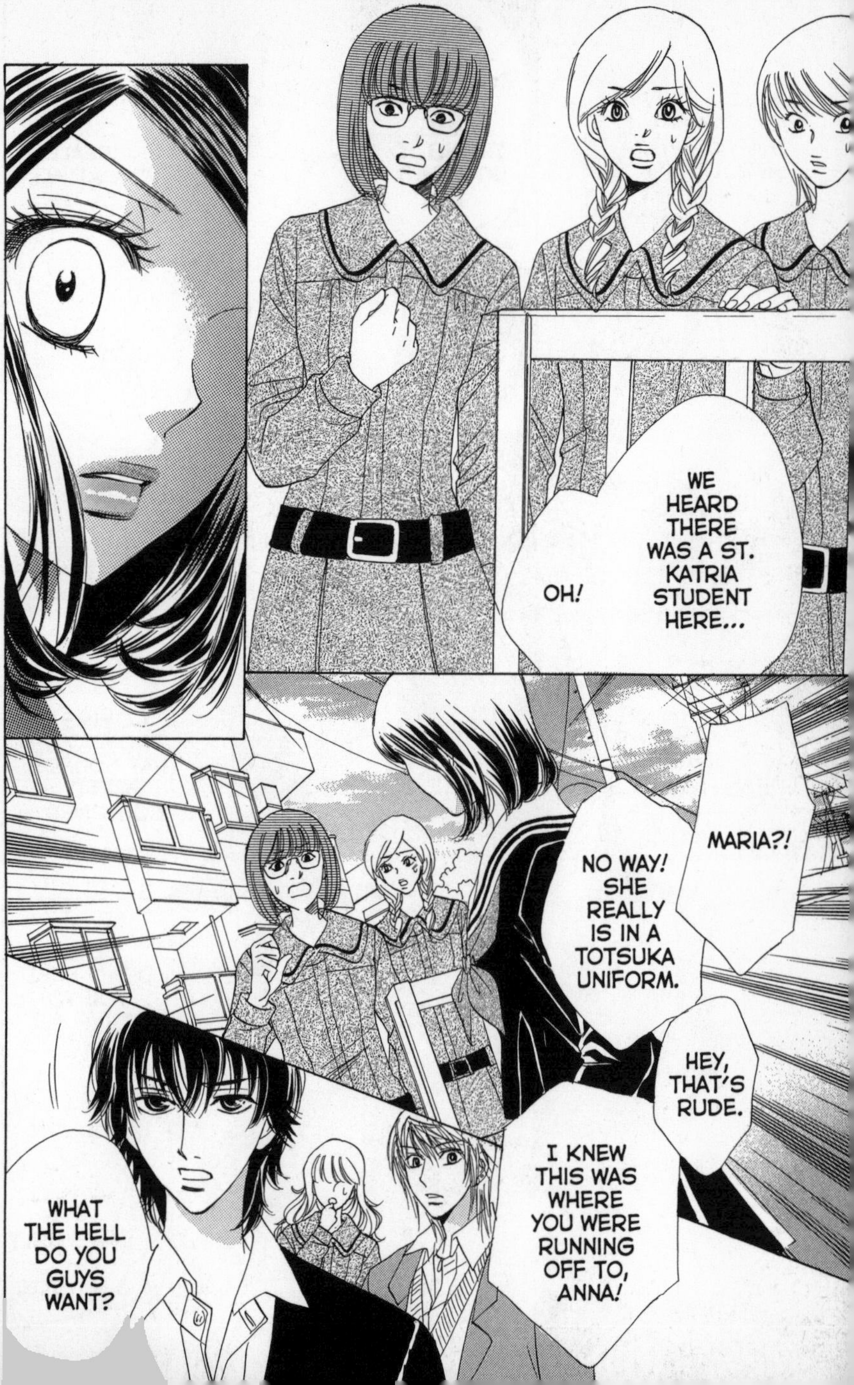
WE HEARD THERE WAS A ST. KATRIA STUDENT HERE...
OH!
MARIA?!
NO WAY! SHE REALLY IS IN A TOTSUKA UNIFORM.
HEY, THAT'S RUDE.
I KNEW THIS WAS WHERE YOU WERE RUNNING OFF TO, ANNA!
WHAT THE HELL DO YOU GUYS WANT?

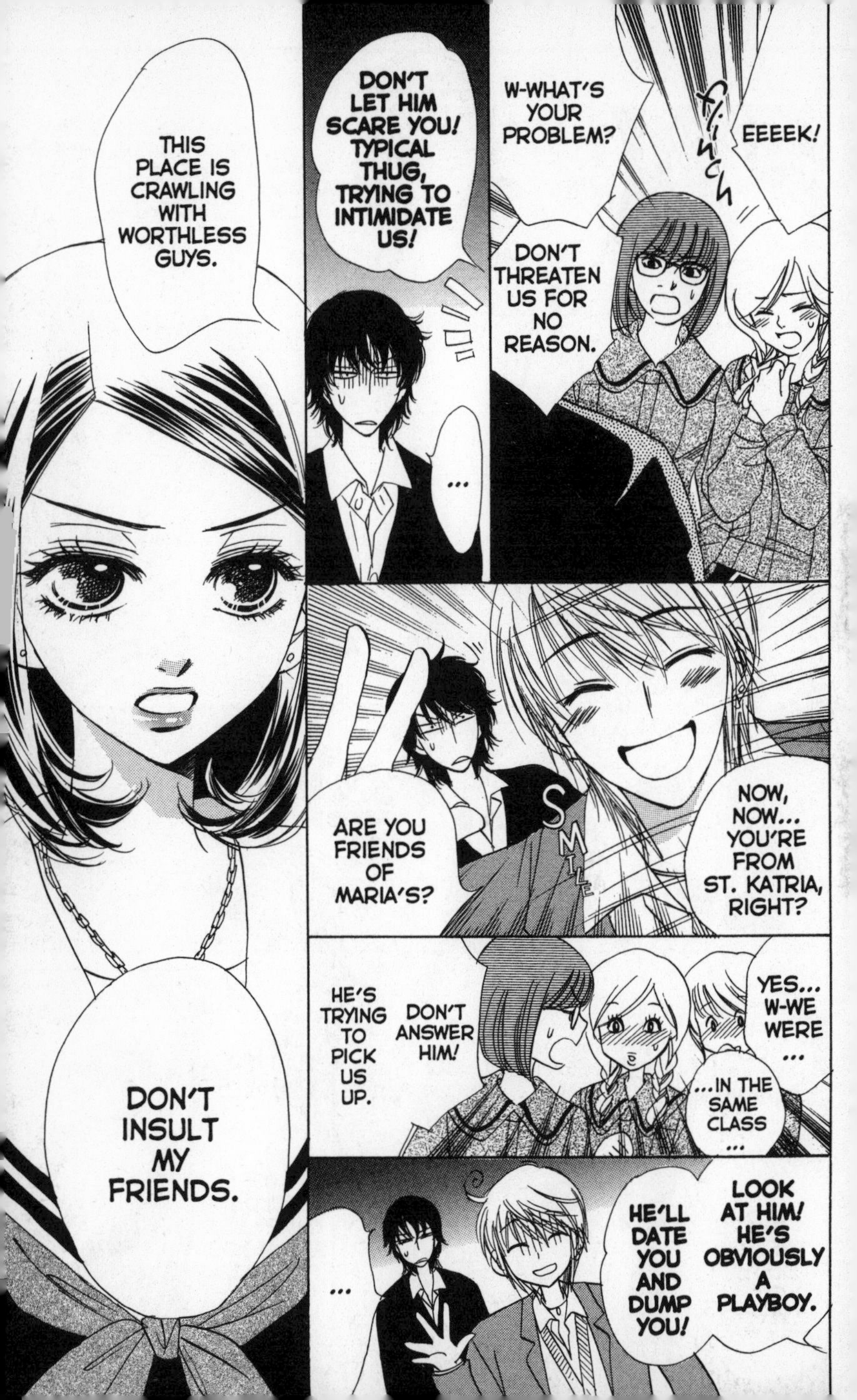
EEEK!
flinch
W-WHAT'S YOUR PROBLEM?
DON'T THREATEN US FOR NO REASON.
DON'T LET HIM SCARE YOU! TYPICAL THUG, TRYING TO INTIMIDATE US!
...
NOW, NOW... YOU'RE FROM ST. KATRIA, RIGHT?
SMILE
ARE YOU FRIENDS OF MARIA'S?
YES... W-WE WERE ...
...IN THE SAME CLASS ...
DON'T ANSWER HIM!
HE'S TRYING TO PICK US UP.
LOOK AT HIM! HE'S OBVIOUSLY A PLAYBOY.
HE'LL DATE YOU AND DUMP YOU!
...
THIS PLACE IS CRAWLING WITH WORTHLESS GUYS.
DON'T INSULT MY FRIENDS.

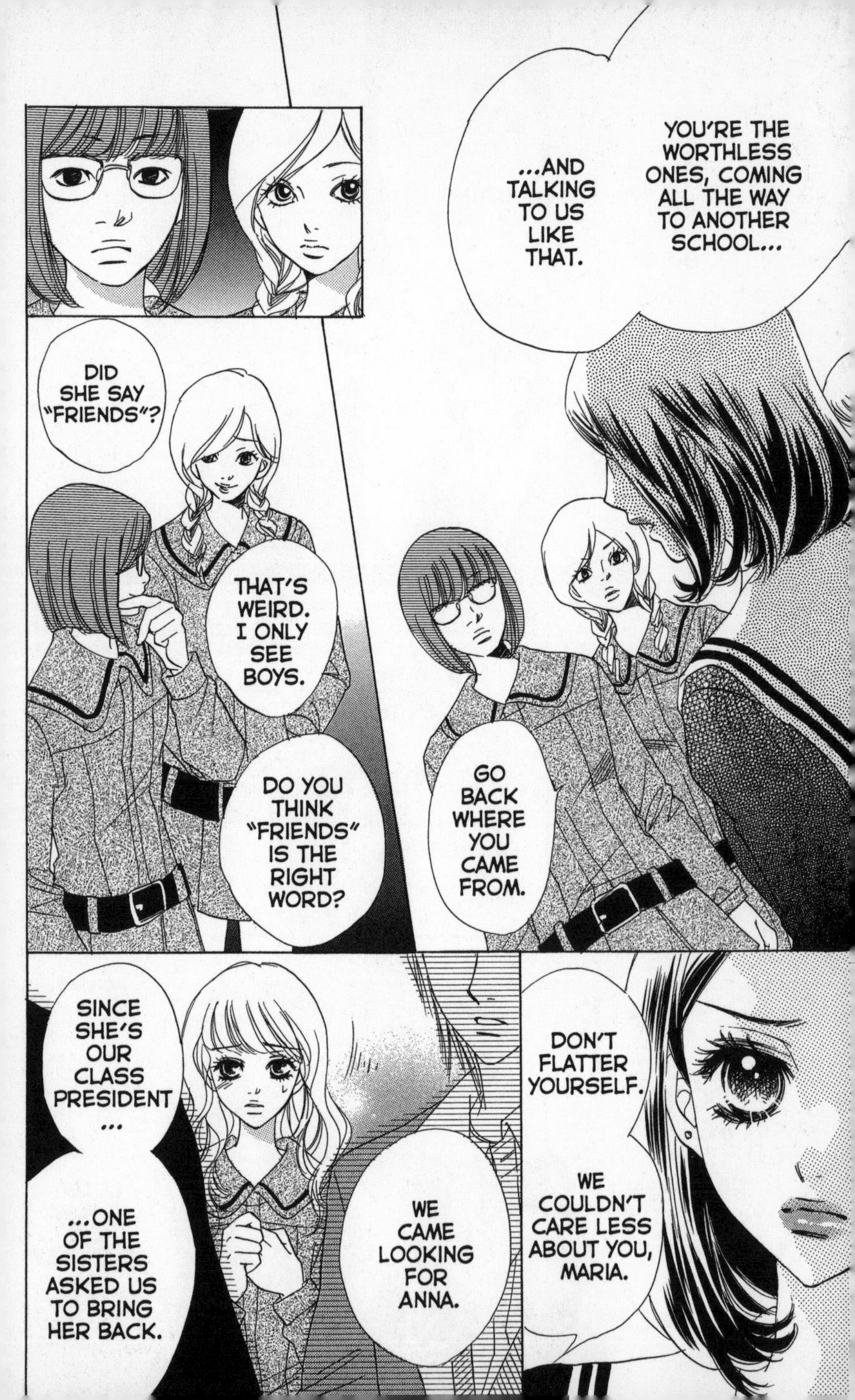
YOU'RE THE WORTHLESS ONES, COMING ALL THE WAY TO ANOTHER SCHOOL...
...AND TALKING TO US LIKE THAT.
GO BACK WHERE YOU CAME FROM.
DID SHE SAY "FRIENDS"?
THAT'S WEIRD. I ONLY SEE BOYS.
DO YOU THINK "FRIENDS" IS THE RIGHT WORD?
DON'T FLATTER YOURSELF.
WE COULDN'T CARE LESS ABOUT YOU, MARIA.
WE CAME LOOKING FOR ANNA.
SINCE SHE'S OUR CLASS PRESIDENT...
...ONE OF THE SISTERS ASKED US TO BRING HER BACK.

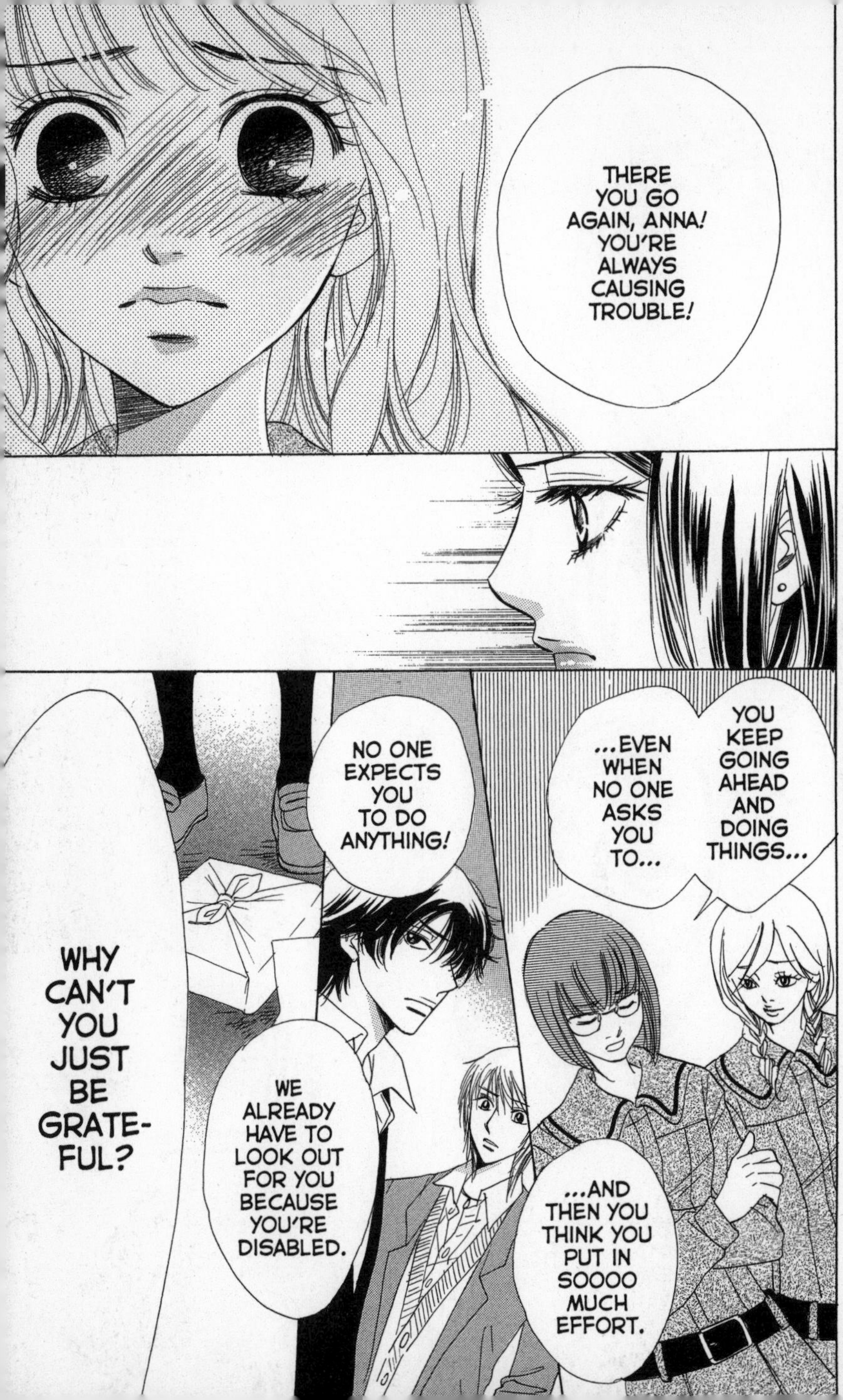
THERE YOU GO AGAIN, ANNA! YOU'RE ALWAYS CAUSING TROUBLE!
YOU KEEP GOING AHEAD AND DOING THINGS...
...EVEN WHEN NO ONE ASKS YOU TO...
NO ONE EXPECTS YOU TO DO ANYTHING!
...AND THEN YOU THINK YOU PUT IN SOOOO MUCH EFFORT.
WE ALREADY HAVE TO LOOK OUT FOR YOU BECAUSE YOU'RE DISABLED.
WHY CAN'T YOU JUST BE GRATE-FUL?

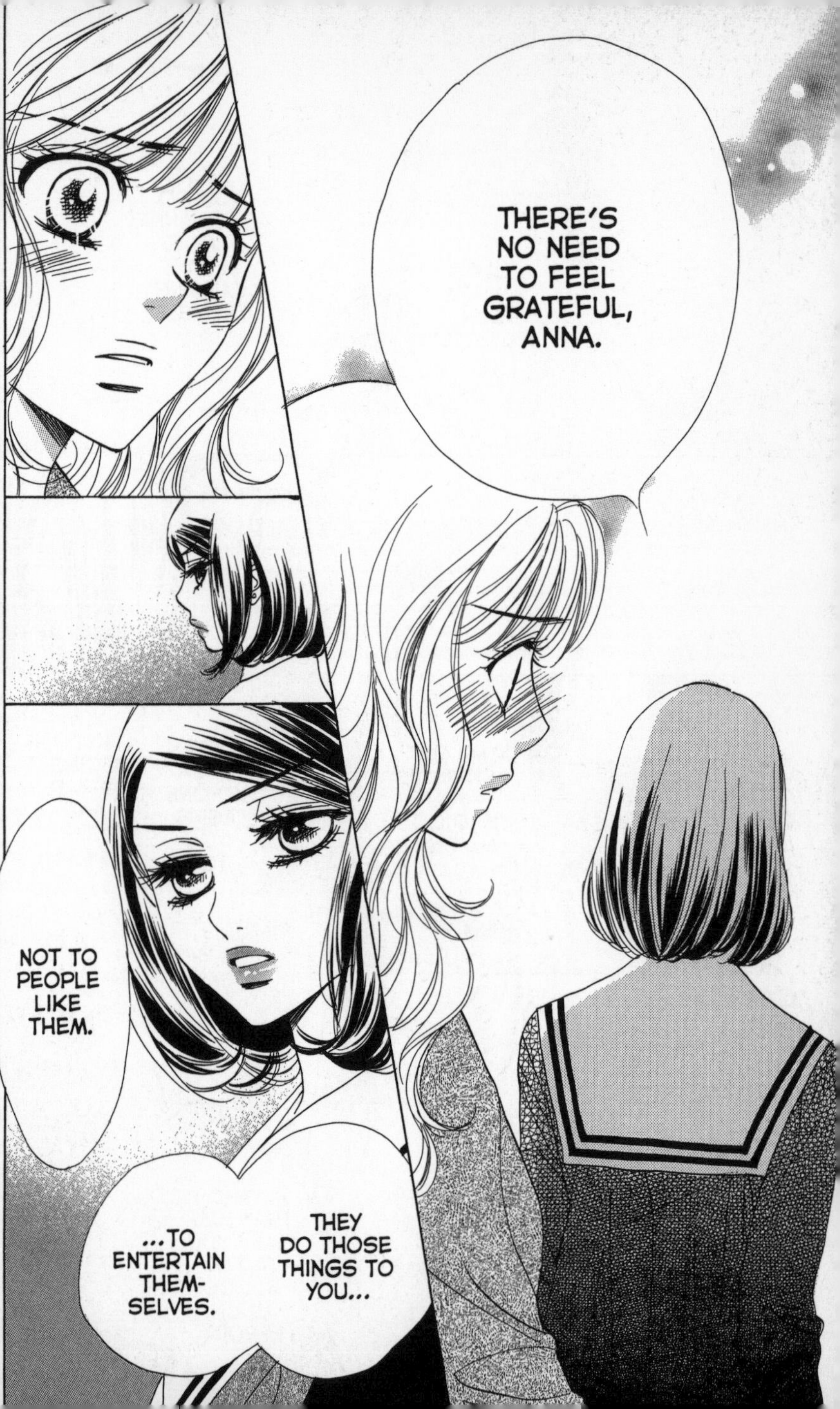
THERE'S NO NEED TO FEEL GRATEFUL, ANNA.
NOT TO PEOPLE LIKE THEM.
THEY DO THOSE THINGS TO YOU...
...TO ENTERTAIN THEM-SELVES.

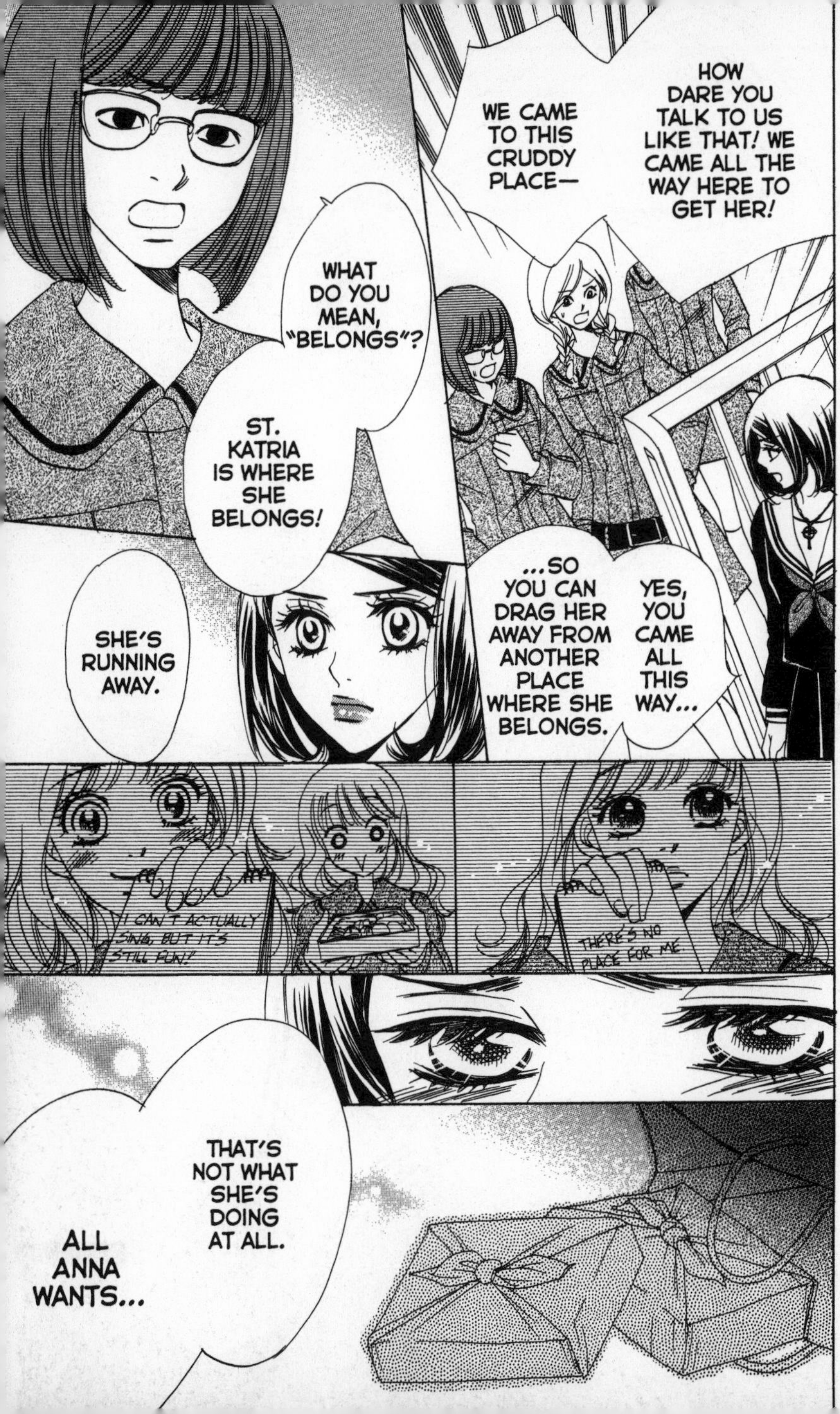
HOW DARE YOU TALK TO US LIKE THAT! WE CAME ALL THE WAY HERE TO GET HER!
WE CAME TO THIS CRUDDY PLACE—
YES, YOU CAME ALL THIS WAY...
...SO YOU CAN DRAG HER AWAY FROM ANOTHER PLACE WHERE SHE BELONGS.
WHAT DO YOU MEAN, "BELONGS"?
ST. KATRIA IS WHERE SHE BELONGS!
SHE'S RUNNING AWAY.
THERE'S NO PLACE FOR ME
I CAN'T ACTUALLY SING, BUT IT'S STILL FUN!
THAT'S NOT WHAT SHE'S DOING AT ALL.
ALL ANNA WANTS...

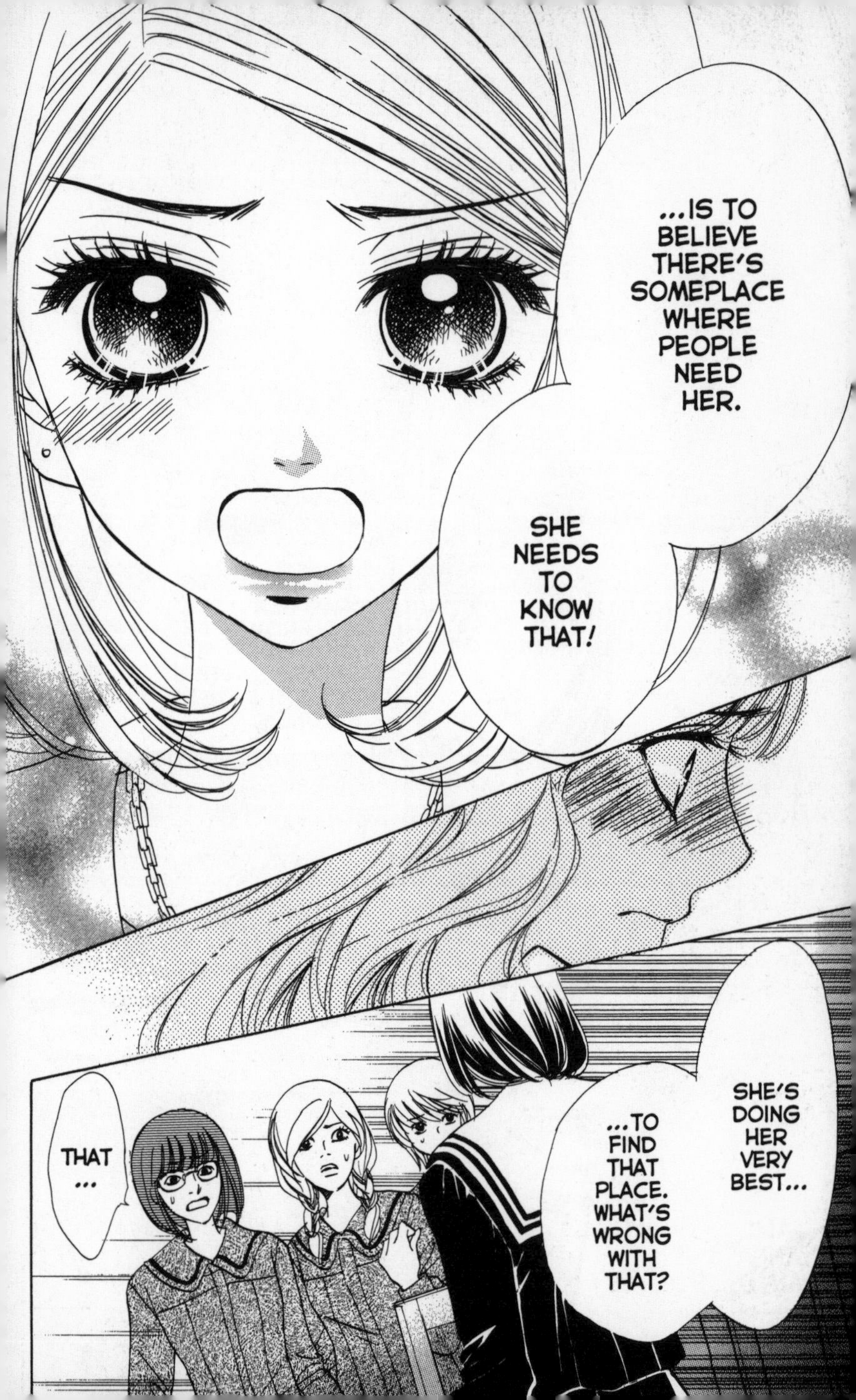
...IS TO BELIEVE THERE'S SOMEPLACE WHERE PEOPLE NEED HER.
SHE NEEDS TO KNOW THAT!
SHE'S DOING HER VERY BEST...
...TO FIND THAT PLACE. WHAT'S WRONG WITH THAT?
THAT ...

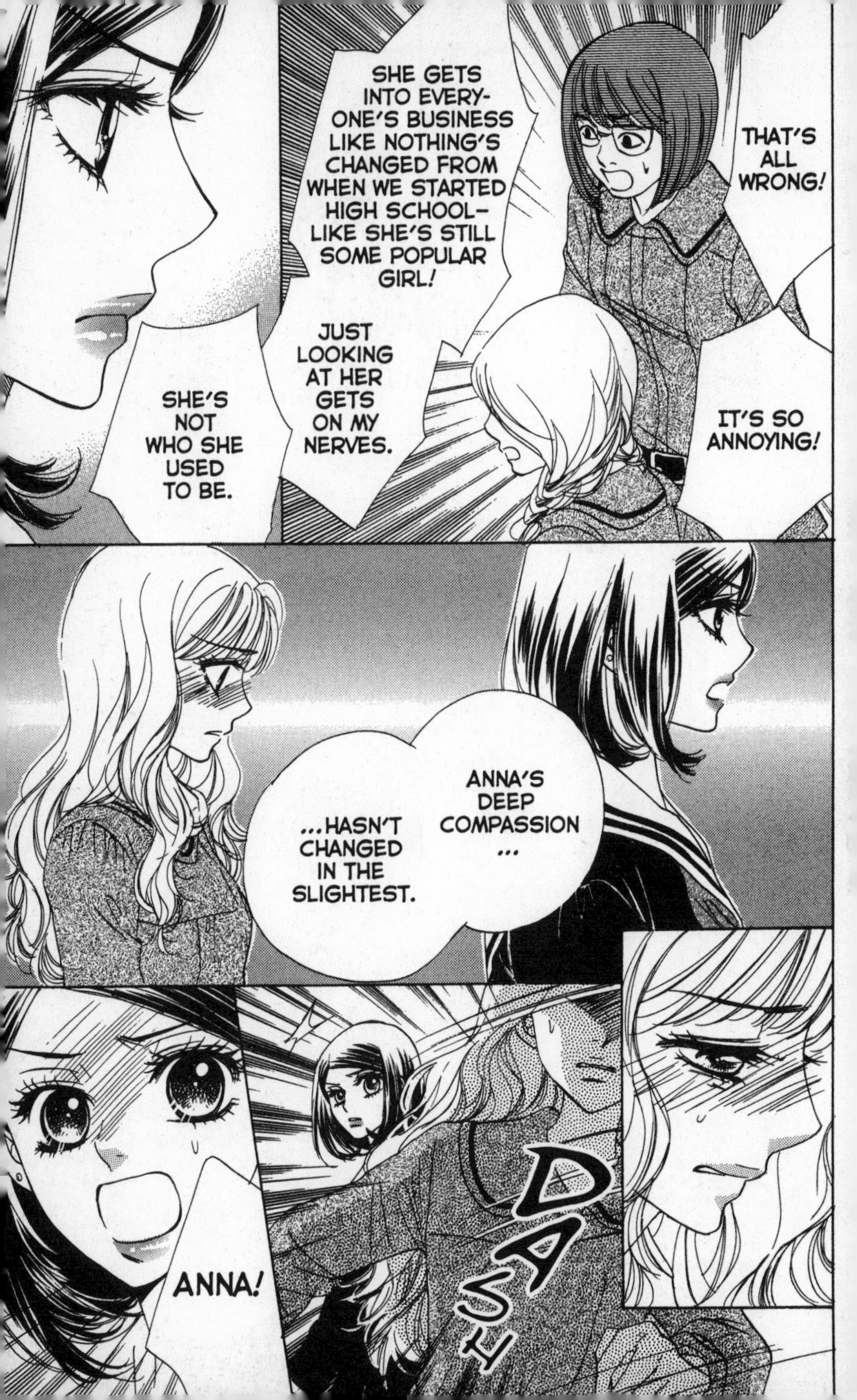
THAT'S ALL WRONG!
IT'S SO ANNOYING!
SHE GETS INTO EVERY-ONE'S BUSINESS LIKE NOTHING'S CHANGED FROM WHEN WE STARTED HIGH SCHOOL–LIKE SHE'S STILL SOME POPULAR GIRL!
JUST LOOKING AT HER GETS ON MY NERVES.
SHE'S NOT WHO SHE USED TO BE.
ANNA'S DEEP COMPASSION ...
...HASN'T CHANGED IN THE SLIGHTEST.
DASH
ANNA!

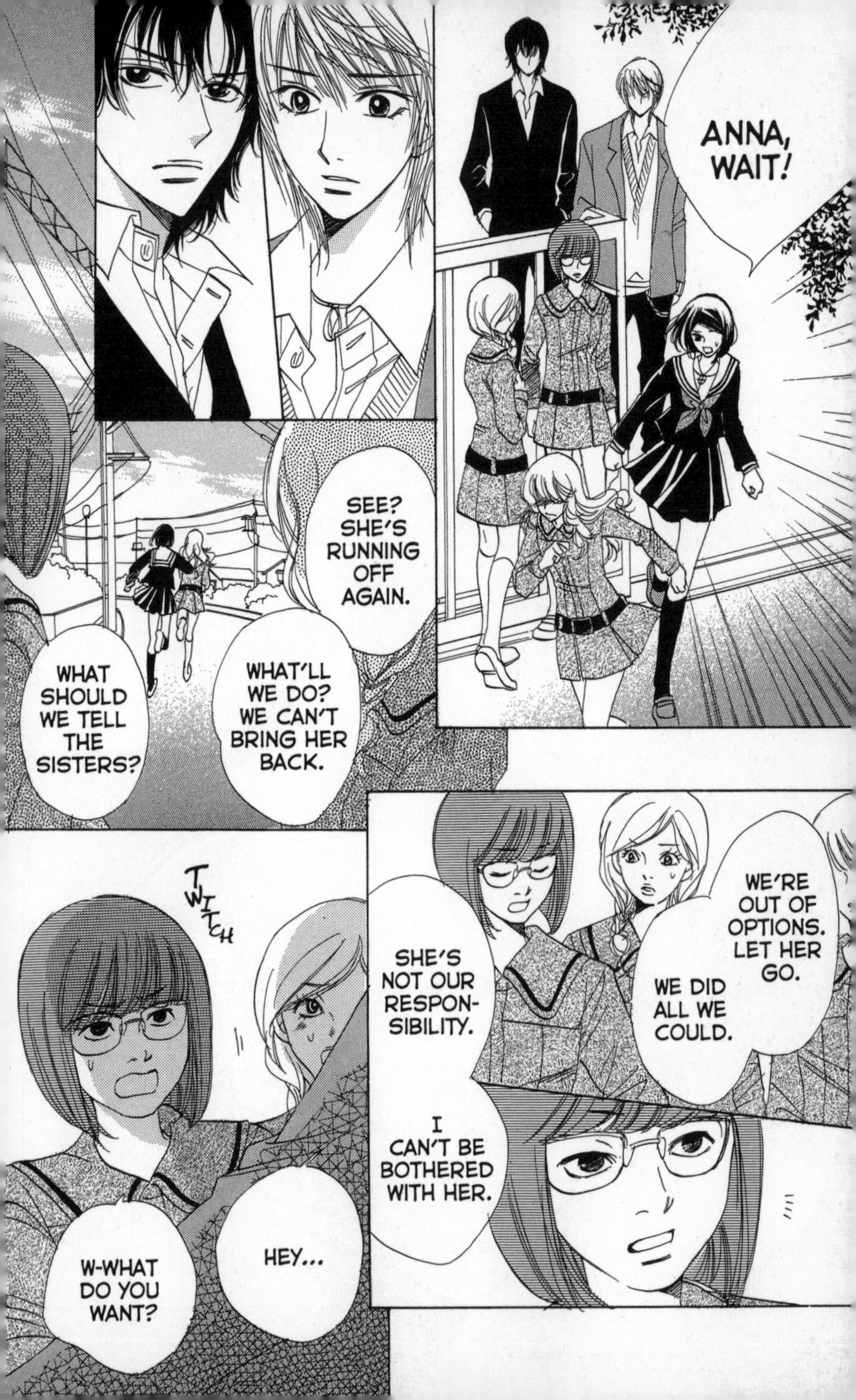
ANNA, WAIT!
SEE? SHE'S RUNNING OFF AGAIN.
WHAT'LL WE DO? WE CAN'T BRING HER BACK.
WHAT SHOULD WE TELL THE SISTERS?
WE'RE OUT OF OPTIONS. LET HER GO.
WE DID ALL WE COULD.
SHE'S NOT OUR RESPON-SIBILITY.
I CAN'T BE BOTHERED WITH HER.
TWITCH
HEY...
W-WHAT DO YOU WANT?

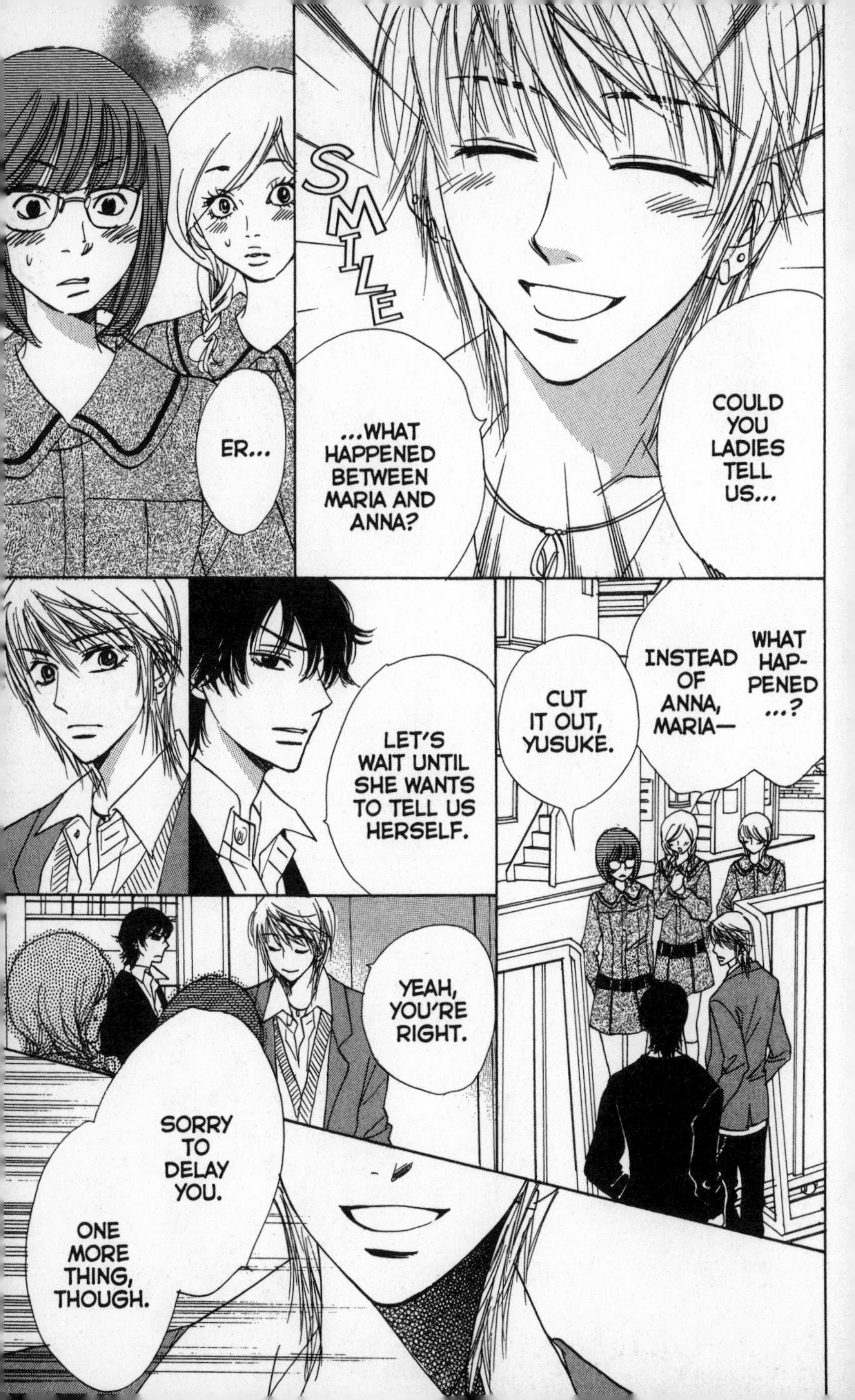
COULD YOU LADIES TELL US...
SMILE
...WHAT HAPPENED BETWEEN MARIA AND ANNA?
ER...
WHAT HAP-PENED ...?
INSTEAD OF ANNA, MARIA—
CUT IT OUT, YUSUKE.
LET'S WAIT UNTIL SHE WANTS TO TELL US HERSELF.
YEAH, YOU'RE RIGHT.
SORRY TO DELAY YOU.
ONE MORE THING, THOUGH.

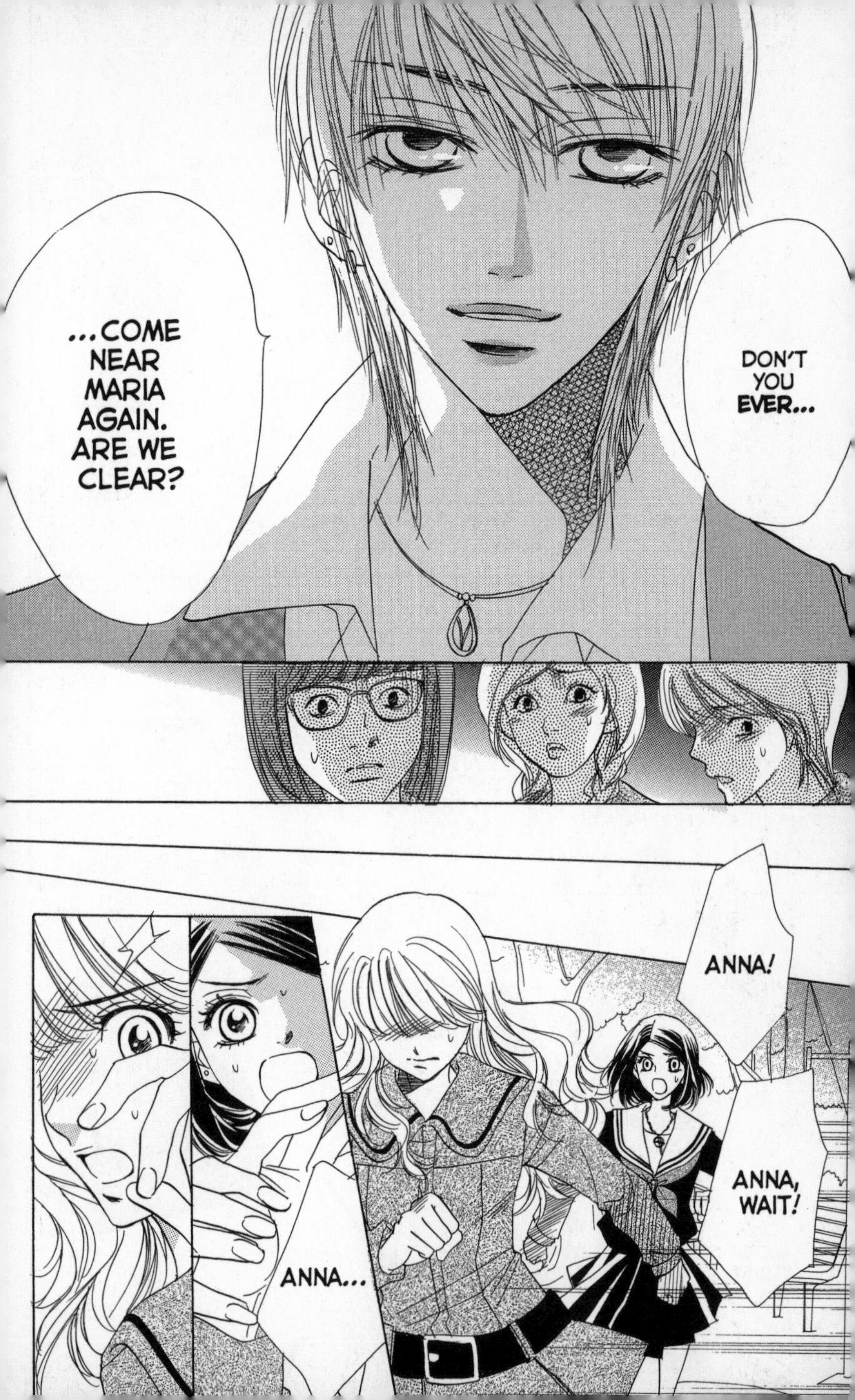
DON'T YOU EVER...
...COME NEAR MARIA AGAIN. ARE WE CLEAR?
ANNA!
ANNA, WAIT!
ANNA...

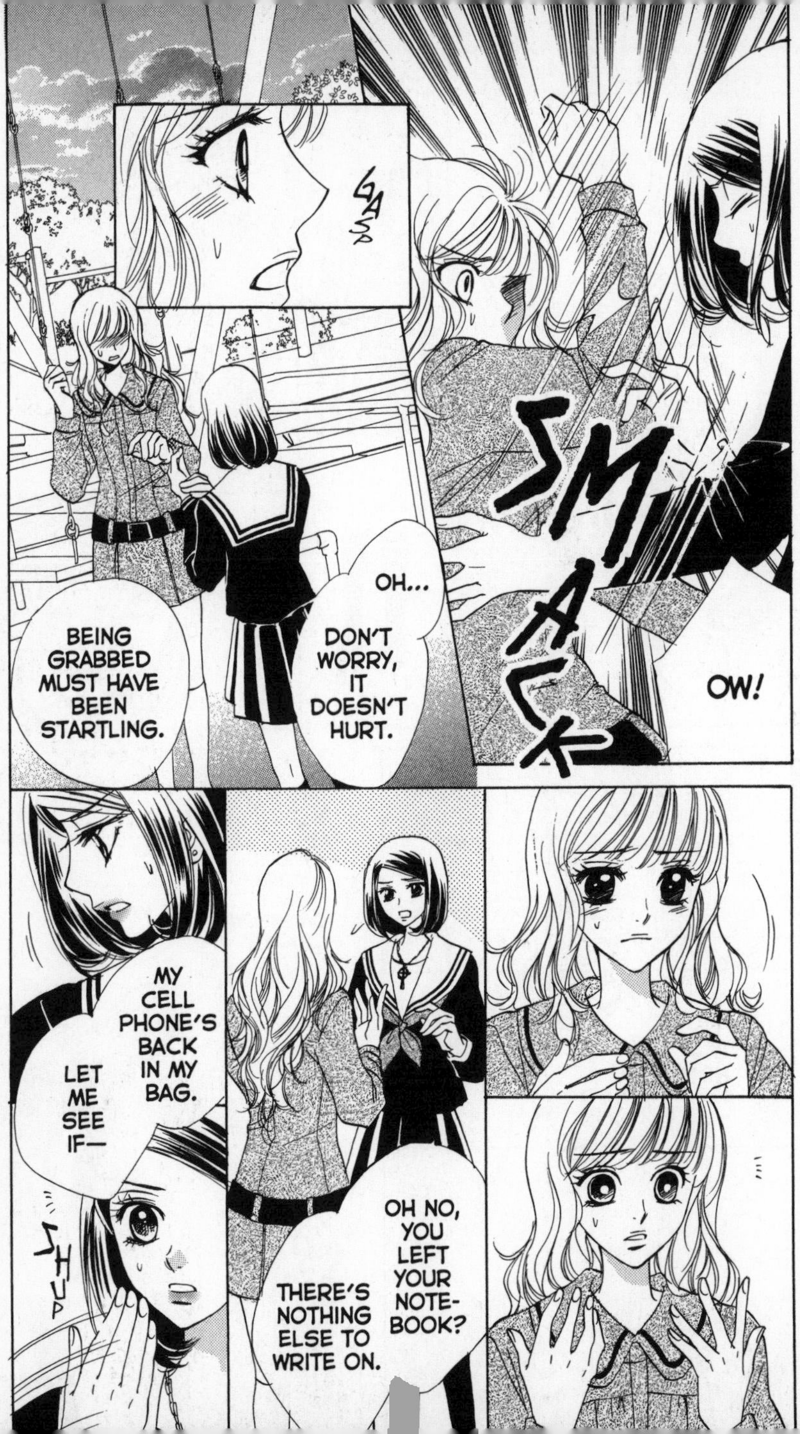
SMACK
OW!
GASP
OH...
DON'T WORRY, IT DOESN'T HURT.
BEING GRABBED MUST HAVE BEEN STARTLING.
OH NO, YOU LEFT YOUR NOTE-BOOK?
THERE'S NOTHING ELSE TO WRITE ON.
MY CELL PHONE'S BACK IN MY BAG.
LET ME SEE IF—
SHUP

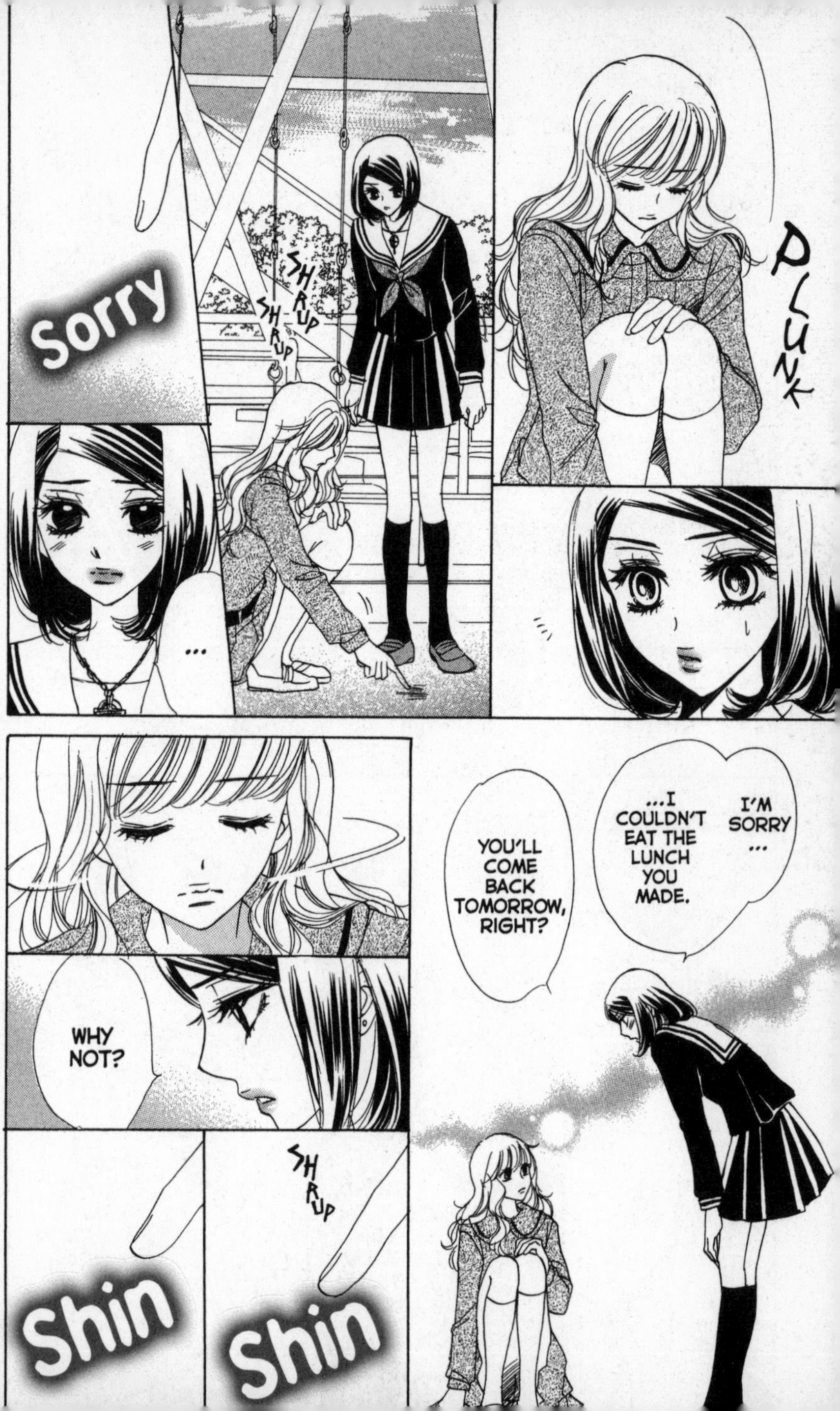
PLUNK
SHRUP
SHRUP
Sorry
...
I'M SORRY ...
...I COULDN'T EAT THE LUNCH YOU MADE.
YOU'LL COME BACK TOMORROW, RIGHT?
WHY NOT?
SHRUP
Shin
Shin

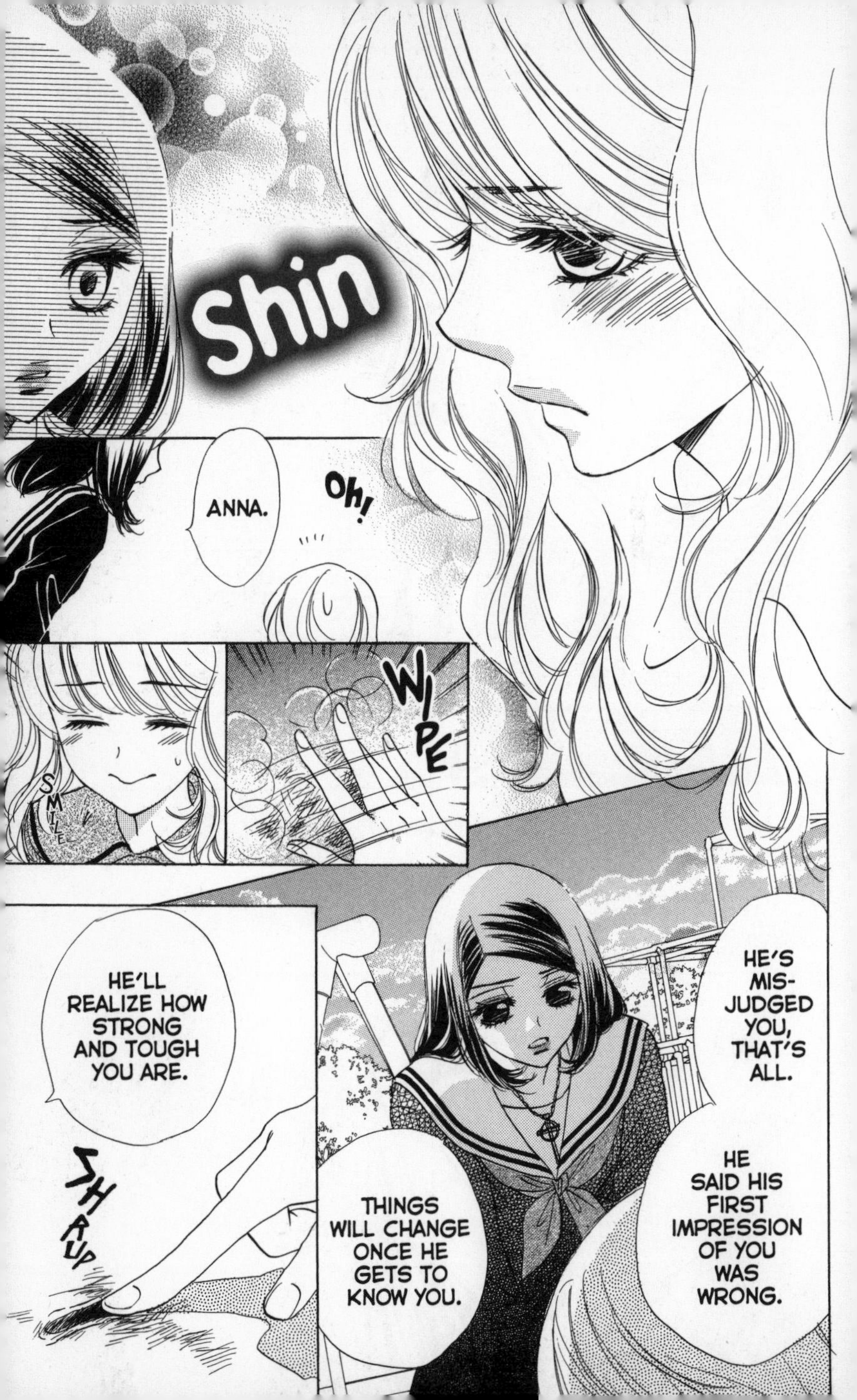
Shin
ANNA.
Oh!
...
WIPE
SMILE
HE'S MIS-JUDGED YOU, THAT'S ALL.
HE SAID HIS FIRST IMPRESSION OF YOU WAS WRONG.
THINGS WILL CHANGE ONCE HE GETS TO KNOW YOU.
HE'LL REALIZE HOW STRONG AND TOUGH YOU ARE.
SHRUP

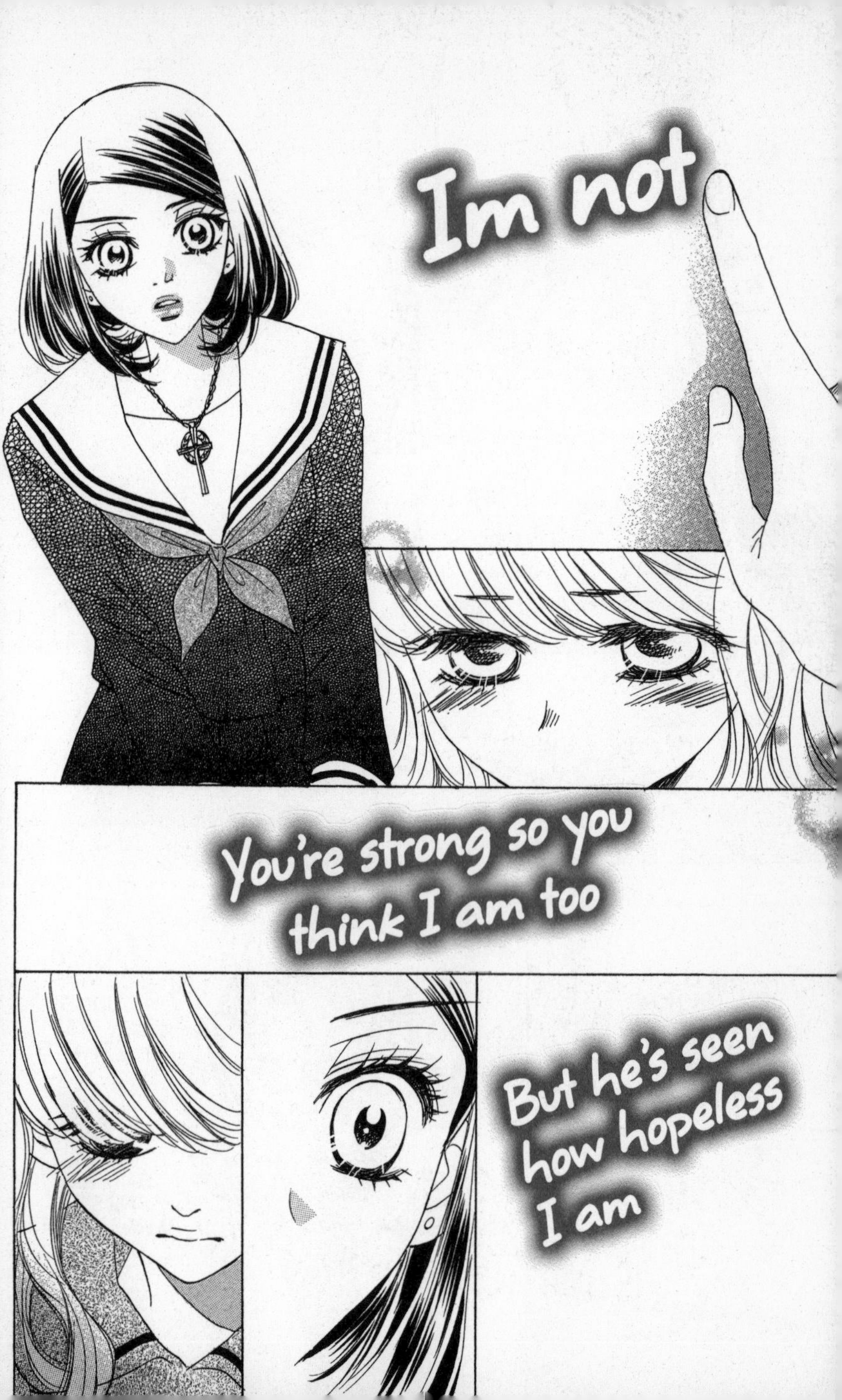
I'm not
You're strong so you think I am too
But he's seen how hopeless I am

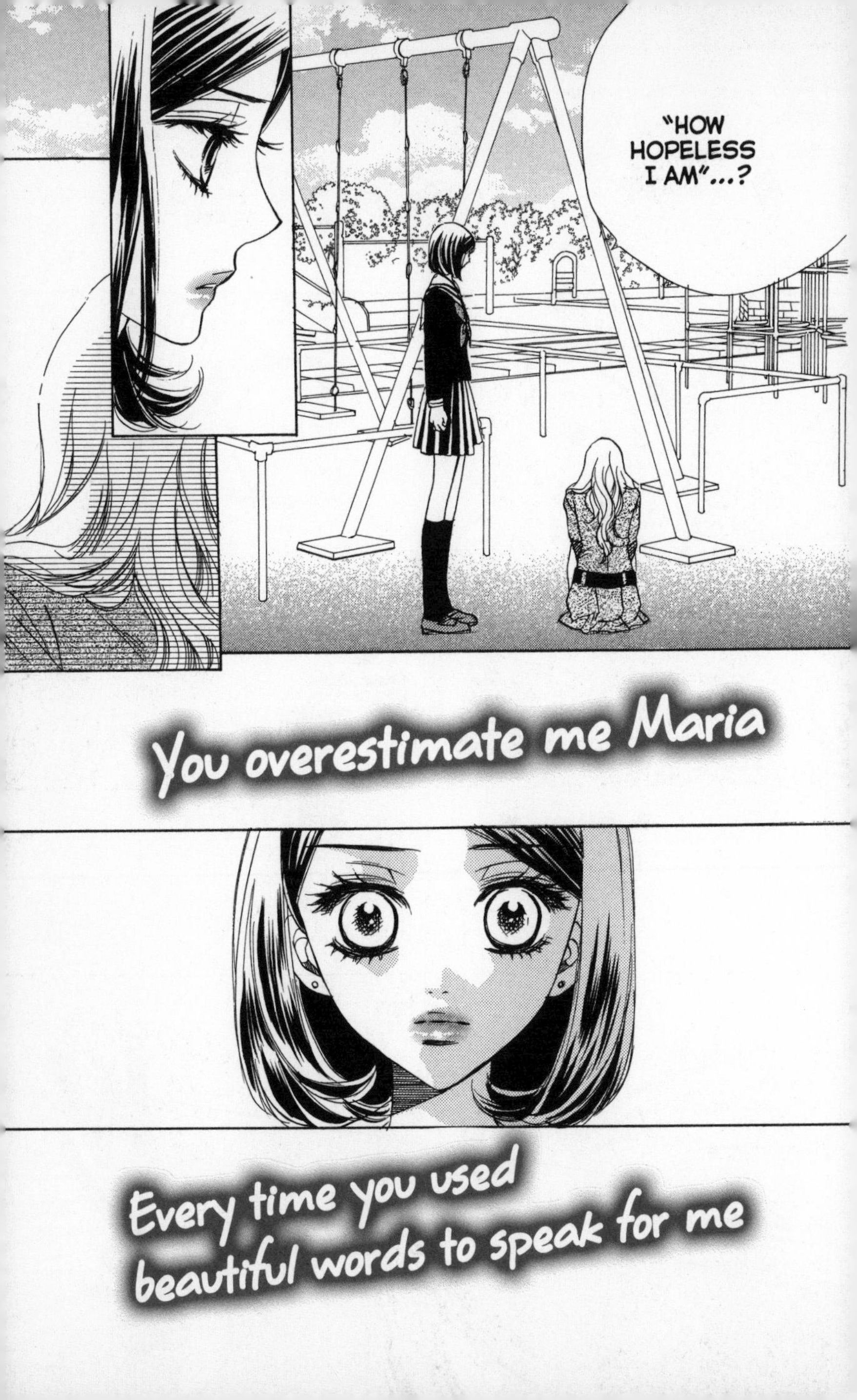
"HOW HOPELESS I AM"...?
You overestimate me Maria
Every time you used beautiful words to speak for me

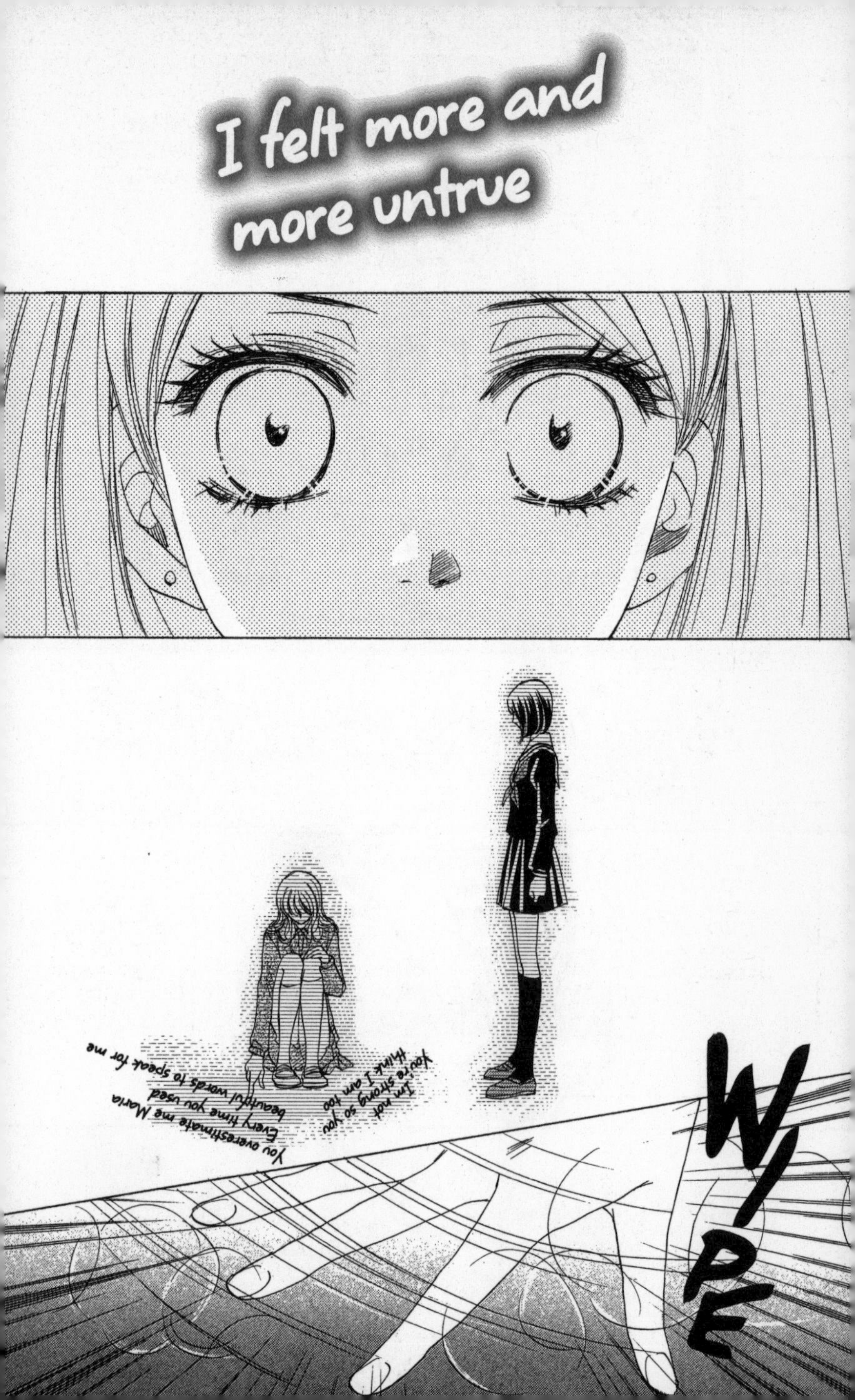
I felt more and more untrue
Im not
You're strong so you
think I am too
You overestimate me Maria
Every time you used
beautiful words to speak for me
WIPE

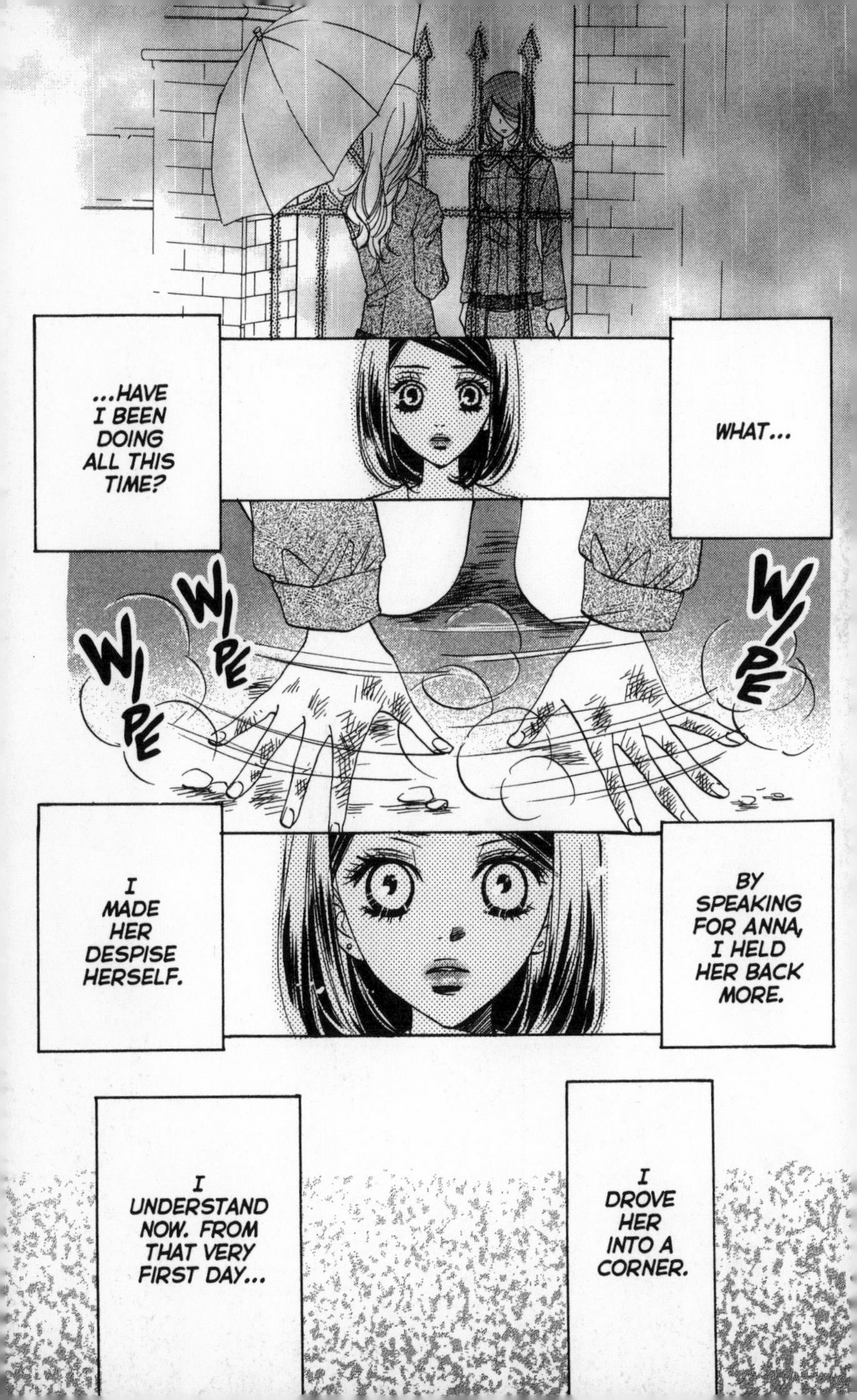
WHAT...
...HAVE I BEEN DOING ALL THIS TIME?
WIPE
WIPE
WIPE
BY SPEAKING FOR ANNA, I HELD HER BACK MORE.
I MADE HER DESPISE HERSELF.
I DROVE HER INTO A CORNER.
I UNDERSTAND NOW. FROM THAT VERY FIRST DAY...

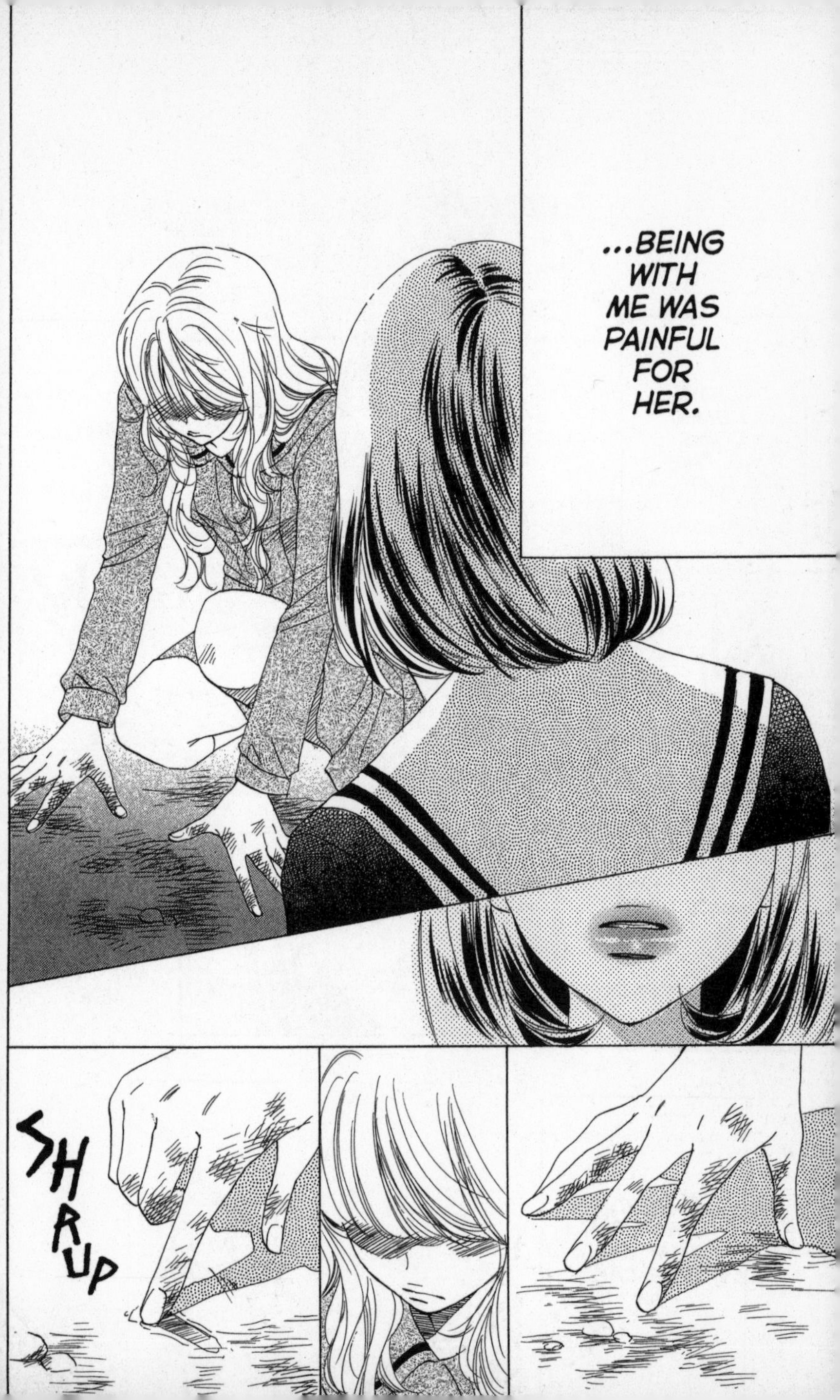
...BEING WITH ME WAS PAINFUL FOR HER.
SHRUP

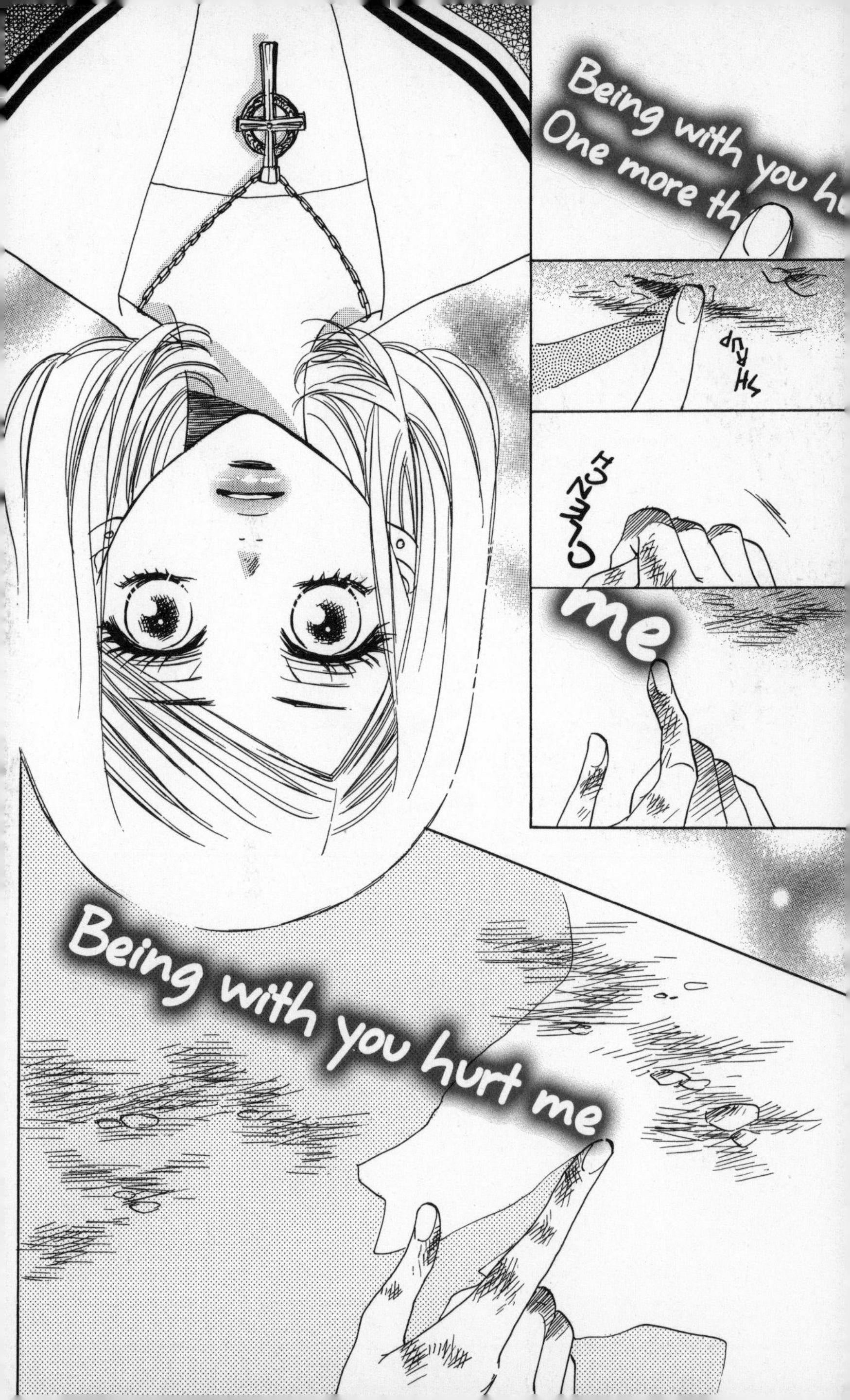

Being with you hu
One more th
SHRUP
CLENCH
me
Being with you hurt me

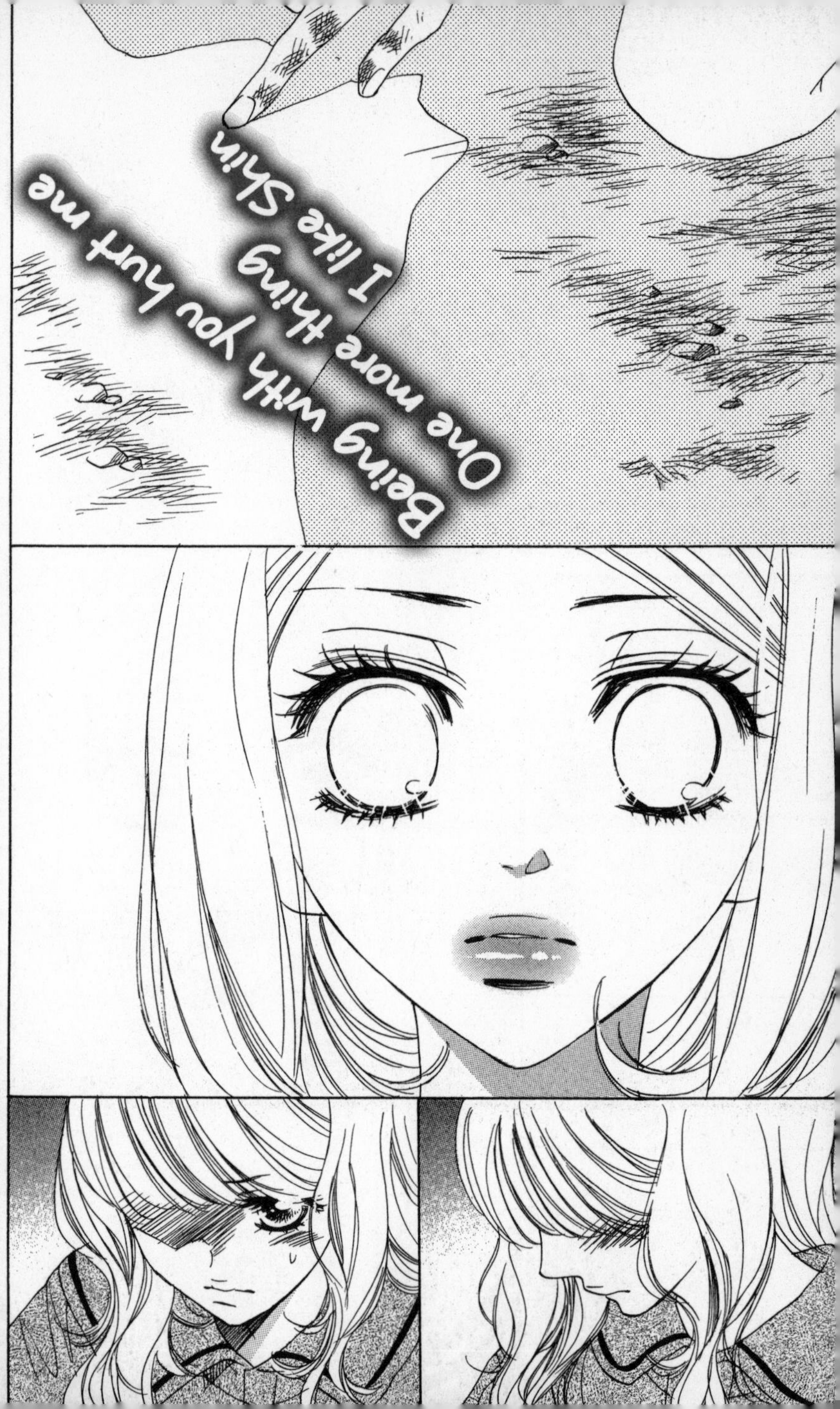
Being with you hurt me
One more thing
I like Shin

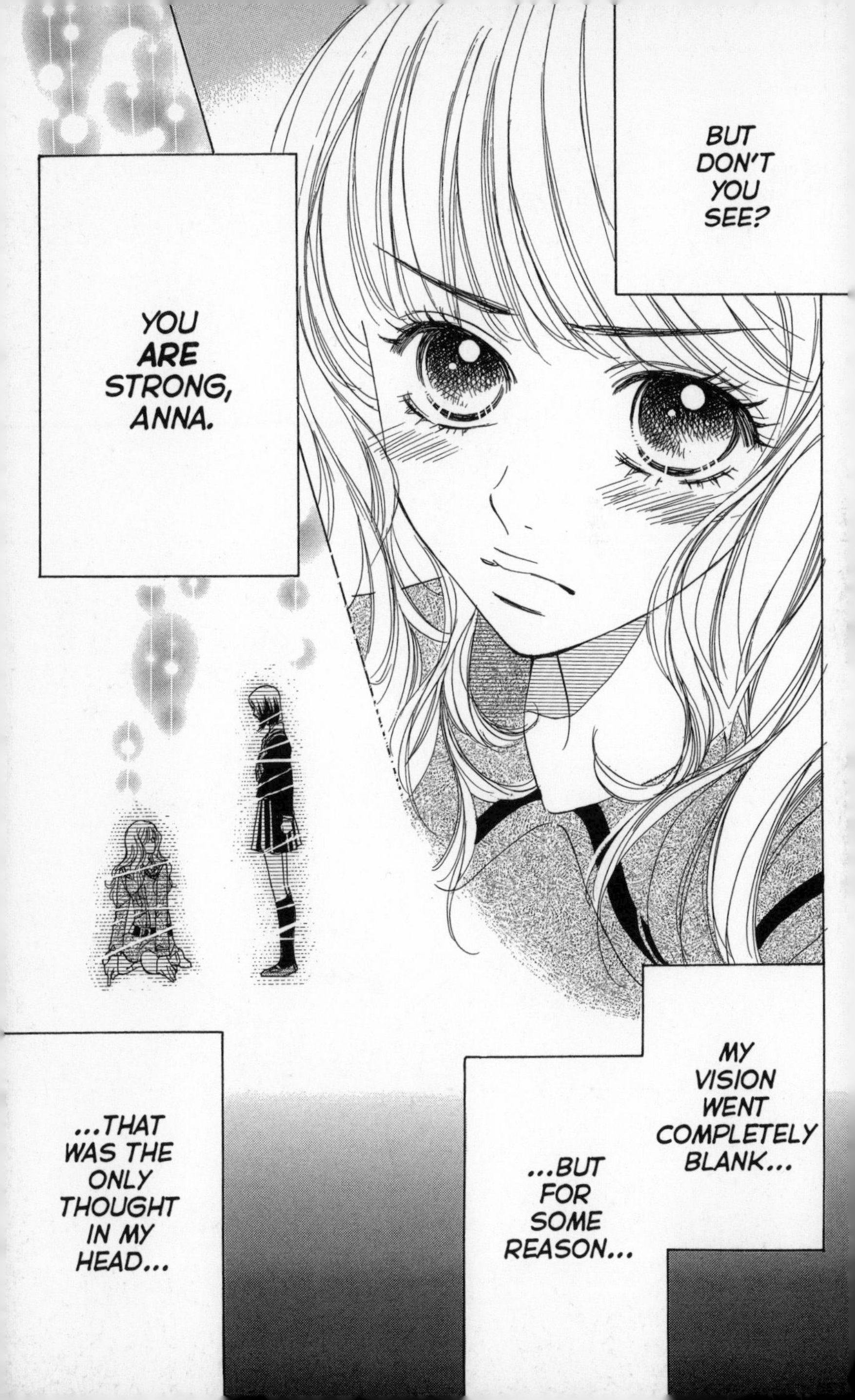
BUT DON'T YOU SEE?
YOU ARE STRONG, ANNA.
MY VISION WENT COMPLETELY BLANK...
...BUT FOR SOME REASON...
...THAT WAS THE ONLY THOUGHT IN MY HEAD...

A Devil and Her Love Song

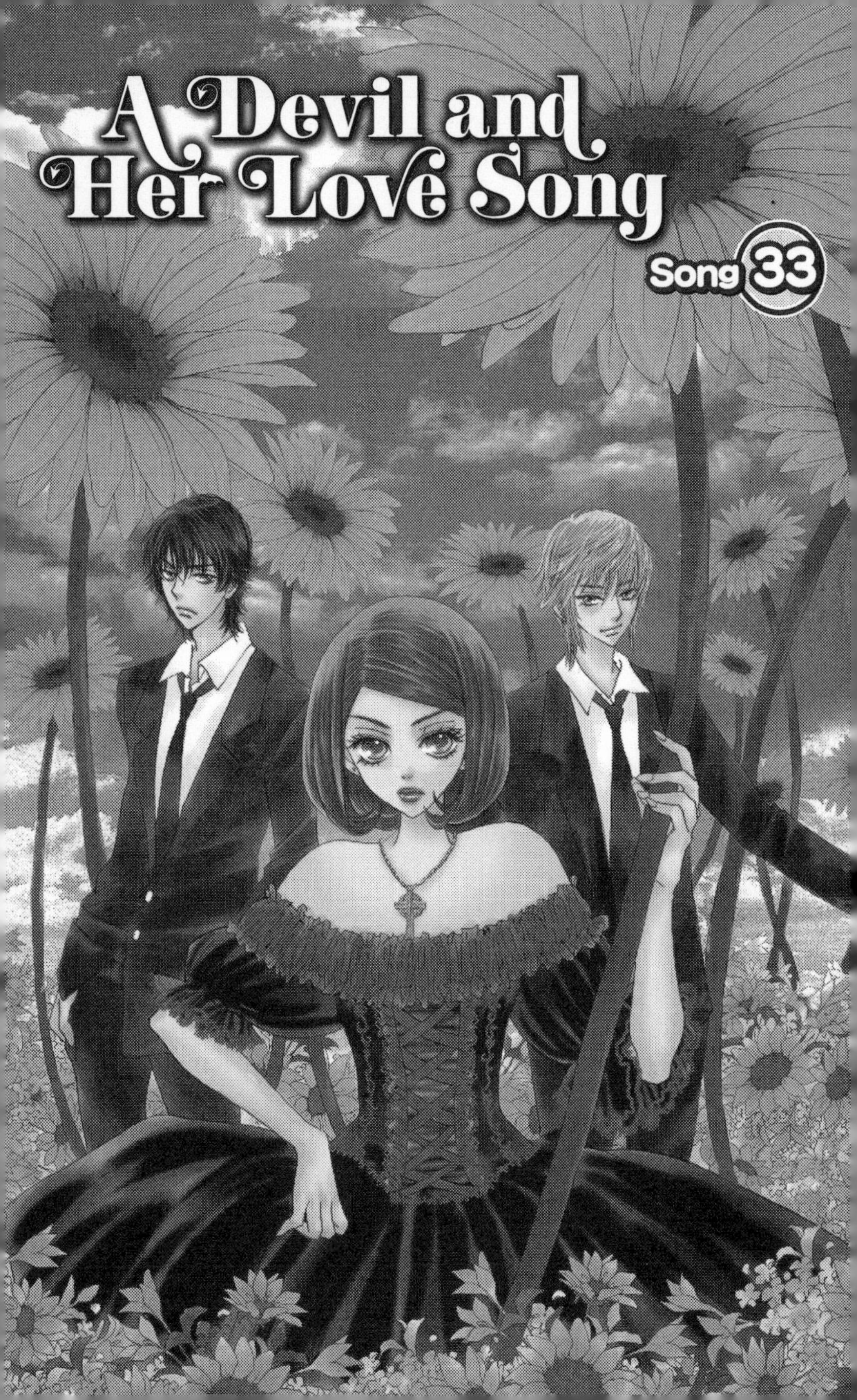
A Devil and Her Love Song
Song 33

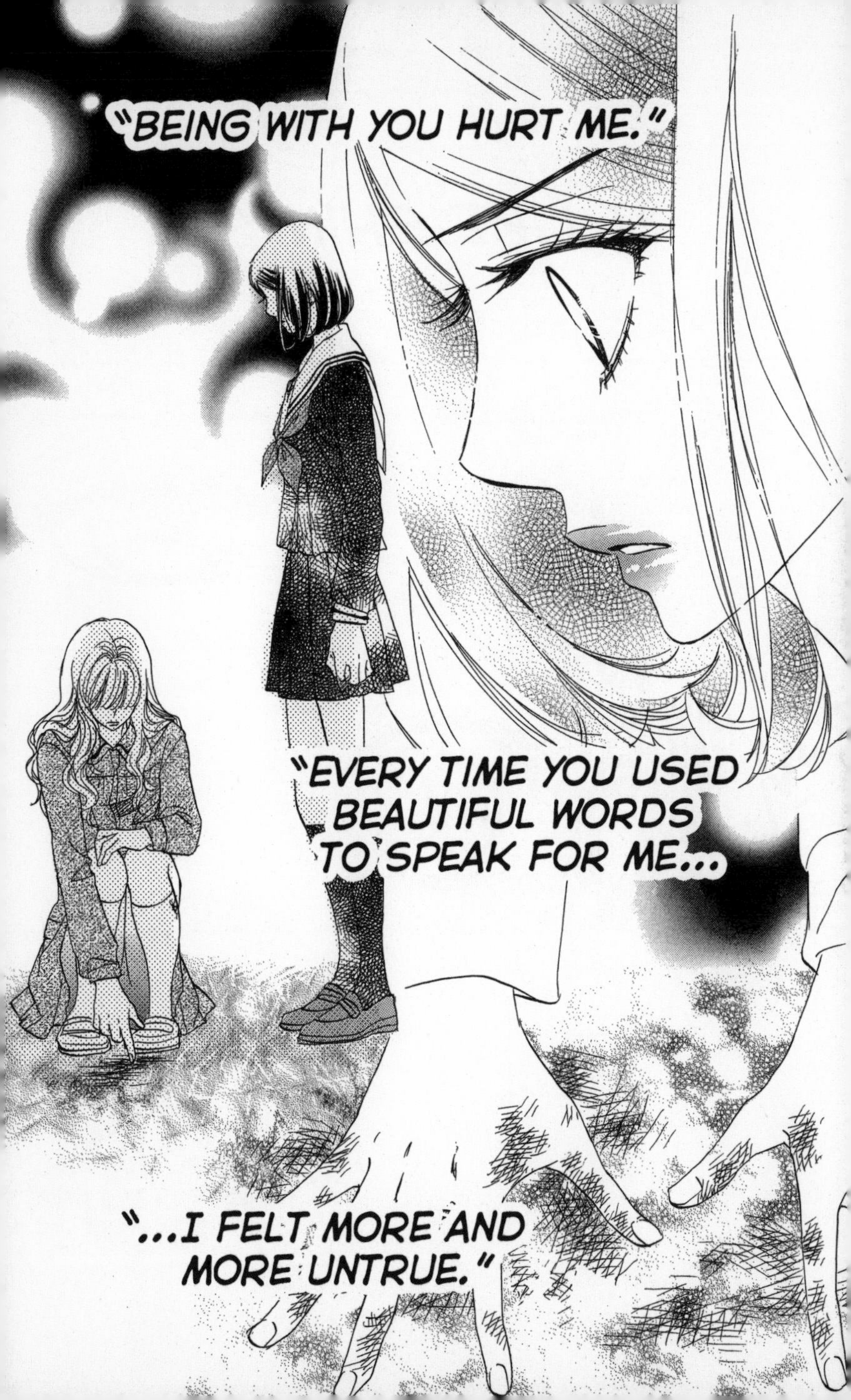
"BEING WITH YOU HURT ME."
"EVERY TIME YOU USED BEAUTIFUL WORDS TO SPEAK FOR ME...
"...I FELT MORE AND MORE UNTRUE."

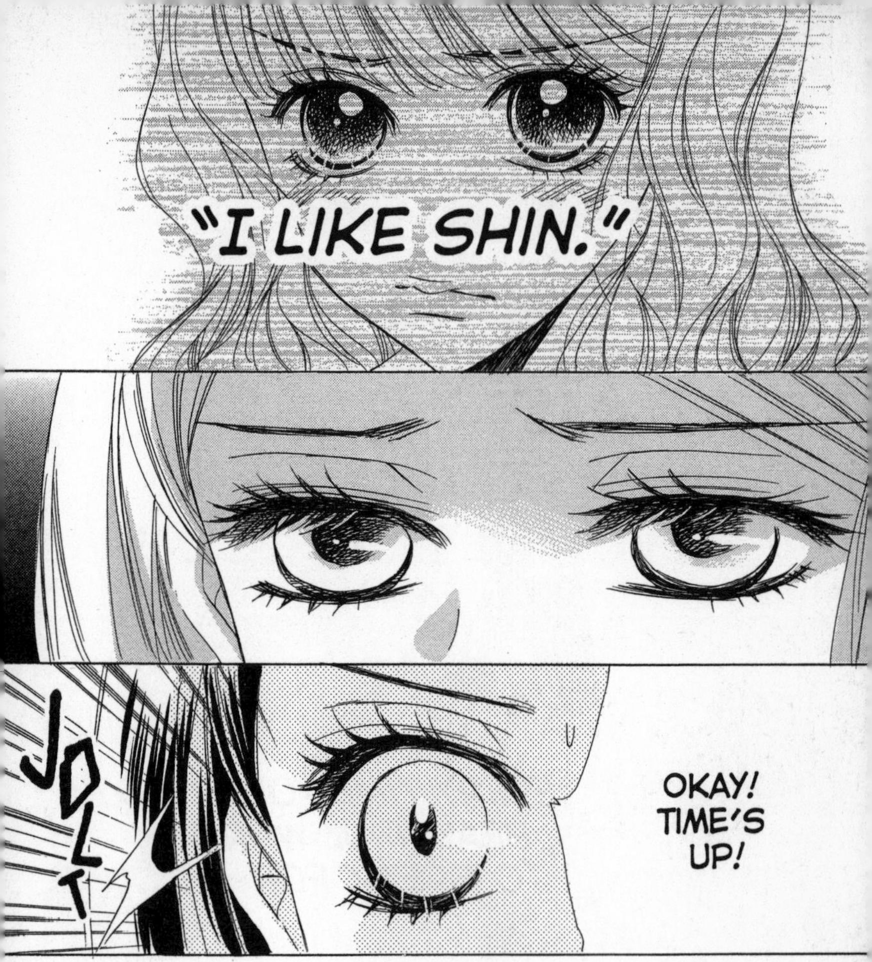
"I LIKE SHIN."
OKAY! TIME'S UP!
JOLT

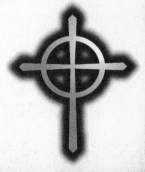

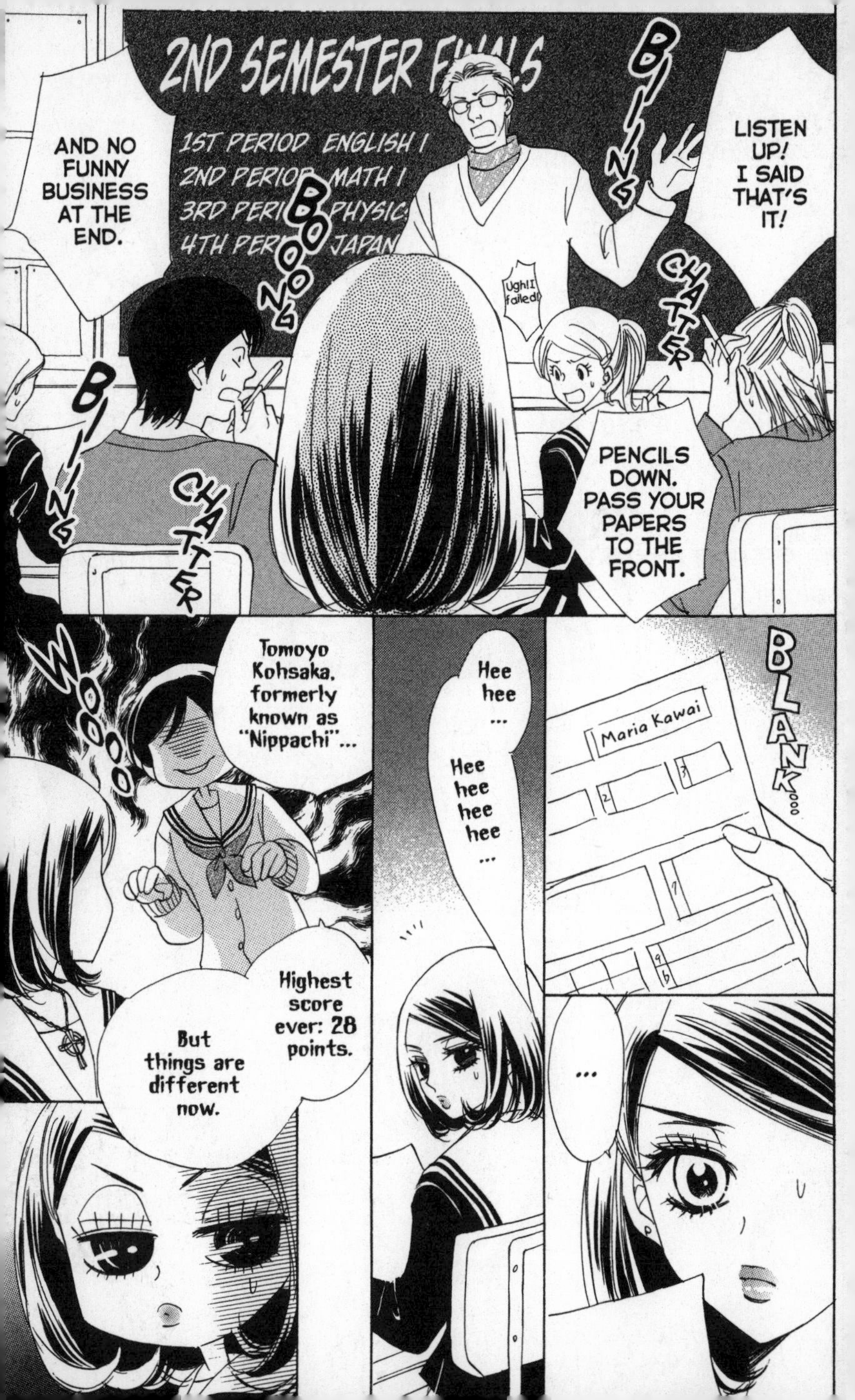
LISTEN UP! I SAID THAT'S IT!
BIIING
CHATTER
PENCILS DOWN. PASS YOUR PAPERS TO THE FRONT.
Ugh! I failed!
BOOOONG
1ST PERIOD ENGLISH I
AND NO FUNNY BUSINESS AT THE END.
BIIING
CHATTER
BLANK...
Maria Kawai
...
Hee hee ...
Hee hee hee hee ...
WOOOOO
Tomoyo Kohsaka, formerly known as "Nippachi"...
Highest score ever: 28 points.
But things are different now.

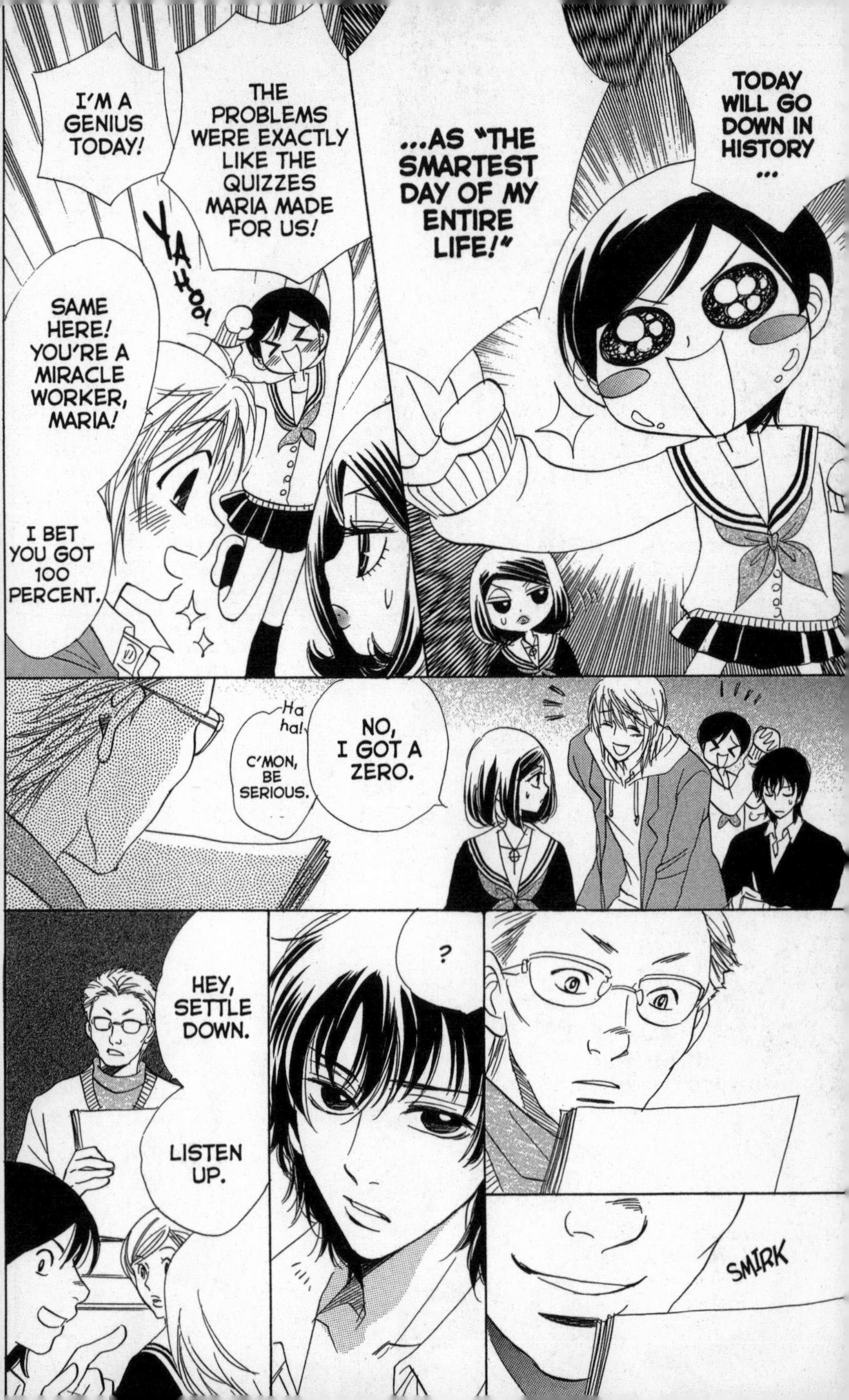
TODAY WILL GO DOWN IN HISTORY...
...AS "THE SMARTEST DAY OF MY ENTIRE LIFE!"
THE PROBLEMS WERE EXACTLY LIKE THE QUIZZES MARIA MADE FOR US!
I'M A GENIUS TODAY!
YAHOO!
SAME HERE! YOU'RE A MIRACLE WORKER, MARIA!
I BET YOU GOT 100 PERCENT.
NO, I GOT A ZERO.
Ha ha!
C'MON, BE SERIOUS.
SMIRK
?
HEY, SETTLE DOWN.
LISTEN UP.

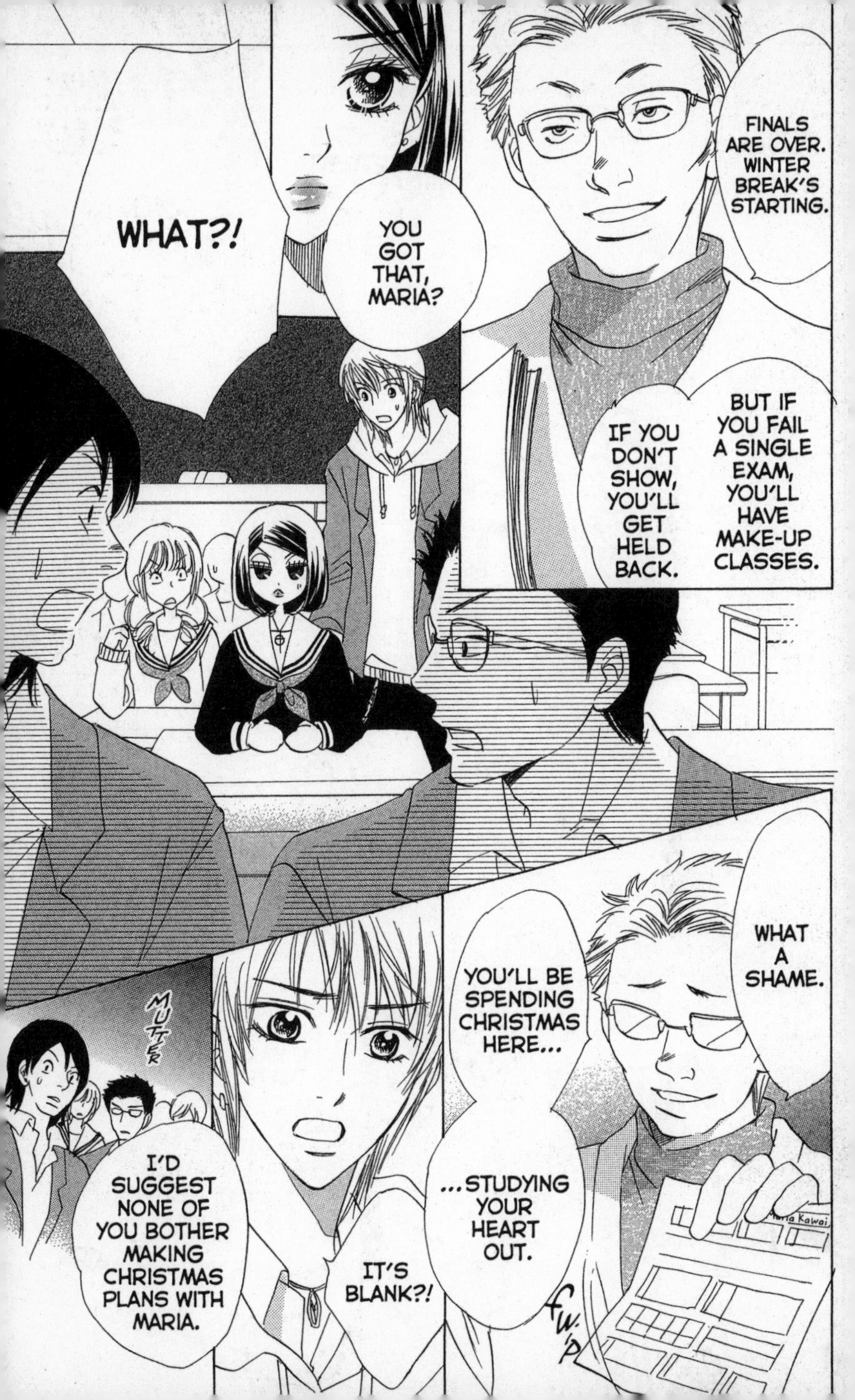
FINALS ARE OVER. WINTER BREAK'S STARTING.
BUT IF YOU FAIL A SINGLE EXAM, YOU'LL HAVE MAKE-UP CLASSES.
IF YOU DON'T SHOW, YOU'LL GET HELD BACK.
YOU GOT THAT, MARIA?
WHAT?!
WHAT A SHAME.
YOU'LL BE SPENDING CHRISTMAS HERE...
...STUDYING YOUR HEART OUT.
Maria Kawai
FWIP
IT'S BLANK?!
MUTTER
I'D SUGGEST NONE OF YOU BOTHER MAKING CHRISTMAS PLANS WITH MARIA.

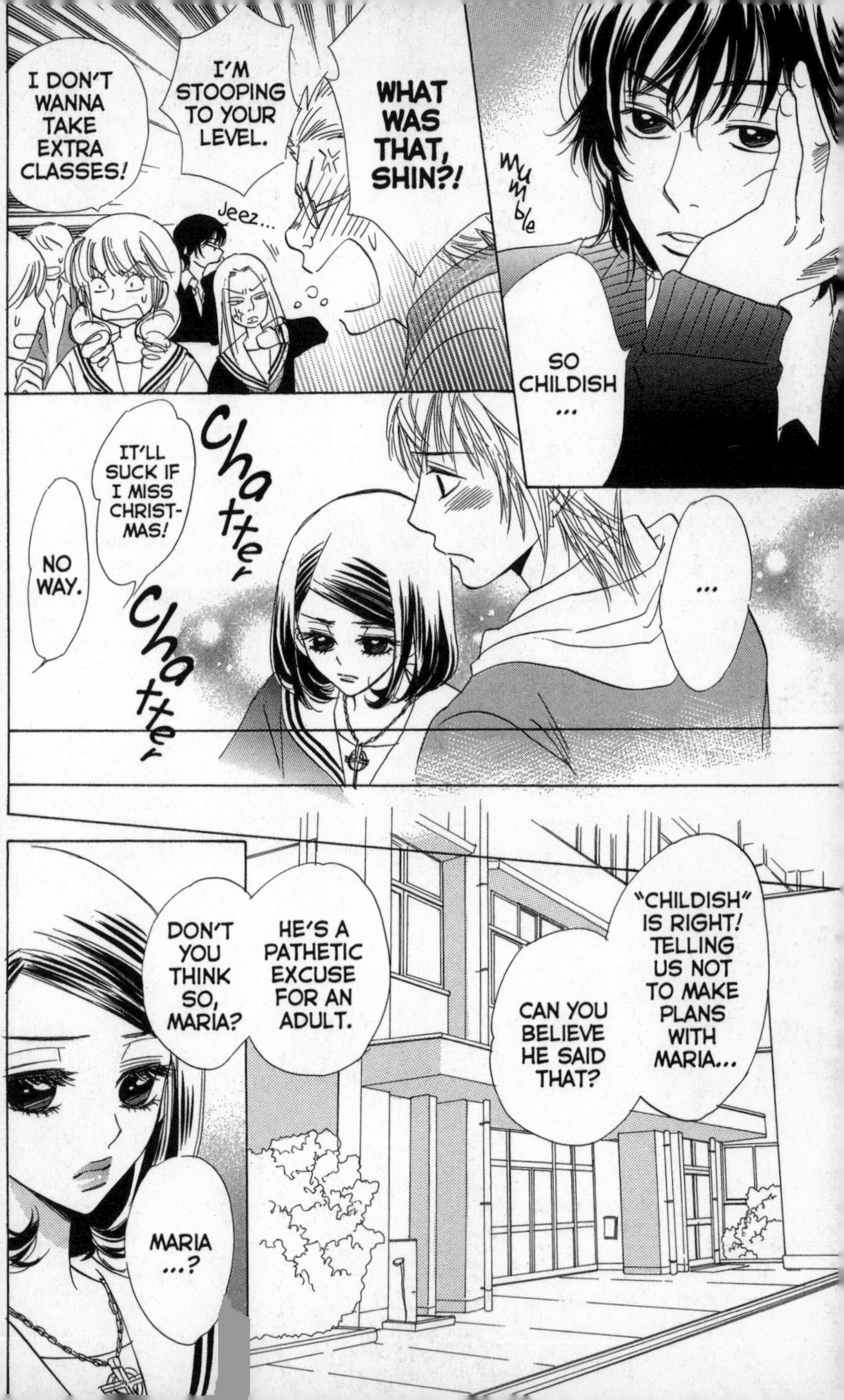
mumble
SO CHILDISH...
WHAT WAS THAT, SHIN?!
I'M STOOPING TO YOUR LEVEL.
I DON'T WANNA TAKE EXTRA CLASSES!
Jeez...
...
Chatter Chatter
IT'LL SUCK IF I MISS CHRIST-MAS!
NO WAY.
"CHILDISH" IS RIGHT! TELLING US NOT TO MAKE PLANS WITH MARIA...
CAN YOU BELIEVE HE SAID THAT?
HE'S A PATHETIC EXCUSE FOR AN ADULT.
DON'T YOU THINK SO, MARIA?
MARIA...?

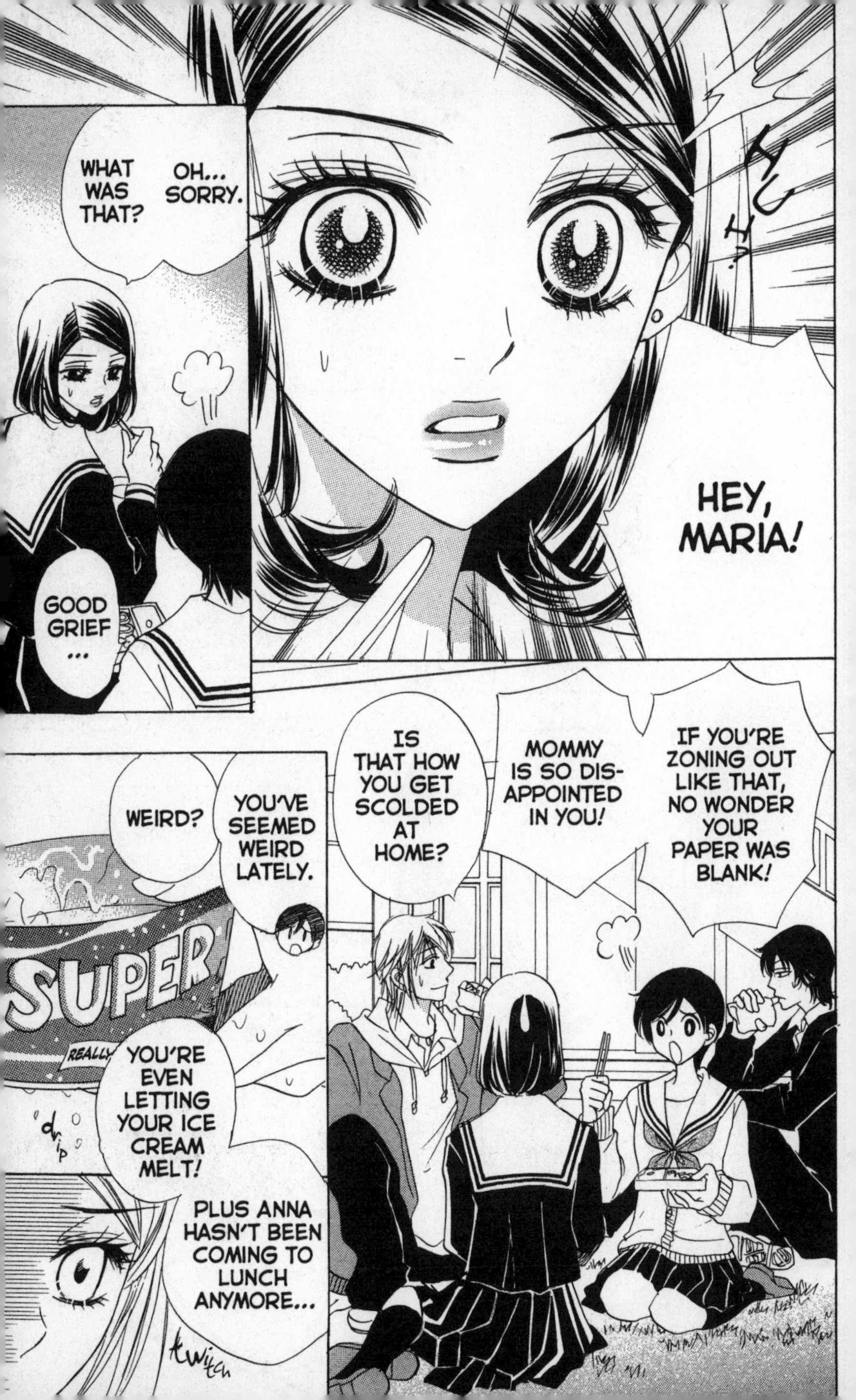
HUH?
HEY, MARIA!
OH... SORRY.
WHAT WAS THAT?
GOOD GRIEF...
IF YOU'RE ZONING OUT LIKE THAT, NO WONDER YOUR PAPER WAS BLANK!
MOMMY IS SO DIS-APPOINTED IN YOU!
IS THAT HOW YOU GET SCOLDED AT HOME?
YOU'VE SEEMED WEIRD LATELY.
WEIRD?
SUPER
REALLY
YOU'RE EVEN LETTING YOUR ICE CREAM MELT!
drip
PLUS ANNA HASN'T BEEN COMING TO LUNCH ANYMORE...
twitch

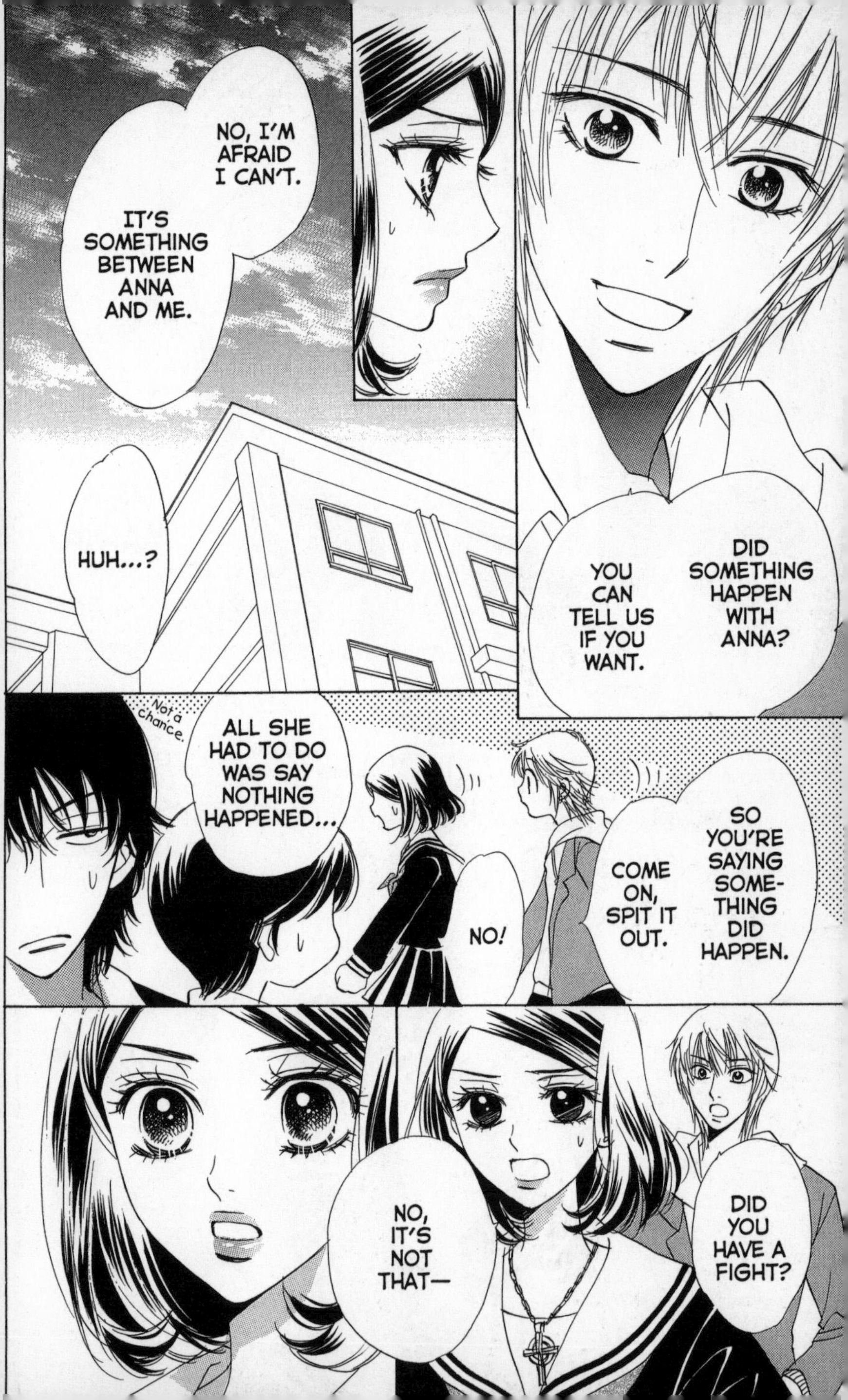
DID SOMETHING HAPPEN WITH ANNA?
YOU CAN TELL US IF YOU WANT.
NO, I'M AFRAID I CAN'T.
IT'S SOMETHING BETWEEN ANNA AND ME.
HUH...?
SO YOU'RE SAYING SOME-THING DID HAPPEN.
COME ON, SPIT IT OUT.
NO!
ALL SHE HAD TO DO WAS SAY NOTHING HAPPENED...
Not a chance.
DID YOU HAVE A FIGHT?
NO, IT'S NOT THAT—

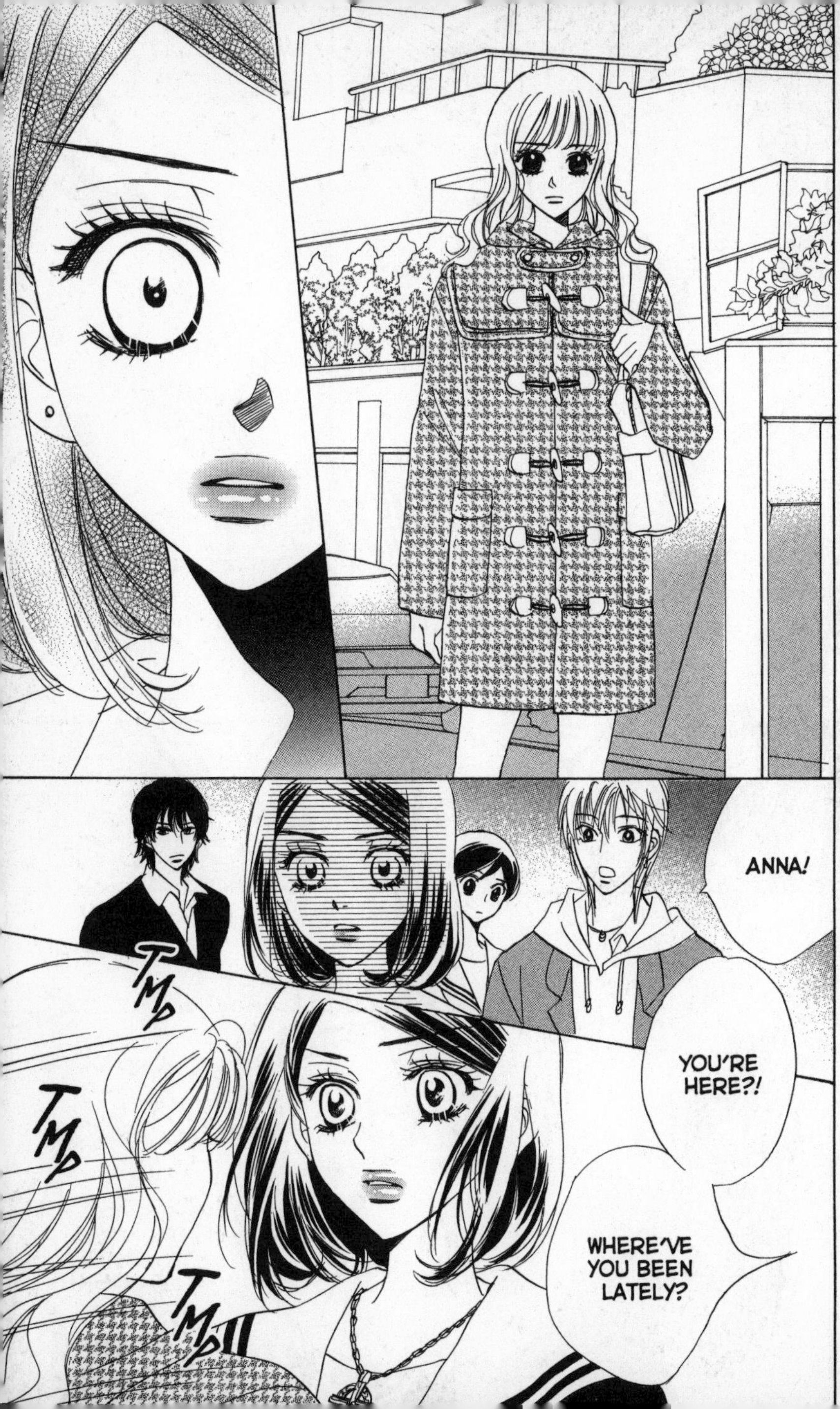
ANNA!
YOU'RE HERE?!
WHERE'VE YOU BEEN LATELY?
TMP
TMP
TMP

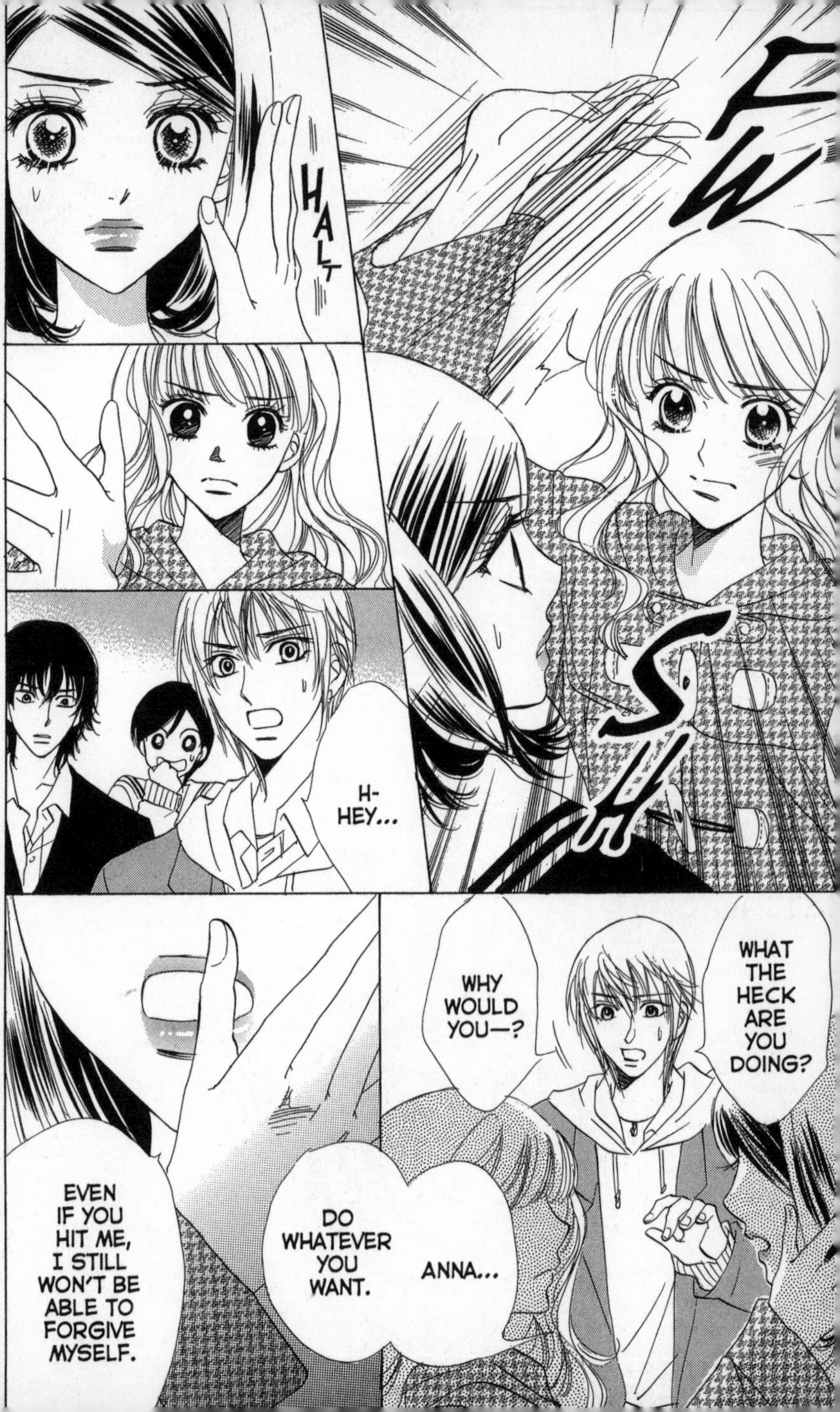

FW
SH
HALT
H-
HEY...
WHAT THE HECK ARE YOU DOING?
WHY WOULD YOU—?
ANNA...
DO WHATEVER YOU WANT.
EVEN IF YOU HIT ME, I STILL WON'T BE ABLE TO FORGIVE MYSELF.

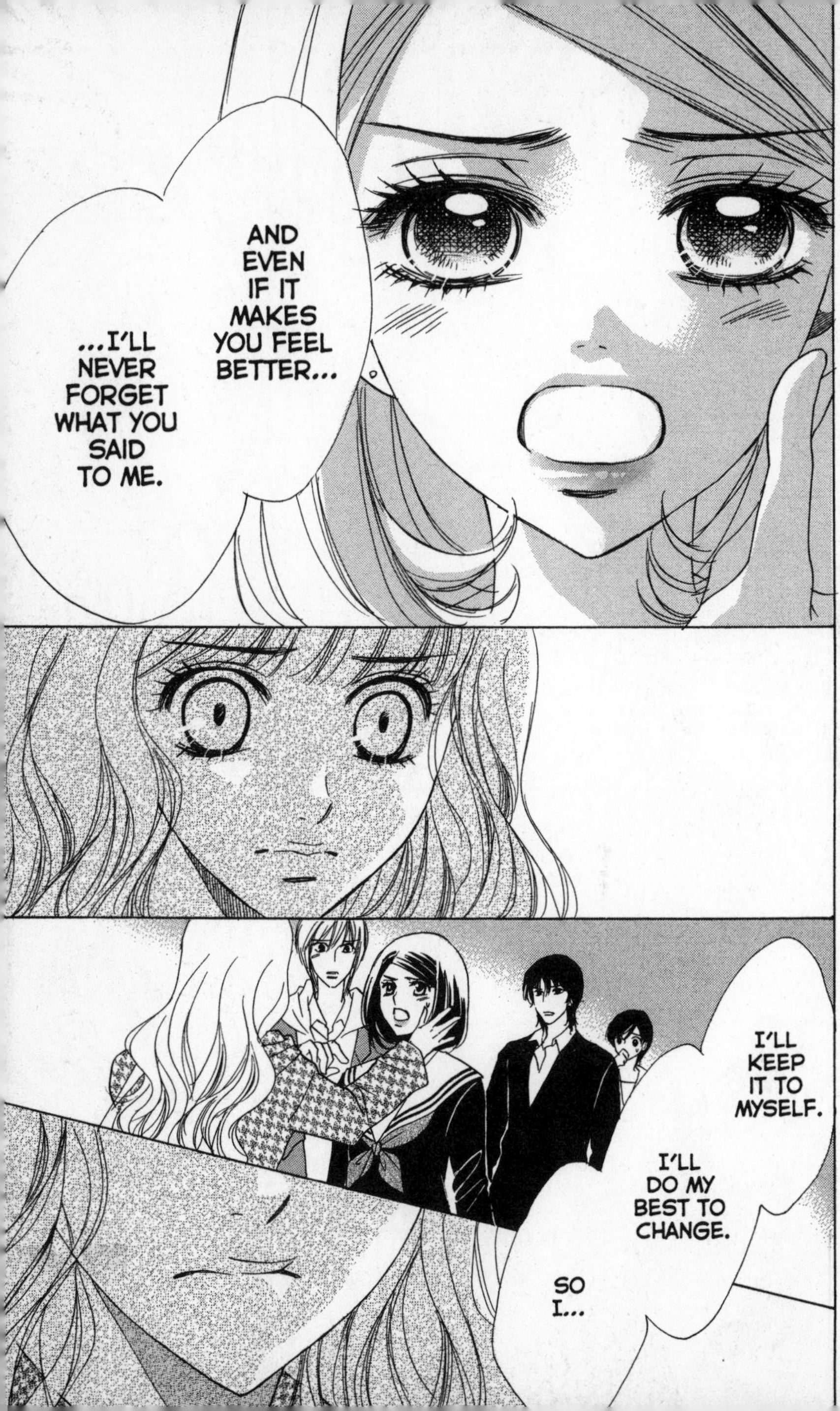
AND EVEN IF IT MAKES YOU FEEL BETTER...
...I'LL NEVER FORGET WHAT YOU SAID TO ME.
I'LL KEEP IT TO MYSELF.
I'LL DO MY BEST TO CHANGE.
SO I...

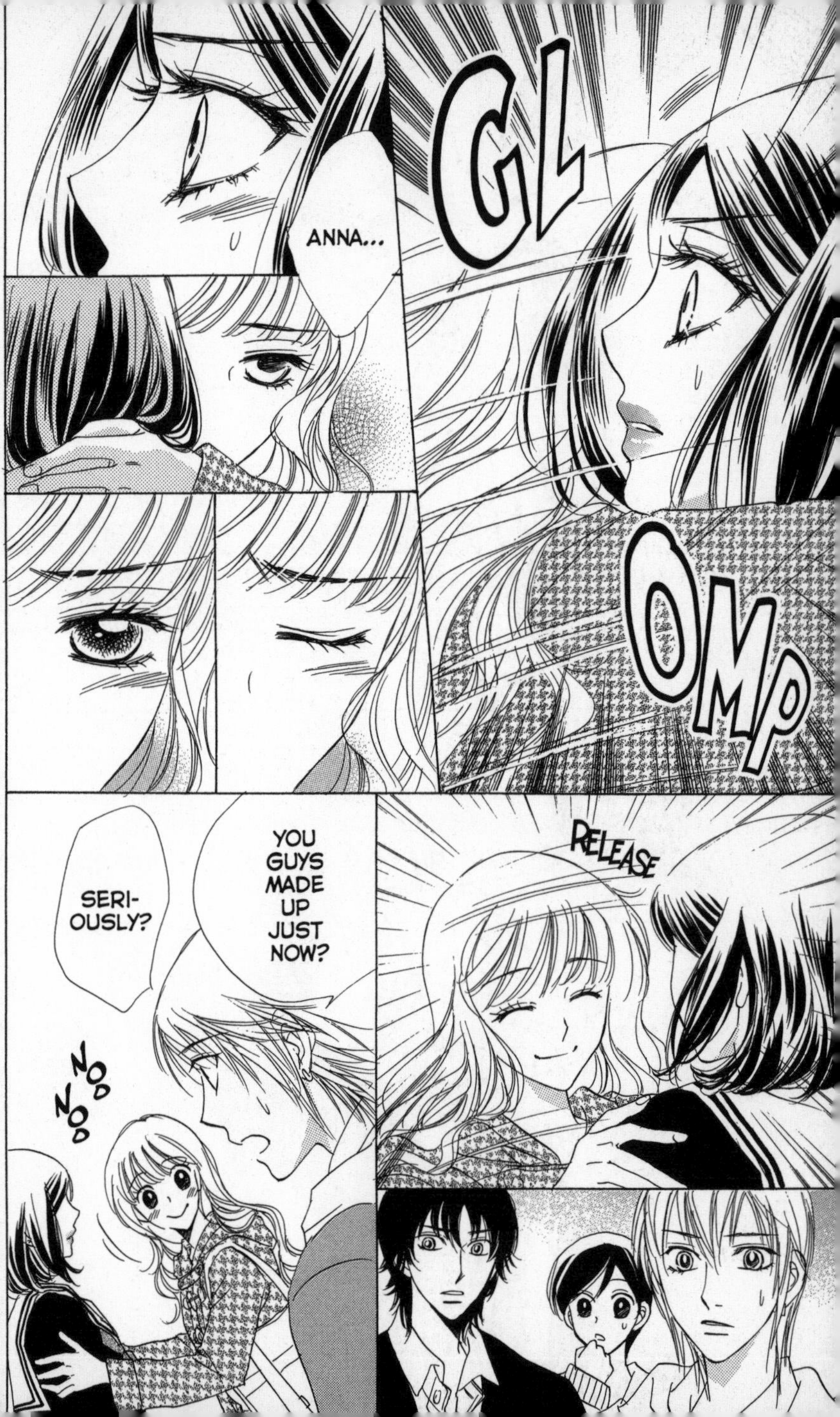
GL
OMP
ANNA...
RELEASE
YOU GUYS MADE UP JUST NOW?
SERI-OUSLY?
NOO NOO

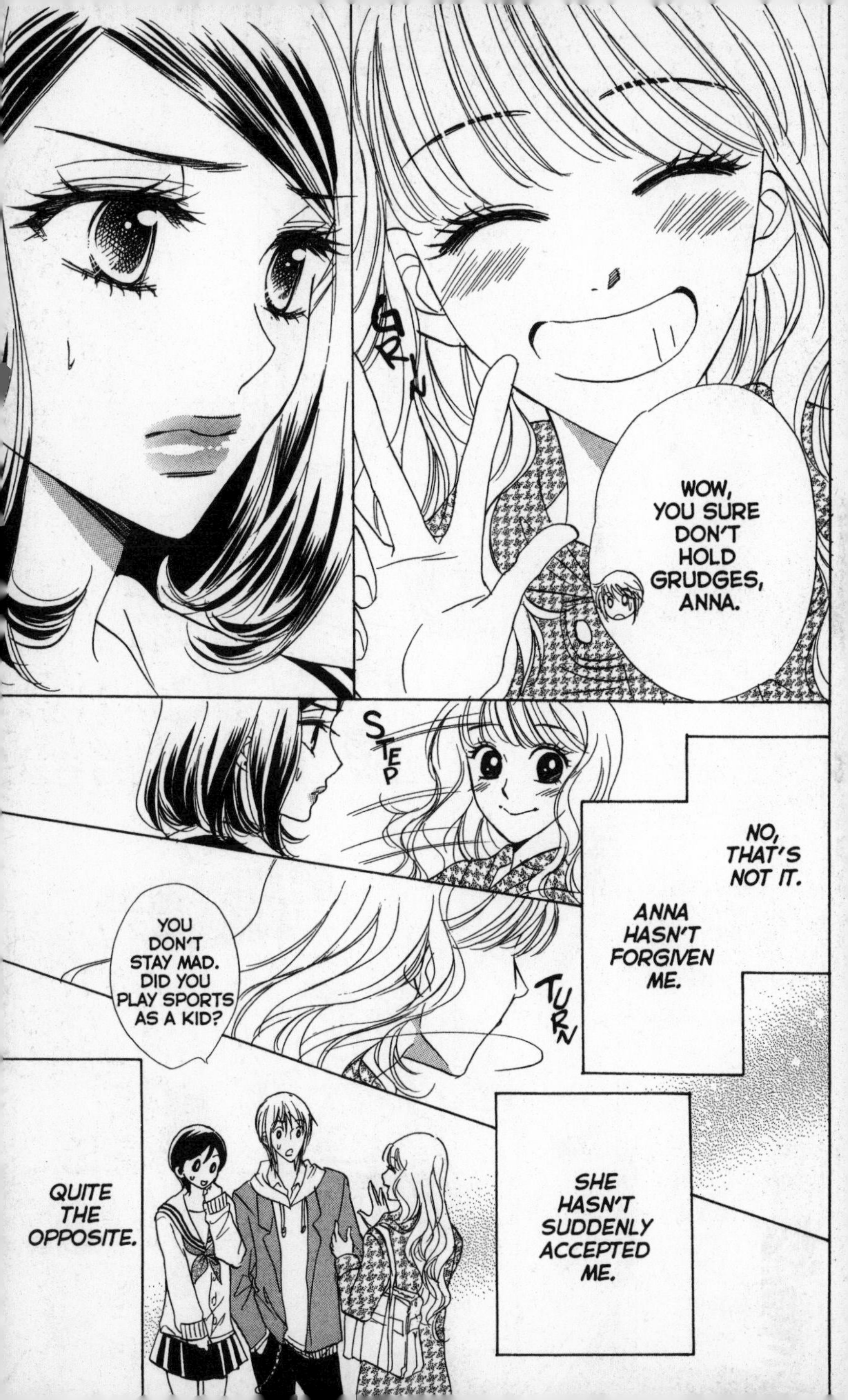
GRIN
WOW, YOU SURE DON'T HOLD GRUDGES, ANNA.
STEP
NO, THAT'S NOT IT.
ANNA HASN'T FORGIVEN ME.
TURN
YOU DON'T STAY MAD. DID YOU PLAY SPORTS AS A KID?
SHE HASN'T SUDDENLY ACCEPTED ME.
QUITE THE OPPOSITE.

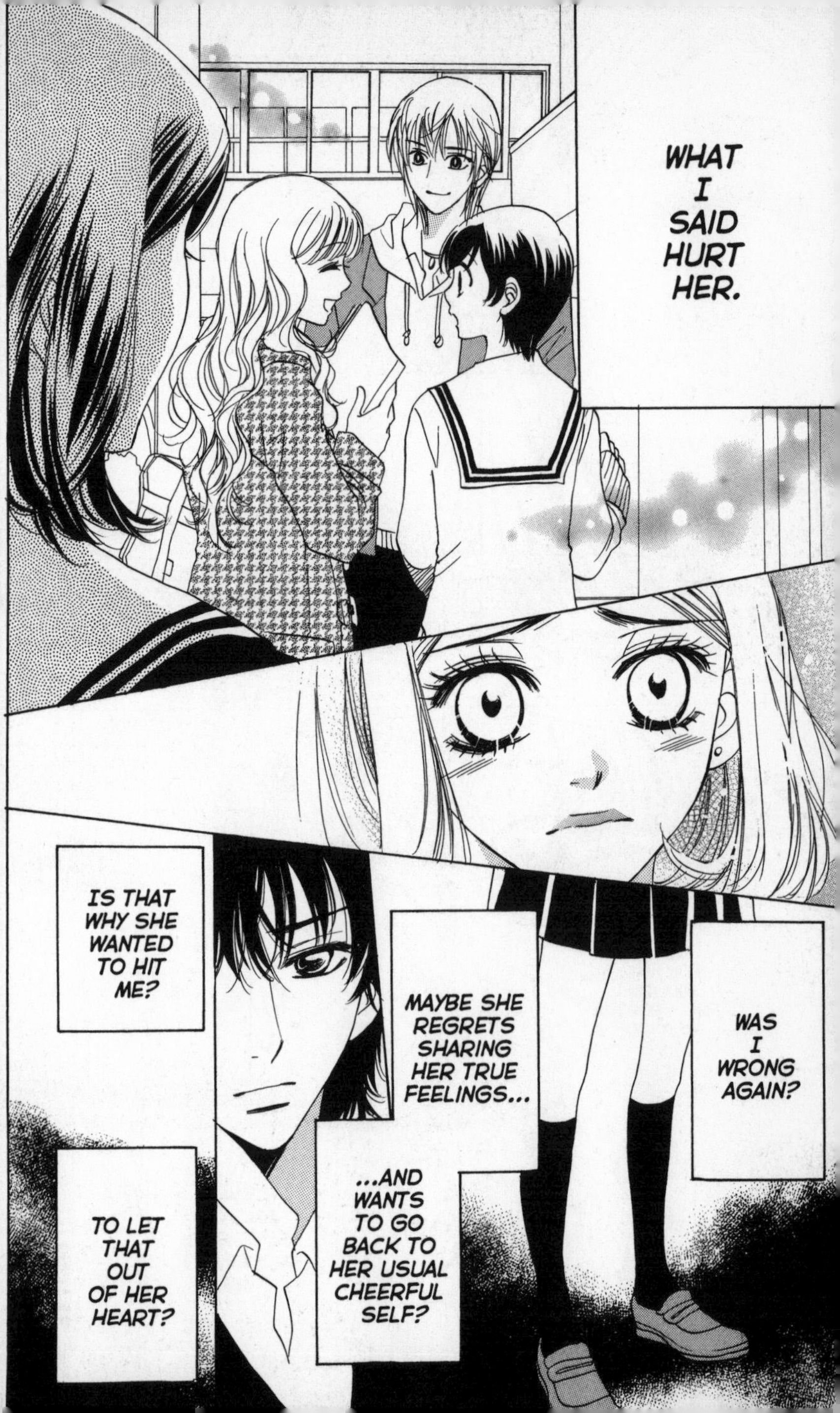
WHAT I SAID HURT HER.
WAS I WRONG AGAIN?
MAYBE SHE REGRETS SHARING HER TRUE FEELINGS...
...AND WANTS TO GO BACK TO HER USUAL CHEERFUL SELF?
IS THAT WHY SHE WANTED TO HIT ME?
TO LET THAT OUT OF HER HEART?

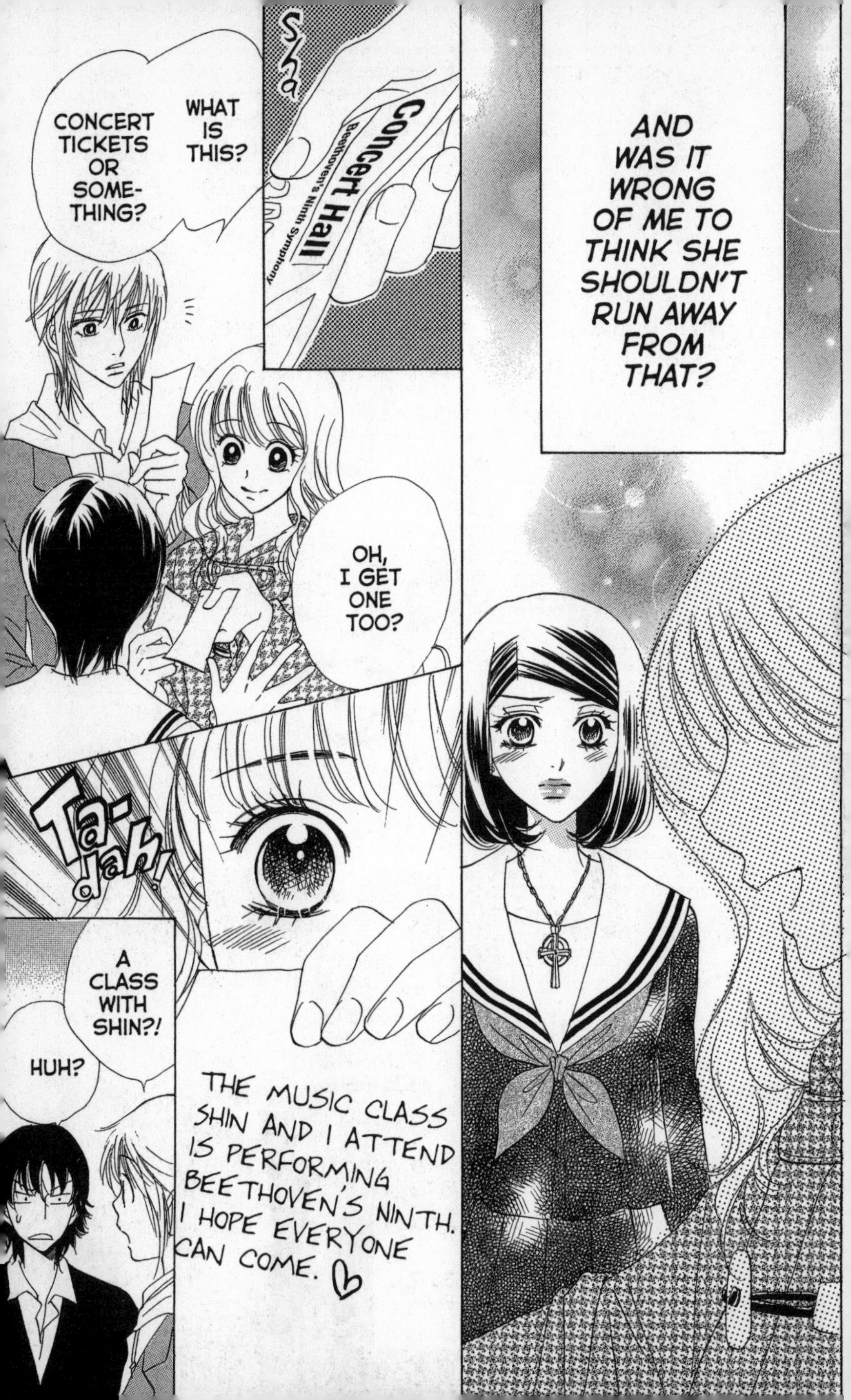
AND WAS IT WRONG OF ME TO THINK SHE SHOULDN'T RUN AWAY FROM THAT?
Sha
Concert Hall
Beethoven's Ninth Symphony
WHAT IS THIS?
CONCERT TICKETS OR SOME-THING?
OH, I GET ONE TOO?
Ta-dah!
THE MUSIC CLASS SHIN AND I ATTEND IS PERFORMING BEETHOVEN'S NINTH. I HOPE EVERYONE CAN COME. ♡
A CLASS WITH SHIN?!
HUH?

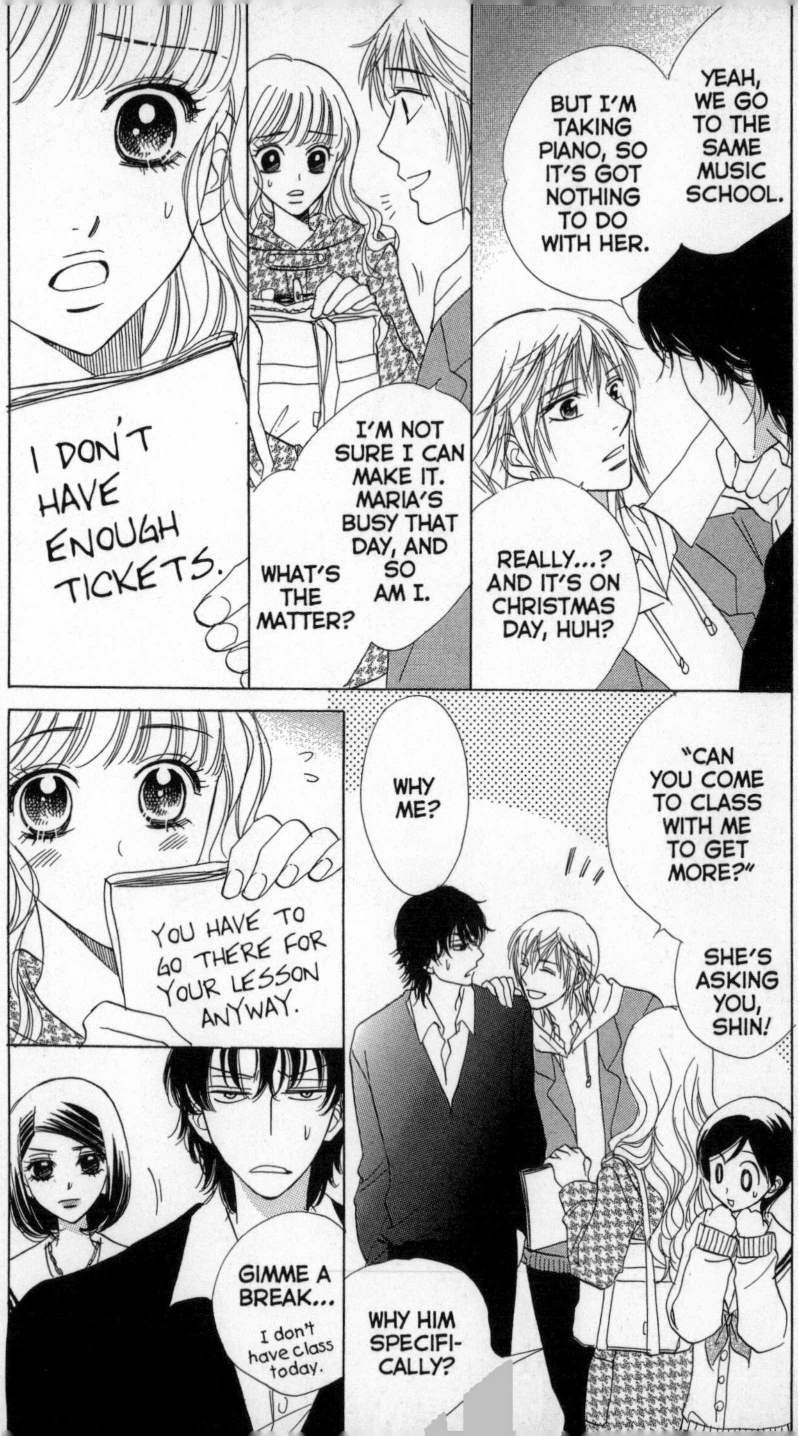
YEAH, WE GO TO THE SAME MUSIC SCHOOL.
BUT I'M TAKING PIANO, SO IT'S GOT NOTHING TO DO WITH HER.
REALLY...? AND IT'S ON CHRISTMAS DAY, HUH?
I'M NOT SURE I CAN MAKE IT. MARIA'S BUSY THAT DAY, AND SO AM I.
WHAT'S THE MATTER?
I DON'T HAVE ENOUGH TICKETS.
"CAN YOU COME TO CLASS WITH ME TO GET MORE?"
WHY ME?
SHE'S ASKING YOU, SHIN!
WHY HIM SPECIFI-CALLY?
YOU HAVE TO GO THERE FOR YOUR LESSON ANYWAY.
GIMME A BREAK...
I don't have class today.

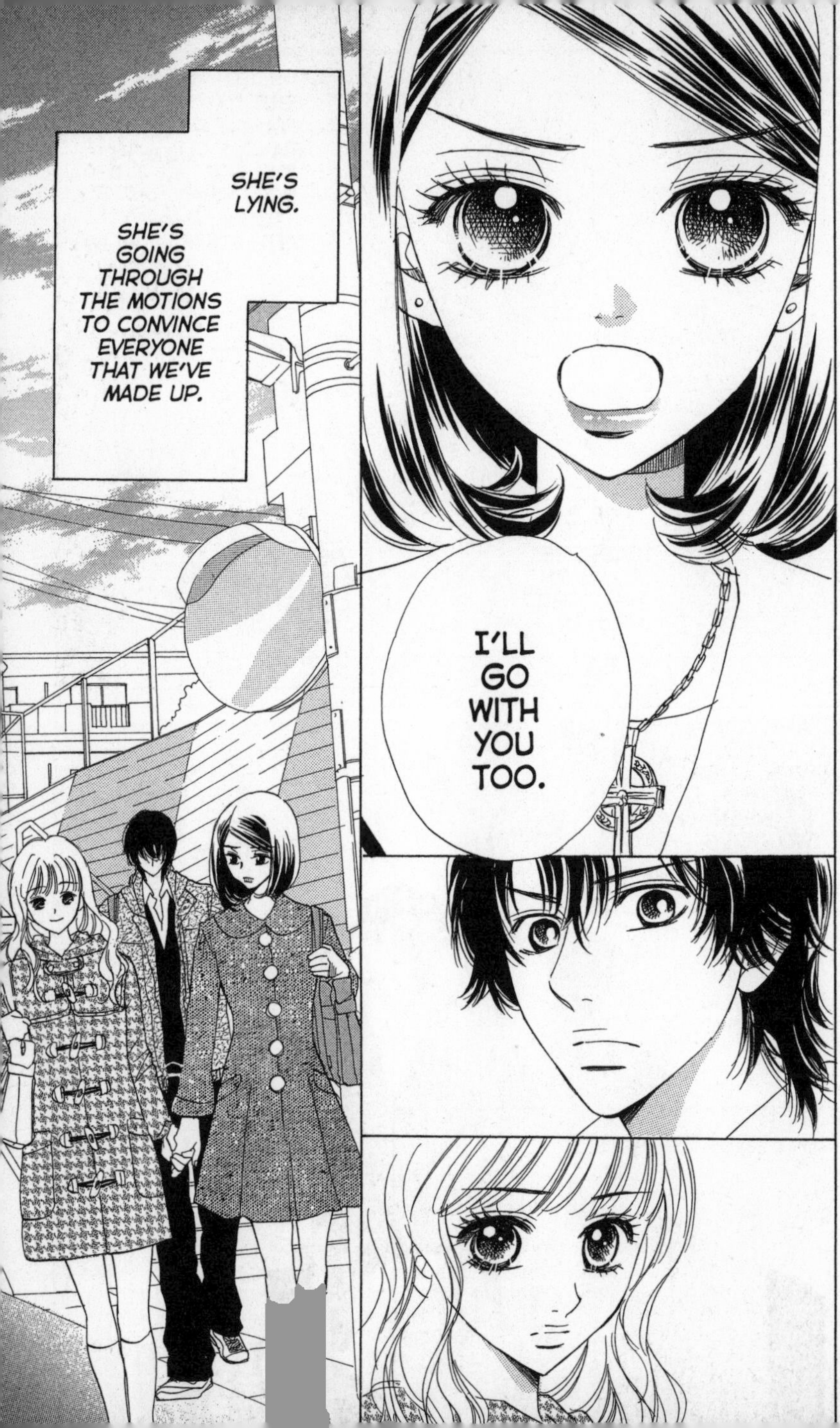
I'LL GO WITH YOU TOO.
SHE'S LYING.
SHE'S GOING THROUGH THE MOTIONS TO CONVINCE EVERYONE THAT WE'VE MADE UP.

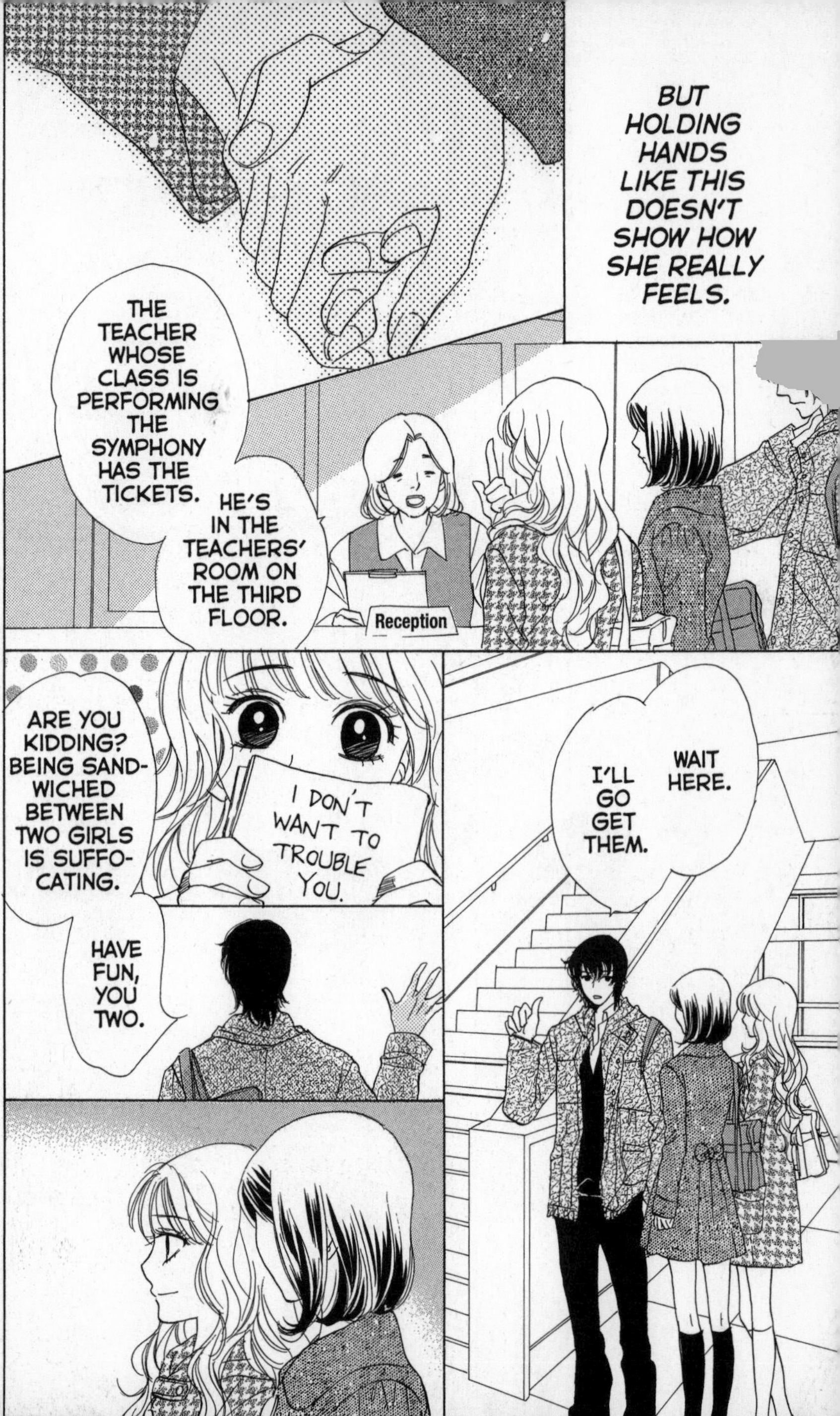
BUT HOLDING HANDS LIKE THIS DOESN'T SHOW HOW SHE REALLY FEELS.
THE TEACHER WHOSE CLASS IS PERFORMING THE SYMPHONY HAS THE TICKETS.
HE'S IN THE TEACHERS' ROOM ON THE THIRD FLOOR.
Reception
WAIT HERE.
I'LL GO GET THEM.
I DON'T WANT TO TROUBLE YOU.
ARE YOU KIDDING? BEING SAND-WICHED BETWEEN TWO GIRLS IS SUFFO-CATING.
HAVE FUN, YOU TWO.

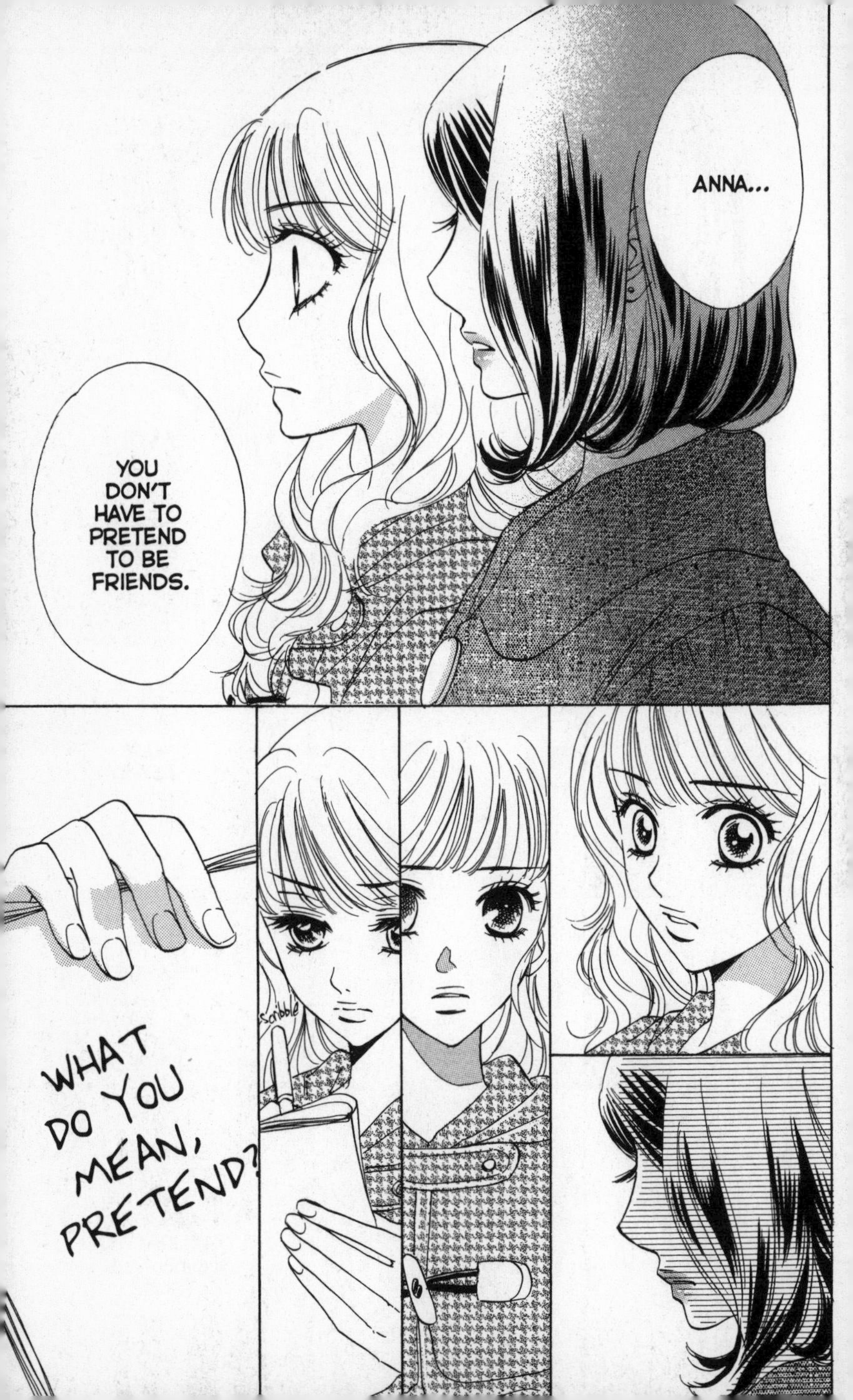
ANNA...
YOU DON'T HAVE TO PRETEND TO BE FRIENDS.
Scribble
WHAT DO YOU MEAN, PRETEND?

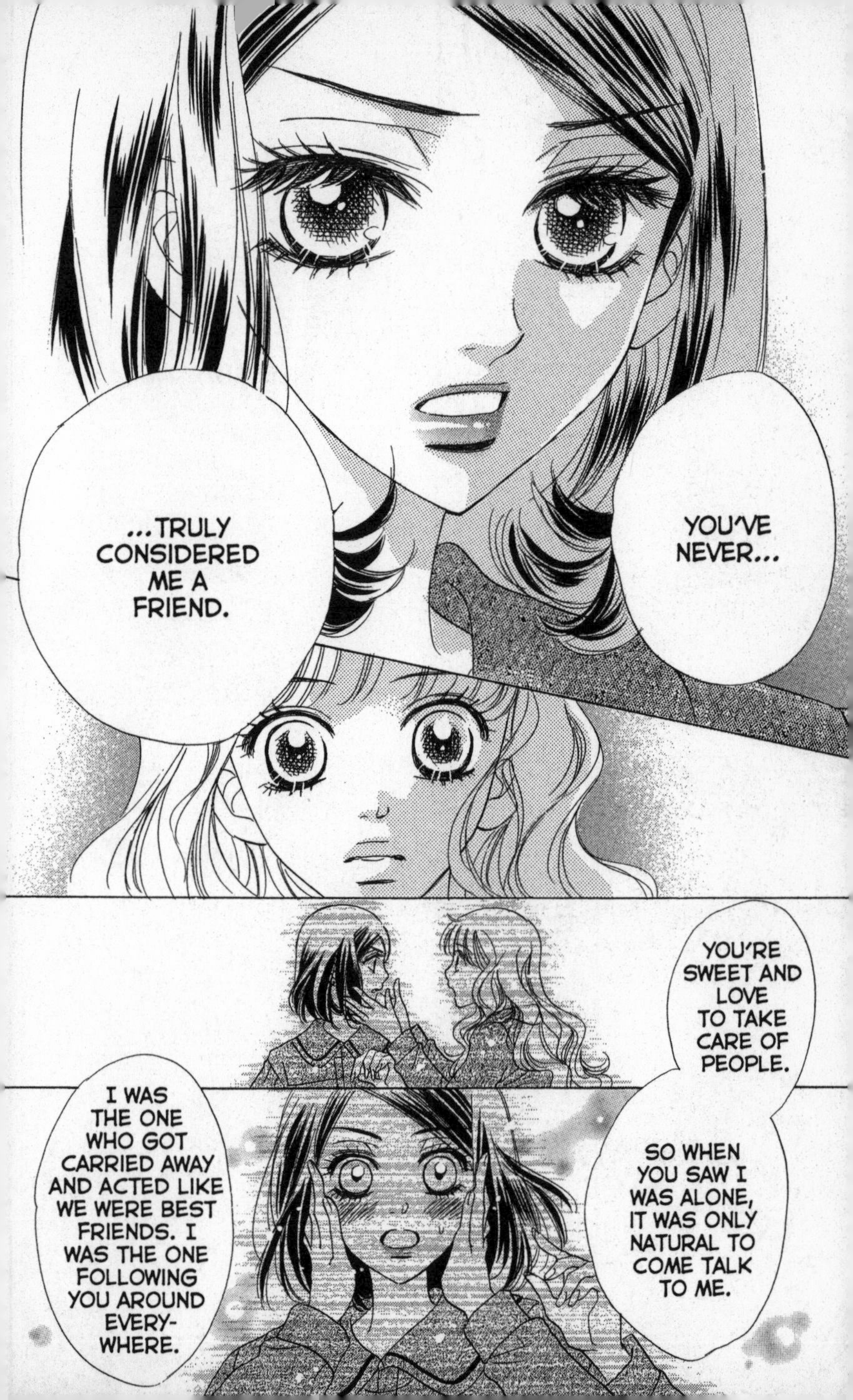
YOU'VE NEVER...
...TRULY CONSIDERED ME A FRIEND.
YOU'RE SWEET AND LOVE TO TAKE CARE OF PEOPLE.
SO WHEN YOU SAW I WAS ALONE, IT WAS ONLY NATURAL TO COME TALK TO ME.
I WAS THE ONE WHO GOT CARRIED AWAY AND ACTED LIKE WE WERE BEST FRIENDS. I WAS THE ONE FOLLOWING YOU AROUND EVERY-WHERE.

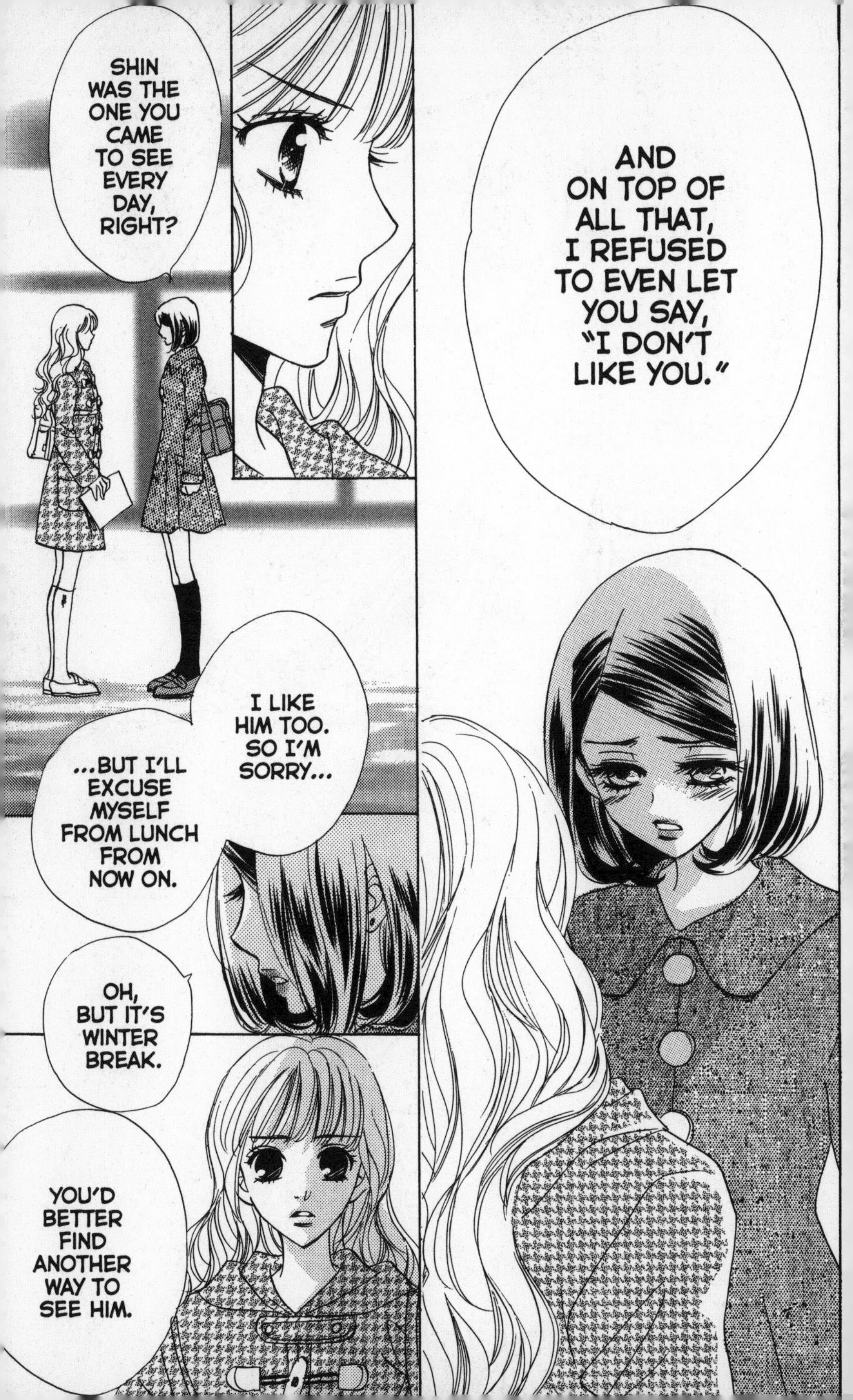
AND ON TOP OF ALL THAT, I REFUSED TO EVEN LET YOU SAY, "I DON'T LIKE YOU."
SHIN WAS THE ONE YOU CAME TO SEE EVERY DAY, RIGHT?
I LIKE HIM TOO. SO I'M SORRY...
...BUT I'LL EXCUSE MYSELF FROM LUNCH FROM NOW ON.
OH, BUT IT'S WINTER BREAK.
YOU'D BETTER FIND ANOTHER WAY TO SEE HIM.

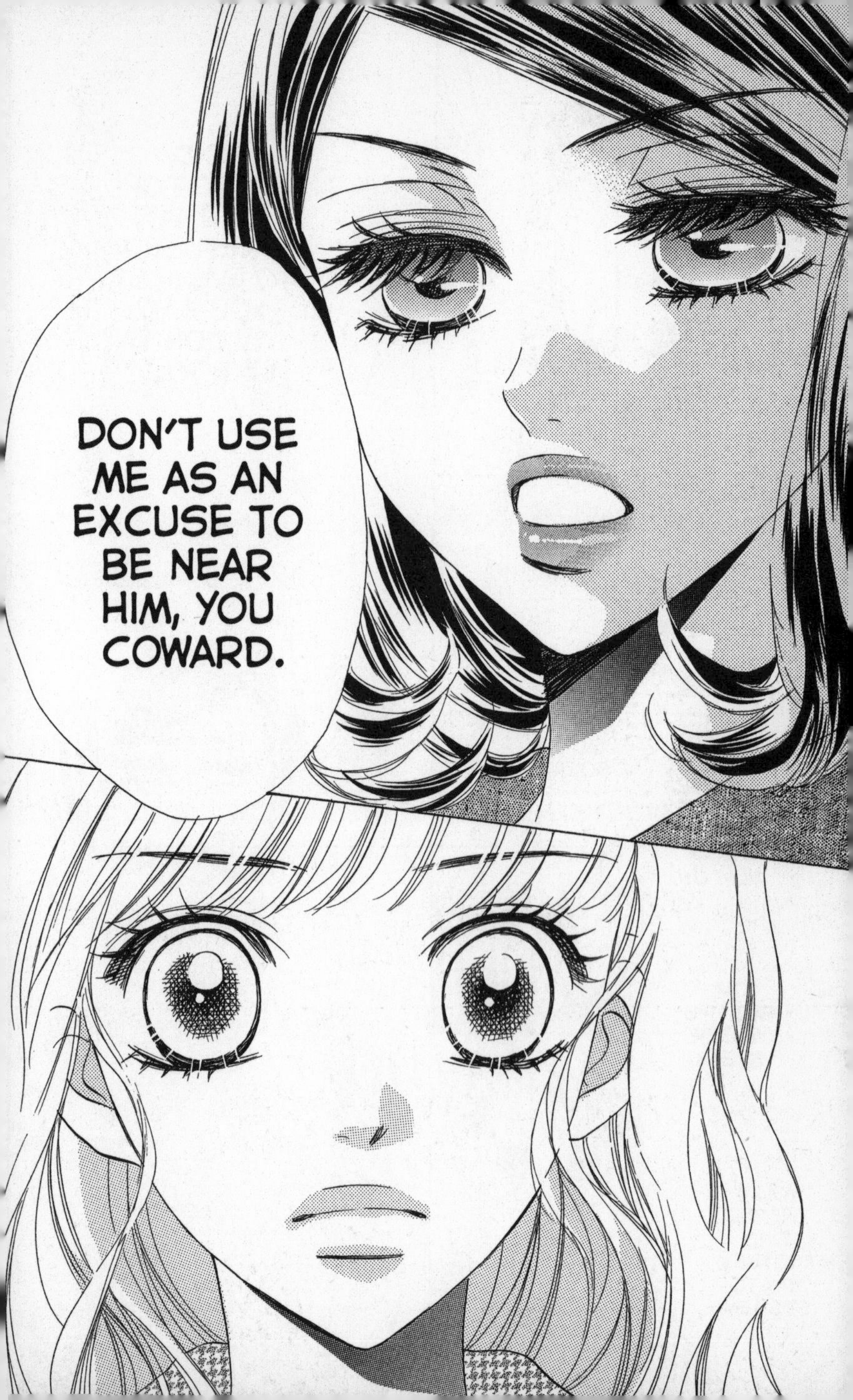
DON'T USE ME AS AN EXCUSE TO BE NEAR HIM, YOU COWARD.

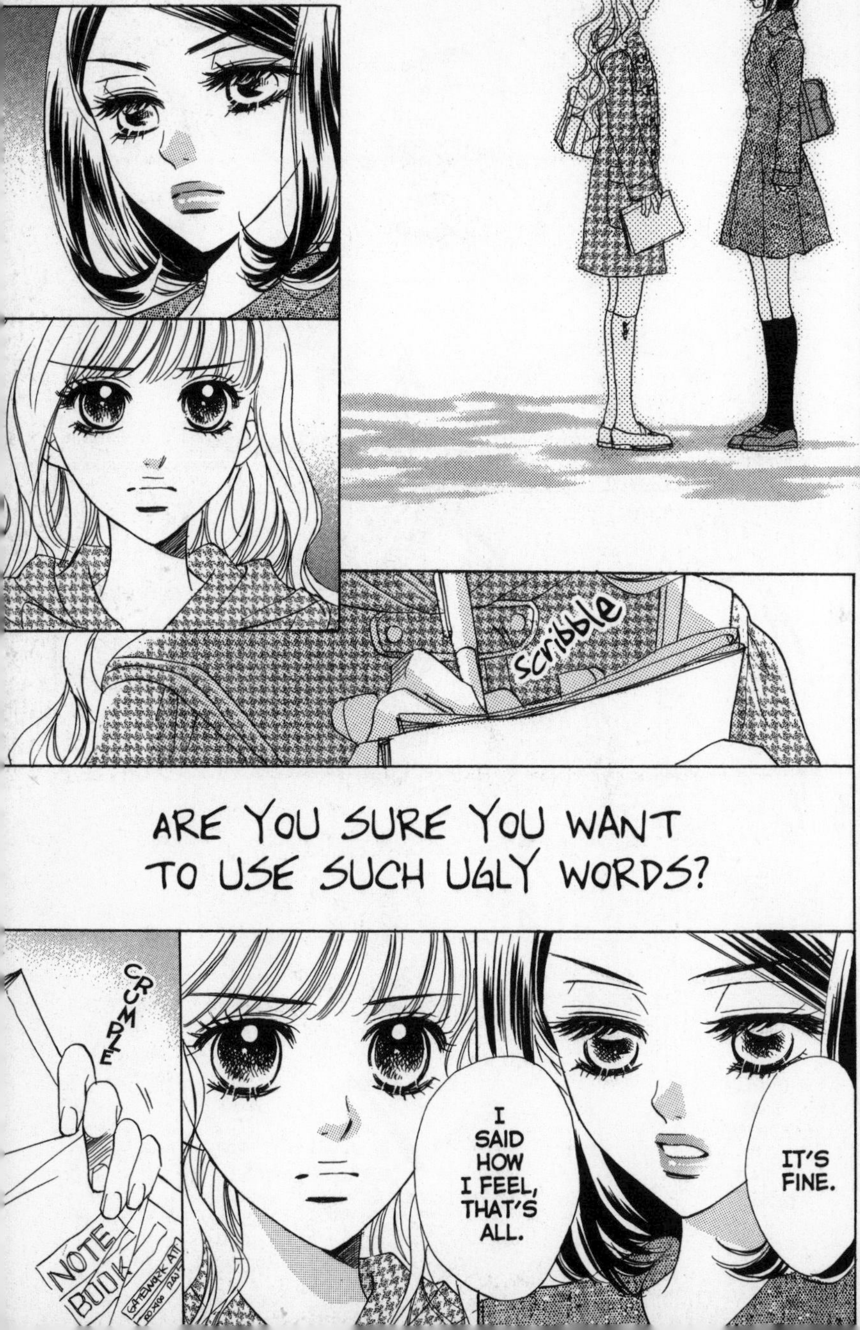
scribble
ARE YOU SURE YOU WANT TO USE SUCH UGLY WORDS?
IT'S FINE.
I SAID HOW I FEEL, THAT'S ALL.
CRUMPLE
NOTE BOOK

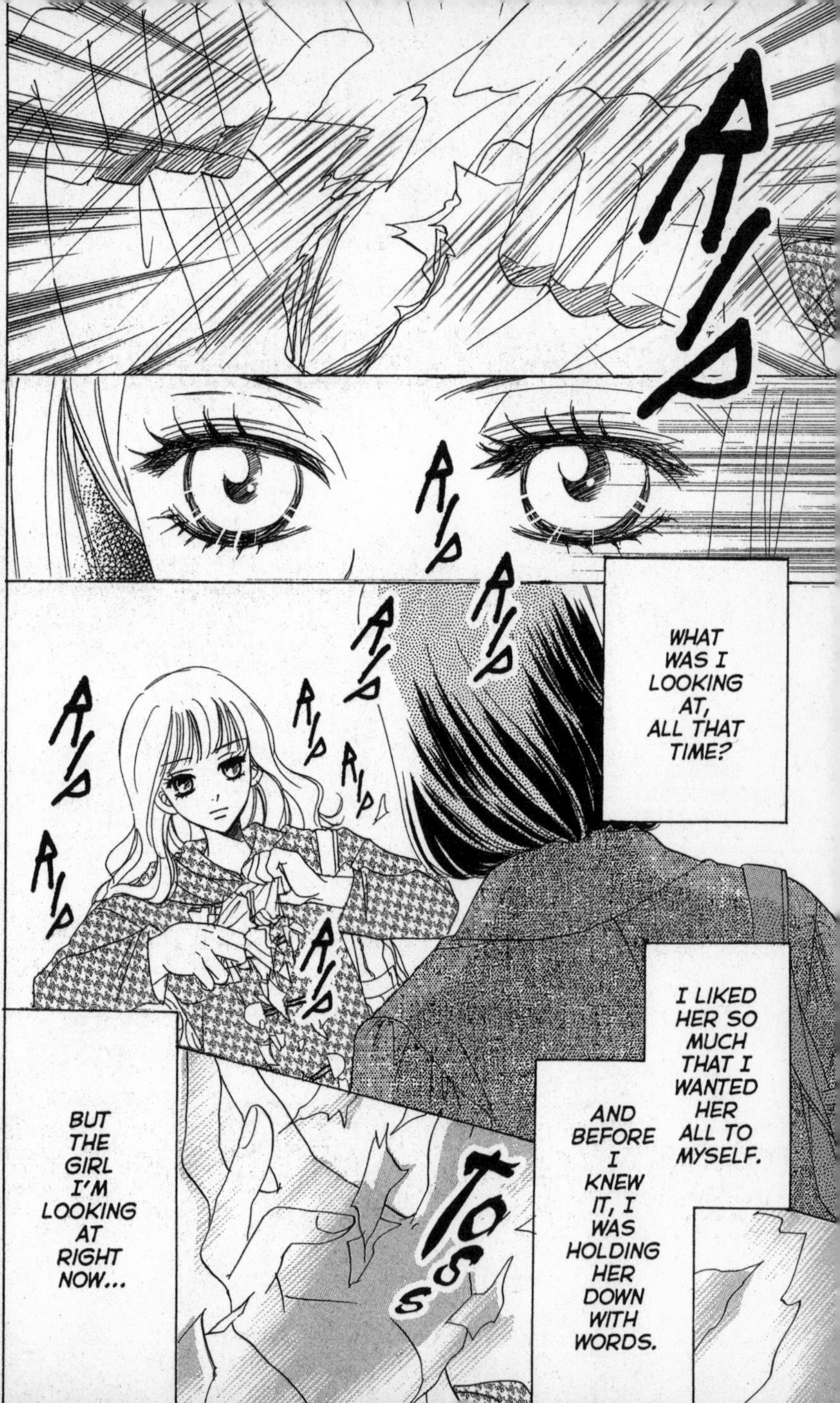
RIP
RIP
RIP
WHAT WAS I LOOKING AT, ALL THAT TIME?
RIP
RIP
RIP!
RIP
RIP
RIP
I LIKED HER SO MUCH THAT I WANTED HER ALL TO MYSELF.
AND BEFORE I KNEW IT, I WAS HOLDING HER DOWN WITH WORDS.
TOSS
BUT THE GIRL I'M LOOKING AT RIGHT NOW...

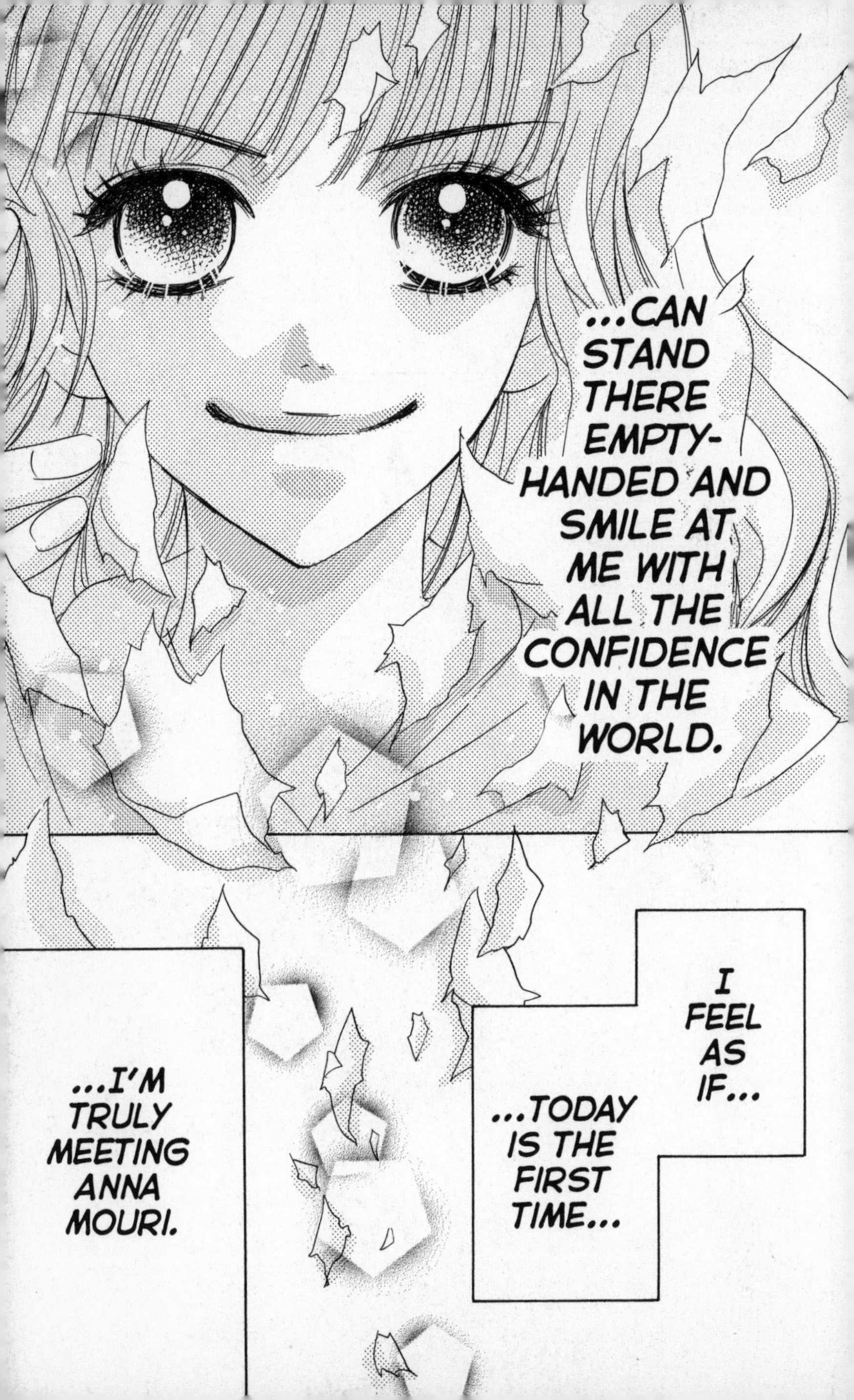
...CAN STAND THERE EMPTY-HANDED AND SMILE AT ME WITH ALL THE CONFIDENCE IN THE WORLD.
I FEEL AS IF...
...TODAY IS THE FIRST TIME...
...I'M TRULY MEETING ANNA MOURI.

Continued in volume 6

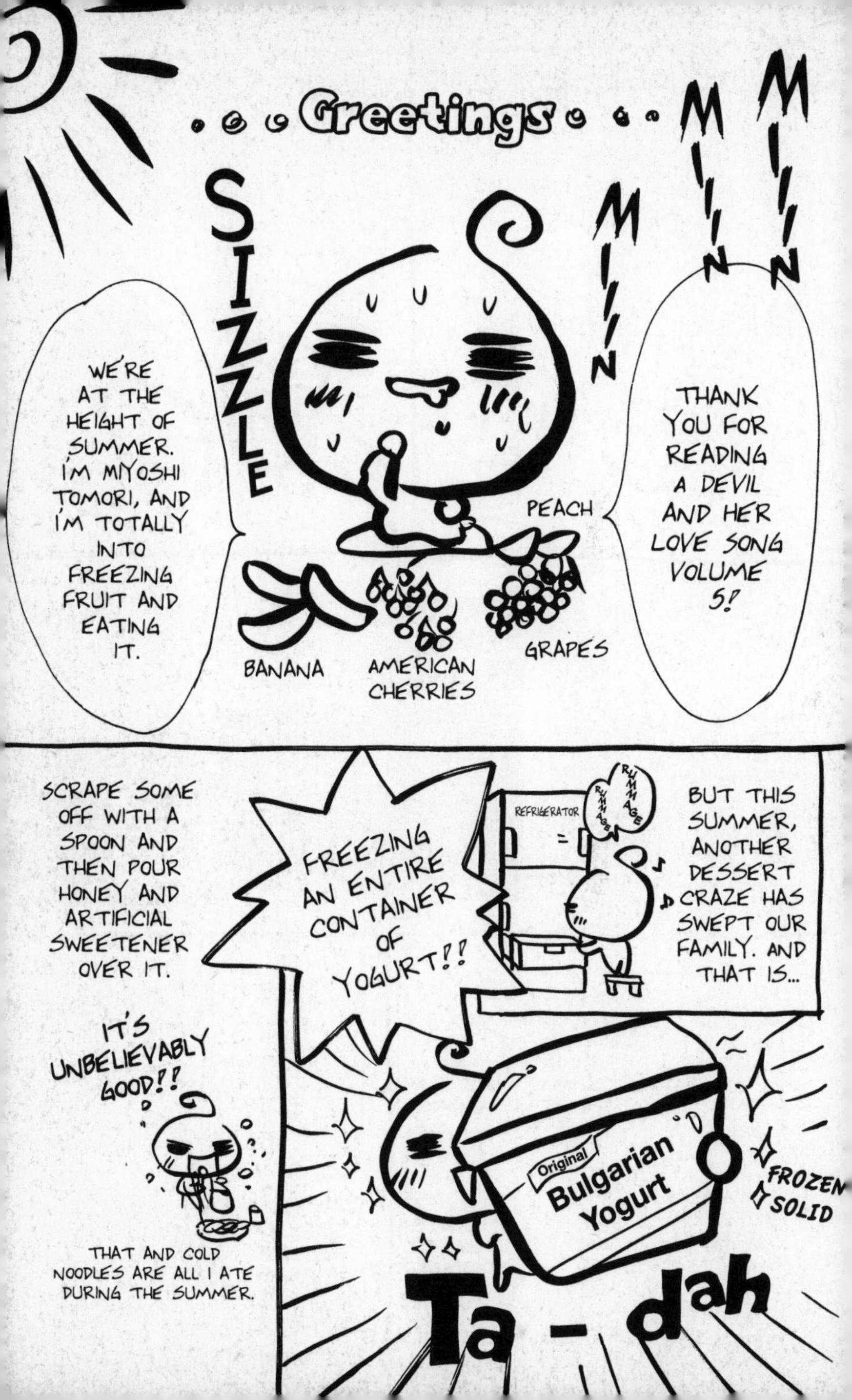
Greetings
MIIIN MIIIN MIIIN
THANK YOU FOR READING A DEVIL AND HER LOVE SONG VOLUME 5!
SIZZLE
WE'RE AT THE HEIGHT OF SUMMER. I'M MIYOSHI TOMORI, AND I'M TOTALLY INTO FREEZING FRUIT AND EATING IT.
PEACH
GRAPES
AMERICAN CHERRIES
BANANA
BUT THIS SUMMER, ANOTHER DESSERT CRAZE HAS SWEPT OUR FAMILY. AND THAT IS...
RUMMAGE RUMMAGE
REFRIGERATOR
FREEZING AN ENTIRE CONTAINER OF YOGURT!!
FROZEN SOLID
Original Bulgarian Yogurt
Ta-dah
SCRAPE SOME OFF WITH A SPOON AND THEN POUR HONEY AND ARTIFICIAL SWEETENER OVER IT.
IT'S UNBELIEVABLY GOOD!!
THAT AND COLD NOODLES ARE ALL I ATE DURING THE SUMMER.

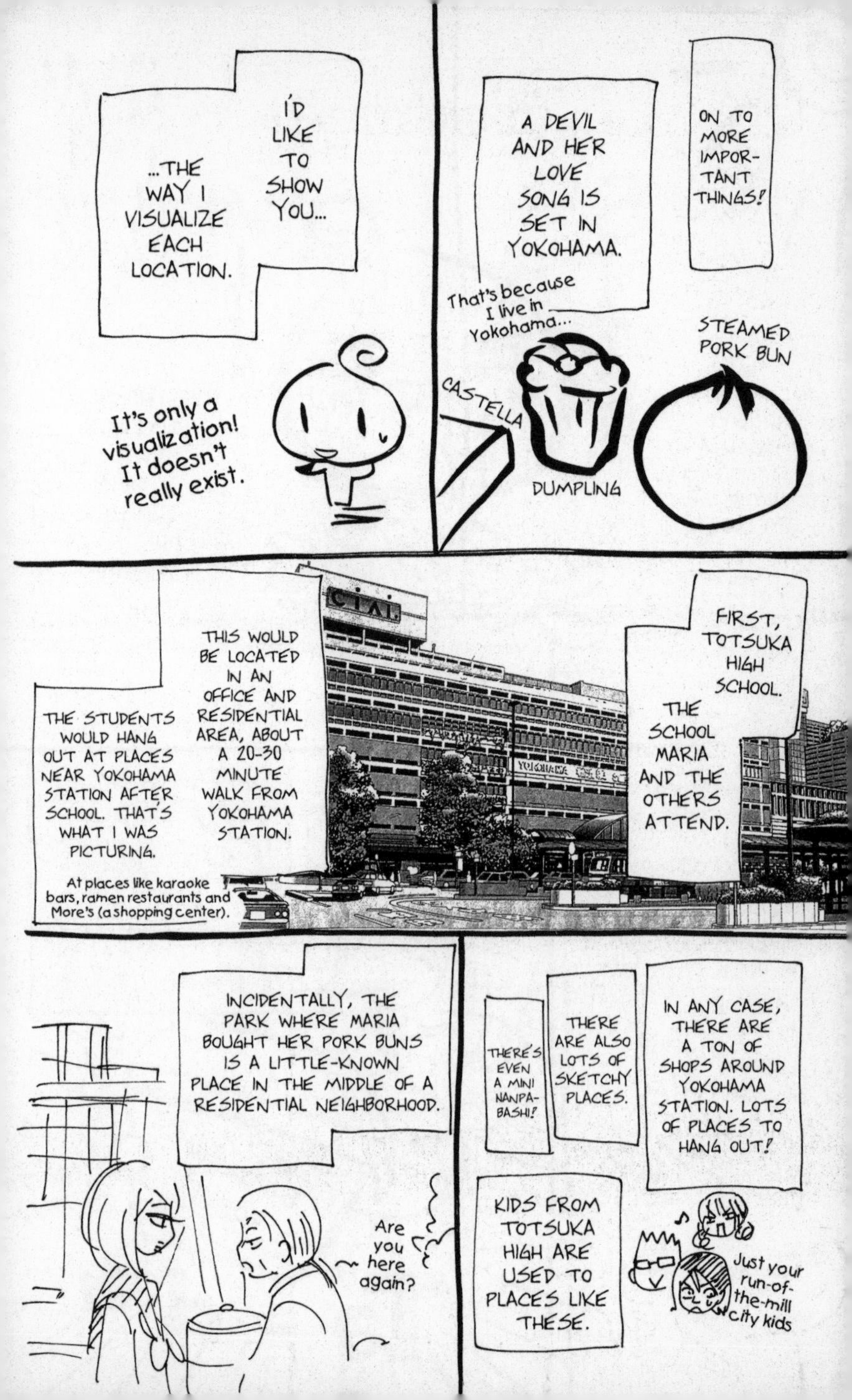
A DEVIL AND HER LOVE SONG IS SET IN YOKOHAMA.
That's because I live in Yokohama...
CASTELLA
DUMPLING
STEAMED PORK BUN
ON TO MORE IMPORTANT THINGS!
I'D LIKE TO SHOW YOU...
...THE WAY I VISUALIZE EACH LOCATION.
It's only a visualization! It doesn't really exist.
FIRST, TOTSUKA HIGH SCHOOL.
THE SCHOOL MARIA AND THE OTHERS ATTEND.
THIS WOULD BE LOCATED IN AN OFFICE AND RESIDENTIAL AREA, ABOUT A 20-30 MINUTE WALK FROM YOKOHAMA STATION.
THE STUDENTS WOULD HANG OUT AT PLACES NEAR YOKOHAMA STATION AFTER SCHOOL. THAT'S WHAT I WAS PICTURING.
At places like karaoke bars, ramen restaurants and More's (a shopping center).
IN ANY CASE, THERE ARE A TON OF SHOPS AROUND YOKOHAMA STATION. LOTS OF PLACES TO HANG OUT!
THERE ARE ALSO LOTS OF SKETCHY PLACES.
THERE'S EVEN A MINI NANPA-BASHI!
KIDS FROM TOTSUKA HIGH ARE USED TO PLACES LIKE THESE.
Just your run-of-the-mill city kids
INCIDENTALLY, THE PARK WHERE MARIA BOUGHT HER PORK BUNS IS A LITTLE-KNOWN PLACE IN THE MIDDLE OF A RESIDENTIAL NEIGHBORHOOD.
Are you here again?

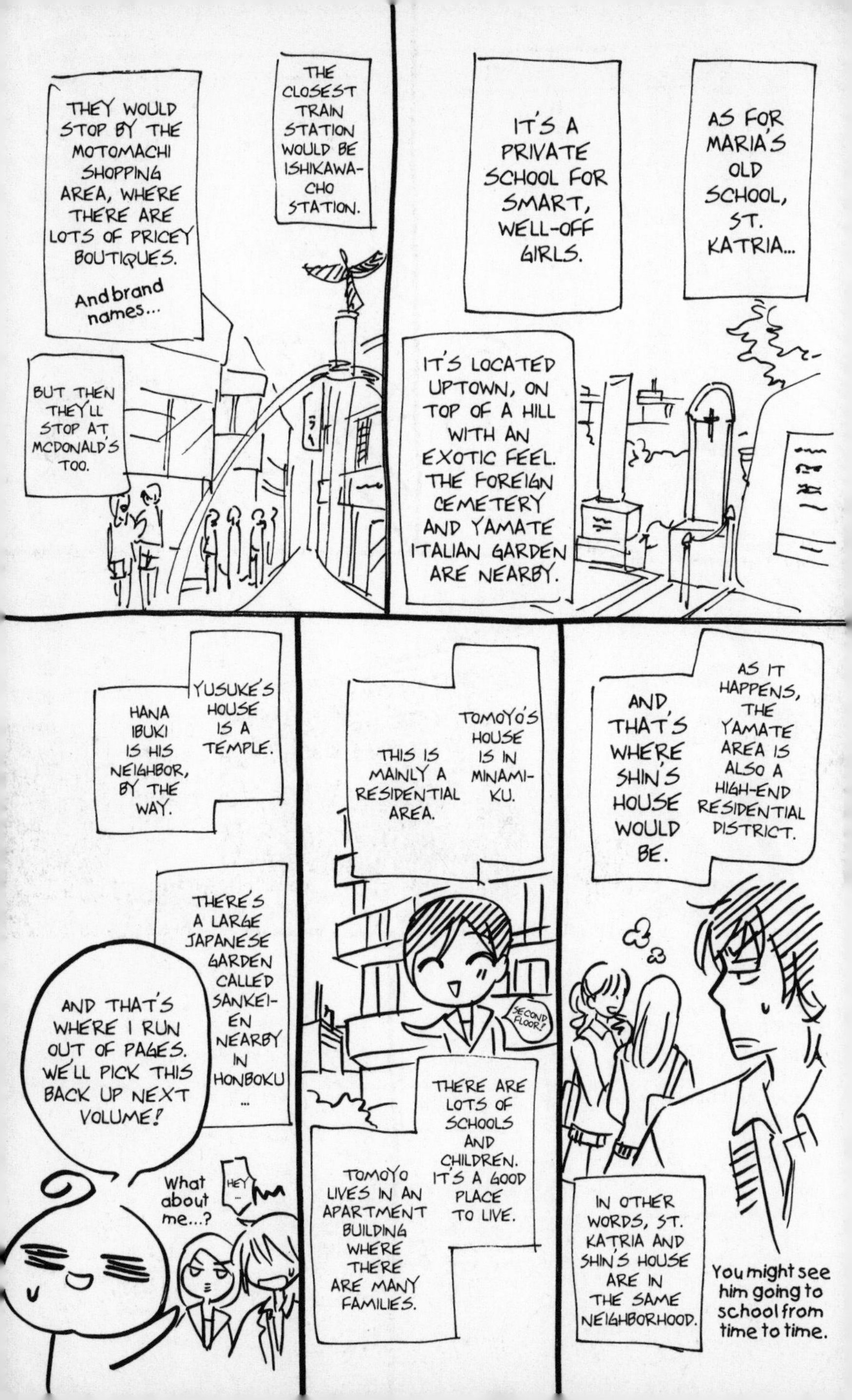
AS FOR MARIA'S OLD SCHOOL, ST. KATRIA...
IT'S A PRIVATE SCHOOL FOR SMART, WELL-OFF GIRLS.
IT'S LOCATED UPTOWN, ON TOP OF A HILL WITH AN EXOTIC FEEL. THE FOREIGN CEMETERY AND YAMATE ITALIAN GARDEN ARE NEARBY.
THE CLOSEST TRAIN STATION WOULD BE ISHIKAWA-CHO STATION.
THEY WOULD STOP BY THE MOTOMACHI SHOPPING AREA, WHERE THERE ARE LOTS OF PRICEY BOUTIQUES.
And brand names...
BUT THEN THEY'LL STOP AT MCDONALD'S TOO.
AS IT HAPPENS, THE YAMATE AREA IS ALSO A HIGH-END RESIDENTIAL DISTRICT.
AND, THAT'S WHERE SHIN'S HOUSE WOULD BE.
IN OTHER WORDS, ST. KATRIA AND SHIN'S HOUSE ARE IN THE SAME NEIGHBORHOOD.
You might see him going to school from time to time.
TOMOYO'S HOUSE IS IN MINAMI-KU.
THIS IS MAINLY A RESIDENTIAL AREA.
SECOND FLOOR!
THERE ARE LOTS OF SCHOOLS AND CHILDREN. IT'S A GOOD PLACE TO LIVE.
TOMOYO LIVES IN AN APARTMENT BUILDING WHERE THERE ARE MANY FAMILIES.
YUSUKE'S HOUSE IS A TEMPLE.
HANA IBUKI IS HIS NEIGHBOR, BY THE WAY.
THERE'S A LARGE JAPANESE GARDEN CALLED SANKEI-EN NEARBY IN HONBOKU...
AND THAT'S WHERE I RUN OUT OF PAGES. WE'LL PICK THIS BACK UP NEXT VOLUME!
HEY...
What about me...?

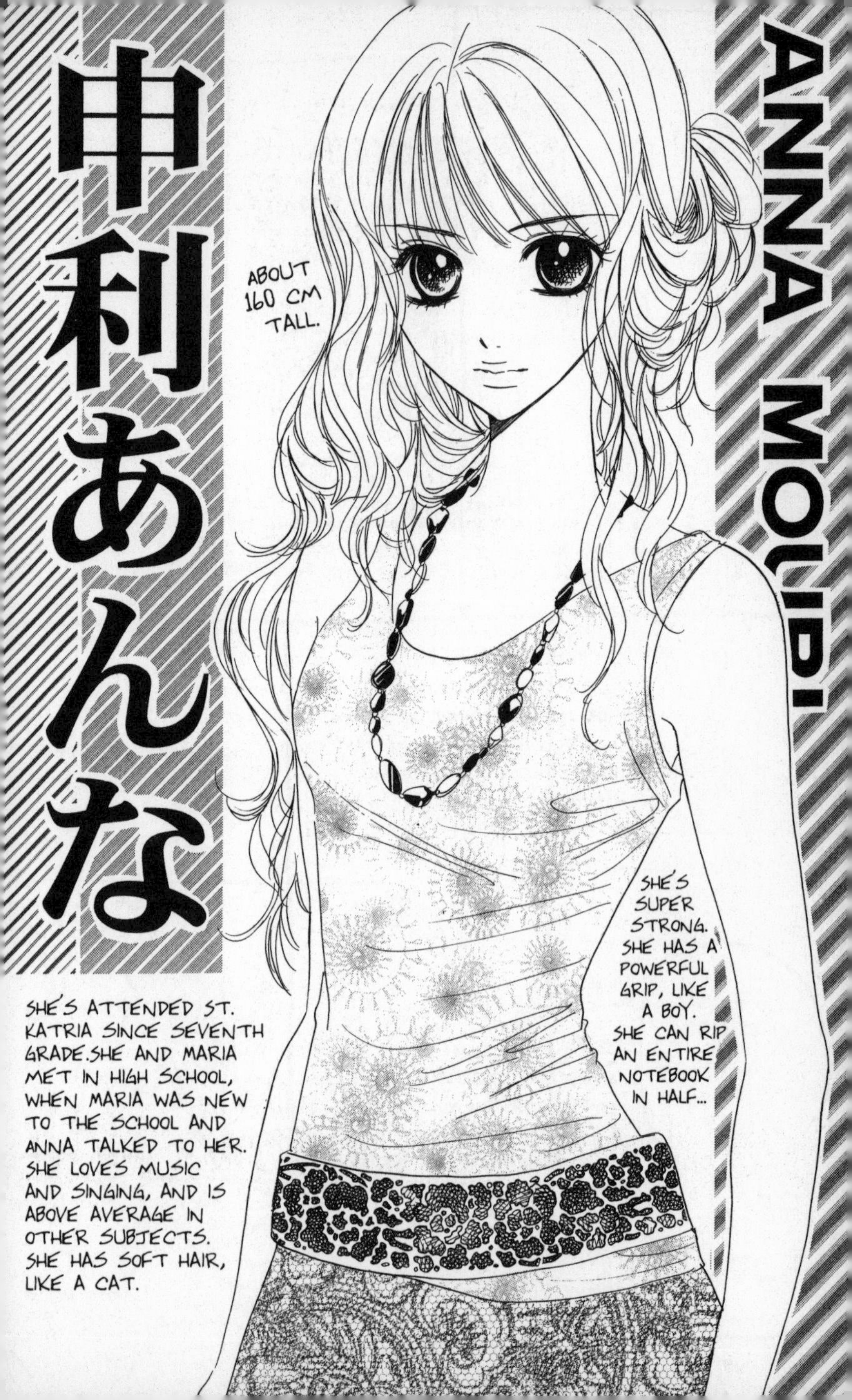
申利あんな
ANNA MOURI
ABOUT 160 CM TALL.
SHE'S SUPER STRONG. SHE HAS A POWERFUL GRIP, LIKE A BOY. SHE CAN RIP AN ENTIRE NOTEBOOK IN HALF...
SHE'S ATTENDED ST. KATRIA SINCE SEVENTH GRADE.SHE AND MARIA MET IN HIGH SCHOOL, WHEN MARIA WAS NEW TO THE SCHOOL AND ANNA TALKED TO HER. SHE LOVES MUSIC AND SINGING, AND IS ABOVE AVERAGE IN OTHER SUBJECTS. SHE HAS SOFT HAIR, LIKE A CAT.

This story is set in Yokohama. In volume 5's bonus pages, I introduce my renditions of various locations that appear in *A Devil and Her Love Song*, so please take a look. If you're interested, you can even visit the actual sites. I wasn't able to introduce all of the locations in this volume, so I plan to feature more in volume 6.

–Miyoshi Tomori

Miyoshi Tomori made her debut as a manga creator in 2001, and her previous titles include *Hatsukare* (First Boyfriend), *Tongari Root* (Square Root), and *Brass Love!!* In her spare time she likes listening to music in the bath and playing musical instruments.

A DEVIL AND HER LOVE SONG
Volume 5
Shojo Beat Edition

STORY AND ART BY
MIYOSHI TOMORI

English Adaptation/Ysabet MacFarlane
Translation/JN Productions
Touch-up Art & Lettering/Monalisa de Asis
Cover Design/Yukiko Whitley
Interior Design/Courtney Utt
Editor/Amy Yu

Printed in the U.S.A.

Published by VIZ Media, LLC
P.O. Box 77010
San Francisco, CA 94107

10 9 8 7 6 5 4 3 2 1
First printing, October 2012

www.viz.com   www.shojobeat.com

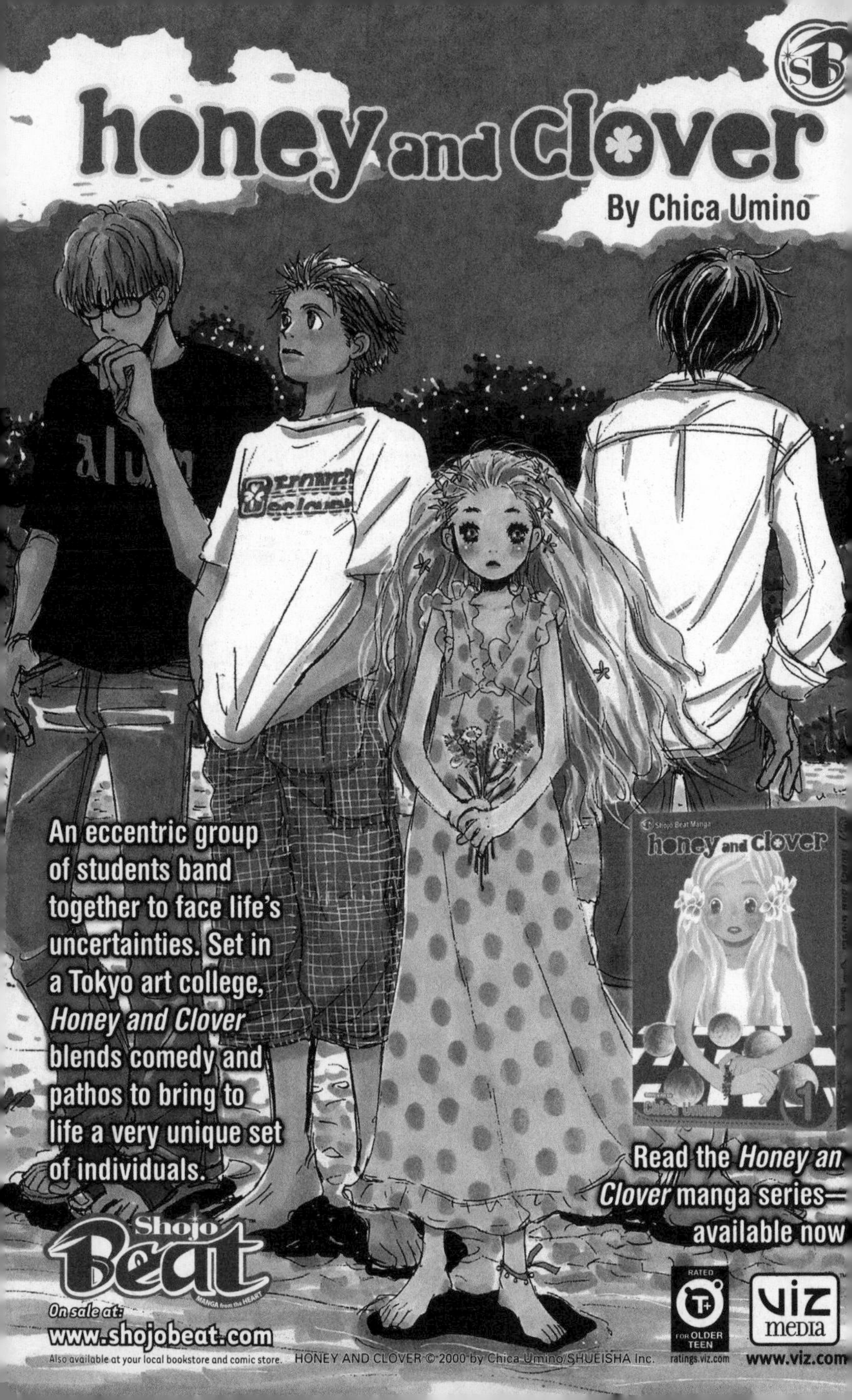
honey and clover
By Chica Umino
An eccentric group of students band together to face life's uncertainties. Set in a Tokyo art college, *Honey and Clover* blends comedy and pathos to bring to life a very unique set of individuals.
Shojo Beat Manga
honey and clover
Chica Umino
1
Read the *Honey an Clover* manga series—available now
Shojo Beat
MANGA from the HEART
On sale at:
www.shojobeat.com
Also available at your local bookstore and comic store.
HONEY AND CLOVER © 2000 by Chica Umino/SHUEISHA Inc.
RATED
T+
FOR OLDER TEEN
ratings.viz.com
VIZ media
www.viz.com

Surprise!

You may be reading the wrong way!

It's true: In keeping with the original Japanese comic format, this book reads from right to left—so action, sound effects, and word balloons are completely reversed. This preserves the orientation of the original artwork—plus, it's fun! Check out the diagram shown here to get the hang of things, and then turn to the other side of the book to get started!

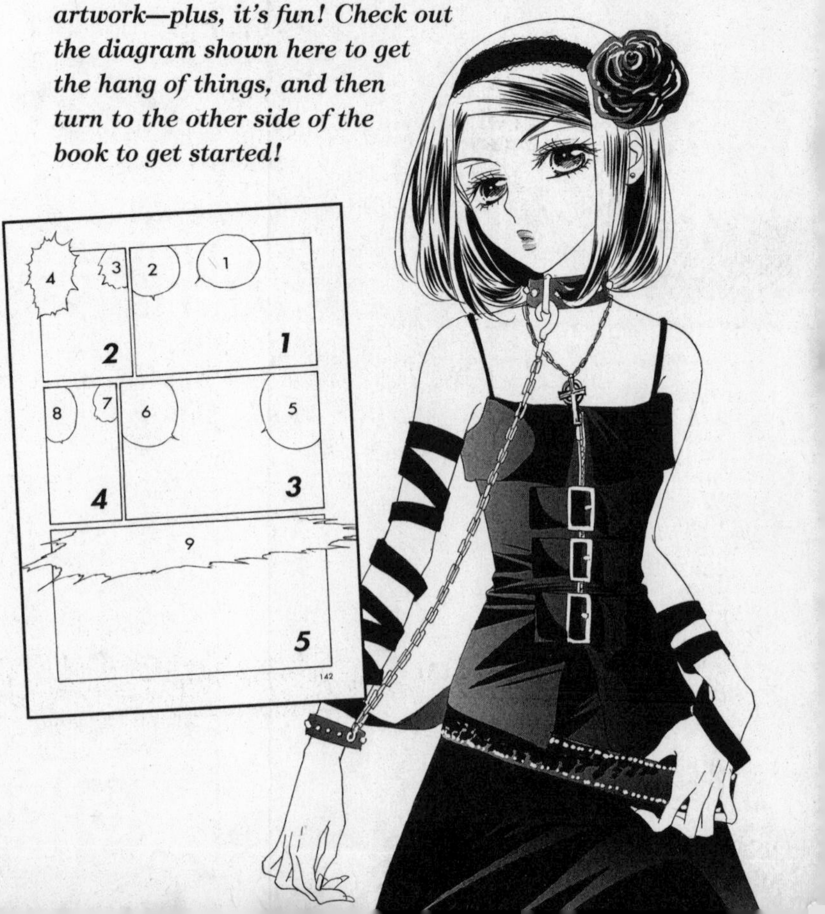
1
2
3
4
1
2
5
6
7
8
3
4
9
5
142